Writing for the
Real World

Writing for the Real World

Instructor's Annotated Edition

Ann Marie Radaskiewicz

Houghton Mifflin Company   BOSTON   NEW YORK

For Suzanne Bartle, Vince Radaskiewicz, and Catherine Radaskiewicz

Senior Sponsoring Editor: Mary Jo Southern
Associate Editor: Kellie Cardone
Editorial Associate: Danielle Richardson
Senior Project Editor: Fred Burns
Senior Production/Design Coordinator: Sarah Ambrose
Senior Manufacturing Coordinator: Sally Culler
Marketing Manager: Annamarie Rice

Cover image: Jim Ward Morris, Artville © 2001

PHOTO CREDITS
Page 1: © Jim Hargan; page 41: © Jim Hargan; page 75: © Milton Heiberg; page 106: © Jim Whitmer; page 130: © Jim Hargan; page 167: © Jim Hargan; page 191: © Jim Hargan; page 226: © Jonathan Ernst; page 250: © Milton Heiberg; page 273: © Jim Hargan; page 296: © Milton Heiberg.

Printed in the U.S.A.

Library of Congress Catalog Card Number: 00-133815

Instructor's Edition ISBN: 0-618-04800-6

Student Text ISBN: 0-618-04797-2

1 2 3 4 5 6 7 8 9—WEB—05 04 03 02 01

Contents

Preface   xiii

1   Creativity and Originality   1

PROFESSIONAL PROFILE: Philip D'Angelo, Graphics Designer   1

IDEA-GENERATION STRATEGIES   3

Talk   4
     Practice 1.1   5
Draw   6
     Practice 1.2   6
Brainstorm   7
     Practice 1.3   8
Cluster   9
     Practice 1.4   10
Meditate   10
     Practice 1.5   11
Freewrite   11
     Practice 1.6   13
Cube   13
     Practice 1.7   14
List   15
     Practice 1.8   16
Use the Journalism Method   16
     Practice 1.9   17
Answer Questions   18
     Practice 1.10   19

TEST YOUR UNDERSTANDING   20

WEB ACTIVITY: Career Exploration   21

GROUP PROJECT AND WRITING ACTIVITIES   22

READINGS   26

"The Power of Goal Setting" Bobbe Sommer   26
     Responding to the Reading   30
     Building Vocabulary   31

"A Worn Path" Eudora Welty   32
     Responding to the Reading   38
     Building Vocabulary   39

2 Vivid Language   41

PROFESSIONAL PROFILE: Buffie Buchanan, Registered Nurse   41

DETAILS   42

General Versus Specific Language   43
    Practice 2.1   44
Factual and Sensory Details   45
    Practice 2.2   47

EXACT ADJECTIVES   48
    Practice 2.3   50

STRONG VERBS   51
    Practice 2.4   53

FIGURES OF SPEECH   55
    Practice 2.5   56

PRECISE WORD CHOICES   57
    Practice 2.6   59

TEST YOUR UNDERSTANDING   59

WEB ACTIVITY: Learning Styles   60

GROUP PROJECT AND WRITING ACTIVITIES   60

READINGS   64

"Time Flies!" Jerry White   64
    Responding to the Reading   67
    Building Vocabulary   68

"How to Drive the Stakes Through the Hearts of Time Vampires"
Dan S. Kennedy   69
    Responding to the Reading   73
    Building Vocabulary   73

3 Four Rules for Clear Sentences   75

PROFESSIONAL PROFILE: Raul Romero, Construction Superintendent   75

RULE 1: USE STRONG VERBS   75

"There is" Sentences   76
    Practice 3.1   77
"It is" Sentences   77
    Practice 3.2   78
Passive Voice Sentences   78
    Practice 3.3   80
Matching Subjects and Verbs   81

RULE 2: AVOID WORDINESS   81

Redundant Words   82
Passive Voice   83
    Practice 3.4   83

RULE 3: VARY SENTENCE LENGTH   84

Short Sentences   85
Long Sentences   86
    Practice 3.5   87

RULE 4: ADHERE TO RULES FOR GRAMMAR, PUNCTUATION, AND SPELLING   88

Grammar and Punctuation   88
Spelling   89
   Practice 3.6   90

TEST YOUR UNDERSTANDING   91

WEB ACTIVITY: Professional Organizations   92

GROUP PROJECT AND WRITING ACTIVITIES   92

READINGS   94

"Talk the Talk" T. J. Saftner   94
   Responding to the Reading   98
   Building Vocabulary   98

"What Ever Happened to Customer Service?" Ralph Kinney Bennett   99
   Responding to the Reading   103
   Building Vocabulary   104

4 Complete Paragraphs — 106

PROFESSIONAL PROFILE: Jamie Johnson, Substance Abuse Counselor   106

ANTICIPATING THE READER'S QUESTIONS   107

LAYERS OF DEVELOPMENT   108
   Practice 4.1   111
   Practice 4.2   115
   Practice 4.3   117

TEST YOUR UNDERSTANDING   117

WEB ACTIVITY: Lifelong Learning   117

GROUP PROJECT AND WRITING ACTIVITIES   118

READINGS   120

"Higher Calling" Osborne Robinson Jr.   120
   Responding to the Reading   123
   Building Vocabulary   123

"Winning for Zora" Collin Perry   124
   Responding to the Reading   128
   Building Vocabulary   129

5 Coherent Paragraphs — 130

PROFESSIONAL PROFILE: L. Lynn Smith, Interior Designer   130

METHODS OF DEVELOPMENT   130

Narration   131
Description   132
Exemplification   133
Process Analysis   134
Comparison/Contrast   135
Cause/Effect   135
Division   136
Classification   137
Reasons   138
Problem/Solution   139
Combining the Methods   140
   Practice 5.1   142

CHOOSING A METHOD OF DEVELOPMENT   143
    Practice 5.2   145

TRANSITIONS   146
    Practice 5.3   147

TEST YOUR UNDERSTANDING   150

WEB ACTIVITY: The Job Search   150

GROUP PROJECT AND WRITING ACTIVITIES   151

READINGS   152

From "Career Intelligence: The Twelve New Rules for Success"
Barbara Moses   152
    Responding to the Reading   159
    Building Vocabulary   161
"Interview Tips and Bloopers" by Jean Ann Cantore   161
    Responding to the Reading   165
    Building Vocabulary   166

6 Cohesive Paragraphs   167

PROFESSIONAL PROFILE: Cindy Carswell, Certified Recreation
Therapy Assistant   167

TYPES OF NONCOHESIVE PARAGRAPHS   168

Digressing from the Main Idea   168
    Practice 6.1   171
Including Extra Main Ideas   171
    Practice 6.2   173

WRITING COHESIVE PARAGRAPHS   174

Planning for Cohesiveness   174
Composing for Cohesiveness   174
Revising for Cohesiveness   174
    Practice 6.3   175

TEST YOUR UNDERSTANDING   175

WEB ACTIVITY: Online Writing Labs   175

GROUP PROJECT AND WRITING ACTIVITIES   176

READINGS   178

From "How Technology Will Change the Workplace"
Samuel Greengard   178
    Responding to the Reading   184
    Building Vocabulary   185
"Journey of an E-Mail" John Dyson   186
    Responding to the Reading   189
    Building Vocabulary   190

7 Organizing Logical Units   191

PROFESSIONAL PROFILE: Phyllis Shuping, Buyer   191

THE THESIS STATEMENT   195

DISCOVERING CATEGORIES FOR IDEAS   196

Natural Organization   197
Logical Organization   198
    Practice 7.1   202

Choosing Natural or Logical Organization   205
Outlining   206
Formal Outlines, 207   Informal Outlines, 208
Practice 7.2   209

USING ORGANIZATIONAL MARKERS   211
Lists, 211   Headings, 212   Combining Organizational Markers, 213

TEST YOUR UNDERSTANDING   214

WEB ACTIVITY: Personality Quiz   215

GROUP PROJECT AND WRITING ACTIVITIES   215

READINGS   218

"Study Reveals Six Types of Workers" Cynthia G. Wagner   218
Responding to the Reading   220
Building Vocabulary   220

"Tactics to Tame Tough People" Sandra Crowe   221
Responding to the Reading   223
Building Vocabulary   224

8 Interesting Openings   226

PROFESSIONAL PROFILE: Mark Radaskiewicz, Engineering
Maintenance Team Leader   226

PURPOSES OF THE OPENING   226

Give Background Information   227
State Thesis   227
Establish Tone   228
Interest the Reader   229
*Tell a Story, 230   Ask Questions, 231   Establish the Significance of Your
Subject, 231   Begin with a Quotation, 232   Use Contrast, 232   Give
an Example, 233   Explain Your General Topic and Narrow to Your Specific
Point, 234   Surprise, Shock, or Startle the Reader, 235   Combining the
Methods, 235*
Practice 8.1   236

TEST YOUR UNDERSTANDING   238

WEB ACTIVITY: Leadership Potential   239

GROUP PROJECT AND WRITING ACTIVITIES   239

READINGS   242

"What It Takes to Become a Successful Manager Today" William M. Pride,
Robert J. Hughes, and Jack R. Kapoor   243
Responding to the Reading   245
Building Vocabulary   245

"Finding Wisdom on Mount Potosi" Bruce Spotleson   246
Responding to the Reading   248
Building Vocabulary   249

9 Effective Closings   250

PROFESSIONAL PROFILE: Russell Barnes, Division Commander   250

TECHNIQUES FOR CONCLUDING A COMPOSITION   251

Describe Effects   252
Make Predictions   252

Make Recommendations   253
Complete a Circle   254
Ask Questions   255
    Practice 9.1   255
TEST YOUR UNDERSTANDING   259
WEB ACTIVITY: Online References   260
GROUP PROJECT AND WRITING ACTIVITIES   260

READINGS   262
"Using the Web to Advance Your Career" John J. Casson   263
    Responding to the Reading   264
    Building Vocabulary   269
"Small Cubicle Is Closing In at the Office" Lenore Skenazy   270
    Responding to the Reading   271
    Building Vocabulary   272

10 Confidence and Assertiveness   273

PROFESSIONAL PROFILE: Starla Hoke, Paralegal   273
COMMUNICATING CONFIDENTLY   274
Avoid Hedging, Apologies, and Disclaimers   274
    Practice 10.1   275
Choose Assertive Words   276
    Practice 10.2   278
Write Assertive Sentences   279
    Practice 10.3   280
Use Varying Typefaces for Emphasis   281
TEST YOUR UNDERSTANDING   281
WEB ACTIVITY: Grammar   282
GROUP PROJECT AND WRITING ACTIVITIES   282

READINGS   284
"Handle Stress Like an Expert" Megan Othersen Gorman   284
    Responding to the Reading   287
    Building Vocabulary   288
"Don't Sweat the Small Stuff at Work" Richard Carlson   289
    Responding to the Reading   294
    Building Vocabulary   295

11 Sensitivity and Tact   296

PROFESSIONAL PROFILE: John King, Systems Administrator   296
MATCH YOUR POINTS TO YOUR READER   297
Types of Readers   298
Types of Arguments   298
    Practice 11.1   299
MAKE CONCESSIONS   299
Advantages and Disadvantages   300
Guidelines   301
    Practice 11.2   302

AVOID OFFENDING OR INSULTING YOUR READER 303

Name Calling 303
Condescending or Dismissive Tone 304
Emotionally Loaded Words 305
    Practice 11.3 306

TEST YOUR UNDERSTANDING 308

WEB ACTIVITY: Resources for Business and Technical Writers 308

GROUP PROJECT AND WRITING ACTIVITIES 309

READINGS 309

"Personal Values and Ethical Choices" Barry L. Reece and
Rhonda Brandt 310
    Responding to the Reading 313
    Building Vocabulary 314

"Coping with a Crooked Boss" Anna Mulrine and
Joannie M. Schrof 315
    Responding to the Reading 316
    Building Vocabulary 317

APPENDIXES   APPENDIX A **Conducting Successful Interviews** 319

APPENDIX B **Preparing Effective Oral Presentations** 321

APPENDIX C **Eleven Serious Errors in English** 325

Error #1: Sentence Fragments 325
Error #2: Run-on Sentences 331
Error #3: Comma Errors 334
Error #4: Semicolon Errors 338
Error #5: Subject/Verb Agreement Errors 340
Error #6: Pronoun Agreement Errors 343
Error #7: Apostrophe Errors 346
Error #8: Inconsistent Verb Tense 348
Error #9: Misplaced Modifiers 350
Error #10: Parallelism Errors 352
Error #11: Awkward Wording 354

Index 357

Preface

You already know how to write.

Before you enrolled in a college English course, before you picked up this book, you had been writing for years, probably since about second or third grade. But now that you're an adult, beginning the education that will help you achieve your career goals, you want to write better.

You want to express your ideas more clearly, more elegantly, and with more sophistication. You want to write documents that make sense, ones that provide readers with what they need. You want to write without errors so that your readers will know you are informed, intelligent, and educated.

This book will show you the essential qualities of good writing. There are only eleven—eleven characteristics to remember each time you sit down to compose a new document. When you can incorporate all eleven qualities into your writing, it will be clear, interesting, and effective, always fulfilling its purpose.

Here are eleven characteristics:

Creativity and originality

Vivid language

Clear sentences

Complete paragraphs

Cohesive paragraphs

Coherent paragraphs

Logical organization

Interesting openings

Effective closings

Confidence and assertiveness

Sensitivity and tact

This book defines, explains, and illustrates these eleven essential qualities of good writing. It includes pieces of writing that demonstrate them, and it gives you many opportunities—in the form of exercises and assignments—to practice them until you can incorporate them easily into your own documents, and write with confidence.

Unlike many other textbooks, this book focuses on career-oriented writing, the kind of writing that will probably make up the majority of documents you'll compose. Regardless of which professional career you pursue, you'll find that you must write on the job. You'll have to compose memos, letters, reports, e-mail messages, and other types of documents. And you'll quickly discover how your writing ability directly affects your career success.

You will find the information in *Writing for the Real World* to be practical and beneficial. May it bring you continued success in your academic and professional fields.

Acknowledgments

I would like to thank my Houghton Mifflin editors, Maggie Barbieri and Mary Jo Southern, for their constant encouragement, insight, support, and advice.

My parents—Suzanne Bartle, Vince Radaskiewicz, and Catherine Radas-kiewicz—all generously contributed their own time and energy so that I could complete this project. I am grateful for their love and sacrifices.

My dearest friend Debra Rose was, as always, an unflagging source of mental, emotional, and spiritual nourishment.

And once again, my inspiration has been Mark, my son.

Ann Marie Radaskiewicz

Writing for the
Real World

1 Creativity and Originality

PROFESSIONAL PROFILE
Philip D'Angelo, Graphics Designer

Before he decided to earn a college degree, Philip D'Angelo had worked as a roadie, a multimedia technician, a commercial photographer, and a computer salesman. "Most of my jobs required hard physical labor," Philip says. "I wanted to get an education so I could focus more on the artistic and creative side of projects." So in his forties, he enrolled in a community college and completed two associate in fine arts degrees, along with an associate in arts degree. Now, working as a graphics designer for a prestigious furniture manufacturer, he often writes memos and e-mail messages to his colleagues and supervisors.

Philip's job requires him to think creatively about the layout and design of the company's documents and then write about his ideas. When his supervisor asked him to redesign the company's price lists, for instance, Philip first jotted his thoughts on a memo pad:

> MORE WHITE SPACE
>
> Widen columns
>
> cluttered! hard to read
>
> HEADING → More space
>
> PRICE LISTS
>
> GRAPHICS— retouch
>
> text →
>
> 8pt. Arial

Then he organized his ideas and composed a memo to his supervisor, Bob Smith.

MEMORANDUM

TO: Bob Smith, Sales Director
FROM: Philip D'Angelo, Graphics Designer
DATE: August 24, 20xx
SUBJECT: Layout and Design of Price Lists

I've been reviewing the price lists you asked me to redesign, and I've come up with some ideas for changing the layout of these lists to improve their readability and make them more visually attractive.

First, I'd like to add more white space around certain elements to separate them and make them stand out. For example, I'd like to increase the

1

space in each heading. Also, I'd like to widen the space in each column for a less cluttered effect.

I'd also recommend that we alter the fonts. In the old price lists, we used 6-point Swiss font for the body text. This size is very small and difficult to read. I'd like to change the font to 8-point Arial. Not only is this font larger and easier to read, it's also the same font we use for our spreadsheets and other company documents, so our price lists will coordinate. As a result, they'll look more professional.

Finally, I want to retouch all of the graphics by re-drawing all vertical and horizontal lines. This will create much crisper images and compensate for shortcomings in the scanning process.

I look forward to your feedback about these ideas. I would be happy to generate a sample page for your review and approval.

Philip used an idea-generation technique to aid his creativity and to help himself find out what he needed to say in his memo. This chapter discusses all of the different strategies you can use to discover new ideas.

The first essential quality of all effective writing is **creativity and originality.** Because readers read to learn or to increase their understanding, all good writing offers them *new information, new insights,* or *new perspectives* about the topic. There's no reason for them to waste their time reading about something they already know, so the writer's job is to offer them something fresh. Being creative doesn't mean producing great masterpieces of literature every time you sit down to write. Instead, creativity involves thinking for yourself, exploring your thoughts, and striving to discover new and interesting ideas.

When you have to write something, do you ever use any of the following techniques? Check anything in the list that you've tried at least once in the past:

☐ I just wait until an idea pops into my head.
☐ I sit and stare at my paper or computer screen until something comes to me.
☐ I wait until the last minute before the paper is due because being under pressure forces my mind to come up with something.

When you use any of these methods, do you ever feel frustrated or upset? Are you satisfied with the writing you produce? Or do you often wish your compositions were better?

The three techniques in the list could be collectively described as the "divine inspiration" method of getting ideas. All three involve passively waiting for the perfect idea to be sent from the heavens straight to the brain. Though writers sometimes *do* get ideas in this way, out of the blue, this particular method more often creates four serious problems.

First, the "divine inspiration" technique often fails the writer. You may remember a time or two when you sat and sat, waiting and getting more frustrated and more stressed by the minute as your mind continued to remain blank. Hours later, still not knowing where to begin, you probably cried, "I can't think of anything to write about!" As a result, you may have concluded that you had no ideas and nothing to say. Actually, *everyone* has important, worthwhile thoughts about a wide variety of topics.

Second, this method makes the actual writing of a paper more difficult and more time-consuming. Trying to think up everything you need to say *while* you're actually composing complicates the whole process and therefore slows it down. It's challenging enough to find the right words to express your thoughts as you're forming your sentences and paragraphs. You don't want to give your brain an additional burden by forcing it to *produce* ideas at the same time.

The final two problems created by the "divine inspiration" method show up as specific weaknesses in the writing itself. People who are dissatisfied with their writing often believe that their compositions are incomplete or unoriginal. If you sense that your writing is not long enough or that your ideas are not fully explained, you're recognizing the lack of completeness. If you believe you're merely repeating the thoughts of others, you're aware of the lack of originality. The roots of these two problems can often be traced back to the very beginning of the procedure, when the writer was still searching for ideas.

Now that you know it's the "divine inspiration" method that's stressing you out and contributing to the poor quality of your writing, what can you do instead? You must use more *active* approaches when you're trying to discover what you want to say. You need to know and use one or more specific strategies that will aid you in getting ideas. Good idea-generation strategies will help you find a topic, narrow a topic, or decide what you need to say about a topic.

IDEA-GENERATION STRATEGIES

When you have written during the past, what active methods did you use to get ideas before you began composing? Describe those methods in the space below.

Answers will vary.

_____

_____

_____

_____

_____

_____

The ten idea-generation strategies described in the rest of this chapter offer you many different techniques for getting ideas. Some of them require paper and pen; others are mental procedures. All of them, however, are active approaches to discovering ideas. All require you to rummage around in your mind to see what's already there, rather than waiting for lightning to strike. All will help you generate complete and creative thoughts about your topic.

There is no one best way of generating ideas. Different techniques work for different writers. The most successful writers, though, are usually the ones who have familiarized themselves with *all* of the possibilities, discovering through practice the methods that work best for them. Also, they don't limit themselves to just one method; they experiment with different combinations of the techniques to achieve the best results.

Before you begin practicing the strategies described in the rest of this chapter, you'll need to select a topic. You'll use this same topic for each exercise so that you can discover

1. which methods work best for you.
2. how different methods produce different kinds of ideas.
3. how combinations of different methods produce more ideas.

Right now, think of a topic that interests you or choose a topic from this list of suggestions.

a current news topic	a new invention	career
home	time	money
my role model	retirement	college
computers	exercise	addiction
health insurance	stress	school reform
investments	safety	vacation
taxes	debt	nursing homes
sports	small business	a budget

Write your topic in this blank: *Answers will vary.*

Some of the activities in this chapter will ask you to choose a specific aspect or example of your topic. For instance, if you choose *exercise* as your topic, examples and aspects include specific types of exercise such as swimming, tennis, and running. Specific equipment includes golf clubs and weightlifting machines. Specific procedures or techniques include aerobic walking and strength training.

Talk

The talk idea-generation strategy involves simply discussing your ideas informally with someone else before beginning to write. Ask a friend, a family member, a co-worker, or a fellow student if you can talk about a paper you need to write. Start by saying, "Here's what I want to say in this paper"; then explain what you hope to accomplish. You could also answer questions your listener may have.

This method is based on the power of language to help us understand our thoughts. Many of the topics we need to write about are ones we've never written about or even discussed. So even though we may have some ideas or opinions about the subject, they tend to be fuzzy, shadowy, and half-formed as long as they stay solely in our minds. Only when someone asks us to express those ideas, either orally or in writing, do they crystallize and take shape.

Can you remember the last time someone asked for your ideas about a particular topic? Maybe a co-worker asked you what you thought about a new company policy. Perhaps a member of an organization to which you belong asked how you felt about an upcoming project. As you searched for the right words for communicating your ideas, you probably clarified in your own mind what you knew or believed about that subject. When we must find the right words to express what we're thinking, our thoughts become clearer, and we have a better idea of what we think—simply by having found the language for sharing those thoughts. As the poet W. H. Auden put it, "How do I know what I think, until I see what I say?"

So talking about your ideas with others prior to composing can be an important first step. You will, of course, have to find the right words when you sit down to write, but you will find this challenging mental task much easier if you've already experimented with them in an informal conversation. Oral discussion will also produce the additional benefit of helping you identify either gaps in your information or aspects of the topic that you're still not sure about. Then you can gather the missing data or spend more time thinking before you begin to write. If you begin writing when you're still fuzzy about what you think, your composition will be fuzzy too.

PRACTICE 1.1
Talk

1. Discuss your topic with a partner for at least five minutes.

2. During your conversation with your partner, what are some things you realized you knew about this topic? *Answers will vary.*

_____

_____

_____

_____

3. Which of your feelings or thoughts about the topic became clearer or more intense during your conversation? *Answers will vary.*

_____

_____

_____

_____

_____

4. What questions did you have about your topic as you discussed it? What gaps in your knowledge did you uncover? *Answers will vary.*

_____

_____

_____

_____

_____

_____

> ## IDEA-GENERATION STRATEGIES FOR COMPOSITION
>
> **TALK:** Explain verbally to another person what you want to write about.
>
> **DRAW:** Picture your subject in images and draw them.
>
> **BRAINSTORM:** Free-associate, writing down images and ideas in any order as they occur to you.
>
> **CLUSTER:** Record ideas in the order in which they occur to you as you free-associate. Explore different trains of thought.
>
> **MEDITATE:** Clear your mind; then focus your full attention on your topic and let ideas and images arise.
>
> **FREEWRITE:** Record your stream of consciousness in response to a suggested topic.
>
> **CUBE:** Explore your topic from different angles: describe it, tell a story about it, analyze its causes or effects or parts, compare it, argue for it, and so forth.
>
> **LIST:** Make lists in response to a suggested topic.
>
> **USE THE JOURNALISM METHOD:** Like a newspaper reporter, ask the questions Who? What? When? Where? Why? How?
>
> **ANSWER QUESTIONS:** Create and answer some very specific questions about your subject.

Draw

Some topics you write about will require you to describe people, places, or objects. The drawing idea-generation technique is especially well suited for compositions that must help the reader visualize something. This method involves sketching pictures to help yourself remember which specific details to include later in your writing.

You do not have to be an artist to use this technique. Your goal is not to produce a work of art but to reproduce your own visual mental image so that you can think about what to describe to the reader.

PRACTICE 1.2
Draw

Think of a person, an object, or a place associated with the topic you selected. Draw that person, object, or place in the space below.

Brainstorm

Brainstorming involves quickly writing down words and phrases that occur to you as you consider your topic. For example, when you hear the word *college,* another word or an image that you associate with college immediately pops into your mind. You may think of assignments, instructors, books, degree, classes, and so on. When you brainstorm, you write all of the associated words on a blank sheet of paper, like this:

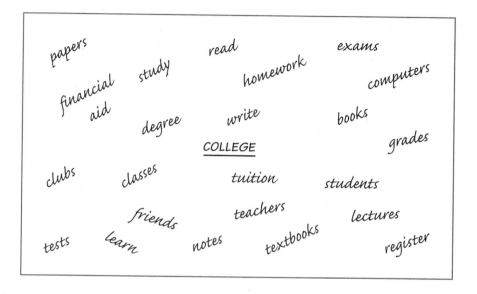

To get the best results from the brainstorming technique, follow these guidelines:

Don't Try to Organize Your Thoughts in Any Way.   Don't try to produce ideas in a certain order. Instead, let them occur randomly. Don't try to organize them, either. Simply write each word or phrase anywhere on the blank page, as the preceding example illustrates, and fill up the whole page with ideas. Your paper may be messy, but that's OK. You're the only one who will be seeing it.

Don't Reject Any of Your Ideas.   As you think of ideas, you'll be tempted to avoid writing some of them on the page. You'll think, "That's a dumb idea," or "That makes no sense," or "That really has nothing to do with my topic." When you brainstorm, though, ignore those thoughts and write down *every* word or phrase that occurs to you. For now, simply take dictation from your mind. You can weed out the silly or irrelevant ideas later. During brainstorming, don't judge your thoughts; just record them.

Do Write As Fast As You Can.   Don't worry about the neatness of your handwriting or about the appearance of the page. Remember that no one but you will see this paper, so record ideas as fast as possible until they stop coming to you. Not only is brainstorming an effective way to explore your thoughts, it's also a great technique for problem solving. If, for instance, your supervisor wants you to come up with some ideas for advertising or marketing your company's product, you could write "Possible New Marketing Strategies" on a sheet of paper and then fill the page with possibilities. Write down even the ideas that seem impractical or extravagant. They may turn out to be innovative later. If you need to solve a personal problem—such as trying to get your family to help you more with housework, get out some paper and brainstorm a variety of potential solutions.

PRACTICE 1.3
Brainstorm

1. In the space below, write your topic on the blank line in the middle. Then use brainstorming to fill up the space around that topic with associated words and phrases.

Answers will vary.

2. Think of a personal problem you need to resolve. In the next space, brainstorm some possible solutions.

Answers will vary.

Cluster

Like brainstorming, clustering is based on the mind's tendency to associate one thought with another. But this method assumes that ideas don't pop into our heads in an isolated, random fashion, but rather in trains of thought or "clusters." A cluster, then, is a related collection of ideas. Clustering is slightly more organized than brainstorming because you link ideas together in a chain in the order in which they occur to you, and you exhaust one set of associations before beginning another. For example, you begin the way you do in brainstorming, with a topic. You write down the first word or phrase you think of when you consider that topic. Then you write down what *that* word or phrase makes you think of. So if you began with the topic *day care*, your clustering would look something like this:

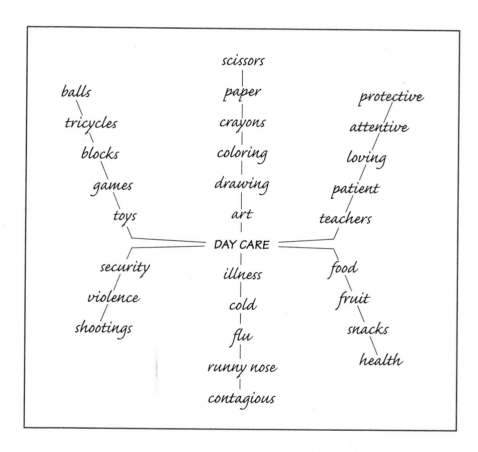

You follow a train of thought as far as you can, then return to your original topic to begin another train of thought. When you finish, you'll have several sets of associations, or clusters. Like brainstorming, this technique is most effective when you don't censor yourself. Instead, write quickly to capture every idea and image you think of.

PRACTICE 1.4
Cluster

Think of a specific example or aspect of your topic. For example, if your topic is *sports*, select one particular game, one specific player, or one piece of equipment. Then, in the space below, create a cluster of ideas for that topic.

Answers will vary.

Meditate

Another useful technique for generating ideas is meditation, which involves clearing your mind, focusing your full attention on your topic, and letting ideas and images surface. Meditation does not necessarily require sitting cross-legged in an incense-filled room and chanting (some people's stereotyped image of this activity). Rather, it requires focused concentration that can be accomplished in a variety of positions and settings.

If you've tried any form of meditation before, you know it can be very difficult to accomplish the first step of clearing the mind. Our brains are always filled with a great many different thoughts competing for our attention. Things to do, plans to make, problems to solve—all jostle each other constantly, each demanding our consideration. Temporarily banishing all of this mental noise to a dark corner of your mind while you concentrate on one specific project, such as an essay you need to write for your English class, can be challenging. But here are some specific techniques you can use for sweeping away the clutter for a while so that you can focus on just one idea.

Before you attempt to focus on one particular idea or project, spend a little time devoting your full attention to all of the unrelated thoughts that might intrude. Either mentally or on paper, take ten minutes to concentrate exclusively on your boyfriend or girlfriend, your problem at work, your upcoming math test, or anything else that could pull your attention away from your writing. If you can't stop thinking about all of the other things you need to be doing, spend five or ten minutes making a "to do" list. Then you may find it easier to focus solely on ideas for your composition.

Try Mental Visualization Techniques to Clear Your Mind. This method is similar to the "counting sheep" procedure some people use to fall asleep. When, for instance, you mentally visualize sheep jumping a fence one after the other, you're attempting to distract your mind from all of the buzzing thoughts that keep you from relaxing. Other visualization techniques ask you to envision certain images or scenarios in order to quiet your mind. One such method tells you to first picture a platform or stage. Then visualize yourself standing on the platform holding a broom. Every time a thought surfaces in your consciousness, picture it as a little gremlin trying to crawl up onto your platform—and see yourself sweeping it back into the shadows with your broom. Sweep off all thoughts that try to get up onto the clear, smooth platform of your mind until they stop trying. Then focus your full attention on your composition topic. Another method involves visualizing yourself in deep, clear water. Imagine going beneath the surface and still being able to breathe. You will sink lower and lower, to deeper, more silent levels as you proceed; but first, envision yourself spending some time just below the surface. Picture your thoughts as aquatic creatures swimming by. Let them drift and swim around you for a while. Keep noticing and watching each one. Then imagine yourself descending deeper, to another level. At each level, the numbers of thought "creatures" will diminish until you feel you're in a still, quiet place too deep for any of them.[1] Then think about your composition topic. If you'd like to know more about visualization methods, many different books about meditation can offer other techniques for clearing the mind of its clutter.

Take Advantage of Mental Down Time. Each day, we engage in many activities that don't require higher cognitive functions. These activities—such as doing the dishes, taking a shower, jogging, or even driving a car—are ones we perform without having to think about what we're doing, as though we're on autopilot. As a result, they afford good opportunities for mini meditation sessions about ideas. While engaged in these activities, try focusing your attention on a topic you need to write about. When you're finished, you can jot down what you came up with, for consideration later.

PRACTICE 1.5
Meditate

You'll need a quiet, interruption-free place to complete this activity. Try one of the three techniques for clearing your mind of clutter; then think of your topic for as long as you can.

1. Which technique did you try? *Answers will vary.*

2. How long did you practice this technique? *Answers will vary.*

3. How effective was this technique? After you used it, were you able to completely focus your attention on your topic? Were you able to generate some ideas about that topic? *Answers will vary.*

Freewrite

Freewriting involves recording the flow of thought in your mind. When you freewrite, you literally take dictation from your brain, letting your thoughts arise freely without controlling them in any way. You can begin with a particular topic to focus on or just record the mental "noise" going on in your head. This technique is an excellent tool for generating ideas for a wide variety of

[1]Wayne Dyer, *Your Sacred Self* (New York: HarperCollins, 1995), 147–152.

writing tasks. It will also help you understand what you already know about your topic.

In order to freewrite most effectively, follow the next two guidelines.

Write for a Prescribed Length of Time. Ten or fifteen minutes is enough. During that time, do not stop writing. If your mind goes blank, write "my mind is blank my mind is blank" over and over until another thought occurs to you.

Don't Censor Your Thoughts. Write down *everything* you're thinking, even if it seems silly or irrelevant. Don't judge or evaluate your thoughts now—just put them on the page. If your train of thought moves away from your original topic to another subject, let it.

Forget About Grammar and Spelling. Don't worry about punctuation, capital letters, or the spellings of words. When you freewrite, you'll be more productive if you forget about the rules. Don't slow yourself down by wondering whether you should use a comma or a semicolon. Write as fast as you can, and don't try to write complete sentences. The brain thinks in fragments and phrases, so your freewriting should be a collection of partial and half-formed thoughts. As a result, you'll probably end up with sloppy, seemingly incomprehensible scribblings. If other people were to read your freewriting, it probably wouldn't make any sense to them. But it's not meant for others to read. You alone will see these pages—this activity is a tool for the *writer* exploring ideas. Later on, you'll sculpt them into a document suitable for the reader's eyes.

Beyond generating ideas, freewriting can be helpful in other ways. Like brainstorming, it can be an effective tool for problemsolving and self-understanding. When something is bothering you, spend some time emptying your thoughts onto paper. This is a good technique for identifying the source of the problem and generating possible solutions. Also, freewriting is an effective tool for clearing your mind of clutter before you begin a task, such as writing a memo, that will demand your full concentration. Freewrite to give your other thoughts some attention. Then they'll be less likely to intrude when you need to focus your mental efforts on one particular project.

The following is a sample of freewriting on the topic *my car*. If you adhere to the guidelines, your freewriting should look something like this example.

---

my poor car its so old worn out making funny noises and rattles transmission is wearing out need a new one but they're so expensive 400 a month how can I afford that much maybe a used car but where can I find a good one maybe Car Max in Charlotte heard they were good should drive over this weekend and take a look before I break down on the side of the road

---

Notice that this freewriting contains no punctuation marks. Also, it does not bother with complete sentences, capital letters, or spelling corrections.

PRACTICE 1.6
Freewrite

Freewrite about your topic for ten minutes in the space below.

Answers will vary.

_____

_____

_____

_____

_____

_____

_____

_____

_____

_____

_____

_____

_____

_____

_____

_____

_____

_____

Cube

In cubing, you begin with a particular topic and then explore its different aspects, as if you were examining the different sides, or faces, of a cube. To examine either the topic itself or some narrowed aspect of that topic, you describe it, tell a story about it, compare or contrast it to something else, tell how to do it, give examples of it, analyze its causes or effects, divide it, classify it, define it, or argue for it. Try to come up with several ideas in each category. For example, if your topic is *Miami*, your cubing might look like this:

MIAMI

Describe it
- distinguishing features
- details about certain areas
- Miami architecture

Compare or contrast it
- Miami vs. New York
- Miami crime rate vs. national crime rate
- Miami beaches vs. California beaches

Give examples of it
- best Miami restaurants
- famous Miami residents

Divide it
- sections of the city

Define it
- what makes Miami unique

Tell a story about it (relate experiences)
- a vacation in Miami
- a recent business trip to Miami

Tell how to do it (explain procedures)
- how to get around in Miami
- how to adapt to the hot climate

Analyze its causes or effects
- reasons for its popularity

Classify it (group it into categories)
- types of Miami residents

Argue for it
- reasons why people should visit

Cubing is a more structured approach than the preceding idea-generation strategies. It will push you to think in specific ways and produce ideas in a systematic manner. It's an excellent method for generating many different ideas about a topic.

What you do with all of the ideas you come up with depends on your reader's needs. If that reader needs or wants a comprehensive report about the topic, your paper will probably include many of the ideas in your lists. If he or she is more interested in a specific aspect of the topic, you would focus on the idea in that area. For example, if your supervisor plans to attend a seminar in Miami and needs more information about the city, you'd want to tell her how to get around, and you might recommend some good restaurants. If she is considering relocating the company, she'll want to know more about Miami residents and reasons for Miami's popularity.

PRACTICE 1.7
Cube

Use either your general topic or one particular example or aspect of that topic. Fill in the blanks below with ideas about it. *Answers will vary.*

Describe it   *Tell a story about it*

_____   _____

_____   _____

_____   _____

_____   _____

Compare or contrast it

_____

_____

_____

_____

Tell how to do it

_____

_____

_____

_____

Give examples of it

_____

_____

_____

_____

Analyze its causes or effects

_____

_____

_____

_____

Divide it

_____

_____

_____

_____

Classify it

_____

_____

_____

_____

Define it

_____

_____

_____

_____

Argue for it

_____

_____

_____

_____

List

Listing is another orderly way to generate ideas. It's like brainstorming because you write down words or phrases related to your topic. However, listing is more structured in two ways. First of all, you usually set a target number of items to produce (for example, ten ways to save money on household utilities, or five reasons for joining a campus club). Second, rather than writing the items randomly across the page, as you do when you brainstorm, you impose order by lining them up in a column and numbering them. You might also arrange your list by using certain patterns, such as most important to least important, or lowest to highest.

Lists can be valuable tools for discovering ideas, arranging them, and pushing yourself to think more about the topic than you would otherwise. If you've numbered your paper from 1 to 10 but have listed only seven items, chances are that you'll continue to ponder the subject in hopes of completing the list.

PRACTICE 1.8
List

Use specific aspects of your topic to fill in the blanks in the following lists. *Answers will vary.*

Five ways to _____

1. _____

2. _____

3. _____

4. _____

5. _____

Four things that _____

1. _____

2. _____

3. _____

4. _____

Ten examples of _____

1. _____

2. _____

3. _____

4. _____

5. _____

6. _____

7. _____

8. _____

9. _____

10. _____

Use the Journalism Method

When a newspaper reporter goes out to collect information about an event or a situation, he or she gets answers to the following questions: Who? What? When? Where? Why? How? Asking (and finding answers to) these questions about your topic can be an effective way to generate ideas. For example, if you've been assigned to evaluate a particular software package for your office, you could explore different aspects by asking questions such as the following.

Who designed this software?

Who manufactures it?

What can the software do?

What are its distinguishing features?

When did it first become available?

When was it last updated?

When can you expect it to arrive after placing an order?

Where should it be installed? (Does everyone in the office need it?)

Why is this company's product better than others?

Why do we need it in our office?

How much does it cost?

How will the manufacturer help us install and maintain it?

How will we pay for it?

Investigating the answers to all of these questions should provide you with an abundance of good ideas for the report you need to write.

PRACTICE 1.9
Use the Journalism Method

Generate specific Who? What? When? Where? Why? How? questions for your topic or a specific aspect of your topic. Then jot down answers to each.

Answers will vary.

_____

_____

_____

_____

_____

_____

_____

_____

_____

_____

_____

_____

_____

_____

_____

_____

_____

_____

_____

_____

Answer Questions

You might view this final invention strategy as a combination of cubing and the journalism approach. As in the journalism method, you answer Who? What? When? questions about your topic. But now these questions are more specific, related to particular aspects or facets of the subject. Here is one possible list of such questions.

1. How can X be described?
2. How did X happen?
3. What kind of person is X?
4. What is my memory of X?
5. What is my personal response to X?
6. What are the facts about X?
7. How can X be summarized?
8. What does X mean?
9. What is the essential function of X?
10. What are the component parts of X?
11. How is X made or done?
12. How should X be made or done?
13. What are the causes of X?
14. What are the consequences of X?
15. What are the types of X?
16. How does X compare to Y?
17. What is the present status of X?
18. How should X be interpreted?
19. What is the value of X?
20. What case can be made for or against X?[2]

As with cubing, your goal is to produce a variety of specific questions so that you can explore different angles of your main topic. For example, if your supervisor at work asks you to find out more about 401(k) investment plans for employees, substitute the phrase _401(k) Plans_ (or specific aspects of that topic) for the X in each of the twenty questions just listed. Then, by considering the answers to the resulting questions, you should discover many significant ideas.

[2]Jacqueline Berke, _Twenty Questions for the Writer_ (San Diego: Harcourt Brace Jovanovich), ix–x.

PRACTICE 1.10
Answer Questions

A. Use the foregoing list of twenty questions to generate specific questions related to your topic.

Answers will vary.

_____

_____

_____

_____

_____

_____

_____

_____

_____

_____

_____

_____

_____

_____

_____

_____

_____

_____

_____

B. Choose five of the specific questions you generated for Part A and jot down some ideas in response to each.

Answers will vary.

_____

_____

_____

_____

_____

_____

_____

_____

_____

_____

_____

_____

_____

_____

_____

_____

_____

_____

_____

The ten different idea-generation strategies presented in this chapter will unlock the ideas in your head in various ways. To use these strategies most effectively, do the following:

1. Practice all of the methods to discover which ones work best for you.
2. If one method fails you, try another.
3. Combine two or more strategies to produce a wider range of ideas for a writing project.

With so many ways to discover what you can say, you'll never again have to stare at a blank sheet of paper in frustration or despair. You'll never again believe you have nothing to say, and your thoughts will be more original and more complete.

TEST YOUR UNDERSTANDING

1. What are four problems that result from not using idea-generation strategies?

   Lack of ideas, more difficult/more time-consuming writing, lack of originality, and

   incomplete writing

   _____

2. What's the difference between brainstorming and freewriting?

Brainstorming involves writing isolated words and phrases in no particular order

all over the page. Freewriting involves using stream of consciousness dictation in

sentence form; however, you do not worry about adhering to the rules of

standard English.

3. What's the difference between brainstorming and clustering?

Brainstorming involves randomly recording words and phrases. Clustering

involves grouping those words and phrases in specific trains of thought.

4. What two idea-generation techniques do not require pen and paper?

Talk and meditation

5. What two techniques both involve asking questions about the topic to get ideas?

The Journalism Method and Answer Questions

WEB ACTIVITY: Career Exploration

If you're unsure of your career goals, or if you're not sure what job within a particular career field is right for you, you can take a quiz that's designed to match your personal preferences with specific positions. Usually, the quiz will ask you about your interests, your likes and dislikes, and your skills and abilities. The results of the quiz help you understand what jobs best match your goals and desires.

1. Go to the College Board Career Search web site at *http://www. collegeboard.org/career/html/searchQues.html* and follow the directions for completing the Career Questionnaire.
2. The web site will suggest some jobs that may be right for you. Which of these jobs interests you? Why?
3. Click on the links to the descriptions of each job. Write a letter to at least one of the Sources for Additional Information to request more information about that job or career field.

GROUP PROJECT AND WRITING ACTIVITIES

Before working with a group of three or four of your classmates to complete some later activities, complete the following five activities on your own.

Make a list of five to ten areas in your city or town that need to be cleaned up, repaired, or renovated.

_____

_____

_____

_____

_____

_____

_____

_____

Choose one of the areas on your list and freewrite about it.

_____

_____

_____

_____

_____

_____

_____

_____

_____

_____

_____

_____

_____

_____

_____

_____

_____

Choose another area on your list and brainstorm about it.

_____

Choose a third area and cluster it.

Draw a fourth area from your list.

In a memo to your group members, briefly describe three of the areas on your list.

MEMORANDUM

TO: _____

FROM: _____

DATE: _____

SUBJECT: Three Areas That Need Improvements

_____

_____

_____

_____

_____

_____

_____

_____

_____

_____

With your group, discuss the areas you all described in your memos. Together, decide on one area the group will focus on for the activities in the next two chapters. Write that area here:

On your own, use one or more of the idea-generation strategies to discover more ideas about the area your group chose. Record your ideas in the space below.

READINGS Do you set specific goals for yourself? Do you write them down? What goals have you already achieved in your life? Think of your personal, professional, and academic achievements.

In the following article, business trainer Bobbe Sommer explains a step-by-step procedure for setting goals.

As you read this article, circle every word that's unfamiliar to you. Look it up in a dictionary and write the meaning in the margin. Put an exclamation point (!) next to any sentence or paragraph you find especially interesting. Put a question mark (?) next to any sentence or paragraph you don't understand.

The Power of Goal Setting

Bobbe Sommer

The difference between success and failure is goal setting. So why don't most people ever bother to set goals? Quite frankly, most don't know how. Find out how you can join the people who are getting what they want from their lives.

1 When baby elephants are trained for the circus, a chain is clamped on one ankle and staked in the ground. Determined, the elephant pulls and pulls and pulls. Each time he tugs the chain, it rubs his sore ankle. Soon, he learns he can't go anywhere. He's stuck. Remember the saying, "Elephants never forget"? As he grows to 2 or more tons, the elephant still thinks he's stuck.

2 To reinforce the elephant's belief, circus trainers never change the size or heaviness of the chain or stake. Yet at any moment, the adult elephant could pick up his foot, snap the chain in half and walk away. But he doesn't. And the result is sometimes tragic. Elephants die in fires because they won't move—they believe they can't.

3 Think about your beliefs. Do you feel stuck in your job or personal life? When you set goals, your life completely changes. Goals provide you with a feeling of control, a sense that you're calling the shots in your life.

4 "A goal is just a dream with a deadline," says Harvey Mackay, author of *Swim With the Sharks Without Being Eaten Alive* (Morrow, 1988). "If you have a clear, concise goal, the probability of success goes up dramatically. This is true at any stage of your life. And it's fun. Don't you think it's fun to continually improve yourself?"

The Seven Steps of Goal Setting

5 Most of us plan our vacations with more precision than we plan our lives. Sometimes "life just happens." Can you influence what happens to you in life? Are you in control or simply a victim of life's circumstances? It all depends on your point of view. If you tell yourself, "I want to get ahead but my boss won't let me," it will happen because you believe it just like the elephant who believes he's stuck.

Bobbe Sommer, "The Power of Goal Setting," from *Women in Business* (January/February 1995): 27. This article was written for WOMEN IN BUSINESS® magazine. WOMEN IN BUSINESS is an official publication of the American Business Women's Association. The mission of ABWA is to bring together businesswomen of diverse occupations and to provide opportunities for them to help themselves and others grow personally and professionally through leadership, education, networking support and national recognition.

6   Start mapping your way to your dreams with these seven action steps to effective goal setting:

1. Identify the Goal

7 The first step in establishing a goal is the one that usually causes most people to stumble: You must figure out exactly what you want to accomplish. Think about setting goals in both your personal and professional life. Ask yourself questions such as, "What do I enjoy so much that I would pay people to let me do it?"

8   When you set goals, make sure they're S.M.A.R.T.:

9   *Specific.* "I want to be happy" is not a specific goal. Be specific: "I see myself working in pleasant surroundings, with positive, uplifting people around me." Target what's going to make you happy. When you state your goal, state it as an ongoing process. Make it sound as if you're doing it now. For example, "I am currently in the process of . . ." or "I'm allowing myself to. . . ." Your goals should be action-oriented in a positive, present tense.

10   *Measurable.* Establishing goals furnishes you with a clear-cut destination, and gives you a yardstick to help measure your advancement. Your goal may be to become a better salesperson. But how do you measure "better"? Instead, your goal should be "I am a salesperson who will meet and exceed the company goal of a 16 percent increase in sales by June 1, 19xx."

11   A measuring system helps you track your progress. If you have a set-back along the way, you can correct your actions and stay focused on your goal.

12   Measurement doesn't necessarily mean harsh judgment. Don't beat yourself up. Just make your measurement process serve as a guidepost, not a judgment call. Use a progress chart to mark each step along your goal path.

13   *Action-oriented.* This is the most important step in goal setting and goal keeping. Your action is the workhorse of your goal-setting venture. It will take time, thought and probably more perspiration than inspiration. As you build your action plan, follow these steps:

14   • Assess your past experiences. Take your last job and list the skills you learned. You'll develop a check-list of experiences you can transfer to a new job or career. If your goal is to get promoted or transferred, take a close look at all the jobs you've had. Examine your work experience, including part time, temporary and summer jobs. Identify all the skills you've learned. Count how many of those skills are transferable to the position you wish to hold when you reach your ultimate dream job.

15   For example, if your last job was working as an insurance agent, you learned skills such as listening, customer service, persuasion and negotiating. How will these skills help you achieve your dream job?

16   •   Determine what you love to do. Think about what you want from your career. List specific tasks you'd enjoy doing in your dream job. What would your title be?

17   *Realistic.* When your goals are realistic, you have to balance them between safe actions and risk taking. How far can you stretch and allow yourself to grow without being too secure? If you don't have a contract or deadline staring you in the face, decide what you can realistically accomplish in a given period, and then push yourself a little more.

18   For example, if you know you can make four sales calls a day, try for 22 calls a week. Small increases like two extra calls a week will be a comfortable stretch, and you'll reach your long-term objective of increased sales faster.

19   *Timing.* Neither your goals nor the time frame should be inflexible. You change. Conditions change. There is no reason why you shouldn't be able to alter your goals. Be sure the timing is right for your goals. If your goal is to complete your college degree, have three children and move into a new home in the next four years, you may want to reexamine your timing. You may need to scrap one or two goals in the short run but keep them as long-range goals.

2. Date the Goal

20 Write the year, day and month that you'll achieve that goal. Without a specific date, how will you know when you've reached your goal? A deadline will help you develop monthly, weekly and daily action steps.

3. What Are the Perceived Obstacles?

21 Will you need more education? Do you need to change jobs? Do you belong to professional organizations that will give you the people connections and credentials you'll need? List every obstacle you might encounter. By identifying potential roadblocks, you can develop specific actions to overcome them. Remember, an obstacle won't stop you unless you let it. When you fall short of your goals, try these four correction steps:

22   •   Figure out what went wrong. Derailment happens to everybody, and determining what knocked you off course will help you get back on track. Was your goal unrealistic? Were there roadblocks you didn't anticipate? Have you simply lost interest? Then determine how you can avoid a wrong turn again.

23   •   Develop a support system. Consult friendly folks with whom you can discuss your failure. Solicit their advice on where you went astray and how to proceed.

24   •   Don't call it a catastrophe if it isn't. It's easy to blow a failure out of proportion. Instead, step back and try to be objective. What's the real likelihood that you're doomed forever? Try to envision the worst-case

scenario that might result from your failure. Draw up a strategy and list possible solutions. If you develop a plan to overcome your worst-case scenario, you'll certainly be able to handle a less-than-worse-case crisis.

25   • Revise your goals. Accept the fact that perhaps a goal is too ambitious, then revise it. Break down your bigger aims into smaller ones that will be easier to achieve.

26   Don't give up. Abandoning your dream is a self-defeating mistake. Remember the words that Babe Ruth once told a reporter: "Every time I miss the ball, I get excited. It means I'm just one swing closer to my next home run."

4. Who Can Help You Achieve Your Goal?

27   Share your goal with people who will help champion your cause. Tap your network in professional organizations to form your own personal board of directors. While you're making connections, you may also meet a mentor.

28   Your friends can help you monitor your progress. After all, the prospect of disappointing someone else may keep you on track.

5. Identify Existing and New Skills

29   How will the skills you currently possess help you reach your goal? Can you blend some of your existing skills with new skills to get what you want?

30   Think about all the jobs you've ever had. Make a list of the key skills you learned in each job. Combine your workplace skills with skills you've learned through experiences, such as serving as president of an American Business Women's Association chapter. Together, this list of workplace skills and experiences is your "skill library"—a resource of talents you can tap. Your "skill library" should always be growing, so jot down one or two skills you might want to acquire or polish that will help you achieve your goal.

6. Develop an Action Plan

31   Where are you going to start? Break your goal into small pieces that form the stepping stones for reaching your goal. Your list of activities, such as developing a new skill, can become part of a daily, weekly, monthly or annual plan. Weave your action plans into your calendar.

7. What's in It for Me?

32   Many of us wander through life, tuned into WIFM—What's in it for me? You must sell yourself on the benefits of reaching your objective. Why would you want to carry through this goal?

33   You may need to revamp or reprioritize your goals to make them fit into your current lifestyle. To determine whether your timing is realistic, ask others who are living the dream you hope to attain. Offer to take that person to lunch so you can find out more about what she does and how she does it. Your lunch meeting may bring more than good advice—you could

discover a mentor. Talking to others will help you identify more resources. Join professional organizations and share your career goals with others who can lead you to new opportunities.

34   Allow yourself ample time to complete one goal before you move on to the next or you'll feel pressed. Constantly update your action plan and look at your goals at least once a month. Remember, no goal is set in concrete. The second your goal gets off course, simply start correcting.

35   If you find yourself procrastinating, sit down and write ways you can stop the procrastination. If you routinely procrastinate working on a specific goal, it's probably a good time to change or delete that goal. By keeping your objectives open for fine-tuning, you'll be less likely to abandon them at a crisis point.

36   When you reach a goal, whether it is a short-term or long-range objective, reward yourself. Achievement and accomplishment don't accidentally happen. Your careful planning, thoughtful strategy and faithful execution helped you succeed.

37   Remember that life is not a dress rehearsal—it's opening night. Get out there and make your goals a reality.

RESPONDING TO THE READING

1. What are the seven steps of setting goals?

   Identify the goal, date the goal, decide what obstacles you perceive, identify people

   who can help you, identify existing and new skills, develop an action plan, and

   determine the benefits of reaching your objective.

2. On a separate piece of paper, use the brainstorming idea-generation strategy described in this chapter for the topic *My Goals*. *Answers will vary.*

3. On a separate sheet, use your brainstorming to create three lists, one for each of the following categories: Personal Goals, Academic Goals, and Professional Goals. *Answers will vary.*

4. From the three lists you created, choose the goal that's most important to you right now. Freewrite for ten minutes about this goal.
   Answers will vary.

5. Write a one-sentence goal statement that meets the author's S.M.A.R.T. criteria.

   Answers will vary.

BUILDING VOCABULARY

To add more creativity to your writing, you can use words that are *metaphoric*. A *metaphor* is a figure of speech that creates an interesting visual image as it compares two things. Metaphoric words or phrases make concise points by saying that one thing is another. For example, the article about setting goals contains the sentence

> By identifying potential **roadblocks,** you can develop specific actions to overcome them. (paragraph 21)

The author uses the metaphoric word *roadblocks* to compare problems or obstacles to physical barriers erected in streets. These obstacles, of course, are not literal roadblocks, but this word makes a point while producing an interesting visual picture for the reader.

A second example is in the sentence

> Just make your measurement process serve as a **guidepost,** not a judgment call. (paragraph 12)

In this sentence, the word *guidepost* is a metaphoric word that compares goal evaluation to a sign at a crossroad.

Each of the following sentences from the goal-setting article contains a metaphoric word or phrase. Circle that word or phrase; then briefly explain the comparison.

1. Establishing goals furnishes you with a clear-cut destination, and gives you a yardstick to help measure your advancement. (paragraph 10)

2. Your action is the workhorse of your goal-setting venture. (paragraph 13)

3. Derailment happens to everybody, and determining what knocked you off course will help you get back on track. (paragraph 22)

4. Break your goal into small pieces that form the stepping stones for reaching your goal. (paragraph 31)

5. By keeping your objectives open for fine-tuning, you'll be less likely to abandon them at a crisis point. (paragraph 35)

6. Remember that life is not a dress rehearsal—it's opening night. (paragraph 37)

Has there ever been a time in your life when problems and obstacles repeatedly held you back from achieving a particular goal? Do you know someone who never gives up on a dream or a goal, even when the going gets tough?

In the next story, writer Eudora Welty describes one woman who refuses to give up.

As you read this story, circle every word that's unfamiliar to you. Look it up in a dictionary and write the meaning in the margin. Put an exclamation point (!) next to any sentence or paragraph you find especially interesting. Put a question mark (?) next to any sentence or paragraph you don't understand.

A Worn Path

Eudora Welty

1   It was December—a bright frozen day in the early morning. Far out in the country there was an old Negro woman with her head tied in a red rag, coming along a path through the pinewoods. Her name was Phoenix Jackson. She was very old and small and she walked slowly in the dark pine shadows, moving a little from side to side in her steps, with the balanced heaviness and lightness of a pendulum in a grandfather clock. She carried a thin, small cane made from an umbrella, and with this she kept tapping the frozen earth in front of her. This made a grave and persistent noise in the still air that seemed meditative, like the chirping of a solitary little bird.

2   She wore a dark striped dress reaching down to her shoe tops, and an equally long apron of bleached sugar sacks, with a full pocket: all neat and tidy, but every time she took a step she might have fallen over her shoelaces, which dragged from her unlaced shoes. She looked straight ahead. Her eyes were blue with age. Her skin had a pattern all its own of numberless branching wrinkles, as though a whole little tree stood in the middle of her forehead, but a golden color ran underneath, and the two knobs of her cheeks were illuminated by a yellow burning under the dark. Under the red rag her hair came down on her neck in the frailest of ringlets, still black, and with an odor like copper.

3   Now and then there was a quivering in the thicket. Old Phoenix said, "Out of my way, all you foxes, owls, beetles, jack rabbits, coons and wild animals! . . . Keep out from under these feet, little bob-whites. . . . Keep the big wild hogs out of my path. Don't let none of those come running my direction. I got a long way." Under her small black-freckled hand her cane, limber as a buggy whip, would switch at the brush as if to rouse up any hiding things.

4   On she went. The woods were deep and still. The sun made the pine needles almost too bright to look at, up where the wind rocked. The cones dropped as light as feathers. Down in the hollow was the mourning dove—it was not too late for him.

5   The path ran up a hill. "Seem like there is chains about my feet, time I get this far," she said, in the voice of argument old people keep to use with themselves. "Something always take a hold of me on this hill—pleads I should stay."

6   After she got to the top, she turned and gave a full, severe look behind her where she had come. "Up through pines," she said at length. "Now down through oaks."

7   Her eyes opened their widest, and she started down gently. But before she got to the bottom of the hill a bush caught her dress.

"A Worn Path" from *A Curtain of Green and Other Stories*, copyright 1941 and renewed 1969 by Eudora Welty, reprinted by permission of Harcourt, Inc.

8   Her fingers were busy and intent, but her skirts were full and long, so that before she could pull them free in one place they were caught in another. It was not possible to allow the dress to tear. "I in the thorny bush," she said. "Thorns, you doing your appointed work. Never want to let folks pass, no sir. Old eyes thought you was a pretty little *green* bush."

9   Finally, trembling all over, she stood free, and after a moment dared to stoop for her cane.

10   "Sun so high!" she cried, leaning back and looking, while the thick tears went over her eyes. "The time getting all gone here."

11   At the foot of this hill was a place where a log was laid across the creek.

12   "Now comes the trial," said Phoenix.

13   Putting her right foot out, she mounted the log and shut her eyes. Lifting her skirt, leveling her cane fiercely before her, like a festival figure in some parade, she began to march across. Then she opened her eyes and she was safe on the other side.

14   "I wasn't as old as I thought," she said.

15   But she sat down to rest. She spread her skirts on the bank around her and folded her hands over her knees. Up above her was a tree in a pearly cloud of mistletoe. She did not dare to close her eyes, and when a little boy brought her a plate with a slice of marble-cake on it she spoke to him. "That would be acceptable," she said. But when she went to take it there was just her own hand in the air.

16   So she left that tree, and had to go through a barbed-wire fence. There she had to creep and crawl, spreading her knees and stretching her fingers like a baby trying to climb the steps. But she talked loudly to herself: she could not let her dress be torn now, so late in the day, and she could not pay for having her arm or her leg sawed off if she got caught fast where she was.

17   At last she was safe through the fence and risen up out in the clearing. Big dead trees, like black men with one arm, were standing in the purple stalks of the withered cotton field. There sat a buzzard.

18   "Who you watching?"

19   In the furrow she made her way along.

20   "Glad this not the season for bulls," she said, looking sideways, "and the good Lord made his snakes to curl up and sleep in the winter. A pleasure I don't see no two-headed snake coming around that tree, where it come once. It took a while to get by him, back in the summer."

21   She passed through the old cotton and went into a field of dead corn. It whispered and shook and was taller than her head. "Through the maze now," she said, for there was no path.

22   Then there was something tall, black, and skinny there, moving before her.

23   At first she took it for a man. It could have been a man dancing in the field. But she stood still and listened, and it did not make a sound. It was silent as a ghost.

24 "Ghost," she said sharply, "who be you the ghost of? For I have heard of nary death close by."

25 But there was no answer—only the ragged dancing in the wind.

26 She shut her eyes, reached out her hand, and touched a sleeve. She found a coat and inside that an emptiness, cold as ice.

27 "You scarecrow," she said. Her face lighted. "I ought to be shut up for good," she said with laughter. "My senses is gone. I too old. I the oldest people I ever know. Dance, old scarecrow," she said, "while I dancing with you."

28 She kicked her foot over the furrow, and with mouth drawn down, shook her head once or twice in a little strutting way. Some husks blew down and whirled in streamers about her skirts.

29 Then she went on, parting her way from side to side with the cane, through the whispering field. At last she came to the end, to a wagon track where the silver grass blew between the red ruts. The quail were walking around like pullets, seeming all dainty and unseen.

30 "Walk pretty," she said. "This the easy place. This the easy going."

31 She followed the track, swaying through the quiet bare fields, through the little strings of trees silver in their dead leaves, past cabins silver from weather, with the doors and windows boarded shut, all like old women under a spell sitting there. "I walking in their sleep," she said, nodding her head vigorously.

32 In a ravine she went where a spring was, silent flowing through a hollow log. Old Phoenix bent and drank. "Sweet gum makes the water sweet," she said, and drank more. "Nobody know who made this well, for it was here when I was born."

33 The track crossed a swampy part where the moss hung as white as lace from every limb. "Sleep on, alligators, and blow your bubbles." Then the track went into the road.

34 Deep, deep the road went down between the high green-colored banks. Overhead the live-oaks met, and it was as dark as a cave.

35 A black dog with a lolling tongue came up out of the weeds by the ditch. She was meditating, and not ready, and when he came at her she only hit him a little with her cane. Over she went in the ditch, like a little puff of milkweed.

36 Down there, her senses drifted away. A dream visited her, and she reached her hand up, but nothing reached down and gave her a pull. So she lay there and presently went to talking. "Old woman," she said to herself, "that black dog come up out of the weeds to stall you off, and now there he sitting on his fine tail, smiling at you."

37 A white man finally came along and found her—a hunter, a young man, with his dog on a chain.

38 "Well, Granny!" he laughed. "What are you doing there?"

39 "Lying on my back like a June-bug waiting to be turned over, mister," she said, reaching up her hand.

40   He lifted her up, gave her a swing in the air, and set her down. "Anything broken, Granny?"

41   "No, sir, them old dead weeds is springy enough," said Phoenix, when she had got her breath. "I thank you for your trouble."

42   "Where do you live, Granny?" he asked, while the two dogs were growling at each other.

43   "Away back yonder, sir, behind the ridge. You can't even see it from here."

44   "On your way home?"

45   "No sir, I going to town."

46   "Why, that's too far! That's as far as I walk when I come out myself, and I get something for my trouble." He patted the stuffed bag he carried, and there hung down a little closed claw. It was one of the bob-whites, with its beak hooked bitterly to show it was dead. "Now you go home, Granny!"

47   "I bound to go to town, mister," said Phoenix. "The time come around."

48   He gave another laugh, filling the whole landscape. "I know you old colored people! Wouldn't miss going to town to see Santa Claus!"

49   But something held old Phoenix very still. The deep lines in her face went into a fierce and different radiation. Without warning, she had seen with her own eyes a flashing nickel fall out of the man's pocket onto the ground.

50   "How old are you, Granny?" he was saying.

51   "There is no telling, mister," she said, "no telling."

52   Then she gave a little cry and clapped her hands and said, "Git on away from here, dog! Look! Look at that dog!" She laughed as if in admiration. "He ain't scared of nobody. He a big black dog." She whispered, "Sic him!"

53   "Watch me get rid of that cur," said the man. "Sic him, Pete! Sic him!"

54   Phoenix heard the dogs fighting, and heard the man running and throwing sticks. She even heard a gunshot. But she was slowly bending forward by that time, further and further forward, the lids stretched down over her eyes, as if she were doing this in her sleep. Her chin was lowered almost to her knees. The yellow palm of her hand came out from the fold of her apron. Her fingers slid down and along the ground under the piece of money with the grace and care they would have in lifting an egg from under a setting hen. Then she slowly straightened up; she stood erect, and the nickel was in her apron pocket. A bird flew by. Her lips moved. "God watching me the whole time. I come to stealing."

55   The man came back, and his own dog panted about them. "Well, I scared him off that time," he said, and then he laughed and lifted his gun and pointed it at Phoenix.

56   She stood straight and faced him.

57   "Doesn't the gun scare you?" he said, still pointing it.

58   "No, sir, I seen plenty go off closer by, in my day, and for less than what I done," she said, holding utterly still.

59   He smiled, and shouldered the gun. "Well, Granny," he said, "you must be a hundred years old, and scared of nothing. I'd give you a dime if I had

any money with me. But you take my advice and stay home, and nothing will happen to you."

60   "I bound to go on my way, mister," said Phoenix. She inclined her head in the red rag. Then they went in different directions, but she could hear the gun shooting again and again over the hill.

61   She walked on. The shadows hung from the oak trees to the road like curtains. Then she smelled wood-smoke, and smelled the river, and she saw a steeple and the cabins on their steep steps. Dozens of little black children whirled around her. There ahead was Natchez shining. Bells were ringing. She walked on.

62   In the paved city it was Christmas time. There were red and green electric lights strung and criss-crossed everywhere, and all turned on in the daytime. Old Phoenix would have been lost if she had not distrusted her eyesight and depended on her feet to know where to take her.

63   She paused quietly on the sidewalk where people were passing by. A lady came along in the crowd, carrying an armful of red-, green- and silver-wrapped presents; she gave off perfume like the red roses in hot summer, and Phoenix stopped her.

64   "Please, missy, will you lace up my shoe?" She held up her foot.

65   "What do you want, Grandma?"

66   "See my shoe," said Phoenix. "Do all right for out in the country, but wouldn't look right to go in a big building."

67   "Stand still then, Grandma," said the lady. She put her packages down carefully on the sidewalk beside her and laced and tied both shoes tightly.

68   "Can't lace 'em with a cane," said Phoenix. "Thank you, missy. I doesn't mind asking a nice lady to tie up my shoe, when I gets out on the street."

69   Moving slowly and from side to side, she went into the big building, and into a tower of steps, where she walked up and around and around until her feet knew to stop.

70   She entered a door, and there she saw nailed up on the wall the document that had been stamped with the gold seal and framed in the gold frame, which matched the dream that was hung up in her head.

71   "Here I be," she said. There was a fixed and ceremonial stiffness over her body.

72   "A charity case, I suppose," said an attendant who sat at the desk before her.

73   But Phoenix only looked above her head. There was sweat on her face; the wrinkles in her skin shone like a bright net.

74   "Speak up, Grandma," the woman said. "What's your name? We must have your history, you know. Have you been here before? What seems to be the trouble with you?"

75   Old Phoenix only gave a twitch to her face as if a fly were bothering her.

76   "Are you deaf?" cried the attendant.

77   But then the nurse came in.

78 "Oh, that's just old Aunt Phoenix," she said. "She doesn't come for herself—she has a little grandson. She makes these trips just as regular as clockwork. She lives away back off the Old Natchez Trace." She bent down. "Well, Aunt Phoenix, why don't you just take a seat? We won't keep you standing after your long trip." She pointed.

79 The old woman sat down, bolt upright in the chair.

80 "Now, how is the boy?" asked the nurse.

81 Old Phoenix did not speak.

82 "I said, how is the boy?"

83 But Phoenix only waited and stared straight ahead, her face very solemn and withdrawn into rigidity.

84 "Is his throat any better?" asked the nurse. "Aunt Phoenix, don't you hear me? Is your grandson's throat any better since the last time you came for the medicine?"

85 With her hands on her knees, the old woman waited, silent, erect and motionless, just as if she were in armor.

86 "You mustn't take up our time this way, Aunt Phoenix," the nurse said. "Tell us quickly about your grandson, and get it over. He isn't dead, is he?"

87 At last there came a flicker and then a flame of comprehension across her face, and she spoke.

88 "My grandson. It was my memory had left me. There I sat and forgot why I made my long trip."

89 "Forgot?" The nurse frowned. "After you came so far?"

90 Then Phoenix was like an old woman begging a dignified forgiveness for waking up frightened in the night. "I never did go to school, I was too old at the Surrender," she said in a soft voice. "I'm an old woman without an education. It was my memory fail me. My little grandson, he is just the same, and I forgot it in the coming."

91 "Throat never heals, does it?" said the nurse, speaking in a loud, sure voice to old Phoenix. By now she had a card with something written on it, a little list. "Yes. Swallowed lye. When was it—January—two—three years ago—"

92 Phoenix spoke unasked now. "No, missy, he not dead, he just the same. Every little while his throat begin to close up again, and he not able to swallow. He not get his breath. He not able to help himself. So the time come around, and I go on another trip for the soothing medicine."

93 "All right. The doctor said as long as you came to get it, you could have it," said the nurse. "But it's an obstinate case."

94 "My little grandson, he sit up there in the house all wrapped up, waiting by himself," Phoenix went on. "We is the only two left in the world. He suffer and it don't seem to put him back at all. He got a sweet look. He going to last. He wear a little patch quilt and peep out holding his mouth open like a little bird. I remembers so plain now. I not going to forget him again, no, the whole enduring time. I could tell him from all the others in creation."

95 "All right." The nurse was trying to hush her now. She brought her a bottle of medicine. "Charity," she said, making a check mark in a book.

96 Old Phoenix held the bottle close to her eyes, and then carefully put it into her pocket.

97 "I thank you," she said.

98 "It's Christmas time, Grandma," said the attendant. "Could I give you a few pennies out of my purse?"

99 "Five pennies is a nickel," said Phoenix stiffly.

100 "Here's a nickel," said the attendant.

101 Phoenix rose carefully and held out her hand. She received the nickel and then fished the other nickel out of her pocket and laid it beside the new one. She stared at her palm closely, with her head on one side.

102 Then she gave a tap with her cane on the floor.

103 "This is what come to me to do," she said. "I going to the store and buy my child a little windmill they sells, made out of paper. He going to find it hard to believe there such a thing in the world. I'll march myself back where he waiting, holding it straight up in this hand."

104 She lifted her free hand, gave a little nod, turned around, and walked out of the doctor's office. Then her slow step began on the stairs, going down.

RESPONDING TO THE READING

1. This story can be read as an *allegory*, a type of story in which the characters, events, and places all represent ideas. Explain how "A Worn Path" can be interpreted as an allegory for perseverance in achieving goals. What does Phoenix represent? Together, what do the things she encounters—such as the terrain she travels, the dogs, and the hunter—stand for?

   Phoenix could represent someone who pursues an important goal. The challenges

   she encounters represent the obstacles that must be overcome in pursuit of a goal.

   _____

   _____

2. Though Phoenix is determined to reach her destination, she stops several times on her journey to rest, to drink the sweet spring water, and to dance with the scarecrow. If you're reading this story as an allegory for setting and achieving goals, how could you interpret Phoenix's brief stops to do these things along the way?

   Even when pursuing an important goal, a person should not forget to take care of

   himself or herself and enjoy life by having some fun.

   _____

   _____

   _____

3. A phoenix is a mythological bird that lives for five hundred years before it dies in flames and then rises from its own ashes to a new life. Why is Phoenix an appropriate name for the main character of this story?

   Phoenix's difficult journey exhausts her and perhaps even brings her closer to her

   own death, but her errand ensures life and renewed strength for her grandson.

4. When Phoenix speaks, she uses an ungrammatical, nonstandard dialect of English. For example, she says, "Here I be," instead of "Here I am." What does this dialect tell you about Phoenix?

   She lacks formal education.

BUILDING VOCABULARY

When you look up an unfamiliar word in the dictionary, you'll often find several different meanings and variations for it. You have to look at the *context* (the words, phrases, and sentences surrounding that word) to determine which definition applies.

Also, you may need to determine the word's part of speech in the sentence. Many words can function as different parts of speech (for example, the word *left* can be a noun, a verb, an adjective, or an adverb), so you'll have to figure out how the word is being used before you can decide which definition applies. For example, the word *furrow* can be either a noun or a verb:

> She kicked her foot over the ***furrow***, and with mouth drawn down, shook her head. . . . (paragraph 28)

In this sentence, the word is a noun, but the noun form has two different meanings: "a long, shallow trench made by a plow," or "a deep wrinkle in the skin." The words that surround *furrow* in the example sentence help you conclude that it refers to the trench made by a plow.

The following sentences all come from "A Worn Path." Look up the italicized words in a dictionary and determine which definition best describes how those words are being used.

1. Down in the ***hollow*** was the mourning dove—it was not too late for him. (paragraph 4).

   Noun: a small valley between mountains.

2. Her fingers were busy and ***intent,*** but her skirts were full and long, so that before she could pull them free in one place they were caught in another. (paragraph 8)

   Adjective: firmly focused; concentrated.

(continued)

3. The deep lines in her face went into a fierce and different *radiation.* (paragraph 49)

   Noun: extension of straight lines from or toward a center.

   _____

4. She *inclined* her head in the red rag. (paragraph 60)

   Verb: bend or lower the head.

   _____

   _____

5. "All right. The doctor said as long as you came to get it, you could have it," said the nurse. "But it's an *obstinate* case." (paragraph 93)

   Adjective: difficult to cure.

   _____

   _____

2 Vivid Language

PROFESSIONAL PROFILE
Buffie Buchanan, Registered Nurse

As a registered nurse in the emergency room of a large hospital, Buffie Buchanan's major responsibilities include assessing a patient's condition through interviews and tests, carrying out doctors' orders, and watching for changes in the patient's status. As she performs these duties, she must write down her actions and observations in meticulous detail.

To communicate accurately with other health care professionals, nurses need to use precise and vivid language. The following example comes from Buffie's narrative notes on a trauma flow sheet for a patient in her care.

> 1652: Patient brought in via EMS after one-vehicle accident. Airway patient oxygen saturation 92% on room air. Oxygen placed on patient at 2 liters via nasal cannula. Cardiac monitor in place. Respiration 22. Heart rate 96. Blood pressure 145/85. Patient with complaint of pain in right lower quadrant of abdomen radiating to right lower back. Abdomen soft and tender to palpation over right lower quadrant. Glasgow Coma Scale score of 12. Pupils equal and reactive to light. Patient denies headache or blurred vision. Distal pulses +2 in upper and lower extremities.

> 1654: Doctor Jones in with patient.
> 1657: X-ray in for portable chest x-ray.
> 1659: Lab in with patient.
> 1702: Patient to CT via stretcher with 2 liters oxygen via nasal cannula. Side rails up x2.

This sample includes strong verbs (*brought, placed, denies*) and exact adjectives (*one-vehicle, soft, tender, reactive*). It also includes considerable specific detail, such as numerical data and the locations of the patient's pain.

Chapter 2 discusses how these types of vivid language will improve your writing.

Why is this passage from a travel guide good writing?

The Florida Keys are a wilderness of flowering jungles and shimmering seas, a jade necklace of mangrove-fringed islands dangling toward the tropics. Take pleasure as you drive down U.S. 1 along the islands. Most days you can gaze over the silvery blue and green Atlantic and its still-living reef, with Florida Bay, the Gulf of Mexico, and the backcountry on your right (the Keys extend east-west from the mainland). At a few points the ocean and gulf are as much as 10 miles apart. In most places, however, they are within one to four miles, and on the narrowest landfill islands, they are separated only by the road.

Things to do and see are everywhere, but first you have to remind yourself to get off the highway. Once you do, rent a boat and find a secluded anchorage and fish, swim, or marvel at the sun, sea, and sky. In the Atlantic you can dive to spectacular coral reefs or pursue dolphin, blue marlin, andother deep-water game fish. Along the Florida Bay coastline you can seek out the bonefish, snapper, snook, and tarpon that lurk in the grass flats and in the shallow, winding channels of the backcountry.

With virtually no distracting air pollution or obstructive high-rises, sunsets are a pure, unadulterated spectacle that each evening attracts thousands of tourists and locals to waterfront parks, piers, restaurants, bars, and resorts throughout the Keys.[1]

After reading this passage, do you want to visit the Florida Keys? Why? To participate in the activities the writer describes? To see the beautiful scenery? The writer of this passage hoped to whet your appetite for his subject by creating very appealing images of the islands. If you'd like to visit the Keys after reading this description, the writer succeeded: he achieved his purpose.

When writers can describe something in a way that paints a picture in the minds of readers, they are communicating with those readers successfully. They create these mental pictures by using *vivid language*. The four kinds of vivid language are *factual and sensory details, strong verbs, exact adjectives,* and *figures of speech*.

In the passage aboout the Florida Keys, the writer uses all four types of vivid language to help the reader form a crisp mental image of the islands. He includes factual details such as the specific names of the trees, the fish, the bodies of water, and the highway. He also includes sensory details such as the colors of the sea and the beauty of the sunsets. This writer also uses strong action verbs such as *rent, find, fish, swim, marvel, dive, pursue,* and *seek* to describe things you can do in the Keys. Precise, exact adjectives such as *shimmering, still-living, secluded, spectacular, shallow,* and *winding* create clear mental images that stimulate the reader's desire to experience this place personally. And early in the passage, the writer uses a figure of speech, a metaphor that compares the Florida Keys to a jade necklace, to help the reader picture the islands and their beauty.

Vivid language brings your ideas alive by painting pictures with words. When you write with vivid language, you'll not only help readers understand you better, you'll also keep their attention by providing them with sentences that are interesting to focus on.

DETAILS

The people who use words—not the words themselves—decide the meanings of those words. Words are arbitrary combinations of letters and sounds that we decide will designate certain things or ideas. The word *truck*, for example, is a combination of five letters that we've all agreed we'll use to name a particular kind of vehicle. However, many of the words in our language can suggest different meanings to different people. For some, the word *truck* calls to mind a two-passenger pickup, while others picture an eighteen-wheeler semi.

[1]*Florida Keys Destination Guide* [Online]. http://dest-excite.previewtravel.com/DestGuides/0,1208,EXC_194,00.html.

That's why when you write, it's important to choose words that leave no doubt about what you mean. When you use specific, detailed language, you will not risk the reader's misunderstanding you by attaching to your words different meanings than you intended.

General Versus Specific Language

Words have different levels of generality. For instance, examine the following list:

food

sweets

junk food

candy

chocolate

Hershey's chocolate bar with almonds

The items in this list move from very general (*food*, a category that includes a variety of things to eat, including meat and fruit) to very specific (one particular brand and type of candy bar). The more general the word, the greater the risk of miscommunication with readers: when you use a word such as *food*, they will at best conjure up in their minds a shadowy image of something on a plate—and at worst, attach a meaning (*peanut butter sandwich*, for instance) that you didn't intend at all. The more specific you can be, the sharper and clearer the image you generate in a reader's mind, and the less likely it is that the reader will misinterpret what you write or say.

Bad writing is often filled with general language, words that are too vague or too broad to create a specific mental picture. If you're writing an e-mail to a co-worker asking her to order lunch for a staff meeting, she might order Chinese food when you mean for her to order barbecue. If you're writing a letter to your customers, they may not respond to your announcement of a *sale* if they don't know you really mean *half-price clearance*. In both cases, the writing would be bad because it could not fulfill its purpose; that is, because one or two general words might allow the readers to decide on meanings you did not intend.

As you compose, evaluate each word choice to determine whether you're choosing a general word when a specific one is more appropriate. Don't write the word *animal* when you really mean *German shepherd*. Don't choose the word *appliance* when you really mean *microwave oven*. Don't write *beverage* when you mean *lemonade*. In the following examples, which are all based on actual newsletters, reports, and letters, note how the meaning becomes clearer when the general language (italicized) is replaced with more specific terms.

General:	Whether you sit down every day to *conventional meals* or *eat throughout the day*, try to include *foods from all Food Pyramid groups*.
More specific:	Whether you sit down every day to *breakfast, lunch, and dinner* or *snack every three to four hours*, try to include *dairy products, meat, vegetables, fruit, bread, and cereals*.
General:	*Cutting Edge* must verify that all *restrooms* comply with *the law*.
More specific:	*Cutting Edge architects* must verify that all *restrooms in their commercial designs* comply with the *regulations of the Americans with Disabilities Act*.

General: One of my first actions as manager of Freeman's was to direct my *staff* to develop a *planning policy* that *involves everyone affected.*

More specific: One of my first actions as manager of Freeman's was to direct my *three assistant managers* to develop a *long-term planning process* that *asks for suggestions from employees of all five store departments.*

General: *Area hospitals* do allow doctors to practice *alternative medicine.*

More specific: *Franklin Memorial Hospital and St. Joseph's Hospital* do allow doctors to practice *acupuncture.*

As a final example, read the following two versions of the same passage from a military recruitment brochure. The first relies heavily on general language (in italics). The second substitutes the more specific words that make the meaning clearer.

General:

My parents always told me I could do *anything.* I *went* to college, but afterward I still had few *marketable skills,* so I worked in *a low-paying job.* Then I found out *what the military offers.* I enlisted, and I'm receiving valuable *training for my future.*

More specific:

My parents always told me I could choose *any career I wanted.* I *graduated* from college, but afterward I still didn't have the *computer and communication skills employers want,* so I worked as a *minimum-wage grocery store cashier.* Then I found out about the military's *career training, medical benefits, higher education options, and travel opportunities.* I enlisted, and I'm receiving valuable training in computer maintenance for a future career in business or industry.

**PRACTICE 2.1
Specific Language**

Rewrite each of these sentences to replace each italicized general word or phrase with a more specific choice. *Answers will vary.*

1. You don't have to eat only *traditional foods* for breakfast. Feel free to enjoy *nontraditional foods,* too.

   You don't have to eat only bacon, eggs, toast, and cereal for breakfast. Feel free to

   enjoy pizza, cheese and crackers, and fried chicken, too.

2. Our office needs the *supplies and equipment* to prepare newsletters and *advertising materials.*

   Our office needs graphic design software, a laser printer, and high-quality paper to

   prepare newsletters, brochures, and magazine advertisements.

3. Students' increased use of *technology* will require that *educational institutions redefine instructional delivery systems*.

   Students' increased use of computer software, the Internet, and e-mail will require

   colleges to offer more online distance education programs.

   _____

4. Please provide *our office* with *information* you want included in our *report*.

   Please provide the Human Resources Office with a list of preferred benefits you want

   included in our annual employee survey for the president.

   _____

5. If you have good employees, one way to keep them is by offering *financial incentives*.

   If you have good employees, one way to keep them is by offering annual bonuses

   and regular pay raises.

6. This *summer, consumers* can expect *transportation costs* to *rise*.

   This June and July, motorists can expect gas prices to increase by ten cents per

   gallon.

Factual and Sensory Details

Clear and interesting writing includes not only specific word choices but also factual and sensory details. Factual details include information such as names, quantities, dates, and dimensions. For instance, in the earlier list, the reader's mental image is sharpened with information such as *Hershey's* (the brand of candy) and *with almonds* (one of the distinguishing ingredients in the chocolate bar). Describing a house as a Colonial with two stories provides factual details that help the reader form a clearer picture of the subject. In the following passage from a town's annual report to its citizens, the writer has not included many factual details. The italicized questions indicate opportunities for more specific information.

> When the current water-bond project is completed *[By whom? When?]*, public water will be available to far more households *[How many? Where?]*. This project will bring public water to a majority *[How many?]* of homes in our county.

Adding the facts brings the subject into crisper focus:

> When the *Public Works Department* completes the current water-bond project *in June*, public water will be available to *1500 more* households in *western Turner County*. This project will bring public water to *90 percent* of households in our county.

Here are two more examples, one from a letter soliciting donations to a medical research organization and one from a computer company's web page.

Not enough facts:	If you are a woman, your chance of developing cancer is high *[How high?]*. If you are a man, it's even higher *[How high?]*.
Effective factual detail:	If you are a woman, you have a *30 percent* chance of developing cancer. If you are a man, your chance increases to *50 percent*.
Not enough facts:	The Professional Series of desktop computers delivers *[How? With what?]* fast performance.
Effective factual detail:	The Professional Series of desktop computers includes a *600MHz Pentium III processor* for fast performance.

Sensory details sharpen the reader's mental image by providing sight, smell, taste, touch (physical sensation), or sound information. For example, that two-story Colonial house you're describing might be built of red brick (a sight detail) next to a babbling brook (a sound detail) and landscaped with fragrant rosebushes (a smell detail). Each detail you add makes the subject come more alive on the page. The following sentences come from advertisements. Notice how the addition of sensory details produces clearer images in your mind.

Example 1:

The IntelliSystem monitors your central air conditioner and alerts you if it detects a malfunction.

Revised to add sound and sight details:

The IntelliSystem monitors your central air conditioner and alerts you *with a piercing beep and a flashing red light* if it detects a malfunction.

Example 2:

You'll love our delicious steaks.

Revised to add taste details:

You'll love every *juicy bite* of our delicious steaks, which are *so tender you can cut them with a fork.*

Example 3:

From head to toe, this statue of Elvis captures his passionate spirit as never before.

Revised to add sight details:

From *glossy jet-black hair* to *studded white bellbottoms,* this lifelike statue of Elvis captures his passionate spirit as never before.

One final example comes from an apartment-complex manager's letter to her tenants. The first version includes a few sensory details.

I've hired a man to pick up trash on the grounds. He has already gathered a lot of trash around the buildings and in the surrounding woods. From now on, please help us keep the grounds clean by putting trash in the dumpsters.

Now notice how adding sensory information, along with a few factual details, makes the subject more vivid and interesting:

I've hired a man to pick up trash on the grounds. He has already filled his pickup truck twice with empty beer cans and soda bottles, greasy oil filters, rotting fruit rinds, soggy cardboard, and other unsightly garbage. Now that the grassy areas and surrounding woods are neat and clean, please help us keep them that way by putting trash in the dumpsters.

Adding details about sights, sounds, smells, tastes, and physical sensations helps the reader visualize the subject for better understanding.

PRACTICE 2.2
Details

Add factual details to the following sentences. *Answers will vary.*

1. A musician *[Who? What kind?]* will perform *[What kind of music?]* live in our lobby *[When?]*.

   Bob Wilson, a guitarist, will perform blues and folk music on Friday from 4:00 until

   7:00 P.M. in our lobby.

2. Now under construction, the park *[Which one? Where?]* will provide *[For whom?]* a number *[How many?]* of recreational and relaxation opportunities *[What kinds?]*.

   Rocky River Park on Highway 126 will provide area residents with opportunities to

   swim, fish, canoe, and picnic.

3. Army soldiers help people *[Who?]* as they travel the world *[Where?]*.

   Army soldiers deliver food and supplies to war victims in countries engaged in civil

   conflicts.

4. I would like to apply for a position *[Which one?]* at your plant *[Which one? Where?]*.

   I would like to apply for a position as an engineering maintenance supervisor at

   your tire plant in Detroit, Michigan.

5. Synthetic motor oil may cost more *[How much more?]*, but it will save us money *[How much?]* on our maintenance of company vehicles.

   Synthetic motor oil may cost a dollar more per can, but it will save us over $10,000

   per year on our maintenance of company vehicles.

Add at least two sensory details of two different types (sights, sounds, smells, tastes, and physical sensations) to the following sentences. *Answers will vary.*

6. When an emergency arises, Turner County ambulances rush to the scene to save lives.

   When an emergency arises, Turner County ambulances rush to the scene, with red

   lights flashing and sirens screaming, to save lives.

   _____

7. The writing team just emerged from the office after an all-night session.

   The writing team, yawning and bleary-eyed with fatigue, just emerged from the

   office after an all-night session.

8. After the fire, the detective examined the remains of the building.

   After the fire, the detective examined the smoking remains of the blackened shell of

   the building.

9. I ordered the shrimp dinner, which I could not eat.

   I ordered the shrimp dinner, which I could not eat because it was mushy and

   smelled like rotten fish.

10. The lakefront property is an excellent location for a new restaurant.

   The long sandy stretch of lakefront property, where motorboats buzz back and

   forth all day, is an excellent location for a new restaurant.

   _____

EXACT ADJECTIVES

The second type of vivid language is exact adjectives. Adjectives are words that describe nouns. They tell how many, what kind, or which one. The italicized words and phrases in this list are all exact adjectives.

the *red* wagon
an *elderly* gentleman
six eggs
these graphs
the airline *offering the discount*
the toy *that everyone wants*

This kind of descriptive information, combined with specific details, helps create clear images in your reader's mind. Adjectives are especially important when we describe an object, a person, or a place. They provide the important information the reader must have if he is to "see" what you saw. Notice how the writer of the following paragraph from a brochure uses describing words (in italics) to help you picture the subject.

As a *new EarthCare Club* member, you will receive a *one-year* subscription to our *award-winning* magazine EARTHCARE. Each *colorful* issue is filled with *stunning nature* photography that will remind you of the *breathtaking* beauty of the plants, animals, and *geographical* wonders of our planet. *EarthCare* members also receive *half-price* discounts on EarthCare Club's *excellent* books and *travel* tours.

The next passage is from an e-mail message warning users about a computer virus. The first version, which includes few adjectives, offers a flat, lifeless description of the subject.

Apparently, a user has manufactured a virus. Other viruses cannot compare to the power of this creation. The FCC says this virus requires no exchange of programs for a computer to be infected. Instead, systems spread it via the Internet. Once the virus infects a computer, it damages the processor by placing it in a loop. Unfortunately, a user will not recognize the problem until his or her system is destroyed.

A few spicy adjectives create a clearer and much more urgent version of the same message:

Apparently, a *warped computer* user has manufactured a *new computer* virus. Other *well-known* viruses cannot compare to the *destructive* power of this *diabolical* creation. The FCC says this *terrifying* virus requires no exchange of *software* programs for a *new* computer to be infected. Instead, *existing e-mail* systems spread it via the Internet. Once the virus infects a computer, it damages the processor by placing it in an *infinite binary* loop that will erase the hard drive. Unfortunately, the *novice computer* user will not recognize the problem until his or her *whole* system is destroyed.

Adjectives are important not only for describing things, but also for clarifying more abstract ideas. Often, the reader would not be able to understand the subject at all without crucial descriptive words. For example, in the following statement from a booklet about legal documents, necessary adjectives have been removed.

A living will is a document. It tells your doctor to stop treatment if you are in a condition.

The removal of the adjectives changes the meaning of the whole statement, which is no longer accurate. Now notice how the meaning becomes clear when the adjectives are restored:

A living will is a *legal* document. It tells your doctor to stop *life-sustaining* treatment if you are in an *incurable, comatose* condition.

Here is another example, from a travel agency's newsletter. In the first version, the adjectives are removed, causing misinformation.

Make your reservation minutes after midnight, when fares are available. Airlines enter fares into their computers in the morning. They also reopen seats people booked but never paid for.

When the adjectives are restored, the whole passage makes sense:

Make your *air* reservations about *thirty* minutes after midnight, when *bargain* fares are most available. Airlines enter *discounted* fares into their computers in the *slow, early-morning* hours. They also reopen *reduced-price* seats people booked but never paid for.

However, beware of overusing adjectives. You don't want to pile too many of them in front of your nouns, for too many can slow the pace of your sentences and bog down your ideas with unnecessary information. In the next examples, many of the adjectives are merely extra words adding no additional meaning. The first sentence comes from an advertisement for a book.

Too many adjectives:
A *miraculous* dream come true for the *passionate* mechanic, this *unique, one-of-a-kind* book mixes *dazzling, eye-catching, color-rich* photographs with *fascinating*, meticulously *researched* details about hundreds of *interesting* tools.

Revision:
A dream come true for the mechanic, this *unique* book mixes *colorful* photographs with *fascinating* details about hundreds of tools.

This next example comes from a report.

Too many adjectives:
In *today's modern* world, the *typical, cost-conscious* shopper expects *good, money-saving* value combined with *easy* convenience.

Revision:
Today's shopper expects both value and convenience.

One final example is from a memo.

Too many adjectives:
She manages with a *conservative, low-risk, nonaggressive* philosophy *that prevents her employees from taking chances and breaking out of the status quo.*

Revision:
She rarely risks letting her *innovative* employees break out of the status quo.

If you're placing two or three adjectives with every person, place, or thing you mention, go back and carefully evaluate each of your describing words. Select only those that seem essential. If you have a tendency to use too many adjectives, you may be relying on them to convey meaning that could be more effectively delivered by verbs. For example, in the last example, not only do the adjectives repeat each other, but a variation of one of them (*low-risk*) would function more effectively as a strong verb for the sentence. (Strong verbs are the topic of the next section.)

PRACTICE 2.3
Adjectives

Fill in the blanks in the following sentences with appropriate adjectives.
Answers will vary.
1. The group signed up for a <u>*three-hour*</u> tour of the <u>*historic*</u> city of Boston.

2. Don't pass up this <u>*amazing*</u> offer to get <u>*educational*</u> books for your <u>*preschool*</u> child.

3. When you bring your car for service, Fast Lube disposes of your <u>*used*</u> oil and filters in a <u>*responsible*</u> manner.

4. The company's *conservative* leaders do not approve of *long*

   hair or *casual* clothes for *male* employees.

5. The *50 percent* increase in *compact disc* orders over the past

   three months signals a *20 percent* increase in our com-

   pany's share of the *teenage* market.

STRONG VERBS

Clear, interesting writing always relies on strong action verbs to express ideas. The verb in a sentence is the part of speech that conveys the subject's action or state of being. The more descriptive the verb, the sharper the image in the reader's mind. Read the following passage from a city's newsletter to its citizens and notice how the italicized verbs add interesting action to the subject.

In February, demolition teams *attacked* the interior brick and concrete walls of the old mill. Workers with jack hammers and sledgehammers *opened* large, airy spaces, and natural light *poured* into the dark corners. Next, the crews *will install* energy-efficient window glass.

Another example comes from an environmental organization's brochure:

Across the country, EarthCare Club members *expand* our national parks and *protect* wilderness areas. They *lobby* legislatures for laws that preserve woodlands and prevent the destruction of wildlife habitats. They also *halt* damaging construction and pollution.

Boring writing is filled with boring verbs. As you write, you might have a tendency to choose some lackluster verbs because they occur to you first. You might be relying on weak "to be" or "to have" verbs. Though *be* and *have* do have their uses (and we cannot write without them), you might be choosing them *instead of* more interesting alternatives. In the following examples, the dull verbs are italicized. Notice how each revision substitutes a much more action-oriented choice.

Weak verb: Turner County *has* about 475 square miles and *has* a population of more than 60,000.

Strong verb: More than 60,000 residents *populate* Turner County, which *covers* about 475 square miles.

Weak verb: This cookout *will be* one with all the trimmings.

Strong verb: At this cookout, you *can pile* your plate with coleslaw, beans, chips, and more.

Weak verb: As a former preschool building, the facility *is* suitable for a learning environment.

Strong verb: As a former preschool building, the facility's environment *encourages* learning.

Weak verb: Military school terms *are* a few weeks to nearly a year.

Strong verb: Military school terms *range* in length from a few weeks to nearly a year.

In this next example, from a company's press release, the writer uses many dull verbs (italicized):

> Office Pro's greatest distinction *is* its staff of office supply experts. Some *have been* with Office Pro since it opened its doors in 1975. These experts *are* eager to answer your questions, and they *are* here to help you increase your office's efficiency.

The writer is relying too heavily on weak "to be" verbs. Note how the paragraph gets more interesting with the substitution of action-oriented verbs:

> A staff of office supply experts *distinguishes* the Office Pro team. Some *have worked* with Office Pro since it opened its doors in 1975. These experts *will* gladly *answer* your questions, and they *will help* you improve your office's efficiency.

Many times, the best verb for the sentence is lurking *within* the sentence, masquerading as another part of speech such as an adjective or noun. Creating a more interesting sentence, then, becomes a matter of rearranging the words to put the action where it belongs: in the verb.

Weak verb:	We *have been having* complaint calls from people who live in District 14. *[The best verb for this sentence is either* call *or* complain. *The first is disguised as a noun, and the second is hiding as an adjective.]*
Strong verb:	Residents of District 14 *are calling* to complain.
Weak verb:	California Chemical always *has* full inventories, ready for shipment from ten different warehouses. *[The most interesting verb is hiding as a noun.]*
Strong verb:	California Chemical always *warehouses* full inventories, ready for shipment from ten different locations.
Weak verb:	At our booth in the mall, we *will have* pencils, key chains, cups, and other giveaway items. *[The best verb is lurking as an adjective.]*
Strong verb:	At our booth in the mall, we *will give* away pencils, key chains, cups, and other items.
Weak verb:	Dynamic load testing *is* an effective method for troubleshooting problems and discovering wiring deficiencies. *[The best verbs are disguised as nouns.]*
Strong verbs:	Dynamic load testing effectively *troubleshoots* problems and *discovers* wiring deficiencies.

You can easily select strong verbs when you're describing action, such as that in a story. But get into the habit of evaluating your verbs in everything you write, from summaries to professional reports. In the next examples, from a brochure, note how the subject is made clearer and more interesting simply by substituting more vivid verbs.

Dull verbs:

If you want to be a leader, then the management program *may be* for you. There *is* hotel management, restaurant management, and even office management. If you're interested in retail sales, you *are* in luck. We *have* a six-month course that prepares you for leadership roles in department stores or smaller ones.

Revised for more interesting verbs:

If you want to be a leader, *sign up* now for our management program. *Study* for a career in hotel management, restaurant management, or even office management. If you're interested in retail sales, *prepare* for leadership roles in department stores or smaller ones by completing our six-month course.

Another example comes from a doctor's examination notes.

Dull verbs:

She *is* comfortable sitting, and she *does not have* discomfort when she moves her neck and shoulders. However, she *has* lumbar scoliosis, and her leg lengths *are* different. She *had* a leg-lengthening operation on her right femur when she was eight years old. She *has* soreness when she moves her back or raises her legs.

Revised for more interesting verbs:

She *sits* comfortably and *can move* her neck and shoulders without pain. However, scoliosis *curves* her lumbar spine, and her leg lengths *differ*. A surgeon *lengthened* her right femur when she was eight years old. She *complains* of soreness when she moves her back or raises her legs.

As you try out action-oriented verbs in your sentences, be prepared to experiment with the wording of each entire sentence. Often it's necessary to rearrange, delete, and add other parts of speech as you search for the best action word.

PRACTICE 2.4
Verbs

A. Rewrite the following passages to substitute more interesting verbs for those italicized. *Answers will vary.*

Rocky Mountain spotted fever *has* flulike aches and pains, headache, fever, chills, and vomiting. It *is* a condition that makes the person feel terrible. She *will have* a bumpy red rash all over her body.

Rocky Mountain spotted fever announces itself with flulike aches and pains,

headache, fever, chills, and vomiting. This condition makes the person feel terrible.

A bumpy red rash will cover her body.

Art classes at the academy *are* completely full, and there *are* now 175 children enrolled. Our newest curriculum *is* for kindergartners. We now *have* 25 of them painting, pasting, and coloring!

We have filled all art classes at the academy, and 175 children are now enrolled.

The kindergartners love our newest curriculum. Twenty-five of them can paint,

paste, and color.

B. In the following sentences, the best verb is disguised as another part of speech, such as a noun or an adjective. Locate that word; then rewrite the sentence so that the verb conveys the action. You may need to completely rearrange or add to the sentence to accommodate the best verb. *Answers will vary.*

1. The 911 Emergency System *is* under the supervision of the Information Management Office.

   The Information Management Office supervises the 911 Emergency System.

   _____

2. A regularly maintained vehicle *has* a higher resale value.

   A regularly maintained vehicle will sell for a higher value.

3. The focus of the seminar *is* practical tax-saving ideas for small business owners.

   The seminar focuses on practical tax-saving ideas for small business owners.

4. An e-mail message called "Free Vacation" *has* a virus that will wipe out your hard drive.

   The virus in an e-mail message called "Free Vacation" will wipe out your hard drive.

   _____

5. Elementary school children *may become* afraid to go to school after watching violent scenes on the news.

   Elementary school children may fear going to school after watching violent scenes

   on the news.

6. Creating an effective web page *should be* of utmost concern and importance to us.

   Creating an effective web page should concern us.

7. We *will have* a short meeting to get organized and decide on our priorities.

   We will meet briefly to get organized and decide on our priorities.

8. My intentions *are* to contact our customers with a survey by the end of the year.

   I intend to contact our customers with a survey by the end of the year.

   _____

9. Any supplies or equipment purchases *should be done* by Friday.

   All employees should purchase supplies and equipment by Friday.

   _____

10. The success of this program *is* dependent upon your support.

    The success of this program depends upon your support.

FIGURES OF SPEECH

Figures of speech are the fourth type of vivid language that adds interest and clarity to writing. Metaphors and similes, two specific types of vivid language, will create images in your readers' minds to help them understand your ideas. Both metaphors and similes creatively compare two things to reveal their similarity. Metaphors are direct comparisons. Similes are indirect comparisons that use the word *like* or *as*.

Metaphors:	Budget constraints have put this project *on the back burner.*
	Because our facility employs only fifteen people, the regional office considers us only *a small blip on the screen.*
	EarthCare Club members *are on the front lines*, battling greedy corporations that dispose of toxic waste illegally.
Similes:	Local residents named the train "Screech" because its shrill whistle pierced the night *like a woman's scream.*
	The children squirmed at their desks *like worms in a bait can.*
	Attending the managers' meeting is *like tiptoeing through a minefield.*

It is unlikely that you'll use much figurative language in professional writing such as memos or reports. However, this type of creative comparison often adds punch to persuasive writing in documents such as advertisements and sales letters. For example, the following example from an advertisement for Angel Soft toilet paper includes both metaphors and similes:

Bathroom flora (germs) are *fearsome little devils.* They spread *faster than an office rumor* and once they get around, they're hard to root out. . . . Once microscopic *beauties* like *E. coli*, *shigella*, and *salmonella* get loose and find a nice, damp place to live, they go crazy and start multiplying *like caffeinated rabbits.*[2]

A second example comes from a sales letter:

Let yourself be tempted with an affordable, totally irresistible grown-up treat. Hollywood's brightest hits. Over 250 of them. At a penny apiece, just *like old-fashioned candy.* It's the sweetest deal since the good old days.[3]

[2] Georgia-Pacific Corporation, advertisement for Angel Soft toilet paper in *Family Fun* (April 1999), 7.
[3] Columbia House Company, letter from Dennis Chandler (July 1999).

As you attempt to include more metaphors and similes in your writing, beware of clichés. A cliché is a phrase that's no longer fresh or interesting because it has been overused; therefore, it no longer creates a picture in the reader's mind. Clichés include similes such as the following.

as busy as a bee
as mean as a snake
as clear as a bell
as white as a ghost
spread like wildfire
slept like a log
cried like a baby

Instead of including dull, hackneyed phrases that everyone's heard before, strive for creativity in your comparisons. Make intriguing connections that startle or delight the reader with their originality.

PRACTICE 2.5
Figurative Language

Fill in the blanks below with original, descriptive metaphors or similes:
Answers will vary.

1. The angry director shouted like _____.

2. The scathing e-mail message shot through cyberspace like _____.

3. The line of people waiting to buy tickets was _____.

4. His small, windowless office is _____.

5. The computer screen remained as blank as _____.

6. Munchie potato chips are as crisp as _____.

7. Our new sweaters are as soft as _____.

To sum up these sections on details, adjectives, strong verbs, and figurative language, note how the following sentences all dramatically improve when they are revised to include various types of vivid language.

Example 1:
The work we did, clearing vegetation in the hot sun, was very hard.

Revised to add vivid language:
Soaked with sweat, we toiled in the blazing tropical sun, hacking down brush with machetes and raking it into piles for giant bonfires.

Example 2:
Summer is a good time for sky watching because of pleasant viewing conditions.

Revised to add vivid language:
Summer brings clear, balmy nights, perfect for gazing at the bright web of constellations in the southern sky.

Example 3:

With Telecentral, you will get good sound, connections, and customer service.

Revised to add vivid language:

Telecentral promises you crisp, clear sound quality and fast, solid connections. And you can call our friendly customer-service representatives at any time of the day or night.

Example 4:

The Central Command Office is responsible for recording all problems that come up.

Revised to add vivid language:

The Central Command Office will record on spreadsheets the severity, status, and response for all power outage problems.

Example 5:

Pristine's formula cleans dirt and kills germs.

Revised to add vivid language:

Pristine's new concentrated formula cuts through grease and grime, killing germs like staphylococcus.

Example 6:

Many people have sleep apnea, a breathing and snoring problem.

Revised to add vivid language:

About 20 million Americans suffer from sleep apnea, a dangerous disorder that causes interrupted breathing and loud snoring.

PRECISE WORD CHOICES

As you experiment with vivid details, exact adjectives, strong verbs, and figures of speech to enliven your writing, carefully evaluate the words you choose: make sure what meaning they convey. The English language contains over one million words, providing us with many fascinating options. However, this very variety of choice can increase the danger of selecting a word that does not accurately convey the intended meaning. As Mark Twain said, "The difference between the right word and the almost-right word is the difference between lightning and a lightning bug." Words have various shades of meaning that we must take into account as we search for the language to best express our thoughts.

Imprecise word choices will "sound" like wrong notes in a musical performance. For example, examine these sentences from brochures and letters:

The Occupational Safety and Health Administration (OSHA) *contemplates* that all health care providers offer free, confidential HIV tests for their employees. *[The writer probably wanted the word* stipulates.*]*

Politics is *inherit* in the Sheriff's Office. *[The word should be* inherent.*]*

They are making a *conscience* effort to improve handicapped accessibility. *[The word should be* conscious.*]*

Imprecise word choices come in a variety of flavors. Sometimes a writer accidentally chooses the wrong word through mistaking it for another that sounds very similar. For example:

If we *loose* tonight, we're out of the semifinals. *[Instead of* loose, *the writer means* lose.*]*

Or in the same vein, he might choose a homophone, a word that sounds like the intended word choice but is spelled differently.

One applicant graduated from the *Navel* Academy. *[The word should be* Naval.*]*

Other word choices are imprecise because they violate the tone of the rest of a document. For instance, when we toss an informal slang term into the middle of a serious report, or when we select a very formal word for a more conversational-sounding message, those inappropriate words sound wrong. One writer included this statement in her report about searching high school students for weapons:

Female students may object to physical searches for fear that security guards may try to cop a feel.

The phrase *cop a feel* is inappropriate slang, too conversational for a formal document like a report. Conversely, another writer included this sentence in an e-mail to his colleagues:

We will partake of a luncheon this Friday at the noon hour.

This sentence (particularly the use of the word *partake*) is too stiff and formal for a message of this type.

Another category of imprecise words includes synonyms with subtle but significant shades of meaning. Consider this list of words:

house
hut
shack
cabin
cottage
condominium
mansion
villa

Although they're all types of dwellings, they can't necessarily replace each other without significantly altering the meaning of the sentence. If you consult a thesaurus (a synonym dictionary) as you write, make sure you're selecting the word that most accurately reflects *your* intended meaning.

Finally, many imprecise word choices are ones writers think they know, but don't. Make sure you know the *exact* meaning of each word you select. When she wrote the following sentence in a report, the next writer clearly did not know the meaning of the italicized word:

A *precocious* child was pulling merchandise off the shelves and damaging it. *[The word* precocious *means "unusually mature," which does not fit the meaning of this sentence.]*

Think about the mental picture an imprecise word choice could conjure up for your readers—not only confusing them but even leaving them chuckling over a silly mental image. An example is this sentence from a memo:

The recent raise in salaries should improve employees' *morals*. *[The word should be* morale.*]*

PRACTICE 2.6
Precise Language

In the following sentences, choose the correct word from each pair in brackets:

1. Andy thought of an [ingenious/ingenuous] idea to save copying costs in the [Personal/Personnel] Department.

2. The state legislature just [past/passed] a bill requiring companies [to/too/two] provide insurance benefits for some part-time employees.

3. I [accept/except] your offer of the engineering position.

4. This decision will [effect/affect] everyone.

5. We can [proceed/precede] no [further/farther] without getting approval.

6. Can we [illicit/elicit] any more information about [their/there] plans for next year?

TEST YOUR UNDERSTANDING

1. Put this list in order from most general to most specific: printer, computer hardware, assets, computers, equipment, Hewlett-Packard LaserJet printer

   assets, equipment, computers, computer hardware, printer, Hewlett-Packard

   LaserJet printer

2. What is the difference between sensory details and factual details?

   Sensory details provide information about sights, smells, sounds, tastes, and

   physical sensations. Factual details provide information such as names, quantities,

   dates, and dimensions.

3. Why are adjectives important?

   They help readers form mental images, and they clarify the writer's ideas.

TEST YOUR UNDERSTANDING (continued)

4. What are two common weak verbs?

   "To be" verbs and "to have" verbs.

5. What is the difference between a metaphor and a simile?

   A metaphor is a direct comparison stating that one thing is another. Similes are

   indirect comparisons that use the word like *or* as.

6. What is one kind of imprecise word choice? Give an example.

   Answers will vary. Sample answer: Using a wrong homonym, such as principle *for*

   principal.

WEB ACTIVITY: Learning Styles

People do not all learn in the same way. Some people are auditory learners; they learn most easily when information is presented in the form of songs, poems, or sayings. Some people are visual learners; they need to see the information in writing, in graphs, or in pictures. Others are kinesthetic learners who learn best through hands-on activities that allow them to directly participate.

As a student, you should identify your learning style to help yourself know how to study information so that you'll remember it.

1. Go to the web site at http://silcon.com/~scmiller/multiple/ multiple_choice_questions.cgi and follow the directions to complete the Learning Style Survey.
2. Read the description of your learning style. Does it seem accurate? Why or why not?
3. Read the Learning Strategies list, which describes actions you can perform to help yourself learn better. How could you apply this advice to one of the classes you're enrolled in now?

GROUP PROJECT AND WRITING ACTIVITIES

In Chapter 1, you and your group selected an area in your city or town that needs to be cleaned up, repaired, or renovated. You'll be focusing on that area for the following activities.

Complete this activity on your own.

Go to the area your group chose. Closely examine it. In the space below, jot down notes about the details you notice.

SIGHTS:

SOUNDS:

SMELLS:

TASTES:

PHYSICAL SENSATIONS:

With your group, discuss the notes each of you recorded. If someone else noticed something you missed, add that detail to your own list.

On your own, write a detailed description of the area you examined. Use all four types of vivid language (factual and sensory details, exact adjectives, action verbs, and figures of speech) to create clear mental images for your reader.

_____

_____

_____

On your own, find a person who lives near, travels through, or uses the area you have just described in detail. Interview that person to discover his or her impressions or observations of this area. (See Appendix A for tips about conducting a successful interview.)

In the space below, write a summary of your interviewee's impressions or observations.

_____

_____

_____

_____

_____

_____

_____

_____

_____

_____

_____

_____

_____

_____

READINGS Do you feel as though you never have enough time to get things done? Do you put things off until the last minute? What are some of the ways you waste time?

The next article offers tips about using three different kinds of schedules to better manage your time.

As you read, circle every word that's unfamiliar to you. Look it up in a dictionary and write the meaning in the margin. Put an exclamation point (!) next to any sentence or paragraph you find especially interesting. Put a question mark (?) next to any sentence or paragraph you don't understand.

Time Flies!

Jerry White

Here's the buzz on how to keep it under control.

1 Beth's week was typical. On Sunday night, she was cramming for a Monday test and writing a paper that was due the Friday before.

2 On Monday, after the test, Beth had two free hours between classes, so she did a little shopping and had coffee with a friend. In the afternoon Beth did her laundry and talked with friends until dinner. The evening brought more distractions, and she finally began studying at 9 p.m. But she quit at 10:30 since no pressing assignments were due Tuesday.

3 Beth slept through Tuesday's first class, but made it to her 10 a.m. class. At noon she had a Bible study, and stayed to talk until her lab at 2. She studied well after dinner.

4 Wednesday was much like Monday.

5 On Thursday, Beth panicked: A paper was due the next day, and she had quizzes in her two toughest subjects. She studied two hours between classes and skipped lunch. That night, Beth had no time to study for her two quizzes because the paper took longer than expected. She finished at midnight.

6 Beth frantically reviewed between Friday's classes for the quizzes, and with a sense of relief, she took Friday evening off.

7 On Saturday, she slept till noon, went to a football game in the afternoon, and studied for an hour before getting ready for a date that night.

8 Sunday was another day of cramming. After church, Beth studied most of the afternoon. She spent some time with friends that night, and once again found herself studying late into the night preparing for Monday's assignments.

9 A busy week. But Beth was discouraged by how little she accomplished. And she hadn't even started the term paper that was due in three weeks.

10 Is there any possible way to avoid all these frustrations? Probably not all. But a scheduling strategy can help.

Easy as 1-2-3

11 I think it's a good idea to use three schedules throughout each term: 1) a basic calendar, with major events and assignments highlighted for the entire

Jerry White, "Time Flies," from *Making the Grade*. Reprinted by permission of the author.

term; 2) weekly plans, from which you'll work to plan each week; and 3) daily schedules, which will be revised according to that day's needs.

12   Here's a brief description of each:

13   A calendar is just that—a wall calendar, a desk calendar, whatever. Anything you can look at and see the entire term at a glance.

14   At the beginning of each term, write in the due dates for projects, term papers and exams. You may not know them all at first, but record them as soon as you do. You may even want to plan so that vacations can be free of studying. Also, note special activities you want to attend, like weekend retreats or athletic events.

15   Weekly plans will help you throughout the term. As soon as you know your class schedule for the term, make a master weekly planning chart of mandatory and important activities. (A sheet of paper with the days of the week divided into one-hour blocks will work fine.)

16   On your weekly plan, include such things as devotional time, church, classes, labs, and your work schedule (if you have a job). After charting your typical week, make enough copies on a copy machine to last you for the term.

17   Throughout the term, at the beginning of each week, add any additional activities for the coming week to your weekly plan. Some hints:

18   • Concentrate on doing most of your academic work Monday through Friday. (See "How Much Study Time?" below.)

19   • Plan extra study time for exams, but don't neglect your other subjects.

20   • Plan a day of rest—and that includes time off from studying. We all need times of spiritual and physical refreshment.

21   • Plan time for laundry, shopping, and other daily responsibilities.

22   • Plan for adequate rest and avoid all-nighters. Try to quit by 11 every night, no matter what remains undone. This forces you to study earlier in the day or week.

23   A daily schedule includes specific demands of each day:

24   • Each evening, jot down a time plan reflecting the needs of the next day. Remember: The busier you are, the tighter you must schedule.

25   • For each class, estimate what must be accomplished that day. You won't always finish in the allotted time, but stop and go on to the next subject anyway. Return to unfinished work later.

How Much Study Time?

26 Study time shouldn't be measured by whether we "feel" we have done enough. We must set goals to guide us in time allocations.

27   Most college students can do fine with 40–50 hours of class and study time per week. So, in terms of time invested, school is almost like a job.

28   A rule-of-thumb I recommend is 1½ hours of study outside of class for every hour spent in class. Certainly some courses require more than 1½ hours, and some considerably less.

29   Figure out your own required study time, using the above guidelines and depending on the difficulty of each course. Then make sure your schedule allows for that much study time per week. Early in the term, you may not have to study as much. But discipline yourself to use the time studying anyway; when things get tougher later in the term, you'll be glad you studied hard early in the term. During tough weeks with tests, projects and term papers, you'll probably need to increase your study time by several hours.

Some Good Ideas

30 Most of us develop techniques and habits that save time. Here are some of the things that worked for me:

31   Make good use of time between classes. The time between classes frequently escapes us due to conversations or lack of planning. Always plan to use that time constructively. Even the few minutes before your first class starts are a good time. When you have some free time, go directly to the library or study area and begin work. And think twice about going back to your room during the day. Daytime study there is rarely effective; you might be tempted to use the time unwisely.

32   Use Fridays well. The most universally wasted time is Friday afternoon between the end of classes and dinner. Most use it as a time to relax. But by studying hard during this time, as well as earlier in the day, you may find all your weekend work is done by Friday night. And unless you schedule a Friday night activity, use that time for study too. Your goal is to free up the weekend as much as possible for personal activities.

33   Use each weekday afternoon. Next to Friday, late afternoon is the most wasted time for students. What you do from 3 to 6 p.m. determines whether you study late that night or not. The more you do earlier in the day, the more free your evening will be for other activities.

34   Study in prime time. During study time, there are always a hundred other things to distract you, such as telephone calls, laundry and letters. Resist the temptation to do routine things during prime study times.

35   Find a place to study. Not everyone can study well where he lives. In any group living situation, interruptions are the norm. If it's difficult to concentrate where you live, find another place to study. And once you find this other place, use it regularly, not just when frustrations and interruptions get to you. Use it every night or on selected evenings.

36   One final tip: As you make your schedules, don't be too inflexible. A schedule is designed to serve you, not to be your master.

RESPONDING TO THE READING

1. Describe the three different types of schedules the author recommends for students.

   A calendar for the entire school term will allow you to see at a glance several

   months' worth of major due dates and events. A weekly plan allows you to block

   out regularly scheduled activities such as classes, church activities, and work.

   A daily schedule includes tasks you need to accomplish that day.

2. Follow the author's directions in the article to fill out the following monthly calendar. *Answers will vary.*

Sunday	Monday	Tuesday	Wed.	Thursday	Friday	Saturday

3. Follow the author's directions in the article to create your weekly plan for either this week or next week. *Answers will vary.*

4. Follow the author's directions to create your schedule for either today or tomorrow.

   Answers will vary.

**RESPONDING TO
THE READING**
continued

5. Do you waste time late in the afternoon (from 3:00 to 6:00 P.M.), especially on Fridays? What do you usually do then?

   Answers will vary.

6. In the following sentences, which all come from the article, underline the factual details, circle all of the adjectives, and draw boxes around the strong verbs:

   On Sunday night, she was cramming for a Monday test and writing a paper that was due the Friday before. (paragraph 1)

   But she quit at 10:30 since no pressing assignments were due Tuesday. (paragraph 2)

   During tough weeks with tests, projects and term papers, you'll probably need to increase your study time by several hours. (paragraph 29)

   The time between classes frequently escapes us due to conversations or lack of planning. (paragraph 31)

**BUILDING
VOCABULARY**

Knowing the meanings of prefixes can help you determine the meaning of a word. The *re-* prefix means "back or again." For example, the word *reviewed* in paragraph 6 of the preceding article means "viewed or looked at again."

What do the following words from the article mean?

1. revised (paragraph 11) *reconsidered and changed or modified*

2. retreats (paragraph 14) *a period of seclusion, retirement, or solitude*

3. refreshment (paragraph 20) *restoration or renewal*

4. reflecting (paragraph 24) *throwing or bending back*

5. remember (paragraph 24) *to think about again*

6. resist (paragraph 34) *to keep from giving in*

When you're at work, do people ever waste your time? In what ways? How do you respond to these people when you have a lot to do?

The next article offers some practical advice for dealing more effectively with people who start to waste your time.

As you read, circle every word that's unfamiliar to you. Look it up in a dictionary and write the meaning in the margin. Put an exclamation point (!) next to any sentence or paragraph you find especially interesting. Put a question mark (?) next to any sentence or paragraph you don't understand.

How to Drive the Stakes Through the Hearts of Time Vampires

Dan S. Kennedy

And even as they looked the thing that tore the throat out of Hugo Baskerville, on which, as it turned its blazing eyes and dripping jaws upon them, the three shrieked with fear and rode for dear life, still screaming, across the moor.

—*From* The Hound of the Baskervilles *by Sir Arthur Conan Doyle*

1   Time vampires are needy, thirsty, selfish, vicious creatures who, given an opportunity, will suck up all of your time and energy, leaving you white, weak, and debilitated. Once they have found a good meal, they start coming back every day. Even though you regenerate yourself with a meal, a night's sleep, and a vial of vitamins, it's to no avail; they will be waiting for you tomorrow, eager to once again suck every ounce of life from your veins.

2   Being able to recognize these vampires on sight is the first step to protecting yourself from them. And being willing to deal with them as you should a vile, evil, bloodsucking creature of the dark is the first step in freeing yourself from them.

"Have You Got a Minute?"

3   Perhaps the most insidious of all the time vampires is Mr. Have-You-Got-A-Minute? He lurks in the shadows in the hall outside your office, near the elevator, near the cafeteria, in the bushes next to the parking lot, wherever it is possible to catch you off guard. If you give in to him a few times, he becomes emboldened and starts "dropping in" to your office or home. He disarms you with: "Have you got a minute?" or "I just need a couple minutes of your time" or "I just have one quick question." He has a unique knack of pulling this stunt right when you are in the middle of doing something incredibly important like getting mentally prepared for a crucial phone call.

4   If you are in his vicinity all day, he will also "drop by" a dozen times a day, each time needing "just a minute." Each time he drops by, picture him sinking his teeth into your neck and sucking out a pint or two. This is the effect he has.

5   The temptation to give in to this particular vampire is almost irresistible. First of all, it just seems easier to deal with his "one quick question" immediately than to put him off and have it hanging over you for later. Second, it feels rude and unreasonable to refuse him. But the truth is, he deserves no courtesy whatsoever. He is telling you that your time is less valuable than his, that whatever you are doing is unimportant and easily interruptible. So go ahead and stick a stake through his heart without remorse.

6   Here's the stake: "I'm busy right now. Let's meet at 4:00 p.m. for 15 minutes and tackle everything on your list at one time." This tactic stops this bloodthirsty vampire in his tracks. It freezes him like a deer caught in the glare of headlights. Next, it "teaches" this vampire a new discipline. Of course, he

Dan S. Kennedy, "How to Drive Stakes Through the Hearts of Time Vampires," *The Small Business Journal.* Reprinted by permission.

won't get it the first time, or the second. He will keep trying for a while. But if you whip out this same stake every time, over and over again, eventually he will get the message. Someday, he will call you and say something like: "I have five things I need to go over with you. When can we get together?" After you pick yourself up off the floor, you can congratulate yourself on having de-fanged and housebroken a vampire.

"She's in a Meeting"

7 The next most dangerous time vampire is Ms. Meeting. Some people are always in meetings. Just this week, as I was finishing this book, a client dragged me into a 20-minute, four-person conference call to discuss when we could have the next, longer conference call, to plan a meeting.

8   Being in meetings is seductive. It's a way to feel important. It's also a great way to hide from making and taking responsibility for decisions. "Meetingitis" is a disease that turns businesses into unproductive, slow-moving, indecisive coffee klatches. The toughest CEOs I know hold only "stand up" meetings.

9   According to a study published in *Corporate Meetings* magazine, people spend an average of 20 to 40 hours per month in meetings, an increase over previous years. The average time spent in meetings by managers is 1.7 hours a day, and executives spend 50% of their time in meetings. Those surveyed said that the most productive meetings lasted under an hour, but most meetings lasted two hours or longer.

10   The other day I called a company, pressed for some information, and got this response from the frazzled receptionist: "Everybody's in meetings. I don't know anything. Please call back some other time when there might be somebody available who knows something."

11   You need to stop and ask yourself: Do I really need to be in (or hold) this meeting? Is there a more time-efficient way to handle this? A conference call? A memo circulated to each person?

12   If you are going to hold a meeting, there are things you can do to keep it from being an endless "blood klatch" for the other vampires:

13   (a) Set it up for immediately before lunch or at the end of the day, so the vampires are eager to get it done and over with so they can turn into bats and fly out of there.

14   (b) Don't serve refreshments.

15   (c) Circulate, in advance, a written agenda.

16   (d) Communicate a clear, achievable objective for the meeting.

17   If you must attend a meeting, there are things you can do to get in and out fast. First, determine in advance what information you are to contribute, then do it with a prepared, concise presentation. Second, have an exit strategy. Get someone to come in to get you at a certain time or make sure your beeper goes off or receive a call on your cell phone. You can excuse yourself to make a call, promising to return but you probably won't.

Playing Trivial Pursuit

18 Another time vampire to watch out for is Mr. Trivia. He either can't or doesn't want to differentiate between the important or unimportant, the major and the minor.

19 This guy's talent is getting others off-track, getting you to set aside your carefully organized list of priorities in favor of his own. More often than not, his priorities will be of minimal importance. Mr. Trivia can interrupt to tell you just about anything, ranging from "The building is on fire" to "The office supply store has delivered blue pens instead of black pens," and usually it'll be the latter.

20 The best way to deal with this one is to drop a big silver cross around his neck and kick him off the parapet of your castle. But failing the opportunity to do that, you need another stake, interrupting the interrupter: "I have an exceptionally busy day, so I am only dealing with the nines and tens on a one to ten scale. Everything else must wait until tomorrow. Are you convinced that what you want to talk to me about is a nine or ten?"

21 He will say, "No, but . . ." and then you must again rudely interrupt him: "No buts. Thanks. We'll get to it tomorrow." Then physically get away. If he's in your office, *you* leave.

22 He will be offended. Good. The odds of his holding the trivial matter over until tomorrow and bringing it back to you are less than 50-50. He'll go sink his teeth into somebody else's throat. He may even resolve it on his own. But he won't patiently wait until tomorrow.

Oh Boy, It's Soap Opera Time!

23 Have you ever watched a soap opera diva overact? Someone can walk into a room and say, "Ronald has just been murdered and is lying outside on the lawn with a pink flamingo stuck through his chest." Or the statement might be, "It's raining outside." Either way, you get to watch the same overreaction: crying, sobbing, pulling hair, chest heaving, and body twisting.

24 Some people are just like soap opera actors in real life. They turn everything into an emotional crisis. They react to everything emotionally. They magnify everything's importance. If you're not careful, they'll pull you right into the drama. When they do, visualize them sticking in the IV and taking out a quart.

25 The other problem with these particular vampires is that at the very least, you give up some of your time putting them back together emotionally. They play on your guilt until you give them your shoulder to cry on. But while they're resting their head on your shoulder, they're sticking their teeth into your neck.

26 Some people have the amazing ability to turn every molehill into a mountain. If you happen to have some of these overreactive, emotionally wrought weepers in your organization, get rid of them if you can. If you can't do that, then stay away from them.

27   There are two ways to drive them away. First, cut to the core of their problem (which is usually glaringly obvious) and tell them what to do. This is not what they want. They don't want solutions; they want soap opera. Spoil their fun and they will go looking for blood elsewhere. Second, take over the conversation by launching into a long, boring, pointless story. Say something like, "That reminds me of a time when my Uncle Harold was in the dust bowl during the Great Depression. This story will help you . . ." In other words, turn into a vampire yourself and start sucking.

Are There Other Time Vampires?

28   There are almost as many different varieties of time vampires as there are birds or butterflies. Your productivity multiplies as you get more skilled at spotting them and driving stakes through their hearts.

How I Stupidly Put Out the Welcome Mat for the Time Vampires and Let Them Suck Me Dry

29   An article in *Business Today* magazine describes how Bill Arnold, in one of his first acts as president of the Centennial Medical Center, yanked his office door from its hinges and suspended it from the lobby ceiling to demonstrate his commitment to an open door policy. This was applauded by the magazine as some giant act of courage and creativity. I chuckled when I read this. Mr. Arnold has my sympathy. To the management theorists who get all excited when they hear this sort of thing, I say, "Come on out into the real world, where they eat their young every day, and try this yourself. You won't last a week."

30   This is nothing new or revolutionary or innovative. In fact, I made that same mistake about 15 years ago. I pried the office door off the hinges, nailed it to the wall sideways, and proclaimed that from now on the president's office had a true "open door policy." High drama. Incredible stupidity.

31   All day long, an endless parade of time vampires came in. Suck, suck, suck. By the end of the day, my neck looked like a pin cushion. I was whiter than typing paper. Slumped over my desk, I didn't even have enough energy left to sit upright. I'm telling you they just lined up, marched in, and happily took turns siphoning me dry. The only thing that stopped them from slicing me up and consuming me completely was the clock reaching 5:00 p.m. I put out the vampire welcome mat and they took me up on the invitation. It was all my fault, of course.

32   Ideas like open door policies look great on paper. Unfortunately, a lot of these ideas are put on paper by authors who lack real world experience, are safely nestled on a college campus somewhere, and have a good time dreaming up clever-sounding psychobabble buzz words and hot, new management theories to baffle and bedazzle us with. Well, don't believe everything you read.

33   Ask yourself if you're doing something now to invite the vampires in for a feast. If so, stop doing it.

**RESPONDING TO
THE READING**

1. Describe a time vampire you've known in your personal, professional, or academic life. By acting on the advice in this article, how could you prevent that particular vampire from wasting your time?

   Answers will vary.

   _____

2. Underline the simile in paragraph 6.

   "like a deer caught in the glare of headlights"

3. Underline the cliché in paragraph 26.

   "every molehill into a mountain"

4. In the following sentences, underline the sensory details, circle the adjectives, and draw boxes around the strong verbs.

   He lurks in the shadows in the hall outside your office, near the elevator, near the cafeteria, in the bushes next to the parking lot, wherever it is possible to catch you off guard. (paragraph 3)

   But while they're resting their head on your shoulder, they're sticking their teeth into your neck. (paragraph 25)

   I pried the office door off the hinges, nailed it to the wall sideways, and proclaimed that from now on the president's office had a true "open door policy." (paragraph 30)

   By the end of the day, my neck looked like a pin cushion. I was whiter than typing paper. (paragraph 31)

**BUILDING
VOCABULARY**

When you encounter an unfamiliar word as you read, you may be able to figure out its meaning by using *context clues*. The context of a word is its relationship to the other words, phrases, and sentences that surround it. Four different types of context clues can help you draw conclusions about the unfamiliar word.

One type of context clue is *example*. You may find an example nearby that makes the word's meaning more clear. For instance, look at this sentence from paragraph 10 of "Time Vampires":

> The other day I called a company, pressed for some information, and got this response from the *frazzled* receptionist: "Everybody's in meetings. I don't know anything. Please call back some other time when there might be somebody available who knows something."

The receptionist's frustrated response gives you an example of *frazzled*.

A second type of context clue is *contrast*, which gives you a clue to a word's meaning by revealing what it does *not* mean. For example, look at a sentence from paragraph 29:

> To the management *theorists* who get all excited when they hear this sort of thing, I say, "Come on out into the real world, where they eat their young every day, and try this yourself."

(continued)

BUILDING VOCABULARY *continued*

This sentence contrasts the world of the theorists with the "real world," which helps you understand that the word *theorists* means "someone who speculates or thinks in abstractions."

A third type of context clue is *definition/restatement*. In this type of clue, either the word's meaning is directly stated, or synonyms are used to restate it. Paragraph 30 contains a sentence that uses restatement:

This is nothing new or revolutionary or *innovative*.

The word *innovative* means "new and revolutionary," so other words in the sentence restate its meaning.

A final type of context clue is *explanation*. Sometimes the context will explain enough about a word for you to figure out its meaning. For example, in paragraph 20, look at this sentence:

The best way to deal with this one is to drop a big silver cross around his neck and kick him off the *parapet* of your castle.

The sentence tells you that a parapet is part of a castle and that you can kick someone off it; therefore, you can conclude that it's some type of raised architectural structure.

How do the context clues in the following sentences from "Time Vampires" help you understand the meanings of the italicized words? For each word, tell what type of context clue is included, along with what appears to be the word's meaning. *Meanings will vary.*

1. And being willing to deal with them as you should a *vile*, evil, blood-sucking creature of the dark is the first step in freeing yourself from them. (paragraph 2)

   Definition/restatement; "disgusting"

2. Even though you *regenerate* yourself with a meal, a night's sleep, and a vial of vitamins, it's to no avail; they will be waiting for you tomorrow, eager to once again suck every ounce of life from your veins. (paragraph 1)

   Contrast; "revive"

3. All day long, an endless parade of time vampires came in. Suck, suck, suck. . . . I'm telling you they just lined up, marched in, and happily took turns *siphoning* me dry. (paragraph 31)

   Explanation; "draining"

4. Time vampires are needy, thirsty, selfish, vicious creatures who, given an opportunity, will suck up all of your time and energy, leaving you white, weak, and *debilitated*. (paragraph 1)

   Explanation; "showing impairment of energy or strength"

5. Here's the stake: "I'm busy right now. Let's meet at 4:00 for 15 minutes and tackle everything on your list at one time." This *tactic* stops this bloodthirsty vampire in his tracks. (paragraph 6)

   Example; "an expedient for achieving a goal"

3 Four Rules for Clear Sentences

PROFESSIONAL PROFILE
Raul Romero, Construction Superintendent

After working as a tile contractor, Raul Romero earned a degree in building construction technology and now oversees entire residential construction projects. His duties include meeting with homeowners to determine their needs and then reviewing blueprints and making adjustments. He also supervises and coordinates the activities of contractors, subcontractors, and inspectors. These responsibilities require him to write daily summaries, reports, memos, and letters. Here is a paragraph from a letter he sent to a glass subcontractor.

> Please finish up the two houses in the Meadow Woods subdivision by this Friday. Lot #72 still lacks glass in the front door and in the kitchen cabinets. The homeowners requested that you install both with clear silicone only. Also, you'll need to measure the opening for the TV in the master bedroom and then cut a 2-way mirror to fit. Lot #73 needs glass in the small cabinet doors in the garage.

To ensure that his readers understand his instructions, Raul must be careful to adhere to the four rules for clear sentences. Those rules are the subject of this chapter.

"I wish my writing flowed better." Many people have uttered these words, but most aren't sure what makes writing "flow" or how to achieve this effect in their own compositions. Some might relate it to smoothness or clarity or readability. Writing that flows well is writing that does not have to be read twice. It doesn't get in the readers' way as they attempt to understand the ideas on the page.

So how do you achieve this quality in your own writing?

Writing that flows well is no mystery. It's created by the way you put words together in sentences, carefully constructing those sentences according to four simple rules.

RULE 1: USE STRONG VERBS.

Chapter 1 discussed the importance of choosing action-oriented verbs to stimulate the reader's interest. When constructing sentences, writers should be aware of some common habits that will *always* force them to settle for dull, weak verbs.

"There is" Sentences

Any time you begin a sentence with "There is (are/was/were)," stop! These sentences allow the writer to rely on a weak "to be" verb, often burying the best verb possibility somewhere else in the sentence. For example:

Weak: *There are* outside influences, such as school and extracurricular events, that can affect a child's choice of food. *[The best verb is hiding as an noun,* influences.*]*

Better: School and extracurricular events *influence* a child's choice of food.

Weak: *There appears to be* a productive economic advantage to military service. *[The best verb is lurking as an adjective,* productive.*]*

Better: Military service *produces* economic advantage.

Weak: *There have been* only phone calls and no face-to-face contact with the client. *[The best verb is disguised as a noun,* calls.*]*

Better: We *have phoned* the client but *have not met* face-to-face.

In addition to relying on a weak "to be" verb, "there is" phrases are often unnecessary. We can improve a sentence dramatically by merely deleting one.

Unnecessary: *There are* three ways in which we evaluate our performance.

Better: We evaluate our performance in three ways.

Unnecessary: *There is to be* no smoking in this building.

Better: Do not smoke in this building.

Finally, "there is" phrases often produce sentences clogged with other unnecessary words. Note how each of the following revisions not only improves the sentence's verb but also communicates the idea in fewer words.

Wordy: According to research studies, *there is* a close correlation between the rate of aging and the rate at which cancers develop. (21 words)

Better: Research *proves* a close correlation between the rate of aging and the rate of cancer development. (16 words)

Wordy: *There is* a possibility that employees who work this Thursday evening will receive comp time. (15 words)

Better: Employees who work this Thursday evening *may receive* comp time. (9 words)

Wordy: *There are* codes entered that need for you to put in additional data to make the calculations come out correctly. (20 words)

Better: Certain codes *require* the entry of additional data to produce correct calculations. (12 words)

"There is" sentences are very common, and we often write too many of them because they're the first opening words we think of. Get into the habit of noticing when you write sentences that begin this way; then experiment with the wording until the verb conveys the action.

PRACTICE 3.1
"There is" Sentences

Rewrite each of the following sentences to eliminate the "there is" phrase, substitute a better verb, and reduce wordiness. You may have to add more information to the sentence as you revise. *Answers will vary.*

1. There has been a lot of variance in time-sheet hours from week to week.

   Time-sheet hours vary from week to week.

2. Effective January 1, there will be a video camera installed in the reception area.

   Effective January 1, a video camera will monitor the reception area.

3. Throughout the night, while most of us are sleeping, there are people in the Office of Emergency Services who guard our county's safety.

   Throughout the night, while most of us are sleeping, people in the Office of

   Emergency Services guard our county's safety.

4. There are many opportunities to learn new skills in Girl Scouts.

   Girl Scouts provides opportunities to learn new skills.

5. There is a detective in the Sheriff's Department who does nothing but handle crimes involving children.

   A detective in the Sheriff's Department handles nothing but crimes involving

   children.

6. There are several organizations that offer assistance to parents in dealing with troubled teenagers.

   Several organizations offer assistance to parents in dealing with troubled teenagers.

"It is" Sentences

Sentences that begin with "It is" often suffer from the same problems—dull verbs and wordiness—that plague "there is" sentences. The following examples all come from memos.

Weak verb:	*It will be* easier for me to have more effective monitoring and feedback by dividing all of you into three groups.
Better:	I *can* more easily *monitor* and *give* feedback if I divide all of you into three groups.
Weak verb:	*It's* our policy to have as many different styles as we have customers.
Better:	Our customers *can choose* from many different styles.

Wordy: If *it is* solely a cost issue, *it would be* worth it to reduce a few of our expenses to the point where we can purchase the higher-quality materials. (30 words)

Better: If cost alone prevents us from purchasing the higher-quality materials, we *should reduce* our other expenses. (17 words)

Wordy: For the mechanics, *it will* no longer *be* necessary to complete the Work Order form as previously requested. (18 words)

Better: Mechanics *can stop completing* the Work Order form as previously requested. (11 words)

PRACTICE 3.2
"It is" Sentences

Rewrite each of the following sentences to eliminate the "it is" phrase, substitute a better verb, and reduce wordiness. You may have to add more information to the sentence as you revise. *Answers will vary.*

1. Sometimes it is necessary to handwrite a note to the customer.

   Sometimes you must handwrite a note to the customer.

2. It is a more specialized position that will require you to use different types of skills.

   This more specialized position requires you to use different types of skills.

3. As useful as the Internet can be, it can also be overwhelming in its immensity.

   Though useful, the Internet can overwhelm users with its immensity.

4. It was helpful information for all of us.

   The information helped all of us.

5. I live on a dirt road that nine other families live on also, and it's only a half mile long, but it's not paved.

   I live on a half-mile long, unpaved road with nine other families.

6. It is with regret that the Board of Directors has accepted the resignation of our chairman.

   The Board of Directors has regretfully accepted the resignation of our chairman.

Passive Voice Sentences

We can write sentences in either of two different basic ways. The first uses active voice, in which the subject of the sentence is the doer, or performer, of the action:

Phil mowed the lawn.

The active voice, which shows the subject performing an action, is clear and direct. The passive voice shows the subject of the sentence *receiving* the action. Using the passive voice, we can rewrite the example sentence to read:

The lawn was mowed by Phil.

In a passive voice sentence, what *should be* the object becomes the subject—and therefore the focus—of the sentence. Passive voice sentences are usually less interesting and less action-oriented than active voice ones. Also, we often have to read all the way to the end of the sentence before we find out who the doer of the action is. Note the difference between the following versions of the same sentence.

Passive:	Your investment *will be managed* by financial experts.
Active:	Financial experts will manage your investment.
Passive:	Important lessons about nutrition *are learned* by children who try new foods often.
Active:	Children who often try new foods learn important lessons about nutrition.
Passive:	Funds *are requested* for these new programs, but the requests *are turned down* by the county commissioners each year.
Active:	Our office requests funds for new programs each year, but the county commissioners turn them down.

Passive voice also tends to be ineffective because it doesn't emphasize the performer of the action. The following examples from brochures and newsletters all omit the doers of the action, which should be the subject of the sentence.

Jim Clark *was given [by whom?]* a watch as a token of gratitude for his many years of faithful service.

Courses *may be taken [by whom?]* at a community college or technical school.

The military's promises about jobs or training *are written [by whom?]* in a contract so that the recruit *can be assured [by whom?]* that the promise *will be kept [by whom?].*

This type of passive voice sentence asks the reader to fill in some blanks. If he or she can't figure out the answers, there's no choice but to wonder what they are, as in the following example:

The Information Management Office *is to be called [By whom? Family members? Friends? Newspaper reporters? Attorneys? Everyone?]* for any details about a patient's status.

One final reason for being careful about using the passive voice is that it tends to result in wordy sentences. Using the indirect, passive construction often requires you to pile on unnecessary words to get the sentence to make sense. The next section of this chapter will discuss this problem further.

Many inexperienced writers mistakenly believe that the passive voice sounds scholarly or professional. On the contrary, overusing it results in writing that is pretentious or plodding. The writer of the next passage, from a memo, probably thought her sentences sounded official and intelligent.

All work-related accidents *are to be reported* to your supervisor and to me. Should you incur a work-related injury that requires medical treatment, you *will be asked* to contact the Occupational Health Department. In the case of a serious injury, you *will be taken* to the emergency room. If I *cannot be reached,* the matter *will be handled* by the Executive Vice President.

That writer probably wanted the passive voice sentences to lend authority to her message. Instead, the passage sounds unnecessarily formal.

When you occasionally write in the passive voice, do so purposefully. Do not use this pattern when the active voice would produce a clearer, more interesting sentence.

PRACTICE 3.3
Passive Voice
Sentences

Rewrite each of the following sentences, using the active voice. You may have to add information to the sentence as you revise.

1. Release of information regarding a patient's condition is governed by hospital policy.

   Hospital policy governs release of information regarding a patient's condition.

   _____

2. Cooling-system maintenance should be completed by the end of next week.

   Our staff should complete cooling-system maintenance by the end of the week.

   _____

3. Last year, over sixty thousand people were served by United Way agencies.

   Last year, United Way agencies served over sixty thousand people.

   _____

4. This software will be used to maintain calibration records and schedules.

   Engineers will use this software to maintain calibration records and schedules.

   _____

5. The video equipment will be stored in the supply closet until a decision is made about where its permanent location will be.

   We will store the video equipment in the supply closet until Dr. Smith decides on its

   permanent location.

   _____

6. The final budget draft is presented by the president to the Board of Trustees.

   The president presents the final budget draft to the Board of Trustees.

   _____

7. College credit is sometimes granted for some of the military's technical training programs.

   Universities sometimes grant college credit for some of the military's technical

   training programs.

8. Often overlooked are the hundreds of volunteer firefighters who serve this county.

   The public often overlooks the hundreds of volunteer firefighters who serve this

   county.

Matching Subjects and Verbs

When you're experimenting with strong verbs in your sentences, make sure your subjects and verbs match. In other words, decide whether your subjects can actually perform the action conveyed by the verb. In the following examples, all drawn from student writing, note the mismatch between subject and verb, which results in a confusing or meaningless sentence.

Appropriate *use* of the copying machine *needs* clarification. *[The instructions for use—not the use itself—need clarification.]*

The wage *gap transpired* over a period of several years. *[A gap can spread or widen, but it cannot transpire.]*

To ensure effective communication, any student *request* for special accommodations during counseling sessions *is provided*. *[The use of passive voice causes the problem here. The sentence says that* requests *are provided, but the writer meant that* accommodations *are provided.]*

RULE 2: AVOID WORDINESS.

The French writer Pascal once penned to a friend, "I have made this letter longer than usual, only because I have not had the time to make it shorter." His statement reminds us of a paradox about writing: it actually takes *more* time and effort to write less. When we're trying to find the words to communicate our ideas, we usually use too many of them in our first attempt. That's understandable, of course, when we're engaged in finding language for thoughts we've never expressed before. We should go ahead and write down the sentences as we think of them, recording our ideas quickly. However, good writing always expresses an idea in as *few* words as possible. We never want to make our readers wade through a lot of unnecessary words to arrive at the meaning. So we must be willing to reexamine a first version and experiment with different wordings to get rid of any debris that merely clogs up the sentence. Note how the meaning of the following sentences remains the same even after each revision strips away unnecessary words.

Wordy: We would like to impress upon you the need to prevent the recurrence of such noisy party incidents in the future. (21 words)

Better: We urge you to stop your noisy parties. (8 words)

Wordy:	The strengths of this new planning policy are that it requires input from all employees, it is regularly reviewed by a committee of representatives, and it is revised annually. (29 words)
Better:	The new, improved planning policy allows for employee input, regular committee review, and annual revision. (15 words)
Wordy:	Jordan Janitorial Services was the best as far as quality and customer service were concerned, and they were informed of our decision to use them as our cleaning crew. (29 words)
Better:	We hired Jordan Janitorial Services because of their superior quality and customer service. (13 words)
Wordy:	In order to facilitate the setting-up of this system, I have created a document that lists all of the equipment to be installed and the people responsible for the installation of that equipment, along with the dates when we need to have listed the instruments, completed written procedures, and calibrated the instruments. (52 words)
Better:	To set up this system, I have created a document that lists equipment, installers, and dates for completing written procedures and calibrating the instruments. (25 words)

To excise wordiness from your sentences, try to find one word that can substitute for several. For instance, in the third example you just read, the word *hired* substitutes for the wordy phrase *were informed of our decision to use them*. In the last example, the word *installers* replaces *people responsible for the installation of that equipment*.

After you compose your first draft, expect to reevaluate each sentence for possible wordiness. Many sentences will need to be rearranged or pruned to better state your ideas.

Redundant Words

As you search for wordiness in your writing, look for words and phrases that simply repeat ideas or information you've already stated. The italicized parts of the following sentences are redundant.

Wordy:	I have become rather overwhelmed, *and I have found that my time is overcommitted to the point that I am overworked* and need additional help *and assistance. [The words* overwhelmed, *over-committed, and* overworked *all merely repeat the same point over. Also, the words* help *and* assistance *mean the same thing.]*
Better:	My time is now overcommitted, so I need additional help.
Wordy:	Volunteers *who are donating their time and energy* will be asking for your pledge soon. *[The italicized phrase merely gives information already implied by the word* volunteers.*]*
Better:	Volunteers will be asking for your pledge soon.
Wordy:	I am planning on scheduling trainees into their classes next week *so that we can get training schedules out to everyone.*
Better:	I plan to notify everyone of trainee class schedules next week.

If you express an idea clearly the first time, you should not need to repeat it.

Passive Voice

Passive voice tends to produce wordy sentences. When we use the passive voice, we often write sentences that are far longer than they have to be.

Wordy: Your lunches with clients *are to be done* on your own time unless approval *is obtained* from the director. (19 words)

Better: Unless you have the director's approval, lunch with clients on your own time. (13 words)

Wordy: Many customers *are enticed* into accepting credit card offers when they *are told* about low "teaser" interest rates, but they *are not told* by the company that this low rate is only temporary. (33 words)

Better: Credit card companies entice new customers with low "teaser" interest rates but fail to mention that this rate is temporary. (20 words)

Wordy: In order to provide the best service for our customers, it *has been decided* that quality communication training *will be completed* by all employees. (24 words)

Better: All employees will complete quality communication training to improve our customer service. (12 words)

Composing your sentences in the active voice, whenever appropriate, prevents weighting them with unnecessary words.

PRACTICE 3.4
Wordy Sentences

Rewrite each of the following sentences to reduce wordiness. Eliminate both needless use of the passive voice and redundant phrases, and try to substitute one word for several.

1. She has taught for twenty-nine years, and those years have been spent in the second grade at Wolf Glade Elementary School.

   She has taught second grade for twenty-nine years at Wolf Glade Elementary

   School.

2. The Sheriff's Office has the responsibility for the patrol of officers and the investigation of crimes, and the operation of the county jail is also a responsibility of the sheriff.

   The Sheriff's Office is responsible for the patrol of officers, the investigation of

   crimes, and the operation of the county jail.

3. The need for highly skilled people to be a part of today's armed forces is greater than ever before.

   Today's armed forces need highly skilled people.

4. During the past year, I have had the opportunity to complete classes in real estate, and I have become certified.

   During the past year, I obtained my real estate certification by completing classes.

5. A lot of money has been spent on this top-of-the-line equipment in an effort to ensure that maintenance has the equipment necessary for completing jobs efficiently, safely, and without accidents.

   This expensive, top-of-the-line equipment allows maintenance to work safely and

   efficiently.

6. I am the lab technician who has been assigned to the task of ensuring that this process is implemented.

   I am the lab technician assigned to this job.

7. We are planning on making a final decision next week on the service that will be awarded the maintenance contract.

   We will award the maintenance contract next week.

8. Please make requests for repairs by written request put in the office mail slot.

   Please submit your written requests for repairs in the office mail slot.

9. Locations related to hiring processes are in areas that are physically accessible to all job applicants with disabilities.

   The Human Resources Office is physically accessible to all disabled applicants.

10. There are procedures and plans to ensure that safety features and elements such as alarms, fire extinguishers, and sprinkler systems are maintained.

    The staff regularly maintains safety features such as alarms, fire extinguishers,

    and sprinkler systems.

RULE 3: VARY SENTENCE LENGTH

We can use any of three basic ways to construct a sentence. Simple sentences are those with just one independent clause. Compound sentences, a second type, contain two or more independent clauses. The third type of sentence is the complex sentence, which contains both an independent and a dependent clause.

Simple:	Golf is definitely a very challenging sport.
Compound:	I enjoy the challenges of all sports, but I especially enjoy that one.
Complex:	At first, I thought that hitting that little white ball would be easy.

Mature, sophisticated writing combines all three types of sentences. To create writing that flows, mix a variety of sentence types and lengths. But avoid the two extremes of length in your sentences.

Short Sentences

If your writing contains a great many short sentences, one after another, your reader will judge your composition to be monotonous and unsophisticated. Consider the following example from a letter of application:

> I would like to apply for a job at ABC Day Care. I think I am very qualified. I found out about your opening in the newspaper.
> I am majoring in education at Clark Community College. I am on the Dean's List. I like working with children. I worked at another day care center for a year. I helped with infants and toddlers.
> I would like to meet with you. My résumé is enclosed. Perhaps we could schedule an interview. I look forward to talking with you.

Although an adult wrote this passage, it sounds as though a third grader composed it. The short, choppy sentences are childlike and dull. Notice how much more mature the letter sounds when some of the short sentences are combined:

> I would like to apply for the job at ABC Day Care. I read about the opening in the newspaper, and I think I am very qualified for this position.
> I am majoring in education at Clark Community College, where I am on the Dean's List. I like working with children; I worked with infants and toddlers at another day care center for a year.
> I would like to meet with you for an interview after you review my enclosed résumé. I look forward to talking with you.

Another example comes from a medical report:

> Bernice Jones came in today. She did not improve after her last injection. She brought in her medication. I reviewed it. She has taken ten pills too many. I counseled her about the dosage. She understands. She will take the prescription according to the directions.

Again, these short simple sentences could be combined to produce a more sophisticated style:

> Bernice Jones came in today because she did not improve after her last injection. She brought in her medicine, which I reviewed. She has taken ten pills too many, so I counseled her about the dosage. She understands now that she must take the prescription according to the directions.

The revision of these shorter sentences into complex and compound sentences also helps the reader understand the relationships of the ideas better. By connecting thoughts with words such as *because, which, so*, and *that*, we communicate more effectively how the ideas are related and therefore achieve a more flowing style.

One final example comes from a newsletter:

> You are in for a treat. This summer, the Budding Artists summer camp will be held in Asheville, North Carolina. This is a camp for all ages. We'll

have programs for very young children. There will be activities for teenagers and adults, too. Every morning will include at least three classes. We group students by age. Every afternoon, we'll swim, play volleyball, and hike. Don't miss it!

This passage consists of nine simple sentences. This lack of variety not only creates a monotonous style, it also causes the writer to settle for too many weak verbs. However, we can combine and reorganize several of the sentences to improve the sophistication of the writing:

You are in for a treat this summer at the Budding Artists summer camp in Asheville, North Carolina. We welcome all ages because we'll provide programs for all ages, from very young children to teenagers and adults. Every morning will include at least three classes grouped by age. Every afternoon, we'll swim, play volleyball, and hike, so don't miss it!

This revision contains four sentences, of various types: two are simple, one is compound, and one is complex, all contributing to increased variety.

Long Sentences

At the other extreme is the overuse of long sentences. Whereas too many short sentences are monotonous and immature, too many long sentences can be rambling or confusing or pretentious. An overly long sentence packs too much information into what should be more than one sentence. Because the purpose of a sentence is to help readers understand separate units of thought, we defeat that purpose when we ask them to take in too much at one time. Readers can become impatient with writing that doesn't let them pause and digest thoughts in reasonable doses. The following sentence from a memo, for instance, forces the reader to take in too much information.

Bob Wilson from the Corporate Office will meet with us at 8:00 A.M. on September 16 in the conference room to provide us with an update and overview of the corporate planning session, and this meeting is mandatory for all managers, and all other employees should attend if their schedules allow.

This sentence is breathlessly wordy and rambling.
Another example is from a letter:

Pathways Health Services is a licensed, Medicare-certified, accredited home health care agency that provides nurse or health aide home visits for treatment or therapy, as well as licensed nurses for private duty care. Pathways is a national agency, and every county in Virginia is served by a Pathways office, but your local office located in Richmond serves Hanover, Henrico, and New Kent counties with quality care and competitive prices.

These sentences overwhelm the reader with too much in one unit. The passage is much easier to understand when the details are divided into smaller segments:

Pathways Health Services is a licensed, Medicare-certified, accredited home health care agency. We provide nurse or health aide home visits for treatment or therapy, and we also offer licensed nurses for private duty care. Pathways is a national agency that serves all of Virginia; your local office in Richmond serves Hanover, Henrico, and New Kent counties. We offer quality care and competitive prices.

One final example comes from a bank's newsletter:

A check card is not a credit card, although it works like a credit card when you make an offline, non-PIN transaction and sign the sales receipt, but when you're paying at a register with a PIN pad, you select the "debit" button and enter your PIN number, and then the money is deducted from your checking account.

That writer tried to link too much information together in one overly long compound-complex sentence. The reader needs a break long before one arrives.

PRACTICE 3.5
Sentence Length

Rewrite the first passage to combine some of the short sentences. Rewrite the second passage to break up overly long sentences into shorter ones. *Answers will vary.*

You don't have to continue your subscription. There's no obligation. This trial offer is risk-free. If you cancel, you pay nothing. You keep the three sample issues. It's that simple.

You don't have to continue your subscription. There's no obligation, so this trial offer is

risk-free. If you cancel, you pay nothing and keep the three sample issues. It's that

simple.

The 2002 Turner County United Way campaign will begin soon, and Taft Furniture Company has always played an integral part in each year's fundraising effort, and this year should be no different, so our company will serve as a Pacesetter Organization, which is one that agrees to run a campaign before the normally scheduled campaign kickoff in order to set an example for the rest of the community and prove how the results of focused efforts make the fundraising a success.

The 2002 Turner County United Way campaign will begin soon. Taft Furniture has

always played an integral part in each year's fundraising effort, and this year should

be no different. Once again, our company will serve as a Pacesetter Organization,

which is one that agrees to run a campaign before the normally scheduled campaign

kickoff. By doing so, we set an example for the rest of the community and prove how

the results of focused efforts make the fundraising a success.

RULE 4: ADHERE TO RULES FOR GRAMMAR, PUNCTUATION, AND SPELLING

Standard English is defined as English that is widely used in business, academia, and the media. We expect writing we see on the job, in the classroom, and in magazines and books to conform to grammatical rules and to be spelled correctly. Readers of your writing will bring similar expectations to what you compose.

If your writing contains grammatical or spelling errors, your reader will form one or more of the following conclusions about you.

1. You did not care enough about your document to make it conform to the rules for Standard English.
2. You were too lazy to take the time to make your writing correct.
3. You obviously do not know how to use Standard English, so you must be unintelligent or uneducated.

All would be harsh, perhaps unfair, criticisms of you and your work. Nonetheless, readers *will* make these judgments if errors plague your writing. Even if your thoughts are creative or downright brilliant, your reader may fail to understand or believe you if you do not express them in Standard English.

Grammar and Punctuation

Contrary to popular belief, rules for grammar and punctuation were not devised to make your life miserable! The rules for Standard English are logical and necessary because they provide the form for expression of your ideas.

Failing to make your subjects and verbs agree or using semicolons improperly will lead the reader to form the judgments just listed. In addition, grammatical mistakes can also prevent the reader from understanding your meaning. Writing that flows well is writing that doesn't get in a reader's way. But if he or she is constantly noticing your run-on sentences or other mistakes, that reader will be distracted from the thoughts you're trying to express. She or he will have to reread the sentences that contain errors, mentally correcting those sentences in order to understand them. The following sentences all contain errors that force the reader to stop and figure out what the writer really meant.

Due to a desire for service and a good speech from the Reverend Mr. Brown, the group has decided to volunteer at the homeless shelter. *[The wording of this sentence suggests that the group decided to volunteer in hopes of finally hearing a good speech from the clergyman!]*

She came home from the hospital and prepared herself along with family members to die. *[This sentence suggests that family members will die, too.]*

Covered completely with leather, I feel these chairs will create an elegant look for our waiting room. *[Is the person making the recommendation covered with leather?]*

Grammatical mistakes, such as a usage error or a misplaced or missing comma, can also completely alter the meaning of a sentence:

That completed my focus on training issues shifted.

Because of one missing comma, the whole sentence is unintelligible. Notice how the sentence suddenly makes sense when the comma is inserted:

That completed, my focus on training issues shifted.

For more information about common grammatical errors, refer to the "Eleven Most Common Grammar Errors" section at the back of this book.

Spelling

Are you a good speller? Did you know that the majority of people are *not* good spellers? That's because spelling requires a kind of photographic memory. People who spell well can easily picture words in their minds; they literally "see" the word, so they know the exact order of its letters. As a matter of fact, national spelling bee champions claim to visualize words this way.

So if you aren't a good speller, you probably don't possess this type of memory. But that doesn't let you off the hook! Correct spelling is a requirement in every piece of writing you compose. If you know you don't spell well (and by now, you know), you'll have to get into the habit of checking and double-checking your spelling before sending off your documents to their destinations.

You can spell-check three ways. The modern way is to use your word processor's spell-checker. Many software programs now include features that alert you to possible misspellings even as you type them. However, remember that these spell-checkers are not foolproof. As the following poem humorously illustrates, computers are often wrong.

SPELL CHEQUER

Eye halve a spelling chequer;
It came with my pea sea;
It plainly marques four my revue
Miss steaks eye kin knot sea.
Eye strike a kee and type a word
And weight four it two say
Whether eye am wrong oar write—
It shows me strait a weigh.
As soon as a mist ache is maid
It nose bee fore two long,
And eye can put the error rite
Its rare lea ever wrong.
Eye have run this poem threw it;
I am shore your pleased two no
Its letter purfict awl the weigh.
My chequer tooled me sew.

The other two ways to spell-check are old-fashioned but effective. You can either look words up in the dictionary or ask someone who's a good speller to proofread your documents.

**PRACTICE 3.6
Grammar,
Punctuation,
and Spelling**

Rewrite each of the following sentences to correct the errors. Refer to Appendix C for a review of the most serious grammatical mistakes. You may also use a dictionary.

1. Give our tole-free number to client's, customer's, and any other professional's who you feel it important.

   Give our toll-free number to clients, customers, and any other professionals who

   need it.

2. I tried to schedule a meeting for two o'clock one of the secretarys however could not be their then.

   I tried to schedule a meeting for two o'clock; one of the secretaries, however, could

   not be there then.

3. Only one of the guards were patroling the building last night.

   Only one of the guards was patrolling the building last night.

4. The staff wants a better benefits package. Including tuition reimbursement and dentel insurance.

   The staff wants a better benefits package that includes tuition reimbursement

   and dental insurance.

5. We didn't take memorial day off, because we had to finish the inspection.

   We didn't take Memorial Day off because we had to finish the inspection.

6. Each employee should take their lunch brake by 1:30 P.M.

   Each employee should take his or her lunch break by 1:30 P.M.

7. I'll send you a memo which includes instructions for arming the security system.

   I'll send you a memo that includes instructions for arming the security system.

8. Its critical that you're team meet it's deadline.

   It's critical that your team meet its deadline.

9. Being a nontraditional field of study, women can receive additional financial aide for enrolling in the program.

   Women can receive additional financial aid for enrolling in a nontraditional field

   of study.

10. Assistant Manager, Captain Hook's seafood restaurant, July 1991—
Febuary 1995. Weekly payroll. Supervised eight employees. Training
of new employees. In charge of advertising specials.

Assistant Manager, Captain Hook's Seafood Restaurant, July 1991—February

1995. Handled weekly payroll. Supervised eight employees. Trained new

employees. Determined advertising specials.

TEST YOUR UNDERSTANDING

1. What two problems do "there is" and "it is" sentences cause?

   Weak verbs and wordiness.

2. What is the difference between passive voice and active voice?

   In the active voice, the subject of the sentence is the doer of the action. In the

   passive voice, the subject is acted upon.

3. What problems does the passive voice cause?

   Less interesting sentences, wordiness, missing doer of the action.

4. What are three things you can do to sentences to reduce wordiness?

   Find one word that can substitute for several, look for redundant words, and try

   writing in the active voice.

5. What is the effect of too many short sentences?

   Monotonous, unsophisticated style.

6. What is the effect of too many long sentences?

   Confusing or pretentious style.

7. Why should your writing adhere to the rules for grammar and
   spelling?

   Errors increase the possibility of confusion or misunderstanding. They also might

   encourage readers to doubt your writing ability.

WEB ACTIVITY: Professional Organizations

Consider joining a professional organization for people in your field of study. These organizations can enhance your skills by providing you with publications, conferences and seminars, and contacts with other people in your line of work. Many of them offer student memberships at reduced rates.

1. Search the World Wide Web for a professional organization in your field of study.
2. What publications and activities are available to members of this organization?
3. Does the organization offer student memberships? What are the benefits of student membership?
4. E-mail the organization to ask questions or to request a sample publication.

GROUP PROJECT AND WRITING ACTIVITIES

In Chapters 1 and 2, you and your group selected, observed, and described an area of your city or town—an area that needs to be cleaned up, repaired, or renovated. In the next set of activities, you'll focus on improvements to that area.

With your group, brainstorm in the space below ideas for improving the area. *What* needs to be repaired or cleaned? *Who* could do it? *How* could the area be repaired or cleaned? Think of as many ideas as possible.

Complete this activity on your own.

Gather information about companies or organizations in your city or town that could get involved in the renovation of the area. Below, make a list of those companies or organizations. Then find out *which* companies might participate, *how* they could get involved, and *how much* they would charge for their services.

_____

_____

_____

_____

_____

_____

Together with your group, compose a letter to persuade someone in your city or town to support the renovation of the area. You could write to a local elected official or to the leader of a civic organization. Or you could write a letter to your local newspaper's editor. In your letter, describe the needed improvements and make suggestions about how to make them.

_____

_____
       (Your Address)

_____
          (Date)

_____ (Recipient's Name)

_____ (Recipient's Address)

Dear _____ :
      (Recipient's Name)

_____

_____

_____

_____

_____

_____

_____

Sincerely,

_____
(Your Name)

Together with your group, prepare for your class an oral presentation about the area you selected. See Appendix B for more information about oral presentations.

Divide your presentation so that each group member speaks. For example, one person could describe the area. A second person could describe the needed improvements. A third person could discuss ways to make the improvements, and another person could discuss ways to fund them.

READINGS How important is communication on the job? Do you believe you're an effective communicator, or do people sometimes misunderstand you?

The next article discusses the importance of good communication skills and offers four characteristics of effective communicators.

As you read this article, circle every word that's unfamiliar to you. Look it up and write the meaning in the margin. Put an exclamation point (!) next to any sentence or paragraph you find especially interesting. Put a question mark (?) next to any sentence or paragraph you don't understand.

Talk the Talk: How Well Do You Communicate?

T. J. Saftner

What Kind of Communicator Are You?

Consider each of the following scenarios, and decide which response would be the most effective:

1. Just as you are leaving for the day, your boss hands you a report and asks you to have it on his desk by 8 a.m. You need to tell your boss that you cannot possibly meet the deadline. What would you say?

   a) I don't think Sarah has anything to do.

   b) I can't stay late. I have plans with a friend tonight.

   c) That's a really tight deadline, and I know you are in a hurry. It could take a couple of hours to type up. Would 10 a.m. be soon enough?

T. J. Saftner, "Talk the Talk: How Well Do You Communicate?" *Career World* (January 1998), 24. © 1998 by Weekly Reader Corp. All rights reserved.

2. A customer is expecting you to deliver a product by the middle of the month. You've just been informed that your supplier cannot get the product to you on time. How do you explain this problem to your customer?

   a) It's really out of my hands. I've called the supplier, but can't get any answers.

   b) I'm sorry. We'll try harder next month.

   c) I'm sorry. I hope this delay doesn't cause you a great deal of inconvenience. Our supplier has run into a few problems, but I assure you I will get the product to you as soon as possible.

3. You are applying for a cashier position at a local gas station. You've been asked to fill out a job application. One of the questions on the form is: "Why would you like to work here?" How might you respond?

   a) The hours fit well into my sports schedule and fitness routine.

   b) The new cash registers make it look really easy.

   c) I enjoy working with people and I feel confident I can do a good job.

If you answered "c" to each of these situations, you obviously put some careful consideration into what you were going to say. If you answered "a" or "b," you are responding too quickly, and need to spend some time considering how others will react to off-the-cuff answers.

1 When Gary applied for a job as a payroll clerk at a manufacturing firm, he thought he was a shoo-in. He had excellent math and computer skills, making him a perfect candidate. But much to his surprise, Gary didn't land the job. Why? He had poor communication skills. And just how important is the ability to communicate—even if the job description doesn't include it?

2 Employers rate oral communication as the number-one skill they look for in prospective employees, according to the National Association of Colleges and Employers. Just why are employers so big on communication skills?

What's the Big Deal?

3 Employers are generally selling a product or a service. Business is all about economics and profit. They want their employees to be able to convey to potential customers what that product or service is all about. It's important that their employees come across as professional and knowledgeable. When customers deal with employees who are difficult to understand, or who can't answer their questions adequately, they will take their business to someone else.

4 So why would Gary, as a payroll clerk, have to be able to communicate? He doesn't interact with customers or clients. No, but he may need to clarify the information on an employee's time sheet, speak with the firm's accountant, or talk to government agencies regarding unemployment insurance or income tax. To do this, he would have to ask or answer questions of others.

5   The question is not whether or not you are communicating—you are always communicating, even when you don't say a word—the question is what are you communicating, and are you getting across the message you really want to?

Gift of Gab

6   The gift of gab isn't really a gift at all. It is a learned skill. Here are some ideas on how you can evaluate your own communication skills and improve them, too.

Are you sensitive?

7   Communication is not a one-way street. Not only do you need to be aware of how you are presenting yourself, you need to be aware of the other person's frame of mind. Just as you don't ask your mother for the car keys 5 minutes after she's announced she's been laid off from her job, you don't try to discuss an important topic such as marketing strategy the day after the boss comes down with a cold. Try to make sure the person you wish to communicate with has the time and isn't distracted by other concerns.

8   When you want to talk to someone, it is sometimes a good idea to ask him or her, "Have you got a few minutes?" or "Do you have time to talk to me now about the latest shipment?"

Are you clear?

9   We've all heard the expressions, "Choose your words carefully" and "Think before you speak." The language or words you choose are an important part of effective communication. Whether you are writing it down, or voicing it aloud, take the time to get clear in your own mind the communication you want to deliver. One strategy to hone your oral communication skills is to tape your statement and then replay it to hear how you sound. Do you sound professional? How is your tone?

10   Have you ever heard someone say, "That was smart," in a sarcastic tone? The words alone could be taken as a compliment, but add the tone, and you've got a very different meaning. That's why the tone of your voice is more critical than the actual words you say. The fact is, certain tones are more likely to result in people taking offense or tuning you out. If you want people to listen to you, it's important that your tone is not whiny, demanding, sarcastic, condescending, or urgent.

Are you considerate?

11   Remember to be polite and considerate when communicating with people at work, home, or school. The easiest way to turn off a conversation is to be rude, abrupt, or to discount what someone has said. Everyone wants his or her thoughts heard.

Listen Up!

12 Listening often seems to be the forgotten communication skill. You cannot communicate effectively with people if you don't understand what they are saying. Making assumptions about what the speaker means is a sure way to find yourself in trouble.

13 Consider this scenario: Your boss says, "I'd like you to finish up that project you started last week." You were working on several projects last week but you assume he means the filing. There's quite a stack of it, and it's been bothering you, too. So you put your other work aside to finish the filing. At the end of the day, the boss asks to see the advertising copy, so he can send it to the printer. When you tell him you've been filing all day, he demands, "Why have you been working on the filing when I specifically told you to finish the copy?" The best way to avoid this kind of miscommunication is to clarify the person's instructions. Listen, ask questions, and, if necessary, paraphrase what he or she says.

14 Distractions are another reason we fail to listen effectively. Pay attention. If you are considering what movie to go to next weekend instead of considering what someone is saying to you at that moment, you are not listening effectively.

15 If you are easily distracted, experts offer this unusual but effective tip. Watching the mouth (instead of the eyes) of the person speaking will help to quickly refocus your mind on the conversation. You want to focus on the mouth just long enough to let yourself concentrate on what is being said.

16 Whether you are applying for a job, [or] talking with a teacher, parent, boss, or friend, take the time to develop effective communication skills. They will improve your relationship and add to your future success.

Nonverbal Communication: Let Your Body Do the Talking

17 Our attire, our posture, our facial expressions, the tone of our voice all communicate a message to those around us. Imagine you are conducting a job interview. Here are some tips on how you can communicate positively without saying a word:

- Make eye contact.
- Smile often, but don't over-do it.
- Stand (and sit) straight—good posture counts.
- Don't fold your arms across your chest. It signals a defensive, standoffish attitude.
- Use a firm handshake.
- Look interested; nod, smile, use your body to acknowledge that you're listening . . . and interested!

RESPONDING TO THE READING

1. Why do businesses seek employees with good communication skills?

   Employees with good communication skills can interact more effectively with

   customers or clients.

2. According to the article, what are the four characteristics of effective communicators?

   Sensitivity, clarity, consideration, and good listening skills.

3. Rewrite the following sentences from the article so that they follow all four rules for clear sentences. *Answers will vary.*

   When you want to talk to someone, it is sometimes a good idea to ask him or her, "Have you got a few minutes?" or "Do you have time to talk to me now about the latest shipment?" (paragraph 8)

   When you talk to someone, ask him or her, "Have you got a few minutes?" or "Do

   you have time to talk to me now about the latest shipment?"

   There's quite a stack of it [work], and it's been bothering you, too. (paragraph 13)

   The huge stack of work has been bothering you.

BUILDING VOCABULARY

Idioms are groups of words that have a unique meaning when combined. Many of them are conversational expressions or slang terms used in informal communication. For example, read this sentence from paragraph 2 of the article.

   Just why are employers so *big on* communication skills?

The phrase *big on* is an idiom that means "enthusiastic about."
   To find the meaning of a specific idiom, look up one of its words and examine the dictionary entry for that word. Are any of the definitions labeled either *idiom* or *slang*?

Look up each of the following italicized idioms in these sentences from the article. What does each one mean?

1. It's important that their employees *come across* as professional and knowledgeable. (paragraph 3)

   give an impression

2. . . . you don't try to discuss an important topic such as marketing strategy the day after the boss *comes down with* a cold. (paragraph 7)

   develops

3. The fact is, certain tones are more likely to result in people taking of-
    fense or *tuning you out.* (paragraph 10)

    ignoring you
    _____

4. If you answered "a" or "b," you are responding too quickly and need
    to spend some time considering how others will react to *off-the-cuff*
    answers. (page 95)

    without preparation
    _____

Do you often experience bad customer service when you go shopping? Do
you ever do anything about it?

The following article from *Reader's Digest* magazine explores the reasons
for deteriorating customer service.

As you read this article, circle every word that's unfamiliar to you. Look it
up and write the meaning in the margin. Put an exclamation point (!) next to
any sentence or paragraph you find especially interesting. Put a question
mark (?) next to any sentence or paragraph you don't understand.

What Ever Happened to Customer Service?

Ralph Kinney Bennett

1   You need a new vacuum cleaner. Several are on display—different prices, different features—but there are no clerks to be found. Finally a guy in a store
vest slips past, trying to avoid eye contact. You begin to ask questions, but he
knows even less about vacuum cleaners than you do.

2   You stand at the jewelry counter, waiting to look at a bracelet in the case.
Two young women are giggling at the cash register. You clear your throat, but
they keep talking. At last, a clerk turns to help you. Her forced smile says
you're intruding.

3   You call a department store's customer-service line. A recording tells you,
"Your call is important to us . . ." Then comes the elevator music. Five minutes later you're still waiting.

4   Retailing is big business in the United States. Every day, billions of transactions take place in the nation's 1.4 million stores. Ingenious technology—from
cash-register scanners to computer-generated stock replenishment—speeds a
staggering $2.5-trillion-a-year flow of purchases. But why do those bad encoun-
ters with salespeople continue to bother us so?

5   When Yankelovich Partners asked 2500 shoppers what was "most important to you regarding customer service," people ranked courtesy, knowl-
edgeability and friendliness at the top. Almost two out of three said that
salespeople "don't care much about me or my needs."

6   The American Customer Satisfaction Index, developed in 1994 at the
University of Michigan's National Quality Research Center, shows customer

Reprinted with permission from the January 1998 *Reader's Digest*. Copyright © 1998 by The
Reader's Digest Assn., Inc.

satisfaction declining about a point a year. Retailers now average a less-than-satisfactory 71 out of 100. Even top performers have slipped.

7   To look behind the figures, *Reader's Digest* traveled to malls, discount chains, home centers and neighborhood stores across the country. We spoke with customers and sales personnel. And, as we repeatedly encountered the same customer-service deficiencies, we asked industry experts to explain the poor service that plagues us.

The Invisible Shopper

8   Leah Uhrig of Alexandria, Va., wanted a special dress for her wedding. She began her search in high spirits, hitting a dozen pricey stores, including Neiman Marcus, Macy's and Saks Fifth Avenue. In not one did a salesperson acknowledge her, let alone ask to help. "I thought it was sad," says Uhrig—herself a 14-year sales veteran at Brooks Brothers.

9   "It really comes down to one word—respect," says Leonard Berry, director of Texas A&M University's Center for Retailing Studies. "We've collected the most common service complaints, and every one of them is rooted in lack of respect for the customer."

10   Even though shoppers are now weaned on the self-service culture, most told us that, while uncomfortable with "pushy" salespeople, they still expect a courteous recognition. There is no excuse for clerks to ignore shoppers, says Dana McLendon, a corporate manager for Fossil watch and accessories stores. "Customers must be acknowledged, even if it's just a smile."

Hello . . . Is Anybody Here?

11   Robert Odom, shopping at the Southcenter Mall near Seattle, finds "it's harder to get waited on now. Many stores have one person covering a tremendous area. You've got to go looking to find a clerk."

12   Karen Danielson, a shopper at the Cumberland Mall near Atlanta, agrees. "What I miss most," she says, "is the way you used to be able to try on clothes in the dressing room and there was someone there to help you find another size."

13   Even salespeople notice. Jean Schepp of Chesapeake, Va., a 24-year sales veteran with Sears, is proud of her company's renewed emphasis on customer service. She realized just how much things had changed when she helped a customer try on a coat. The woman turned in surprise and said, "How nice! It's been years since somebody helped me in a store."

14   What happened? John Goodman, president of Technical Assistance Research Programs, a customer-service consulting firm, told us, "To cut costs, many retailers made the mistake of trimming staff to the bone—with obvious consequences."

15   How good is the help once you find it? Carol Cherry, founder of Shop'n Chek, which monitors customer service for retailers and other clients, says, "One of the biggest problems we encounter is unknowledgeable and un-

trained salespeople." Bruce Van Kleeck, a vice president of the National Retail Federation, says, "We're not training as much as we used to," and urges more ongoing training for veteran salespeople.

Needed: Attitude Adjustment

16 When 23-year-old Capitol Hill staffer Ken Schulz entered a Florsheim shoe store in Washington, D.C., he knew what he wanted—a pair of brown loafers. There were two salesmen, one waiting on a customer, the other looking out the window. The window-gazer neither greeted Schulz nor offered help.

17 Finding a shoe he liked on display, Schulz asked to see a pair. Without a word, the clerk disappeared into the back, returned a few minutes later with an unopened box, gave it to Schulz and walked away. When Schulz decided on his purchase, the clerk rang up the sale and handed over the shoes. Transaction completed. Not a word from the clerk. "I got my shoes," Schulz concludes, "but I felt I didn't get what you would call customer service."

18 People we talked to on both sides of the counter concurred that salespeople are less courteous than they once were. Vickie Henry, CEO of Feedback Plus, a Dallas-based shopping research firm, says, "Managers defining what is expected of clerks often assume they don't have to remind people of their manners. But with the younger generation of clerks, we tell clients you'd better put manners in the job description."

The Wait of the World

19 "The thing that bugs me most," says nurse Andrea Remeta, leaving the South Shore Center in Alameda, Calif., "is when there are long lines and there's one person at the cash register, and they call for help and nobody comes."

20 Remeta echoes the feelings of almost every shopper we spoke to. After picking out more than $200 worth of clothing late one day at the Hecht's "Red Dot" sale in Wheaton, Md., John and Jean West stood in line with five other customers. Only one of two cash registers was open. Two employees were talking nearby, ignoring the customers.

21 Jean West asked a clerk why the other register wasn't open. She was told it was "policy" to shut registers down a couple of hours before closing time. "But you're having a big sale," West protested.

22 West went to the customer-service counter, but it was vacant. She then tried the management office, where someone finally answered her page. "Without a hint of sympathy she just repeated, 'That's our policy,'" says West. "I felt I was treated badly, both for the time lost and the indifference." (Hecht's later told *Reader's Digest* it is not store policy to shut down registers early.)

23 According to Texas A&M's Leonard Berry, the chain of service starts with "who's managing the store." If a manager is people oriented, it will be reflected in his employees and from them to the customer.

24   Jerry Sharp, manager of the Wal-Mart outside Meadville, Pa., tries to "overschedule" cashiers on heavy traffic shifts and is ready to man a register himself if necessary. "No matter what we've got on the shelves," says Sharp, "the customer's last impression of us is the cashier at the checkout."

25   At the huge Meijer hypermart in Lexington, Ky., Gwen Taylor is "guest service" manager. She patrols the aisles with a walkie-talkie, counting shopping carts to anticipate crowds at the store's 28 checkouts. "I love it when we're able to get people through despite the rush," Taylor says. "I've waited in too many lines myself."

What's Going On?

26   Studies confirm what shoppers and customer-oriented retailers instinctively know: shopping is a social experience, not merely the transfer of goods. From the souk in ancient Samarkand to the mall in Paramus, N.J., the marketplace has always been one of civilization's most important social centers—the place where we most frequently interact with strangers. Despite the rise of television, catalogue and Internet buying, shoppers want to be among people. And the moments that make or break the experience involve how they are treated.

27   Ed Spangler, a partner with the retail-consulting unit of Arthur Andersen, adds that retailers who lead in customer service, whether large or small, often give employees the chance to have a stake in the company, and always enthuse [sic] them about its culture of service. "The formula is deceptively simple: happy employees make the best shopping environment, which satisfies customers, and satisfied customers equal shareholder value."

28   The sad fact is, stores can get away with poor customer service because customers let them. Customer-service expert John Goodman estimates that about half of customers continue to do business with firms they feel have mistreated them. This is "behavioral loyalty," explains Jeff Ellis of Maritz Marketing Research Inc. "We may bad-mouth a store after a bad experience, but we go back because it's close to our house or carries items we like." Many shoppers we interviewed admitted they returned to stores where service was poor.

How to Get Treated Right

29   Here are three weapons that customers can wield in the battle for better service:

30   1. Complain. Very few wronged customers—Goodman estimates five percent—formally complain. Most of us decide it's not worth our time. But top management at most of the retailers mentioned in this story were genuinely concerned about incidents where service had fallen short, and they were eager to redress the problem. So, overcome that sense of futility and make the call, write the letter or send the e-mail.

31   2. Be civil. There is no evidence that the decline in bad manners began with store clerks. "The attitude of the customer makes it a lot easier to

treat him well," says Leah Uhrig of Brooks Brothers. And tell managers when a clerk has performed well.

32   3. Take your business elsewhere. Retailers are counting on your "behavioral loyalty." But think about it: Shoppers have never had so many choices. Whether it's a pair of jeans or a bottle of perfume, many stores offer the same goods. And remember, as your credit card sweeps through that register slot, the money is transferring from you to the store, not vice versa.

33   Busy interviewing part-time people in preparation for the holiday shopping crunch, Gwen Taylor of the Meijer hypermart says, "We try to find people with something inside that's not in the rules and won't come through training. You have to like helping people. I think good customer service is addictive. I just want to do more. And the 'secret,' when you think about it, is just treating people like you'd want to be treated."

RESPONDING TO THE READING

1. According to the article, what are the qualities of bad customer service?

   Lack of assistance, bad attitudes of employees, and long waits.

2. What specific retail store or company has given you good customer service? Why?

   Answers will vary.

3. Why do stores get away with poor customer service?

   People continue to shop there even after receiving poor service.

4. What three things should you do to improve the customer service you receive?

   Complain, be civil to store employees, and stop patronizing stores with poor service.

5. Rewrite the following sentences from the article so that they follow all four rules for clear sentences.

   There is no excuse for clerks to ignore shoppers . . . (paragraph 10)

   A clerk should never ignore shoppers.

   "Customers must be acknowledged, even if it's just a smile." (paragraph 10)

   Clerks must acknowledge customers with a smile at the very least.

   "Many stores have one person covering a tremendous area." (paragraph 11)

   In many stores, one person covers a tremendous area.

(continued)

RESPONDING TO THE READING *continued*

There were two salesmen, one waiting on a customer, the other looking out the window. (paragraph 16)

One salesman waited on a customer and the other looked out the window.

"The thing that bugs me most . . . is when there are long lines and there's one person at the cash register, and they call for help and nobody comes." (paragraph 19)

Long lines and a lack of cashiers bother me most.

"You have to like helping people. I think good customer service is addictive. I just want to do more." (paragraph 33)

You have to like helping people. I'm addicted to good customer service, and I just

want to do more.

BUILDING VOCABULARY

When you look up a word in a dictionary, you will often see several different definitions listed for that word. Dictionaries arrange these different meanings, using some type of logical order to help users quickly find the information they need.

Some dictionaries arrange the meanings from the *most common* to the least common. For example, when you locate the word *clerk* in the *American Heritage College Dictionary*, which lists the more common meanings first, you'll find that the noun form of the word has five different meanings, or "senses." The third entry is "a person who works at a sales counter or service desk," the meaning the word has in the preceding article.

Other dictionaries arrange meanings from the oldest to the newest one. *Webster's Third New International Dictionary*, for instance, organizes meanings in this way. The same definition of the word *clerk* is the fifth entry of six in that particular dictionary. Each dictionary will explain its arrangement pattern in an introductory guide at the front of the book.

1. Locate the introductory guide in the front of your own dictionary. According to this guide, how does your dictionary organize a variety of meanings for one word?

2. Determine the part of speech for each italicized word in the following sentences from "What Ever Happened to Customer Service?" Then look each word up in your dictionary. If your dictionary uses the "most common to least common" pattern, write down the most common meaning of the italicized word and explain whether that meaning fits the context of the word in the sentence. If your dictionary uses the historical "oldest to newest" pattern, explain how the word has changed or evolved in meaning over time.

Karen Danielson, a shopper at the Cumberland *Mall* near Atlanta, agrees. (paragraph 12)

Most common to least common: a large, enclosed shopping area. This definition

matches the meaning of the word in this sentence.

Oldest to newest: an outdoor public walk for pedestrians.

Jean West asked a clerk why the other *register* wasn't open. (paragraph 21)

Most common to least common: a formal or official recording of items, names, or

actions. This definition does not match the word in the sentence.

Oldest to newest: a written account or entry. This evolved into the meaning of

"a machine that automatically records information."

She then tried the management office, where someone finally answered her *page*. (paragraph 22)

Most common to least common: a boy who acted as a knight's attendant. This

meaning does not fit the sentence.

Oldest to newest: a youth in service to a knight. This meaning evolved into

describing one who delivers a message and then into referring to the actual

message itself.

"I've waited in too many *lines* myself." (paragraph 25)

Most common to least common: the path traced by a moving point. This meaning

does not match the word in the sentence.

Oldest to newest: biological family strain. This came to refer also to the placement

of people or things in an orderly series.

Ed Spangler, a partner with the retail-consulting unit of Arthur Andersen, adds that retailers who lead in customer service, whether large or small, often give employees the chance to have a *stake* in the company, and always enthuse [sic] them about its culture of service. (paragraph 27)

Most common to least common: a piece of wood or metal pointed at one end. This

doesn't fit the sentence.

Oldest to newest: a pointed piece of wood. This evolved into the meaning of

"something gained or lost."

4 Complete Paragraphs

PROFESSIONAL PROFILE
Jamie Johnson, Substance Abuse Counselor

After witnessing the suffering caused by a family member's drug and alcohol addiction, Jamie Johnson decided to become a substance abuse counselor. She now works for a county agency that provides individual, group, and family counseling and educates the community about the dangers of substance abuse. Her responsibilities require her to write a variety of documents, including summaries of counseling sessions and materials distributed to the public. For example, she wrote the following paragraph for a fact sheet she hands out to middle school students when she speaks to them about drugs.

> Marijuana is a drug that damages your brain. The chemicals in marijuana travel through your blood to the parts of your brain that control memory, concentration, coordination, and judgment. If you smoke marijuana, you'll start having trouble in school. You'll find it difficult to remember information, so your schoolwork will suffer and your grades will drop. If you play sports, you'll see that smoking marijuana interferes with your coordination and reduces your overall performance. You'll also be more accident-prone because marijuana alters your perception and reaction time. For example, if you drive a car after smoking marijuana, you're likely to be involved in a serious accident. Marijuana also impairs your ability to make good decisions, so you'll be more likely to engage in unsafe sex. That could lead to pregnancy or to life-threatening diseases such as HIV.

Jamie's paragraph is effective because it's complete. Chapter 4 explains how to write complete paragraphs that fully explain your ideas.

Now that we've examined the kinds of words and sentences found in good writing, we'll turn, in the next three chapters, to the characteristics of effective paragraphs.

A paragraph can be defined as a group of sentences that develops one main idea. That idea is often stated in a topic sentence, and the other sentences in the paragraph provide the details, facts, statistics, examples, or reasons that explain and prove it. Therefore, when a paragraph is complete, it offers readers enough information to help them understand and accept the main idea.

Good writing contains complete paragraphs that leave no doubt about the author's meaning because they provide sufficient information. Complete paragraphs anticipate and answer all of the reader's questions and use layers of development to explain ideas.

ANTICIPATING THE READER'S QUESTIONS

As you compose, you must put yourself in your readers' shoes. As they read about your ideas, what will they *need* to know? What will they *want* to know? Writers must try to be mind readers as they determine what information they should communicate. Most of the time, they will not be present when the audience reads the document, so they will not be able to explain or add to what's on the page. That's why writers must anticipate the readers' questions and be sure to provide answers as they write.

For example, the following paragraph attempts to explain how to cook on a barbecue grill. Yet the writer has left out so many important details (see the questions in brackets) that the reader doesn't learn enough.

To grill a hamburger, you first have to get the fire going. Remove the rack *[On what?]* and stack *[How?]* charcoal briquets *[How many?]* in the center of the grill. Next, squirt charcoal lighter fluid *[How much?]* over the briquets. Wait until the fluid soaks the charcoal *[How long?]*. Then toss in a lighted match. The flame will burn for a few minutes before it goes out. When this happens, let the briquets sit for a while *[How long?]*. Don't squirt any more lighter fluid on the burning briquets *[Why?]*. As the briquets get hot *[How can you tell?]*, spread them out with a stick so they barely touch each other *[Why?]*.

When we assume too much about the reader's level of knowledge, we risk omitting important information. The writer of the paragraph on barbecuing intended to explain how to use a grill, but he assumed that his readers would already know a lot about charcoal, lighter fluid, and the grill itself.

This next paragraph, which comes from a supermarket's nutrition brochure, also leaves the reader with unanswered questions.

You can use your imagination to create fun and healthy snacks. Try using cereal or low-fat crackers. Also, include different fruits such as apples or apricots.

The first sentence—the topic sentence—raises questions the paragraph never answers. It doesn't say *how* you can create these snacks; it merely mentions a few ingredients and leaves you to wonder what to do with them. Also, it never explains how to make the snacks *fun*. Therefore, the reader is left wondering. Compare this revised paragraph:

You can use your imagination to create fun and healthy snacks. For example, you can mix dry cereal, oyster crackers, goldfish crackers and raisins for a tasty, low-fat cure for the munchies. You can serve pretzels with yogurt dip. Fruits can be fun, too. Sprinkle apple slices with cinnamon, or dip raw carrots in peanut butter.

This next example comes from a travel agency's newsletter.

Inexpensive public transportation is available to and from every major airport. Find it, and you can save a lot of money.

This little two-sentence item raises three questions it fails to answer. What kind of public transportation (bus, subway, train)? *How* do you find it? How much money can it save a traveler?

One final example comes from a letter from a day care center, addressed to parents.

> This January, ABC Day Care will begin participating in the U.S.D.A. School Food Service program. This program allows us to serve all children healthy, well-balanced meals.

After reading these two sentences, parents are surely wondering: What is this program? How does it work? Who is eligible? Who pays for it? To answer such questions, the writer should add details about "who, what, when, where, why, and how."

Examine your own writing for places where you've offered only general ideas, without providing enough details or explanation. Readers get frustrated when they have to fill in the blanks. And they shouldn't have to fill them in. That's the writer's job.

LAYERS OF DEVELOPMENT

Paragraphs may contain sentences at various levels of generality. In other words, some sentences express general ideas, while others provide specific information that explains those general ideas. For instance, look at the following passage from an article in a business magazine about temporary workers.

> One of the few surveys found big complaints from temps. In 1994, a South Carolina communication group called the Carolina Alliance for Fair Employment (CAFÉ) paid some two dozen temps for a week to detail problems they had encountered. They said that agencies tell temps to take jobs they're not trained for and don't provide that training. Agencies also don't give written notice of what the wage will be, put temps in unsafe working conditions, and often place them based on race, age, or sex. The group tried to implement a code of conduct based on the findings but gave up after agencies refused to comply.[1]

This paragraph begins with a general idea: surveys of temps reveal big complaints. The writer then adds another sentence to describe one particular survey. In that second sentence, the word *problems* is a general term that needs to be further explained, so the writer adds two more sentences to reveal what these problems are. The last sentence develops the statements about the specific problems by telling about the response to those problems. This series of increasingly specific sentences helps the reader understand the general idea in the first sentence.

We can visually demonstrate these relationships between the sentences by lining them up according to how general or specific they are:

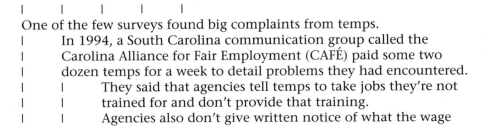

One of the few surveys found big complaints from temps.
    In 1994, a South Carolina communication group called the
    Carolina Alliance for Fair Employment (CAFÉ) paid some two
    dozen temps for a week to detail problems they had encountered.
        They said that agencies tell temps to take jobs they're not
        trained for and don't provide that training.
        Agencies also don't give written notice of what the wage

[1]Aaron Bernstein, "A Leg Up for the Lowly Temp," *Business Week* (June 21, 1999): 103.

| | | | | will be, put temps in unsafe working conditions, and often place them based on race, age, or sex. |

The group tried to implement a code of conduct based on the findings but gave up after agencies refused to comply.

It's helpful to think of imaginary margin lines that indicate how general or specific a sentence is. The most general statement is the first one, so we place it at a left imaginary margin line. The second sentence develops the first, so we indent it to indicate that it's more specific. We place the third and fourth sentences even with a third imaginary margin line to show that they both provide more information to explain the second sentence.

The relationships of general and specific sentences will vary, depending on the paragraph. The next passage, from a book, develops ideas by using a different pattern:

Our property meets all ADA requirements.
Parking lots include accessible parking spaces and curb cuts.
All facility entrances are wheelchair accessible.
Staff are trained in procedures for emergency evacuation of mobility-impaired persons.
All elevators accommodate wheelchairs.
Fire alarms are both visual and auditory.
Letters on all signs are in the large block style for the visually impaired, and some include Braille or raised letters.

All of the sentences that follow the first offer examples of ADA requirements. They are all equal, or *coordinate*, to each other, so they all line up along a second imaginary margin line.

Another example, this one from a bank's newsletter, uses yet another pattern of general and specific sentences:

On the Bank of Burke home page, you will find a wealth of useful information.
You can find a description of Bank of Burke's services, as well as an up-to-date list of interest rates.
Also included is a list of branch and ATM locations.
Furthermore, the web site offers an online access system.
This service allows you to check your account balances, review transactions, transfer funds, order checks, or request copies of your statements.
In addition, you can request services, such as a stop payment, through a secure e-mail system.
Online access *also* includes several calculators.
These calculators will help you figure finance charges and monthly payments for vehicle, mortgage, and other loans.
They can help you figure the interest on your investments.
Finally, the web site will soon offer a vehicle pricing guide and a traveler's cheque order service.

The passage about the bank includes many *clue words* to help the reader understand how the sentences are related to each other. These clue words indicate the subordinate and coordinate relationships between sentences. Words such as *and, also, too, first/second/third, but, however,* and *in other words* indicate coordinate relationships. These words signal that a sentence is equal to one that preceded it. Words such as *for example,* and *for instance* indicate subordinate status; the sentences further develop or explain a preceding sentence. Also, demonstrative adjectives such as *this* and *that* and pronouns such as *he, she,* and *they* often reveal subordinate-type relationships by referring to something that came before. These kinds of words help the reader see that a sentence is more specific than the one that preceded it. In the paragraph about the bank's web site, the clue words are in italics.

In the following passage, from a newsletter article about a type of tax increase called "bracket creep," the general and specific relationships of the sentences are, once again, different.

> Bracket creep can also sometimes affect married couples after they are wed, creating the problem known as the "marriage penalty."
>> The tax brackets are laid out in such a way that it is possible for a couple filing a joint return to pay more income tax than if they were still single.
>>> *This* usually occurs when the two individuals are making roughly the same amount of money.
>>>> *For example*, the 1998 tax year limit for the 15% tax bracket was $25,350 in taxable income for singles and $42,350 for married filing joint.
>>>>> *Therefore*, two single people with $25,000 each in taxable income would only have paid 15% tax on 100% of their income as singles but would have to pay a 28% tax rate on the portion of their combined income over $42,350 if they got married.[2]

The sentences we include to explain more general ideas are called *layers of development*. As you write each sentence, ask yourself, "Is there an idea in this sentence that I should explain further or give an example for?" If there is, add another "layer," another sentence that clarifies the more general idea that preceded it.

Mature, sophisticated writing includes many rich layers of development. For example, look at this paragraph from a hospital's newsletter. It contains six layers.

> Not everyone has the same sleep needs.
>> Most people need eight hours of sleep a night.
>>> Only 10 percent of the population needs more or less.
>>>> Newborn babies average 16 to 18 hours a day.
>>>>> *This* declines over the adolescent period and levels off at eight hours until they reach their teens.

[2]Jeffery Boyd, "Tax Talk," *Grassroots* (May 1999), 3.

| | | | | | Between the ages of 12 and 20,
| | | | | | young people need an hour more
| | | | | | sleep than do most pre-teens.[3]

**PRACTICE 4.1
Layers of
Development**

Rearrange the following paragraphs along imaginary margin lines to show the general and specific relationships between the sentences. Circle each clue word that helps you determine coordinate and subordinate relationships.

Example: The County is committed to protecting local lakes and streams by monitoring growth and adopting standards that builders and developers must follow in constructing homes and subdivisions. Among measures taken to assure that Lake James and other lakes and streams in the County retain their pristine quality, the Commissioners worked with other entities in extending sewer lines to the Lake James area. Commissioners also adopted a Subdivision Ordinance that establishes requirements for home and subdivision construction and sets forth sizes for lots either served by water and sewer, served by one or the other of those services, and lots served by neither, which are required to install septic tank systems. These restrictions are designed to prevent uncontrolled growth and septic tank spillage that would contaminate lakes and streams.[4]

Rearranged into layers of development:

The County is committed . . .
| Among measures taken . . .
| Commissioners (also) adopted . . .
| | (These) restrictions . . .

1. Hospital patients have responsibilities, too. The patient must provide health care professionals with accurate information about his health, including previous illnesses and current medications. Also, the patient is responsible for asking questions when he does not understand information or instructions. Last, the patient is responsible for telling the doctor if he can't follow through on prescribed treatments.

    Hospital patients . . .
    | *The patient must provide . . .*
    | (Also,) *the patient . . .*
    | (Last,) *the patient . . .*

2. North Carolina's Electric Power Communities have been providing reliable, quality service to one million North Carolina electric customers for more than 100 years. In the aftermath of devastating storms like Hurricanes Fran, Bertha, Hugo and Bonnie, we consistently restored power quickly, giving our customers one less thing

[3] Charles Sherrill Jr., M.D., "Sleep and Dreams," *Health Scene*, Valdese General Hospital (Summer 1999): 3.
[4] Burke County Public Information Office, *Burke County Annual Report 1998*, Morganton, North Carolina.

to worry about. After Hurricane Fran, the most devastating storm in decades, cities . . . restored power to more than 240,000 homes and businesses much quicker than other power providers in North Carolina.[5]

> *North Carolina's Electric Power . . .*
> | *In the aftermath . . .*
> | | *After Hurricane Fran . . .*

3. I decided to run the marathon for the Leukemia Society for two reasons. First, my best friend was diagnosed with leukemia in 1995. He and his family suffered helplessly while he bravely fought the disease. I want to make sure other families don't have to go through that pain. A second reason I want to raise money by running is that leukemia is the #1 killer of children under 14. The survival rate is only 40%, so I want to help raise funds for research to find a cure for a disease that inflicts terrible pain upon innocent kids.

> *I decided to run . . .*
> | (First) *my best friend . . .*
> | (He) *and his family . . .*
> | | *I want to make sure . . .* (that) *pain.*
> | *A* (second) *reason . . .*
> | *The survival rate . . .*

4. The best way to take your mind off your work is with a hobby that fills your free time. Pick something you can't get on the job. For example, if you sit at a desk all day, try hiking, camping, bicycle riding or some other physical activity. If you feel your job doesn't provide an outlet for your creativity, take up painting, music, or another activity that satisfies your creative side. People should not restrict their leisure pursuits solely to work activities.[6]

> *The best way . . .*
> | *Pick something . . .*
> | (For example) *if you sit . . .*
> | *If you feel your job . . .*
> | | *People should not . . .*

Ineffective writing includes very few layers of development; if you were to rearrange it as we have the foregoing example paragraphs, it often would contain only about two levels of development. Consequently, because it's not specific enough, it leaves the reader wondering what the writer really means.

For example, examine the following paragraph from a day care center's parent handbook:

> We introduce sensory, motor, perceptual, and language skills through *age-appropriate materials and activities. Concrete, hands-on activities* meet the children's needs for *meaningful learning experiences.* We *emphasize the process rather than the end product* to give each child a feeling of pride and accomplishment.

---

[5]ElectriCities of North Carolina, *Hurricane Preparedness Test* brochure (1999).
[6]Robert W. Bly, "10 Ways to Reduce Stress on the Job," http://www.smartbiz.com/sbs/arts/bly61.htm. Reprinted by permission of the author.

The italicized phrases are all general ideas that need to be further explained. Layers of development are needed to give examples of the materials and activities. Because of not seeing these examples, we don't know much more about the day care center's methods than we did before reading the paragraph.

Another example paragraph, from a mutual fund company's newsletter, also lacks layers:

> Investors learned some important lessons from the *1998 stock market drop*. First, don't panic when the stock market declines. Investors who feared further losses and sold their stocks missed out on the *huge, quick increase* in stock prices. Second, *build a solid foundation* with *longer-term investments* so you won't have to worry about short-term ups and downs.

That paragraph lacks specific data and examples to explain the general ideas shown in italics. The writer needs to add more details about what happened in the 1998 stock market drop, along with numbers such as percentages and prices. Also, he needs to mention specific kinds of *longer-term investments*. All of this additional information will help the reader grasp the ideas.

Another example comes from a finance company's brochure about the differences between leasing and buying a car. In this case, the italicized phrases need to be developed with specific examples.

> Buying—rather than leasing—your car is a good idea for people who have certain plans for the vehicle. Buy if you intend to keep the car for *a while*. Buy if you prefer no *mileage restrictions*. If you know you'll subject your car to *rough treatment*, you should buy it. Also, buy it if you want to *change its appearance*.

Right now, this paragraph offers only two layers of development. We could improve it by including additional layers, along with a few more clue words to help the reader follow the relationships between the sentences:

> Buying a car is a good idea for people who have certain plans for the vehicle. *First*, buy it if you intend to keep the car for more than a few years. Leases run for only two or three years, so if you know you'll keep the car for over three years, buying is a better option. *Second*, buy the car if you prefer no mileage restrictions. Typical leases limit you to only 12,000 to 15,000 miles per year. If you know you'll put more than 15,000 miles on the car per year, buy it. *Also* buy the car if you know you'll subject it to rough treatment. *For example*, regularly driving it over unpaved or challenging mountain roads may cause excess wear and tear that will cost more money under a lease agreement. *Finally*, you should buy if you want to change the vehicle's appearance. *For instance*, adding a spoiler or creating a "low-rider" may violate the lease agreement; buying the car allows you to alter it in any way you like.

The following example from a letter is arranged to show where ideas need to be further developed.

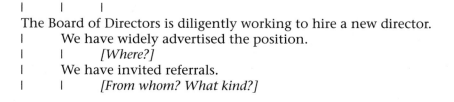

| | We are designing an interview format.
| | | *[What format? What will it include? Why?]*
| | |

The writer offers a thorough second layer of development (the three things the Board is doing); however, she stops short of providing the more specific information that would explain these activities. Note also the absence of clue words that will be essential to helping the reader understand coordinate and subordinate relationships when layers are added.

An e-mail message offers this example:

| | | |
We've made the stuff.com web site easier to explore by adding handy navigational tools on each page.
| New links to key sections of the web site now appear in the same place on every page.
| | *[Give examples of these links.]*
| | These links will prevent you from having to click on your browser's "Back" button.
| | | *[How? Give an example.]*
| A search engine at the top of every page allows you to find what you're looking for immediately.
| | *[Give an example.]*
| Furthermore, a site map explains the organizational structure of the web site.
| | *[What is a site map? What is this structure?]*
| | | |

This writer should have added third and fourth layers of development to give examples and more details for each general statement.

Another underdeveloped example comes from a report:

| | | |
Our increasingly diverse society will require changes in community colleges.
| *[Give examples of "increasingly diverse."]*
| Work and family demands interfere with a student's education.
| | *[Give an example of a particular student in this situation.]*
| | Therefore, colleges must be more flexible.
| | | *[How? Add examples:*
| | | *times of classes, length of classes,*
| | | *places classes meet, or distance education*
| | | *options.]*
| | Also, colleges should offer more support services.
| | | *[Like what? Add examples, such as child care or*
| | | *financial aid.]*
| | | |

The writer should add more layers at every level to give more information about the general statements.

Even professional writing sometimes lacks adequate layers of development:

| | | |
Don't back down from bullies [at work].
| Let them vent their anger, but don't take it personally.
| | *[How?]*

| Try to look for the facts in what they say, aside from the
| emotion.
| | *[Give an example.]*
| Explain the benefits of your point of view, express your
| disagreement in factual terms, and make sure your facts are
| correct.
| | *[Give an example.]*
| Allow the other party to save face because he may have a self-
| esteem problem.[7]
| | *[Give an example.]*

When you don't include adequate layers of development, you present ideas that are only half-explained.

PRACTICE 4.2
Adding Layers of Development

A. The following examples all lack adequate layers of development. Insert sentences (layers) to explain or to give examples. *Answers will vary.*

1. | | |

Joining a club, an organization, or a team helps you in school and prepares you for the future.

| Joining these kinds of groups will help you establish immediate
| bonds and friendships with some of the other students.

| | *Add an example:* _____

| | _____

| It will also help you develop the teamwork skills necessary in
| the work force.

| | *Add an example:* _____

| | _____

| Rather than taking time away from your studies, it will
| help you learn to manage your time more efficiently.

| | *Add an example:* _____

| | _____

| | |

2. | | |

You can use journal writing to explore emotions or to develop intelligence.

| You can write for catharsis—that is, to release your troubling
| thoughts and feelings.

[7]"How to Handle Difficult People," *Executive Edge Newsletter* (1996), http://www.smartbix.com/sbs/pubs/n125.htm.

| | *Like what? Give an example:* _____

| | _____

| You can use your journal to reflect about ideas.

| | *Give an example:* _____

| | _____

| Or your journal can be a problem-solving tool.

| | *Give an example:* _____

| | _____

| Finally, you can write to explore your creativity.

| | *Give an example:* _____

| | _____

| | |

3. | | |

Regular fitness walking produces mental benefits.

| It gives you more confidence.

| | *About what? Explain and add details:* _____

| | _____

| It also relieves stress and helps you maintain a positive attitude.

| | *How?* _____

| | _____

| Walking helps you sleep better at night.

| | *Why? How?* _____

| | _____

| | |

4. Choose one of the underdeveloped paragraphs in this chapter (pages 112–115) and on separate paper, add layers of development to answer the questions. *Answers will vary.*

To ensure that you are including sufficient layers of development in your own writing, try the following techniques:

1. When you compose your first draft, you may want to *arrange your sentences along imaginary margin lines* in order to evaluate how many layers of development you're including. Doing so will also remind you to review each sentence for any thoughts that need further clarification.

2. *Count the sentences in your paragraphs.* While there is no magic maximum or minimum number, your paragraphs probably are not adequately developed if they often contain only three or four sentences apiece.

3. *Scan your drafts for the phrase* for example. This phrase often begins sentences that really help your reader grasp your ideas. If you never begin sentences this way, you may not be including the specific information in the form of particular instances or anecdotes that your reader needs in order to understand you.

PRACTICE 4.3
Examining Your Writing for Layers of Development

Select three different paragraphs from reports or essays you've written. Arrange them into layers of development. *Answers will vary.*

TEST YOUR UNDERSTANDING

1. What are layers of development?

   Sentences that offer specific examples or explanation of more general statements.

2. What's the difference between *coordinate* statements and *subordinate* statements?

   Coordinate statements are equal in generality. A subordinate statement more

   specifically develops the statement that precedes it.

3. Give three examples of clue words.

   Answers will vary. Also, for example, these *are possible responses.*

4. What are three ways in which you can check your own writing for adequate layers of development?

   Arrange sentences along imaginary margin lines, count the sentences in your

   paragraphs, and scan your drafts for the phrase for example.

WEB ACTIVITY: Lifelong Learning

If you want to ensure employment for yourself in an ever-changing, competitive job market, you'll have to continually update your skills. Keeping your knowledge and skills current will often require you to pursue formal training or education. Fortunately, distance education

WEB ACTIVITY: *continued*

via the Internet makes learning opportunities more widely available and more convenient.

1. Go to the web site http://www.lifelonglearning.com.
2. Click on *Search for Courses.*
3. Follow the directions to find courses in your current field of study or in a subject of interest to you. Research the institutions or organizations offering these courses.
4. Write a summary about the results of your research. Include details about "who, what, when, where, why, how, how many"—and "how much" (the cost).

GROUP PROJECT AND WRITING ACTIVITIES

In the next three chapters, you'll be focusing on a specific community service in your area.

Form a group with three or four of your classmates. Together, use one or more of the invention strategies described in Chapter 1 to think of local, national, and international ways you'd like to help other people. For example, think of diseases that need cures; crisis or catastrophe situations; difficult circumstances requiring counseling or support; and needed skills, training, or information. Generate as many ideas as possible in the space below.

On your own, choose two of the ideas your group generated. Find organizations or agencies in your community that work to help people in those ways. Write the names and addresses of those organizations here:

Write a letter to one of the organizations you found. Request more information about its mission, activities, and services. Use the following model to create your letter.

Your street address
Your city, state, ZIP code
Month, day, year

Name of organization
Street address
City, state, ZIP

To whom it may concern:

First paragraph: Tell who you are, why the organization interests you, and what you want.

Second paragraph: Ask for information about specific activities or services. Ask for some of the organization's literature (such as brochures, reports, or flyers).

Third paragraph: Thank the reader.

Sincerely,

(Sign your name.)

Type your name here.

> Make a copy of your letter; then mail it. Share the copy with your group members. When you receive a response to your letter, meet with your group to share the information the organization sent to you.

READINGS   How do the academic demands of high school and college differ? Do you know anyone who was a good student in high school but struggled in college?

The following selection tells the story of a man who overcame his academic troubles to become a renowned pediatric neurosurgeon.

As you read this story, circle every word that's unfamiliar to you. Look it up and write the meaning in the margin. Put an exclamation point (!) next to any sentence or paragraph you find especially interesting. Put a question mark (?) next to any sentence or paragraph you don't understand.

Higher Calling

Osborne Robinson Jr.

1   *"More blood! Stat!"*

2   The silence of the [operating room] was smashed by the amazingly quiet command. The twins had received 50 units of blood, but their bleeding still hadn't stopped!

3   . . . A quiet panic erupted through the room. Every ounce of type AB negative blood had been drained from the Johns Hopkins Hospital blood bank. Yet the 7-month-old twin patients who had been joined at the back of their heads since birth needed more blood or they would die without ever having a chance to recuperate. This was their only opportunity, their only chance, at normal lives. . . .

4   Many of the 70-member team began offering to donate their own blood, realizing the urgency of the situation. . . .

5   Fortunately, within a short time the city blood bank was able to locate the exact number of units of blood needed to continue the surgery. Using every skill, trick, and device known in their specialties, the surgeons were able to stop the bleeding within a couple of hours. The operation continued. Finally, the plastic surgeons sewed the last skin flaps to close the wounds, and the 22-hour surgical ordeal was over. The Siamese twins—Patrick and Benjamin— were separate for the first time in their lives!

6   The exhausted primary neurosurgeon who had devised the plan for the operation was a ghetto kid from the streets of Detroit. . . .

7   *Ben Carson. Just an ordinary name—but one that is recognized and respected throughout America's medical community.*

8   *He is not an ordinary person. His story may assist you in deciding how you would like to spend the rest of your life. As you learn about Ben's calling and listen to his words, think about whether you are still on track in fulfilling your own early*

"Higher Calling" is taken from GIFTED HANDS by Dr. Benjamin Carson. Copyright © 1990 by Review and Herald ® Publishing Association. Used by permission of Zondervan Publishing House.

dreams. If you're not on track, if you have some regret about your present direction, seriously explore the reasons for the decisions, events, or circumstances that have changed your life's path. Be sure to listen closely to Ben's following conversation with his mother because that conversation determined his destiny. He was twelve years old at the time and fascinated by the stories about missionary doctors he had been hearing at church.

9   "That's what I want to do," I said to my mother as we walked home. "I want to be a doctor. Can I be a doctor, Mother?"

10   "Bennie," she said, "listen to me." We stopped walking and Mother stared into my eyes. Then laying her hands on my thin shoulders, she said, "If you ask the Lord for something and believe He will do it, then it'll happen."

11   "I believe I can be a doctor."

12   "Then, Bennie, you will be a doctor," she said matter-of-factly, and we started to walk on again.

13   *Benjamin Carson never forgot for one moment his dream of becoming a healer, a doctor, and he never stopped believing in himself and his plan. He was convinced that if he did well in school, the Lord would bless him and he would become a doctor. From his earliest teens, every thought, nerve, and muscle was focused on finishing high school and going to college.*

14   *College was to be the giant step. College would be the ticket to his life's work, and college was his target. Not just any college, either, but an Ivy League one where, Ben Carson knew, he would be a star and move closer to his calling. The day finally came: high school study and certain sacrifices were all behind him and Ben was ready—or at least he thought he was ready—for Yale.*

15   I strode onto the campus, looked up at the tall, gothic-style buildings, and approved of the ivy-covered walls. I figured I'd take the place by storm. And why not? I was incredibly bright. . . .

16   But I quickly learned that the classwork at Yale was difficult, unlike anything I'd ever encountered at Southwestern High School. The professors expected us to have done our homework before we came to class, then used that information as the basis for the day's lectures. This was a foreign concept to me. I'd slid through semester after semester in high school, studying only what I wanted, and then, being a good crammer, spent the last few days before exams memorizing like mad. It had worked at Southwestern. It was a shock to realize it wouldn't work at Yale.

17   Each day I slipped farther and farther behind in my classwork, especially in chemistry. Why I didn't work to keep up, I'm not sure. I could give myself a dozen excuses, but they didn't matter. What mattered was that I didn't know what was going on in chemistry class.

18   It all came to a head at the end of the first semester when I faced final examinations. The day before the exam I wandered around the campus, sick with dread. I couldn't deny it any longer. I was failing freshman chemistry; and failing it badly . . . As the realization sunk in of my impending failure, this bright boy from Detroit also stared squarely into another horrible truth— if I failed chemistry I couldn't stay in the premed program.

19   Despair washed over me as memories of fifth grade flashed through my mind. "What score did you get, Carson?" "Hey, dummy, did you get any right today?" Years had passed, but I could still hear the taunting voices in my head.

20   *What am I doing at Yale anyway?* It was a legitimate question, and I couldn't push the thought away. *Who do I think I am? Just a dumb Black kid from the poor side of Detroit who has no business trying to make it through Yale with all these intelligent, affluent students.* I kicked a stone and sent it flying into the grass. *Stop it,* I told myself. *You'll only make it worse.* I turned my memories back to those teachers who told me, "Benjamin, you're bright. You can go places." . . .

21   One glimmer of hope—a tiny one at that—shone through my seemingly impossible situation. Although I had been holding on to the bottom rung of the class from the first week at Yale, the professor had a rule that might save me. If failing students did well on the final exam, the teacher would throw out most of the semester's work and let the good final-test score count heavily toward the final grade. That presented the only possibility for me to pass chemistry.

22   Midnight. The words on the pages blurred, and my mind refused to take in any more information. I flopped into my bed and whispered in the darkness, "God, I'm sorry. Please forgive me for failing You and for failing myself." Then I slept.

. . .

23   The professor came in, and without saying much, began to hand out the booklets of examination questions. . . . At last, heart pounding, I opened the booklet and read the first problem. . . .

. . .

24   I knew the answer to every question on the first page. . . .

25   I was so excited to know correct answers that I worked quickly, almost afraid I'd lose what I remembered. Near the end of the test, . . . I didn't get every single problem. But it was enough. I knew I would pass.

26   During my four years at Yale I did backslide a little, but never to the point of not being prepared. I started learning how to study, no longer concentrating on surface material and just what the professors were likely to ask on finals. I aimed to grasp everything in detail. In chemistry, for instance, I didn't want to know just answers but to understand the reasoning behind the formulas. From there, I applied the same principle to all my classes.

27   After this experience, I had no doubt that I would be a physician. I also had the sense that God not only wanted me to be a physician, but that He had special things for me to do. I'm not sure people always understand when I say that, but I had an inner certainty that I was on the right path in my life—the path God had chosen for me. Great things were going to happen in my life, and I had to do my part by preparing myself and being ready.

RESPONDING TO THE READING

1. Do you, like Ben Carson, feel a calling to pursue a career path you've chosen?

   Answers will vary.

2. How did Ben Carson change his study habits after he almost failed his chemistry class?

   He resolved to grasp everything in detail.

3. What changes have you made in your own study habits since entering college?

   Answers will vary.

4. Arrange paragraph 16 into layers of development.

   But I quickly learned . . .

   | *The professors expected . . .*

   | | *This was a foreign concept . . .*

   | | | *I'd slid through semester . . .*

   | | | | *It had worked . . .*

   | | | | *It was a shock . . .*

BUILDING VOCABULARY

Homonyms are words that sound alike but are spelled differently and have different meanings. Because they sound the same, writers can easily mix them up and use the incorrect word, for they are not interchangeable. For example, the word *principle,* which appears in "Higher Calling," sounds exactly like the word *principal.* These two words, however, have very different meanings.

The following sentences contain often-confused words. In each set of brackets, circle the word that fits the sentence's meaning.

1. I told them I could not [accept/except] their offer.

2. She makes more money [then/than] he does.

3. The loan officer will probably [council/counsel] us to increase the down payment.

4. That unpaid bill will have a negative [affect/effect] on your credit rating.

5. You will [lose/loose] vacation time if you don't take it by the end of the month.

(continued)

**BUILDING
VOCABULARY
*continued***

6. The car [passed/past] the bus at a high rate of speed.

7. [Proceed/Precede] to the next phase of negotiations.

8. The cashiers [continuously/continually] complain about the cold wind when the door opens.

9. [Whose/Who's] going with me to the conference?

10. The clerk called a security officer when the shopper's behavior became [bazaar/bizarre].

Who are the people in your life who have encouraged you to get an education? Who has helped you study or complete assignments?

This next article tells the story of former Chicago Bears football player Chris Zorich, who rose to the top—thanks to his mother's love, support, and encouragement.

As you read this article, circle every word that's unfamiliar to you. Look it up and write the meaning in the margin. Put an exclamation point (!) next to any sentence or paragraph you find especially interesting. Put a question mark (?) next to any sentence or paragraph you don't understand.

Winning for Zora

Collin Perry

Chris Zorich seemed destined to go nowhere. His mother had other plans for him.

1   As the crowd funneled into the Chicago skating rink last February, a thickly muscled man with a bronze, shaved head towered above a gaggle of two dozen kids. The children, who came from Lydia Home Association, had been abused or neglected; some of them were also handicapped. All were the guests of pro football player Chris Zorich, who in his bow tie and sports jacket looked like a cross between the Incredible Hulk and Mother Goose.

2   When the show started, a boy with poor vision settled next to Zorich. From time to time the 28-year-old athlete would gently turn the child's head to help him follow the action on ice. Having grown up on Chicago's tough South Side, Zorich knew all too well the pain of feeling different.

3   "As a child, I had four strikes against me," he says. "I was poor, fat, biracial and speech-impaired." Remembering that pain motivates Chris to work with kids of all income levels and social backgrounds to help them do their best.

4   Chris Zorich always knew he had one crucial thing going for him—someone who lifted his hopes and inspired him with her endurance and devotion. If there was one reason he was here today, she was it.

5   "You better not cry," taunted the teenager one day, holding eight-year-old Chris off the ground as he tried to shake money from his pockets.

6   "I ain't c-c-crying," Chris gasped.

7   On other days a different boy badgered Chris and punched him in the chest. "You honky, you better have some money for me tomorrow, got that?"

8   Such incidents often happened as Chris returned home from school in the predominantly black neighborhood on Chicago's South Side in the late 1970s. To explain his bruises, he would tell his mother, Zora, that he had tripped. He never confessed that other kids were beating him up, as he knew she would demand to know who they were.

9   One day, however, Chris finally asked her why the other kids had such a problem with his skin color. "I get 'white boy' and 'honky' from the guys around here," he said. "And in white neighborhoods they call me n-n-nigger."

10   Chris already knew that his black father had abandoned the family before his birth. Now Zora tried to comfort him. "I'm white. Your father was black. You're biracial, and I love you. And no matter what, always know that I'll be there for you."

"I'm the Class"

11   The bond between Chris and his mother was especially tight, having been forged in the shared adversity of inner-city life. Mice and cockroaches infested the tenement building they lived in; outside, muggings were almost routine.

12   Chris always turned to his mother for guidance and reassurance. Zora responded by putting her son's welfare above everything else. She made ends meet by baby-sitting, not just for the money but to provide Chris with companions she could supervise. She read to him, helped with homework and made sure his hand-me-down clothes were always clean.

13   In school Chris's stuttering proved torturous. When he was ten, he had to read an essay in front of the class. He stuttered and mumbled along. When he heard classmates tittering, he quit halfway through and returned to his seat, his face hot with embarrassment.

14   That evening, when Chris told Zora about the incident, she said, "Try it out on me. Pretend *I'm* the class."

15   Chris began reciting his essay and, though still stuttering, managed to finish it. That was a good start for Zora, but not enough. She asked him to read it again and again, and each time his speech improved. "Now show the class what you can do," she insisted. At the end of the year, Chris found the nerve to ask his teacher for another chance. Telling himself it was only his mother in the audience, he got through the reading with few hesitations.

16   Despite their hardships, Chris noticed that his mother was generous to others. Whenever children approached and offered to carry her groceries, hoping to earn a tip, she'd always give them a dime or a piece of candy—even though she'd carry her own packages. Chris was shocked, but he said nothing. Zora believed in treating the world as she would her own family. It was a lesson he never forgot.

17   Zora tried to do everything for Chris that a father would. She'd watch a lot of sports and television with Chris. She would even take him to the park, where she'd chase passes and hit fly balls. Other kids razzed him for playing ball with his mother, but their taunts barely mattered to him. With Zora he felt secure and happy.

"I'll Get Us Out"

18   Chris returned his mother's affection openly. On Zora's birthday he would make her a card and buy her an inexpensive gift. On Mother's Day he would present her with a bouquet of dandelions.

19   Still, their devotion to each other couldn't stop others from being cruel about Chris's mixed-race background. One winter, as Zora and Chris walked home, a group of kids pelted them with snowballs. One hit Zora square in the face, and Chris saw a tear roll down her cheek. At that moment he vowed he would someday get them out of there.

20   The obstacles in their lives seemed unremitting, especially after Zora was told she had severe diabetes. Overweight and unable to stay on her feet for prolonged periods, she was forced to turn to public assistance. It was barely enough for rent.

21   The two plunged to their lowest. Food became so short that Chris sometimes went to bed at 6 p.m. to sleep through his hunger pangs, knowing he'd wake up to a hot breakfast at school. Other times they would rummage through a supermarket garbage bin for discarded food. "It's fine," Zora would say at the sight of a package of hamburger meat that was well past its "sell by" date. "I'll cut off the bad parts."

22   Ironically, food became an escape for Chris. His ravenous appetite and fear of being hungry compelled him to eat every scrap he could get his hands on. By the time he was 12, his weight had ballooned to 250 pounds.

23   Chris envied gang members, who had the girls, cars and clothes—everything a kid wanted. But his mother had been mugged by neighborhood thugs right in front of him as a toddler. Because of this incident, he knew he could never join a gang.

Fast and Strong

24   Chris's first real glimmer of finding a way out came when he was admitted to Chicago Vocational High School in September 1983. Soon the high school's football coach, John Potocki, noticed the oversized boy. "You playing football?" he asked Chris. "You're big enough to be on the squad."

25   Chris started going to after-school football practice and discovered, to his delight, he was with people who had some real goals in life. He enjoyed the discipline of it and working with others. Potocki found that the sweet-tempered boy was fast, strong and determined—indeed, he had a "killer instinct" on the football field.

26 Zora became the team's biggest fan. Before each game Chris would scan the crowd until he found her in the stands. And he established himself as a standout player. In his junior year five colleges recruited him. After discussions with his mother, he decided on Notre Dame in South Bend, Indiana, partly because he viewed the team's graduation rate—almost 99 percent—as a guarantee that he could get a good job one day and help Zora.

"I Can't Do It"

27 When he started at Notre Dame in August 1987, however, Chris was unprepared for the academic rigors of a first-rate university. As a freshman, he partied on weekends and finished the first semester with a 1.9 grade-point average, which landed him on academic probation.

28 "Mom, I can't do it," he told Zora one night on the phone. "I get these grades again and I'll be kicked out. I'm coming home."

29 Zora was silent for a minute. Finally she said, "And what would you be coming back to?"

30 "You. *You're* there."

31 "Yes, but I won't be here forever," she said.

32 For days Chris mulled over his mother's words. She was right. He knew this was the chance of a lifetime, and in the end he buckled down to his studies and got off probation.

33 Meanwhile, Chris's progress on the playing field was even more impressive. In his sophomore year he became the starting defensive tackle and was named to the 1988 All-America squad.

34 Back home, word got around that the former "fat boy" was an emerging football star. On visits home the now six-foot-one, 260-pound athlete enjoyed strolling through the old neighborhoods, his mother proudly leaning on his arm. Indeed, Zora became something of a neighborhood hero, signing autographs for fans when Chris was away at school.

"Some Game!"

35 Chris went on to make All-America for three consecutive years. During his senior year he won the Rotary Lombardi Award as the nation's top collegiate lineman. That season ended with a one-point loss to the University of Colorado in the Orange Bowl on January 1, 1991. Still, Chris was named Notre Dame's Most Valuable Player for the game, stacking up ten tackles and one sack.

36 Gloomy over his team's defeat, Chris telephoned his mother, who'd watched on TV. "Hey, I saw all those tackles," she said brightly. "You played some game!" Zora's enthusiasm was contagious, and the two talked and laughed.

37 The next morning Chris caught a flight for Chicago. He had expected Zora to meet him at the airport, but she wasn't there. Racing to his mother's apartment, he found the front door locked. He pounded. No answer. Frantic,

he went around the back, pulled the screen off a bathroom window and saw Zora lying on the hallway floor, dead of a heart attack. As Chris knelt beside her, his distress gradually gave way to a feeling of serenity at his core. "Bye, Mom," he whispered, kissing her. "I love you."

38   At Zora's wake, mourners sang "You Are My Sunshine." Later, at the grave site, Chris placed roses on her coffin. Mom, he thought, I hope you'll be proud of what I do with the rest of my life.

RESPONDING TO THE READING

1. Describe four obstacles Chris Zorich faced during his childhood.

   Chris said he was "poor, fat, biracial, and speech-impaired."

2. What incident strengthened Zorich's resolve to make a better life for himself and his mother?

   A group of kids threw snowballs at him and his mother. One hit his mother in the

   face and made her cry.

3. How did playing football help Zorich find a way out of a life of poverty?

   It gave him the ability to discipline himself and work with others toward

   achieving goals.

4. What obstacles have you had to overcome to complete your education?

   Answers will vary.

5. Arrange paragraphs 12 and 17 of the story into layers of development.

   Chris always . . .

   | *Zora responded . . .*

   | | *She made ends meet . . .*

   | | *She read to him . . .*

   Zora tried . . .

   | *She'd watch . . .*

   | *She would even . . .*

   | | *Other kids . . .*

   | | | *With Zora . . .*

BUILDING VOCABULARY

Adding a negative prefix gives a word its opposite meaning. Negative prefixes are *a, ab, dis, il, im, in, ir, non,* and *un.*

inexpensive = not expensive

unprepared = not prepared

abnormal = not normal

disrespectful = not respectful

irrelevant = not relevant

Add the correct negative prefix to each of the following words and write the meaning of the new word.

1. logical *illogical—contradicting or disregarding the principles of logic*

2. believable *unbelievable—not capable of eliciting belief or trust*

3. restrictive *nonrestrictive—not limiting*

4. passable *impassable—impossible to pass, cross, or overcome*

5. eligible *ineligible—disqualified by law, rule, or provision*

6. typical *atypical—unusual or irregular*

7. honest *dishonest—disposed to lie, cheat, defraud, or deceive*

8. responsible *irresponsible—unreliable or untrustworthy*

9. legible *illegible—not decipherable*

10. content *discontent—dissatisfaction*

5 Coherent Paragraphs

PROFESSIONAL PROFILE
L. Lynn Smith, Interior Designer

Lynn Smith operates her own interior design business for both residential and commercial clients. She visits a site, analyzes the project, and then generates layout and design ideas. When a client hires her, she goes to work transforming the site with new floor coverings, wall coverings, furniture, window treatments, and accessories such as lamps and plants. Because she is a business owner and a member of several professional and community organizations, Lynn writes a wide variety of documents, including newsletter articles, brochures, and letters. For each prospective client, Lynn writes a project analysis, a document that summarizes her ideas for a project. The following paragraph comes from her project analysis for a Civil War–era house acquired by a historic preservation society.

> The layout of the Samuel McDowell Tate home suggests remodeling and redecoration for multiple uses that could all preserve the house's three distinct styles: Greek Revival, Second Empire, and Victorian. With appropriate colors, motifs, and furnishings adapted to today's modern commercial applications, the main floor could accommodate an elegant restaurant. The colors and space planning of the second floor suggest office space. The third floor, which resulted from the transition to the Second Empire addition of the mansard roof and turret, could easily transform into a private condominium. The first and second floor baths could become the elevator shaft for access to this space. Other structures on the grounds, such as the garden shed and pool house, could be redesigned into shops or settings for outdoor weddings.

To explain her ideas for this property, Lynn used two methods of development, description and division. Chapter 5 discusses ten different methods of development that writers use.

In addition to being complete, effective paragraphs must be coherent. *Coherent* means that the paragraph makes sense because it offers a clear progression of thought. In other words, the reader can easily follow the writer's ideas from sentence to sentence.

We achieve coherence in our paragraphs in two ways. First, we use methods of development to explain and develop our ideas. Second, we use transitions to help the reader understand the relationships between the sentences.

METHODS OF DEVELOPMENT

Chapter 4 of this book discussed layers of development, which are the facts, data, statistics, details, examples, and anecdotes that a writer uses to explain and develop general ideas or abstract concepts. In this chapter, we examine common patterns for arranging these layers to achieve coherence. These patterns, called *methods of development,* are ones readers recognize easily—so they're effective for explaining ideas.

The next sections give examples of the most common development methods: narration, description, exemplification, process analysis, comparison/contrast, cause/effect, division, classification, reasons, and problem/solution. These methods can even be combined in one paragraph. However, we'll first look at each method in isolation.

You will notice that topic sentences in each paragraph are underlined. Where no topic sentence is underlined, the main idea is implied, rather than stated directly.

Narration

One way to develop an idea stated in a paragraph's topic sentence is by telling a story to explain or illustrate it. For instance, the following passage from a memo makes a statement about a business trip, then narrates the writer's experiences to prove that statement.

> <u>Our trip to the Greenville plant was very productive.</u> On our first day there, we met with Mr. Yamamoto, who spent the whole morning briefing us about the corporate office's plans for next year. That afternoon, we toured the facility and talked to many employees about their successes and needs in each department. On the second day, we met first with department crew leaders to review production goals; then we saw a video presentation about the proposed Augusta facility.

In the next paragraph, from a brochure, the writer also tells a story to develop his point.

> <u>In my opinion, the comedian who makes the most effective use of inferiority [as a source of humorous material] is the scrawny introvert, Woody Allen.</u> The following story from Woody's childhood comes alive when he tells it:

> > Woody was on his way to his violin lesson when he passed the pool hall where "Floyd" and his friends hung out. They were stealing hubcaps (from moving cars). Floyd called Woody an insulting name as he passed, and being a "cocky kid," Woody announced that he didn't take that from anybody! He put down his violin and said, "If you want to address me, you will call me Master Haywood Allen!" Woody said he spent that winter in a wheelchair. A team of doctors labored to remove a violin from his skull. His only good fortune was that it wasn't a cello.

> Hasn't every boy in the world been tyrannized by "Floyd" sometime during childhood? He was certainly well-represented in my hometown.[1]

A final paragraph comes from a brochure about parenting.

> <u>Mark's parents were no strangers to discipline, and they tried every approach on their little rebel.</u> They spanked him, stood him in the corner,

---

[1]James Dobson, Ph.D., *Understanding Your Child's Personality* brochure (Colorado Springs: Focus on the Family, 1992), 11.

sent him to bed early, and shamed and scolded him. Nothing worked. The temper tantrums continued regularly. Then one evening Mark's parents were both reading a newspaper in their living room. They had said something that angered their son, and he fell on the floor in a rage. He screamed and whacked his head on the carpet, kicking and flailing his small arms. They were totally exasperated at that point and didn't know what to do, so they did nothing. They continued reading the paper in stony silence, which was the last thing the little tornado expected. He got up, looked at his father, and fell down for Act Two. Again his parents made no response. By this time they were glancing at one another knowingly and watching junior with curiosity. Again, Mark's tantrum stopped abruptly. He approached his mother, shook her arm, then collapsed for Act Three. They continued ignoring him. His response? This child felt so silly flapping and crying on the floor that he never threw another tantrum.[2]

In that paragraph, the story of one particular family illustrates the idea that the best way to handle a child's temper tantrums is to ignore them.

Description

Sometimes we need to give descriptive details to explain a person, place, or thing. Two types of descriptive details are *factual details* and *sensory details*. Factual details include information such as size, weight, shape, age, brand names or proper names, dimensions, construction materials, parts, percentages, distances, and prices. Sensory details help readers experience the subject with their five senses of sight, sound, taste, touch, and smell. Colors, fragrances, and physical sensations such as heat or cold are all sensory details. Chapter 2 includes more information about sensory and factual details.

The following passage from an eyecare wellness newsletter helps the reader visualize the best computer monitor through factual details such as the type of monitor and its features, and sensory details such as the contrast, flickering, and glare.

Want a monitor that will ease the wear-and-tear on your overworked eyes? Look for the following:

- *A high-quality image.* "The larger, flat-panel LCDs (Liquid Crystal Displays) are the easiest on the eyes because the imaging is more powerfully focused," says Jeffery Anshel, O.D., who treats computer vision syndrome. "But if you have to use an older model, try to get one that doesn't flicker and that features a sharp contrast between the field [background] and the images."

- *Flexible positioning.* Your computer monitor should be positioned at a distance of at least 20 inches from your eyes (about an arm's length). It should be placed so that you look down slightly when you're reading the screen. Position your keyboard directly in front of the monitor to cut down on excessive eye movements as you look from keyboard to screen.

- *Minimum glare.* Some monitors have glare-reducing screens. Others feature hoods or shields that keep light away. Remember to dust the screen frequently—dust buildup reduces image quality.[3]

[2]James Dobson, *The Miracle Parenting Tools* brochure (Colorado Springs: Focus on the Family, 1994), 16.
[3]Vision Service Plan Marketing and Corporate Development Division, "Choose Your Monitor With Care," *Eye on Health* (Rancho Cordova, Calif.: 1999): 3.

Another example, from a letter of complaint addressed to a fast-food restaurant's manager, combines factual and sensory details to describe both people and things.

<u>My family and I have stopped eating at Burger Champ because of the terrible service and poor food.</u> I usually end up sitting in the drive-thru lane for at least 15 minutes. When I finally get to the window and my patience is gone, your employees make matters even worse with their unfriendly attitudes. They never smile; some of them even wear unpleasant scowling expressions. They don't say "thank you;" instead, they thrust my bags of food toward my car window in silence. Many times, they forget an item I ordered or give me the wrong item. When I get the food home, my family is disappointed in its quality. The french fries are greasy and limp, the burger buns are stale and soggy, and the iced tea is either sickeningly sweet or too watery.

A final example, which comes from a report, describes a place. To help readers visualize the subject, this description provides details about its location, dimensions, materials of construction, and parts.

<u>Construction will begin on the new Maintenance Service Center this spring.</u> The site selected for this building is located near the property entrance for easy entry and exit of large trucks. However, a south-facing downward slope will conceal much of the facility from view. The two-story, red brick building will include 15,000 square feet of storage, office, and shipping/receiving areas. It will house equipment, supplies, and a workshop. It will also store hazardous materials in compliance with state and federal regulations.

Exemplification

Some general ideas are best developed by presenting one or more specific examples that illustrate the main point. The key phrases *for example* and *for instance* usually indicate the presence of the exemplification method. This passage from a campaign brochure written by a candidate for mayor offers one specific example to develop the paragraph's main idea.

<u>If I am elected mayor, I will carefully examine projects begun by the current administration.</u> For example, many of our town's residents have expressed concern about renovations to our down-town streetscape. The new brick flowerbeds are attractive, but people don't like the way the new curbs jut out into the street and decrease the number of parking spaces. While I obviously cannot reverse that project, I can take a close look at other proposed renovations to make sure they meet with citizens' approval.

This next paragraph, from a credit union newsletter, uses two examples to illustrate the main idea:

<u>You should understand fully what is required to keep the [low, introductory credit card] rate that is being offered.</u> A recent Platinum MasterCard offer has a six month teaser rate of 3.9% that moves to 13.99% but can move to 25.99% after one late payment or if you go over your credit line. Another card issuer is offering six months at 0% but then moves to 15.65% and can go to 23.99% after a late payment or exceeding your

credit limit. Additionally, both of these cards have $29.00 late payment and over-the-limit fees.[4]

A final passage is from an Army recruitment brochure. It offers three examples to explain the main idea:

> <u>Today's Army also offers a variety of programs to suit your needs and lifestyle.</u> For instance, our Delayed Entry Program lets you sign up as a high school junior, select your area of specialization, then delay your entry until graduation. Our College Loan Repayment plan can help you pay back your federally insured college loan, up to $65,000. And with the Montgomery GI Bill, plus the Army College Fund, you could earn up to $40,000 for college or vo-tech training. Whatever your goals in life, today's Army can help you achieve them.[5]

Process Analysis

Process analysis explains the steps in a procedure. Two types of process analysis are directive or informational. *Directive process analysis* gives the readers "how-to" instructions (directions) so that they can re-create a procedure themselves. For example, you could explain the steps for making a cake or for changing the oil in a car. *Informational process analysis* explains a process so that readers can understand how something is done or how something works. For instance, you might explain how bees make honey or how an air traffic control tower works.

This paragraph from a magazine article is an example of directive process analysis that gives step-by-step directions for the reader to follow.

> [To reduce or prevent work-induced aches and pains,] <u>get up and stretch every 45 to 60 minutes.</u> Inexpensive software can be purchased that not only reminds you that it's time for a stretch break, but even shows you some exercises to do. If you don't have a software program for this purpose, try setting a soft alarm to go off at regular intervals, or simply make a habit of standing up and stretching a little every time you answer the phone. After your call is completed, do some gentle shoulder rolls and neck stretches. Walk around the office briefly and get yourself a glass of water. You'll feel better![6]

Another passage, from an e-mail, also offers directive process analysis with how-to instructions:

> <u>As of today, we have begun a new system of package receipt.</u> We have put a red, three-ring binder in the mailroom. The mailroom staff will record each package in this book as it is delivered. Before you pick up a package and remove it from the mailroom, please sign for it in the red book. If you receive packages from postal workers or delivery persons at the loading dock, please list them in the book with your name as the receiver. If you have any questions about this procedure, please call me or e-mail me.

The next paragraph, from a brochure about anesthesia, is an example of informational process analysis. It explains a procedure so that readers will understand how it works, rather than re-create the process themselves.

[4]North Carolina State Employees' Credit Union Consumer Education Department, "Take Time to Compare the Fine Print," *Grassroots* (Raleigh, N.C.: August 1999): 2.
[5]United States Government Printing Office, *African American Role Models* Army brochure (July 1998).
[6]"Reducing Desktop Injuries," *The Office Professional* (October 1999): 7.

With spinal anesthesia, a very thin needle is placed into the spinal fluid sack 3 to 4 inches below the end of the spinal cord, and numbing medicine is injected into the spinal fluid. The needle is then removed. In just a few minutes, the legs begin to feel warm, then the lower half of the body goes completely numb. You will not be able to feel or move your legs. The area to be operated on will be cleaned thoroughly and sterile drapes placed so that you will not be able to see any of the surgery. Additional sedatives will be given as needed.[7]

Comparison/Contrast

Sometimes we need to develop an idea by showing how two or more subjects are alike or different. *Comparison* involves examining the similarities between two subjects; *contrast* explores the subjects' differences. A paragraph might do one or the other or both to explain a point to the reader.

The following passage from a memo compares two advertisements by discussing only their similarities.

Because our previous newspaper advertisement generated so much business, we'll keep our new advertisement very similar. We'll use the same drawing of our combo platter, our most popular menu item, that we put in the old ad. We'll also keep the restaurant's logo and contact information at the bottom. At the top of the ad, we'll include the same buy-one-get-one-free coupon of the old ad. Also like the old ad, we'll run this ad in the Sunday editions of two local newspapers.

A passage that comes from a home improvement store's circular uses contrast only. It presents differences between a home of the past and a home of today.

Old photos taken in my grandmother's house show me just how much life has changed. Hers: home cooked, sit-down meals, shiny waxed floors, and "don't touch me" fabrics. Mine: often the scene of impromptu take-out dinners and homework done in the middle of the floor. It's a fact, today the pace is faster and the style more casual.[8]

One last paragraph comes from a report. It presents the similarities and the differences of the two subjects, so it uses both comparison *and* contrast.

Our team investigated both Steel Strong and Pressman tools by inviting representatives from each company to bring in samples for our evaluation. We all agreed that Pressman tools were superior in quality. Also, the Pressman salesman promised us that the tools we need are in stock now, so we could get them immediately. The Steel Strong representative thought they could deliver by November. However, both companies' prices are too high. Both of their bids far exceeded the amount we have budgeted for new tools.

Cause/Effect

Another way to develop ideas is to give the reasons why something occurred (examining *causes*), or to explain the consequences of something (exploring *effects*). Some paragraphs discuss only the causes, some discuss only the effects, and some discuss both causes *and* effects. Using the cause/effect method

[7]Frye Regional Medical Center, *An Explanation of Anesthesia* brochure (Hickory, N.C.).
[8]Lowe's Home Centers, Inc., *Designabilities* circular (North Wilkesboro, N.C.: August 1999).

of development often requires the writer to present a chain reaction of events and explain how one thing led to another.

This first paragraph comes from an e-mail message. It explains causes only.

> I have received numerous complaints about the cold temperature in the lab area. <u>This unpleasant temperature is caused by our inability to switch back and forth between our heating and air-conditioning systems.</u> The air-conditioning system is still on during this transitional time between seasons. Therefore, on cooler days, the building is unusually cold. We do not want to switch prematurely to the heating system, though, because on warmer days, interior temperatures would be uncomfortably hot. Until the weather outside is consistently cold, we will not turn on the heating system, so we ask for your patience and tolerance during this time.

The next example, from a doctor's optometric vision report, discusses only effects.

> <u>Precise eye movements are critical to academic success.</u> They allow the eyes to shift quickly and accurately along the lines of print in a book or from desktop work to the chalkboard. Inadequate eye movements prevent a person from easily shifting his eyes from one point to another. This causes him to constantly lose his place while reading, to skip or omit words while reading, and to inaccurately copy information from the chalkboard. As a result, learning decreases.

A final example, from a brochure, presents both causes *and* effects:

> All children are impressionable. <u>But children younger than 7 are especially influenced by what they see on television.</u> Young children are not yet able to distinguish between fantasy and reality. They cannot think critically about people's motives and they have difficulty understanding subtle behavior. Therefore, young children are especially vulnerable to the powerful images of violent behavior portrayed in the media. Adults—parents, teachers, and broadcasters—must assume responsibility for protecting children from potentially harmful effects of exposure to violence through the media—television, movies, and videos.[9]

This paragraph gives the causes of children's susceptibility to television violence in the third and fourth sentences. Then the fifth and sixth sentences discuss two effects of this trait.

Division

Some ideas are best developed by explaining how something can be divided into smaller parts. Often, it's easier to understand a larger entity or concept by breaking it down into its components or stages and then examining each in detail. This first paragraph, which divides a team of people into two parts, is from a report.

> <u>The Corrective Action team will consist of two personnel.</u> The software engineer will be available on an as-needed basis to test applications, report problems, analyze root causes, resolve problems, and communicate

---

[9]Joan Horton and Jenni Zimmer, *Media Violence and Children: A Guide for Parents* brochure (Washington, D.C.: National Association for the Education of Young Children, 1994).

solutions to the affected units. This person may choose to work from home. The system administrator will monitor the CI/600 and log and track any events that occur. This person, who may also work from home, will also submit status reports to the Command Center operator.

Another division paragraph comes from a memo. It divides a meeting into three stages.

<u>Monday's session will be divided into three segments</u>. From 8:00 to 8:30 A.M., Mr. Wilson will present an overview of the issues involved in changing our hiring and training process. From 8:30 to 9:30, we'll break into smaller groups that will work together to brainstorm suggestions about new procedures. Then from 9:30 to 11:00, we'll reconvene to share the results of our small group discussions. We hope to make significant progress toward revising our procedures during that time.

One last paragraph divides its subject into ten different parts:

<u>A successful business plan should include ten sections</u>. The **introduction** gives basic information such as name and address of the business, nature of the business, statement of the business's financial needs (if any), and statement of confidentiality (to keep important information away from potential competitors). The **executive summary** summarizes the entire business plan (a convenience for busy investors), including a justification statement stating why the business will succeed. The **industry analysis** examines the potential customer, current competitors, and the business's future. A **detailed description of the business** provides information on the products or services to be offered, size and location of the business, personnel and office equipment needed, and a brief history of the business. A **production plan** describes and analyzes the cost of the manufacturing process [and] outlines the raw materials, physical plant, and heavy machinery needed. The **marketing plan** discusses pricing, promotion, distribution, and product forecasts. An **organizational plan** describes the form of ownership of the venture and responsibilities of all members of the organization. An **assessment of risk** evaluates the weaknesses of the business and explains how the company plans to deal with these and other business problems. The **financial plan** summarizes the investment needed, forecasts sales and cash-flow, analyzes breakeven points and estimated balances, and summarizes sources of funding. An **appendix** includes supplementary information such as market research results, copies of leases, and supplier price lists.[10]

Classification

Classification places things in groups on the basis of qualities or characteristics they share. When we explain an idea with the classification method, we demonstrate how the subject can be explained in terms of categories. The key word *types* often appears in classification paragraphs. For example, this passage from a newsletter explains the subject in term of two categories.

<u>Two types of canoe races will occur on Saturday</u>. The challenging slalom races require paddlers to weave in and out of gates strung over the water. The exciting downriver races require paddlers to race each other to the finish line, where the fastest time wins.

[10]William M. Pride et al., *Business* (Boston: Houghton Mifflin, 1999), 125.

One more classification paragraph comes from a hospital's newsletter.

<u>Several types of biopsies are performed depending on the site of the tissue that needs to be examined.</u> These include, but aren't limited to, biopsies in which:

- An entire lesion is removed.
- Part of a lesion is removed.
- Cells are drawn through a fine needle.
- A core of tissue is removed from deep within the body using a needle.
- Tissue is removed from the interior of an organ or body cavity using an endoscope, or flexible viewing tube.[11]

A final example classifies different types of stressors.

<u>Psychological stressors can be grouped into four major categories.</u> *Catastrophic events* are sudden, unexpected, potentially life-threatening experiences or traumas, such as physical or sexual assault, military combat, natural disasters, and accidents. *Life changes and strains* include divorce, illness in the family, difficulties at work, moving to a new place, and other circumstances that create demands to which people must adjust. *Chronic stress*—stressors that continue over a long period of time—can involve anything from living near a noisy airport to being unable to earn a decent living because of adverse economic conditions or job discrimination. *Daily hassles* include traffic jams, deadlines, and other irritations, pressures, and annoyances that might not be significant stressors by themselves but whose cumulative effects can be significant.[12]

Reasons

Another method of development involves explaining the reasons why something is true or, in the case of an argumentative topic, why something *should be* true. This first example comes from a sales letter.

<u>If you let us service your Honda, we guarantee your satisfaction.</u> Our staff of technicians is quick, accurate, and gets the job done right the first time. They receive the latest comprehensive factory training and always use quality Honda parts. Our Service Department is conveniently open from 7:30 A.M. to 6:30 P.M. Also, our services are competitively priced.

The writer gives three reasons (competent staff, convenient hours, and competitive prices) to explain his idea that his department offers excellent customer service.

A second example, from an article about taxes in a credit union newsletter, gives two reasons that support the main idea.

<u>Records concerning your real and personal property should be kept until the statute of limitations expires for the year in which you dispose of the property in a taxable disposition, generally, three years.</u> You must keep these records to calculate your basis for gain or loss when you dis-

---

[11]"Medical Tests: Don't Hesitate to Ask," *Health Scene* (Valdese General Hospital, Summer 1999): 5.
[12]Douglas A. Bernstein et al., *Psychology* (Boston: Houghton Mifflin, 1997), 432.

pose of the property. If you do not contemplate disposal of personal property, these records may still be important to your heirs in the future.[13]

A final example, from a report, offers seven reasons in support of the writer's recommendation.

> <u>I recommend that we purchase Pressman Tools for the following reasons</u>:
>
> • Pressman has demonstrated that they are committed to us by repeatedly contacting us after their initial presentation.
>
> • They make tools of superior quality, as indicated by many testimonials from other users of their products.
>
> • Pressman Tools last three to ten times as long as other manufacturers' tools.
>
> • These tools provide strength without adding bulk to the physical dimension of a tool. As a result, they can get into tighter spaces that other tools will not fit into.
>
> • Pressman Tools are safer to use than other manufacturers' tools because their superior strength minimizes slippage. The tools are designed to bend rather than fracture; this minimizes danger to the user.
>
> • Pressman offers a larger selection than any other vendor.
>
> • Pressman will completely install the new tools in our existing toolboxes. We will not have to do any additional work.

Problem/Solution

A final method of development is problem/solution. A paragraph using this method will first explain a problem, then discuss one or more solutions. Problem/solution paragraphs often include other methods of development; for instance, writers may use description or effects to help the reader understand the problem. They may include process analysis to explain the solution.

After mentioning the problem, this first paragraph from an e-mail message uses process analysis to detail the solution.

> The NC LIVE Help Desk has informed me that some AOL users are having difficulty accessing their site. Technicians at both NC LIVE and AOL are working to diagnose and fix the problem. In the meantime, AOL users can still get to the site by using the following procedure:
>
> 1. Log on to AOL as usual.
>
> 2. Minimize your AOL browser, but don't close it.
>
> 3. Open a new browser window using either Netscape Navigator or Internet Explorer.
>
> 4. Type in NC LIVE's address and proceed with remote log-in.

A paragraph from another e-mail message uses description to help the reader grasp the problem.

---

[13]Sallie Clement, "Tax Talk," *Grassroots* (Raleigh: North Carolina State Employees' Credit Union, April 1999): 3.

> <u>Homeowner victims of the flood need help with assessing their property damage and advice about needed repairs</u>. Sheet rock is soaked, electrical outlets are clogged with mud, and wiring may need replacement. These homeowners need to know which damages require cleaning and which will require total replacement. We need people skilled in the building trades to travel from house to house and make recommendations. The Emergency Operations Director can provide volunteers with maps of the affected areas.

A final passage, from a telephone instruction manual, discusses several different problems and solutions.

> <u>If you're having trouble making calls, try these troubleshooting techniques</u>. If you hear one beep when you press the TALK button, the battery is low on power. Replace the handset on the base unit for six hours to allow it to recharge. If you hear no dial tone, make sure the telephone line is connected securely and verify that the battery is fully charged. If you fail to connect to a number you dialed, make sure the number you dialed is correct, and then check to see that the dialing mode is set correctly.

Combining the Methods

Often, instead of using only one method of development in a paragraph, you'll use two or more in combination to fully explain your idea. Well-developed paragraphs will usually include one method as a framework for the entire paragraph and other methods of development within that framework.

For example, read this paragraph about effective leaders, which comes from a small business publication. The writer used the contrast method to provide the overall framework for a discussion of do's and don'ts for good leaders. He then added process analysis to further develop each point:

> <u>To use the standard cliché, effective leaders can't just "talk the talk"; they must also "walk the walk."</u> That is, leaders cannot isolate themselves in their offices and fax bulletins and edicts down to the shop floor. Leaders have to get involved in the life of the organization. It's not enough to loosen your tie, roll up your sleeves, walk the floors and say hello. You've got to stop, listen, exchange information, negotiate and advise. Effective leaders exemplify what they expect from their coworkers: cooperation, effectiveness, and adaptability.[14]

The next example, from a letter, includes description of three different payment-plan options, a process analysis that tells how to select one of these options, and the effects of converting to one of them.

> <u>Customers may find it more convenient to pay with one of our three payment plans</u>. The Annual Plan costs $240 and saves you $36 annually. Under the Semi-Annual Plan, you receive two bills of $126 per year. This plan saves you $24 annually. The Quarterly Plan results in four bills of $66 and saves you $12 per year. To convert to one of these plans, call me at 555-1615 or e-mail me at access@bcc.net. Or you can simply pay the

[14]Al Gini, "Leadership: Keys of an Effective Leader," *The Small Business Journal,* http://www.tsbj.com/03-01/0301-07.htm.

full amount of the plan you choose when you send your next payment, and I will convert your records. It's easy, and it will save you money!

A paragraph from a parents' day care handbook develops the main idea with classification, process analysis, and effects.

> <u>ABC Daycare uses three different discipline strategies in response to unacceptable behavior</u>. One often-used positive procedure is the distraction method, which is most effective for children aged birth to two years. The teacher distracts the child from the inappropriate behavior and tells him or her what behavior she expects. Another form of discipline is the "peace table," which is used with one or more children in conflict who are old enough to verbalize their feelings. The teacher sits down at a table with the children and acts as a mentor while they resolve their differences with each other. A third strategy is "time out." We use this method most often for children three years and older. This involves the teacher isolating the child in a chair apart from the group and requiring him or her to sit there for one minute per year of age. Time out helps the child make connections between bad behavior and its consequences.

The writer classifies three different types of discipline strategies and explains how each one works. She has also added one effect of the last strategy.

A final example, from a hospital newsletter, uses division, contrast, and effects.

> <u>For decades, cancer treatment has involved a three-pronged approach: surgery, radiation and chemotherapy</u>. Although many people have been cured with these treatment methods, they do have drawbacks. Radiation and chemotherapy, for example, can't specifically distinguish between tumor cells and healthy cells. They can damage healthy cells along with cancer cells.[15]

This passage divides cancer treatment into three parts, contrasts the benefits and drawbacks, and explains one negative effect.

And this next example, from a brochure, uses contrast, exemplification, and narration.

> <u>There is a distinct difference between saving and hoarding</u>. . . . During the harvest months, an ant gathers the food she will need during the winter months. She puts aside only what she'll need. I recall an article I read in which an anthill was moved from New England to Florida. During the first year the ants steadily transported and stored food in their chambers. But winter never came, so the next year they cut back on the amount of food they stored. After winter didn't come again the third year, the ants quit storing food. Their supply matched their need. Saving is good stewardship, a hedge against future needs. Hoarding is a lack of trust. Basically, the difference is attitude.[16]

The passage contrasts saving and hoarding by presenting the example of the ant. It tells a story about one group of ants to illustrate the point.

[15]"Beyond 2001: Medicine in the Next Millenium," *Health Scene* (Valdese General Hospital, Fall 1999):4.
[16]James Dobson, Ph.D., *Family Finances: Making Ends Meet* brochure (Colorado Springs: Focus on the Family, 1992), 15.

PRACTICE 5.1
Identifying Methods of Development

For each of the following paragraphs, underline the main idea and identify the method(s) of development used to explain it. Each paragraph uses more than one.

> **Methods of Development**
> Narration
> Description
> Exemplification
> Process Analysis
> Comparison/Contrast
> Cause/Effect
> Division
> Classification
> Reasons
> Problem/Solution

1. You should talk fast when you have a limited amount of time or you want to convey urgency. "Most people are on such tight schedules that they want to hear quickly what you have to say," says Roberta Roesch, author of *Smart Talk: The Art of Savvy Business Conversation* (Amacom). Speedy talking lends importance to your message and makes you and your ideas sound younger and livelier, she adds. But don't overdo it: "Talking way too fast can sometimes make you sound nervous or impetuous," says Roesch. Also, if you're in a meeting and competing with other chatty colleagues for your boss's ear, talking too fast may just confuse her. If your boss has to say, "Excuse me?" more than once during a dialogue, take a deep breath, pause and slow down your delivery.[17]

   Method(s) of development: *Reasons, contrast, process analysis*

2. Barbecue grills are permitted only in some buildings in the apartment complex. In the 300, 400, 500, and 1800 buildings, grills are not permitted. These buildings all have wooden decks on upper floors, which could easily catch fire. However, residents of all other buildings can use grills safely because they have concrete patios on the ground level with easy access to water hoses.

   Method(s) of development: *Description, contrast, reasons*

3. The main safety concern about x-rays is that they expose people to radiation, which is harmful to the body. Today's x-ray machines use the lowest exposures possible, while ensuring good, clear images. The amount of ionizing radiation exposure from a routine x-ray is not enough to be harmful to most people. But even low doses of x-rays can cause birth defects if a fetus is exposed during critical stages

[17]Erin Bried, "Is Your Voice Working For or Against You?" *Glamour* (October 1999): 118.

of development, which is why x-rays aren't advised for pregnant women.[18]

Method(s) of development: *Cause/effect, contrast*

4. The college operates a bookstore on campus that is handicapped-accessible in terms of parking; however, mobility-impaired people have trouble accessing merchandise within the store itself. The aisles are too narrow for wheelchairs, and the height of shelves is too high for the limited reach of disabled people. I saw a girl in a wheelchair in there last week. The store was crowded with students buying books for their new classes, and she was having difficulty maneuvering through the tight spaces. She accidentally knocked over a display of notebooks. The few salesclerks were busy checking people standing in the long line at the register, and this girl could not reach the books she needed. I helped her gather the things she needed, but the bookstore should make some changes to be more handicapped-accessible. One solution would be to expand the store's space and install lower shelving.

Method(s) of development: *Description, exemplification, narration,*

problem/solution

5. As more and more companies send their employees abroad on temporary or permanent assignments, effective communication becomes more critical. Recent studies indicate that more than 25 percent of U.S. corporate overseas assignments fail, at a cost of more than $2 billion a year. Inadequate communication seems to be at the root of many of these failed assignments. For example, learning the language of the new country may be an obvious training need, but more organizations are beginning to realize they must prepare their expatriates—their foreign-based employees—in the language and culture of their host countries. Each country has its own unique view of various aspects of doing business, such as how to spend time, share information, or handle relationships. American employees will function better if they know what to expect. Women should be prepared to cope with far more male chauvinism than they would encounter in the United States. Men and women alike must learn that aggressiveness may be counterproductive in some countries, and that physical contact beyond a handshake is strictly forbidden in many countries.[19]

Method(s) of development: *Cause/effect, exemplification*

CHOOSING A METHOD OF DEVELOPMENT

Good writers choose their methods *consciously.* After you've decided on what main idea you'll discuss in a paragraph, take a moment to reflect upon which method (or methods) you should use to develop it. Making such

[18]"Medical Tests: Don't Hesitate to Ask," *Health Scene* (Valdese General Hospital, Summer 1999): 4.
[19]Barry L. Reece and Rhonda Brandt, *Effective Human Relations in Organizations* (Boston: Houghton Mifflin, 1999), 53.

decisions *before* you compose usually results in paragraphs that are clearer and more complete.

How do you know which method will best develop your idea? The topic sentence will often dictate which method you *must* use. Certain statements lead the reader to form expectations about what will come next. For example, these topic sentences insist that you proceed with a particular method of development.

To make your busy life easier to manage, post one central calendar on which your family members can record their schedules. *(Process Analysis)*

Our preparations for this last furniture market were chaotic and disorganized. *(Narration)*

Young children must eat a healthy breakfast before school. *(Reasons)*

A palmtop computer, or personal digital assistant (PDA), is a convenient new tool for the busy executive. *(Description)*

Office 2000 software includes four useful programs. *(Division)*

We rely on two different kinds of memory to help us process information we'll need to recall later. *(Classification)*

Athletes who need vision correction can choose between soft contact lenses or sports safety glasses. *(Comparison/Contrast)*

Life-sustaining procedures don't cure a patient's terminal condition; they keep him alive with machines. *(Exemplification)*

Electricians can prevent many electrical system fires by pinpointing potential hazards with dynamic load testing. *(Problem/Solution)*

Researchers have linked excessive Internet use to depression. *(Cause/Effect)*

Other topic sentences, however, will allow you to select one or more different methods of development. For example:

Williamsburg, Virginia, is an excellent family vacation destination.

To explain this idea, you could *narrate* highlights of your own family's trip, give *examples* of enjoyable things to do there to illustrate your point, give *reasons* why it's an entertaining place, or *describe* the quaint historic town.

The next topic sentence, too, could be developed with any of a variety of different methods.

Many of us begin to experience a decline in memory at around age fifty.

The writer could *narrate* a personal experience, explain the physiological *causes* of this decline, analyze the *process* of memory loss, or give an *example* of one particular fifty-year-old who experienced memory loss.

PRACTICE 5.2
Choosing a Method of Development

Which method(s) of development could be used to develop each of the following topic sentences?

Methods of Development

Narration

Description

Exemplification

Process Analysis

Comparison/Contrast

Cause/Effect

Division

Classification

Reasons

Problem/Solution

---

1. Cities that have won the National Civic League All-American City award said this award produced several positive benefits for their communities. *Answers will vary.*

   Method(s) of development: *Exemplification, cause/effect*

2. Sudden changes in a teenager's behavior can signal drug abuse.

   Method(s) of development: *Description, exemplification, cause/effect*

3. In the long run, synthetic motor oil provides better protection than conventional motor oils.

   Method(s) of development: *Comparison/contrast, reasons*

4. The next time you clean the lint trap in your clothes dryer, check the vent hose for lint, too.

   Method(s) of development: *Process analysis, reasons*

5. A well-designed yellow pages ad can be a persuasive sales tool.

   Method(s) of development: *Description, exemplification, cause/effect,*

   reasons

6. Sections 500, 501, 502, and 503 of the OSHA Handbook explain guidelines for protecting your employees from falls.

   Method(s) of development: *Description, division*

7. Certain dog breeds are more prone to display aggressive behavior.

   Method(s) of development: *Classification, exemplification*

8. The way you sound on the telephone communicates a great deal about your level of professionalism.

   Method(s) of development: *Description, exemplification, cause/effect,*

   reasons

9. Hurricanes are unpredictable.

   Method(s) of development: *Narration, exemplification, process analysis,*

   cause/effect, reasons

10. Law enforcement is struggling with a huge increase in high-tech computer crimes such as online fraud and cybersmuggling.

    Method(s) of development: *Exemplification, cause/effect, problem/solution*

TRANSITIONS

Chapter 4 of this book mentioned that *clue words* help readers understand relationships between sentences, which enables them to follow the writer's train of thought. *Transitions* are one type of clue word. Together with clear methods of development, they provide coherence to paragraphs. Different kinds of transition words indicate different kinds of relationships between ideas.

COMMON TRANSITIONS

Narration		*Exemplification*
before	then	for example
during	meanwhile	for instance
after	later	
next	while	*Process*
last	now	first, second, third
today		next
		then
Description		after
above	on top	
below	inside	*Comparison*
to the left	outside	similarly
to the right	in front	in like manner
under	in back	likewise
beneath	next to	
over		

Contrast		*Reasons*
on the other hand	but	first, second, third
however	yet	finally
conversely	whereas	last
in contrast	although	furthermore
on the contrary		also

Cause/Effect		*Problem/Solution*
as a result	therefore	so
thus	consequently	therefore
so	because	

Classification and Division
one, two, three (etc.)
first, second, third (etc.)

Use transition words in your paragraphs to help the reader easily understand the relationships between your sentences.

PRACTICE 5.3
Transitions

Add transitions to the following paragraphs to improve their coherence. (Hint: Identify the method(s) of development first; then add appropriate transitions. Refer to the lists in this chapter for some ideas.) *Answers will vary.*

The telecommuting trend is increasing dramatically. The greatest boost to this trend has been the expansion of electronic mail, often referred to as e-mail. E-mail is a message you send or receive through a computer and its modem (the computer's connection to a telephone line). *By the year 2000*, most companies had added e-mail capabilities to their computer networks. In such companies, *for example*, a salesperson calling on a customer can receive up-to-date information on the status of the customer's order by means of a quick e-mail message to the shipping department. An executive could convene an emergency meeting of all department managers by transmitting an e-mail message directly to their computer monitors. With the inception of the Internet, the service that links computers and databases of libraries, universities, and government agencies throughout the world, e-mail can *now* _____ travel on a massive global communications "superhighway."

The advantages of using e-mail, both within an organization and globally, are obvious. *First* _____, time efficiency is unsurpassed, for people can send detailed messages at any time, across all time zones, and the receivers can retrieve their messages as their schedule allows. *Second* _____, the cost of an e-mail transmission is usually less than postage and dramatically less than a trans-Atlantic or trans-Pacific phone call. *Third* _____, the potential for efficient customer service is enhanced because orders can be placed and changed, and shipping tracked, within seconds.

As _____ e-mail use expands, subtle advantages are beginning to surface. E-mail is *now* _____ referred to as the "great equalizer." Because the sender's gender and skin color are not immediately obvious, prejudiced attitudes are less likely to alter the message. *Before* _____ e-mail, lower-level workers had little access to the president or CEO of their organizations. *Today* _____ they can contact these individuals electronically without anyone in between misinterpreting, sabotaging, or blocking the message. *In addition* _____, electronic messages are a wonderful alternative for those individuals who are painfully shy and find it difficult to express themselves when communicating with others face to face.

However _____, e-mail has some disadvantages you should be aware of if you are going to be using it. Because e-mail is used to speed up the communication process, many people compose and send hastily written messages, which can be confusing. If you have to send a second message to clarify your first message, e-mail does not save you any time.

Some people believe electronic mail is reviving the lost art of letter writing. If it has been a while since you had to write a letter to anyone, consider these guidelines before you create an e-mail message:

- *Before* _____ you write, take time to think and compose your thoughts. Don't just "dash out an e-mail."

- *While* _____ you write, summarize your main points, indicate the action or response you are seeking, and be sure you provide all the details the receiver needs to take action. *However* _____, be very careful about the tone of your messages. Remove any potentially offending words and phrasing from your documents. Since correspondents cannot see each other's body language, some mistakenly feel they must use stronger language to get their message across.

- *After* _____ you write, carefully edit your message on the screen before sending it. A typographical error, plural subject and singular verb, or "there" used instead of "their" in a sentence will reflect poorly on your professionalism and intelligence.

- *Another* _____ potential hazard in the use of e-mail is lack of privacy. *However* _____, individuals and organizations are devising safeguards that will maintain every individual's right to privacy.[20]

---

[20]Reece, Barry L. and Rhonda Brandt, excerpts from *Effective Human Relations In Organizations.* Copyright © 1999 by Houghton Mifflin Company. Reprinted with permission.

TEST YOUR UNDERSTANDING

1. What is *coherence*?

   Making sense or providing a clear progression of thought

2. What two techniques produce coherence in paragraphs?

   Methods of development and transitions

3. What are *methods of development*?

   Common patterns of arranging information that readers easily recognize and

   follow.

4. What are ten common methods of development?

   Narration, description, exemplification, process analysis, comparison/contrast,

   cause/effect, division, classification, reasons, problem/solution

5. How does a writer know which methods of development will best explain an idea?

   From what the idea in the topic sentence either dictates or suggests

6. What are *transitions*?

   Words that indicate relationships between ideas

WEB ACTIVITY: The Job Search

When you're ready to search for a new job, you can use the Internet to locate a position you want. Sites such as the Professional Careers Network (http://www.jobs-careers.com), Job Options (http://www.joboptions.com), Monster (http://www.monster.com), the Riley Guide (http://www.rileyguide.com), and Hot Jobs (http://www.hotjobs.com) all contain thousands of openings for job seekers. Many of these sites also allow you to post your résumé for potential employers.

1. Go to the Quintessential Careers web site at http://www.quintcareers.com.

2. Click on *Marketability Test* in the Career Resources list. Take the quiz. What is your score? According to the results of this quiz, are you prepared for a successful job search?

3. Choose and click on one of the links in the Jobs and Career Sites list. Continue to search until you've located a job opening in your current field of study.

4. Write a summary of a specific position that interests you. Include details about the job title; the employer's name and address; the required qualifications for the position; the salary; and the major duties.

GROUP PROJECT AND WRITING ACTIVITIES

In Chapter 4, you wrote a letter to a community service organization or agency in your area. In this chapter, you'll interview a volunteer and write a report about that organization.

With your group, discuss what the public wants and needs to know about community service organizations. Generate a list of ideas in the space below.

On your own, call the organization you selected for the activities in Chapter 4 and arrange to meet and interview a current volunteer. (See Appendix A for more information about conducting a successful interview.) If possible, try to also observe this volunteer as he or she is actually working. Then ask questions based on the list you generated with your group. Take notes as you interview this volunteer.

Write a report about the community service organization you chose. Include complete, coherent paragraphs that inform the public about this organization's goals and activities.

READINGS   You're preparing for a career now by completing your college education. Once you get the job you seek, though, what will you do to ensure that you're happy and successful? Can you make sure you'll always be employed? How can you arrange to move up the career ladder to positions with more authority and better pay? How will you make sure your work matches your personality and your values?

In the next excerpt from an article, author and career-management consultant Barbara Moses tells you how to become a *career activist* to improve your marketability and your own personal satisfaction.

As you read this article, circle every word that's unfamiliar to you. Look it up and write the meaning in the margin. Put an exclamation point (!) next to any sentence or paragraph you find especially interesting. Put a question mark (?) next to any sentence or paragraph you don't understand.

From *Career Intelligence: The 12 New Rules for Success*

Barbara Moses

To keep up with the rapid pace of change, we must become career activists, ever aware of new trends and adept at making changes.

1 . . . The path to career renewal begins with becoming a career activist. At work, we are not passive in terms of initiating projects or looking for cost savings for the company or letting ourselves get away with sloppy work. We only seem to be passive in terms of managing our own careers. In part, perhaps, we are just too tired, busy, distracted, and pressured to look after ourselves, but we are also, typically, ill-prepared to think like a career activist.

2 In fact, we do have control over many aspects of our careers, if we only choose to exercise it. Of course, we will still be affected by external factors, such as fluctuations in the economy, but becoming a career activist can help you survive these ups and downs—and even thrive.

3 Becoming a career activist means:

- **Writing your own script** rather than waiting for someone to write it for you.

- **Being vigilant on your own behalf**, identifying and preparing for opportunities rather than expecting anyone else to guide you along or do reconnaissance.

- **Becoming an independent agent**, defining yourself in terms and concepts that are independent of your job title, your organization, or what other people think you should be. Rather than thinking of yourself as a "level-10 computer programmer for Acme Software," for example, you need to see yourself as a software-builder who has chosen to lease your skills to Acme Software in order to develop project management experience and increase your marketability.

Reprinted with permission of the publisher. From *Career Intelligence: The 12 New Rules For Success*, copyright 1999 by Barbara Moses. Berrett-Koehler Publishers, Inc., San Francisco, CA. All rights reserved. 1-800-929-2929

- **Being entrepreneurial**—looking for opportunity, undertaking enterprises that provide opportunities (as well as risks).

4   Becoming an activist is not a luxury. It's the key to your future career success. It's no longer possible to be a passive player in your own career management. You must be prepared to live in an uncertain work world, where the only certainty is *you*—your skills, your flexibility, your capacity to adapt to change. That requires optimism and belief in yourself.

5   Successful career activists behave more like a guerrilla than a soldier in a regular army. You need to be:

- Informed, vigilant, and flexible.
- Passionate and engaged.
- An unconventional thinker, with no preconceived concepts.
- Opportunistic—always on the lookout for windows of opportunity.
- Mobile, fast, and fluid.
- Well informed about both your own strengths and the environment in which you operate.
- Able to turn advantages into opportunities.

Know Yourself

6 To manage your career effectively, you need to identify the unique talents and personal values that define who you are, what you do, and what you care about. You will then be able to match up your strengths and preferences with the right environment to achieve the maximum work satisfaction. To begin, develop a *personal work ID.*

7   Andrew, an engineer by training, was director of manufacturing for a pharmaceutical company. After a thorough self-assessment, he was able to successfully sell himself as a director of management information systems. His new role fit well with his technical skills: his familiarity with technology, his ability to coordinate between technical and nontechnical colleagues, his knowledge of the manufacturing process, and his personal love of high-tech "toys." But Andrew might not have even contemplated such a move if he had continued to see himself strictly as an engineer in a manufacturing environment.

8   As jobs and roles change, one of the crucial challenges facing us is to look beyond our job titles and identify our key underlying skills. We need to separate our work identity from our jobs and job titles and exchange it for a personal work ID based on our skills, attributes, interests, values, and personal preferences. The job is only the vehicle through which we express those skills and attributes, and the job title is only an outline of what we do at work.

9   Knowing yourself thoroughly will help you identify opportunities that play to your strengths and interests, as well as new skills and knowledge that you may need to acquire in order to ensure your productivity and employability.

You will also realize what is most important to you in a work situation: what makes your work meaningful and makes you feel good about yourself.

10   Self-knowledge liberates opportunities. The more you know about yourself, the more options open up to you. Keisha, a marketing manager for a company selling high-tech medical instrumentation, was able to look at herself as having a *personal portfolio of skills*—technical, interpersonal, financial, managerial—that she could apply in a variety of work settings. As opportunities expand and contract in her industry, Keisha may find herself at times selling more of her marketing skills rather than her technical know-how; at other times, it may be her technical expertise that is most in demand.

11   I like to think that each of us has a personal, self-managed career portfolio containing the unique combination of assets that defines us individually. This combination will ultimately determine what we have to sell.

12   Given that no one is perfect, your portfolio also contains personal liabilities—personality quirks that interfere with your effectiveness, as well as skills and abilities that are not as honed as they might be. To find continuing satisfaction and success at work, to protect yourself from career trauma, and to ensure your future marketability, take stock of your career assets and liabilities. It's important to be able to clearly describe your own strengths, work preferences, and values to find work that best plays to your strengths and assets.

13   You will also need to be able to *reconfigure yourself.* In the future, you will likely have a number of quite different "careers." As your work shifts to meet changing business needs, certain skills will be called to the fore while others recede in importance.

14   Tony, a meteorological research scientist working for an environmental protection agency, found his specialty rendered obsolete by new technology. After conducting a rigorous self-assessment, Tony learned that he had strong investigative, analytical, and data-gathering skills. He found work with the military, collecting data on threats to the environment from chemical weapons—a job that enabled him to apply his existing research skills to solving a different set of problems.

15   Think of your different skills and interests as "modular building blocks"; the way you configure these blocks may change, but their essence will stay more or less the same. . . .

The 12 New Rules for Career Success

16 It is not enough to know what the new emerging careers are for building a successful future for yourself. The job market isn't that stable anyway. The workplace has changed, and the rules of career success have changed along with it.

1. Ensure Your Marketability

17 Ben, 45, was a middle manager in a company that eradicated its entire middle-management ranks. It took him 18 months to find another job—and two years to recover emotionally. Now, Ben says, "Every six months I take out

my résumé, and if I can't think of one thing I've accomplished that I can add, I know that I've been slacking off."

18   It may no longer be realistic to believe that job security exists anywhere anymore. But you can have security in the marketability of your skills. To make yourself marketable:

- Think of everyone you work for as a client rather than a boss.
- Know your product: yourself and the skills you have to offer, your assets, strengths, potential liabilities, and how you can add value to an employer or client.
- Know your market: both current and prospective clients.

2. Think Globally

19 Philip, a Toronto architect, struggled for a few years in what he described as a dying profession. "They're no longer building office towers," he complained. "They were all done in the 1980s." But he secured a new livelihood by going online and networking to find new clients as far away as Saudi Arabia. Philip still lives in Toronto but travels back and forth to the Middle East.

20   Today's technology allows you to work anywhere, anytime. And in a global economy, you may have to. In the borderless work world, where the entire world is a potential market, the ability to speak other languages and be comfortable with other cultures will be crucial. Globalization means an expansion of work opportunities, making you less reliant on the local economy. And living and working internationally helps you gain richer concepts not only in the mechanics of business, but also in the principles of life and work. As organizations increasingly move into new international markets, they will be looking for individuals who can adapt readily to other cultures.

3. Communicate Powerfully, Persuasively, and Unconventionally

21 Adrienne is an international art dealer who is now selling much of her art on the Internet rather than through face-to-face communication; she has had to learn a completely new set of communication skills. In the past, she would build relationships and establish credibility with people over time through "schmoozing," charm, and professional expertise. To do the same thing online, she says, "I had to learn to use the written word the way I speak. I had to learn how to become an evocative writer—to charm, to talk about the feeling of a picture in a few powerful and suggestive words."

22   People with finely honed communication skills have always been valued, but advances in telecommunications, geographically dispersed project work, and everyone's information overload mean that efficient and effective communication is needed more than ever. You must be able to:

- Quickly capture your listener's attention and get your message across.
- Use words to paint a picture, tell a story, make information vivid.

- Write clearly, persuasively, and with impact.
- Zero in on key concepts and translate them appropriately for your listener's requirements.

4. Keep On Learning

23 With constantly changed work and skill requirements, "lifelong learning" will be more than just a catchphrase. It will be a necessity. Rules of lifelong learning include:

- Stay current in your own field, and continue to develop skills and knowledge outside it.
- Take courses, read books and journals, develop and practice new skills.
- Look at periods of full-time education between periods of work not as "time off" but as smart career moves preparing you for the future.

24 When considering learning, don't confine yourself to traditional institutions or modes of learning. Perhaps the most important learning "event" of recent years has been the number of people who have become computer literate—something achieved almost exclusively outside the traditional classroom.

25 As more and more educational institutes are going online, offering diverse learning experiences over the Internet (including graduate degrees), it will be much easier to meet the need for lifelong learning.

5. Understand Business Trends

26 I am always amazed at how many people have only the narrowest knowledge of specific trends in their profession and even less knowledge of broader business trends—whether economic, demographic, or cultural. I routinely ask people, "What international trends will affect your business?" and "Globally, what is your major source of competition?" Even among senior managers, only a handful of people say they are as well informed as they should be.

27 Test yourself: Do you regularly read the business section of your newspaper? Can you identify three trends that will have significant impact on your industry in the next five years? Do you know what new technologies might shape your industry in the next five years? Do you know what the potential threats are to your industry or profession?

28 In a very complex and rapidly changing work world, it is crucial to be aware of key trends in business, society, and politics. Not having the time to keep up simply doesn't cut it as an excuse. Read the business press or keep current through electronic media and keep track of the fast-changing economic and social landscape. Understand the competitive environment. Get information from a variety of sources and maintain an independent and critical perspective.

6. Prepare for Areas of Competence, Not Jobs

29 Recently someone suggested computer animation as a possible future career for Barry, a teenager with storytelling, graphics, and media abilities. Barry replied, "The work I choose now might not even exist by the time I'm old enough to do it. Or if it does exist, the technology may have changed to required completely different skills."

30 Intuitively, Barry understood a key maxim of the new economy: Don't prepare for jobs, prepare for areas of competence. Like many of yesterday's jobs that have now vanished, the "hot jobs" of today may not exist tomorrow.

31 It is important, then, to think of roles, not jobs. You may have a single job title but many, many roles: leader, change agent, coach, problem solver, troubleshooter, team builder, consensus builder, mentor, facilitator, and so on. Think also of marketable skills that are independent of your technical abilities, such as resilient, resourceful, opportunity seeking, time urgent, market driven, high-impact risk taker, and insatiable learner. These are the self-management attributes and skills that employers are looking for and that will determine your future success in the new economy.

7. Look to the Future

32 You can't rely on the accuracy of long-term occupational projections, nor should you try to make career choices based on what kind of work you think will be "hot," rather than what you are best suited to do. But it is still helpful to monitor demographic, economic, and cultural trends.

33 Based on current trends, here are some of the fields that should be fairly buoyant:

- *Medicine.* Many of the new openings will be at the lower end of the scale (e.g., home care workers and nursing assistants), but there will also be openings for occupational and physical therapists, pharmacists, and radiologists, as well as specialties that will help keep an aging population active and youthful looking: plastic surgery, for instance.

- *Education.* School boards are cutting back on jobs for teachers, but educators and entrepreneurs alike will be able to profit from the growth of private tutoring services and centers.

- *Edutainment.* The growth of electronic media and the emphasis on lifelong learning add up to tremendous opportunities for people who can combine the excitement of computer graphics and animation with educational content—everyone from the entrepreneurs who package and market the products to computer programmers, graphic artists, animators, and educators.

34 Other "hot" areas include recreation, the environment, biotechnology, pharmaceuticals, communications, computers, and personal services of all kinds.

8. Build Financial Independence

35 When your finances are in good shape, you can make career decisions based on what is really important to you. A financial planner can help you take steps toward financial independence. Most recommend that you save about 10% of your pre-tax income and keep six months' salary in the bank.

36 Rethink your relationship to money: Does all the stuff you buy contribute to your happiness? If not, could you give up buying it? You might take a lesson from the "voluntary simplicity" movement, in which people have actively decided to pursue a life outside the continual push to "buy, spend, consume." What do you really need?

9. Think Lattice, Not Ladders

37 Corporate downsizing and flattened hierarchies have carved out half the rungs in the traditional career ladder. Now, the career ladder is more like a lattice: You may have to move sideways before you can move up.

38 In a lattice, everything is connected. Each step will take you somewhere, though sometimes in unpredictable directions. You must measure progress in new ways. Each new work assignment should contribute to your portfolio of skills, increasing both your breadth and depth, while you stay motivated and challenged.

39 Be creative in seeking out new opportunities. When 42-year-old Ira was told that he would never make partner at his accounting firm, he looked for opportunities not only to keep himself challenged but also to maintain his visibility and value to the firm. Every two years or so, Ira takes on a high-profile assignment, thus making himself an indispensable contributor to the firm.

40 If you're feeling stuck in your current role, consider the possibilities for job enrichment: a lateral move into a new work assignment that offers opportunities for learning and development, opportunities to mentor younger staff, participation in task forces, and interesting educational programs.

41 Track your career progress by your work, not your level. Judge your progress by the depth of content of your work, its importance to the organization and to customers, and whether you are still learning and having fun.

10. Be a Generalist with a Specialty Or a Specialist Who's a Generalist

42 Will you be better off in the future as a specialist or as a generalist? The answer is both. You need to have strong enough specialist skills to get you in the door—something that makes you unique and puts you in a position to add value to a client. But that is no longer enough.

43 You also need to be able to use those specialist skills in high-pressure environments and in teams of people from different disciplines. You also need to be able to organize your work, manage your time, keep a budget, and sell a

project. So the question is not so much one of either/or, but one of degree. Should you be *more* of a specialist or *more* of a generalist?

44   If you prefer to specialize, conduct a searching self-assessment to make sure you have what it takes to rise to the top of your profession. Take an equally careful look at market conditions to make sure that you are investing your career assets in an in-demand specialty. Stay on top of the newest trends and information in your profession. And don't give up on your general skills.

11. Be a Ruthless Time Manager

45 We are working in a world where fast enough never is and where speed is prized above all else. With so many demands on us, it's crucial to be ruthless in managing time.

46   Evaluate every time commitment. Are you doing something because it needs to be done or because it's there? What are you not doing that may be more important? Become vigilant in saying "no" to excessive work demands. Know your limitations. Work strategically rather than just staying busy. If you are working excessively long hours over an extended period of time, you may lose productivity.

47   Set priorities, including personal priorities. Use the weekend to refresh yourself—turn off the cell phone. Go someplace where you can't be reached.

12. Be Kind to Yourself

48 Instead of beating yourself up over things that didn't work out, remind yourself of your successes. Celebrate them!

49   Set realistic expectations of what's doable. Learn to live with the best you can do at this point, to live with less-than-perfect. Congratulate yourself on your successes. When you've done a good job, pat yourself on the back. Regularly keep track of your successes, no matter how apparently small, and take credit where it's due. Above all, be kind to yourself.

RESPONDING TO THE READING

1. What is a *career activist*? What do career activists do?

   Career activists are people who actively manage their own careers. They

   constantly look for new career opportunities and prepare themselves for those

   opportunities.

2. Why do you need to become a career activist?

   The uncertain, ever-changing work world requires flexibility and ability to adapt to

   change.

   (continued)

**RESPONDING TO
THE READING**
continued

3. Write a current *personal work ID* for yourself.

Answers will vary.

4. How have the global economy and improved technology changed the world of work?

Many companies operate globally through the use of technology, so the ability to

interact with people of other nationalities and cultures increases a person's

marketability.

5. Why has technology made good communication skills more important?

Geographic dispersal and information overload make efficient, effective

communication critical.

6. How can you educate yourself about business trends?

Read business publications and regularly review the electronic media.

7. Why is personal financial stability important to your career?

It allows you to make career decisions based on what's important to you.

8. What is a *career lattice*?

A network of positions that allows you to move sideways as well as up.

9. What method of development does the author use in paragraph 10?

Exemplification

10. What method of development is used in paragraph 20?

Cause/effect

In paragraph 28?

Process analysis

BUILDING VOCABULARY

Jargon is specialized terminology that is usually understood only by people who participate in a particular profession or discipline. For example, nurses use a particular jargon on the job, as do art dealers and computer programmers. However, sometimes jargon words will filter into our everyday language and become mainstreamed, or understood by a more general audience. For example, the word *configure* from the article (paragraph 15) began as a term used in sciences such as astronomy, geometry, and chemistry. Now, we routinely apply the term to computers and even to an individual's skills, as in *reconfigure yourself.*

Each of the following former jargon words appears in the article. Look up each word in a dictionary and find out the profession or discipline in which it originated.

1. portfolio (paragraph 10) *government* _____

2. reconnaissance (paragraph 3) *military* _____

3. guerrilla (paragraph 5) *military* _____

4. lookout (paragraph 5) *military* _____

5. assets (paragraph 11) *business/accounting/law* _____

6. liabilities (paragraph 12) *business* _____

Are your job interviews successful? Or do you often leave an interviewer's office feeling as if you didn't convince him or her that you were the best person for the job?

The following article offers suggestions about how to improve your performance at job interviews.

As you read this article, circle every word that's unfamiliar to you. Look it up and write the meaning in the margin. Put an exclamation point (!) next to any sentence or paragraph you find especially interesting. Put a question mark (?) next to any sentence or paragraph you don't understand.

Interview Tips and Bloopers

Jean Ann Cantore

To get rave reviews at a job interview, you need to know how to avoid the pitfalls.

1 Jessie had her first job interview at a department store. When Jessie got to the interview, she briefly answered the interviewer's questions. She didn't volunteer any information about herself or ask any questions about the store. There were lots of long, uncomfortable moments of silence. In fact, the interviewer mistakenly thought Jessie was shy, something she shouldn't be if she was going to work as a salesperson in the children's department.

Jean Ann Cantore, "Interview Tips and Bloopers," *Career World* (Apr./May 1999): 16-18. © 1999 by Weekly Reader Corp. All rights reserved.

Be Ready with Q's & A's

2   What do you think was wrong with Jessie's approach? She wasn't prepared. She hadn't thought in advance about the kinds of answers she would give or questions she should ask. As a result, Jessie didn't come across well to the interviewer. She came up short, and she didn't get the job.

3   A job interview is a chance for you to let an employer know that you're the right person for the job. A big part of your role as an interviewee is to answer questions, but most often a simple "yes" or "no" isn't enough. Expand on your answer so the interviewer can find out more about your communication skills. You should also be prepared to ask a few questions of your own, such as, "How many people work in the children's department?" or "What is the busiest time of day for the department?" "What would my responsibilities be?" These questions show you are really interested.

4   Here are some more tips to follow in your interview and some blunders to avoid.

Dress the Part

5   Kevin heard that a large auto insurance company was looking for people to train to become adjusters. With his interest in cars and his current job as a mechanic, he thought he was a shoo-in for the job. Kevin was so confident that when he went in for the interview he wore his mechanic's uniform instead of changing into a jacket and tie. He was never called back.

6   One way to make a good impression is to dress appropriately. Even before you start talking, the interviewer forms an opinion about you based on how you look. A good rule to follow is to dress for an interview as you would expect to dress on the job. If you are interviewing at a place where employees wear "business casual" attire, you still want to dress for the interview like you mean business. Guys should wear a sportcoat or suit; girls, a nice dress or suit and dress shoes.

Be on Time

7   Being on time is critical for interviewing. If you're not familiar with the location of your interview, go for a dry run so you know how long travel will take. Also keep rush hour traffic in mind. It's good to arrive a few minutes early but not too early. If you're more than 15 minutes early, stay in the car or lobby. You don't want to appear overanxious.

Mind Your Manners

8   Once you arrive, remember to be polite to everyone you meet. More than likely, your first contact will be with a receptionist. A lot of people don't realize that the person at the front desk actually has power and influence. In

other words, the receptionist or secretary could help you land the job or keep you from getting it. Take Jack, for example. Jack was really nervous and running a few minutes late to meet with the head of the paper company. He wanted a job as a salesperson. When Jack rushed in the door of the company, a polite young woman greeted him with a nice smile and handshake. Jack barely shook her hand and snapped, "I'm Jack, here to see Sam Johnson at 11 a.m."

9   The receptionist was a bit surprised at Jack's abruptness, but she invited Jack to have a seat while she got Mr. Johnson. When she returned to tell Jack that Mr. Johnson was on the phone and would be a few minutes, Jack made a face and said, "And I thought I was running late!"

10   Needless to say, Jack didn't get the job. As Mr. Johnson put it, "How would he act toward front desk people at other companies he calls on for us if he can't be polite to people at his own company?"

Strictly Business

11 A blunder some applicants make during interviews is asking inappropriate or personal questions. Being friendly and talking about the weather is fine, but interviews should be professional and impersonal. Look at Nick's experience. Nick's father had a friend, Blake Stern, who was an editor for a large publishing company. Nick had met Mr. Stern at a family picnic, and they hit it off. When Mr. Stern heard that Nick was interested in the publishing business, he suggested Nick apply for an entry-level job at his firm.

12   At the interview, Nick assumed they would just continue joking and talking as they had at the picnic. When Mr. Stern was more businesslike than he had been before, Nick was thrown for a loop. After answering some standard interview questions, Nick decided to take matters into his own hands and get the scoop on the job.

13   "So, Blake, how much money can I make here?" Nick asked.

14   Mr. Stern told him that a salary hadn't yet been decided for the job, but Nick persisted.

15   "Well, I mean, how much do they pay the other newcomers?" he asked.

16   That question dropped Nick to the bottom of the list of job candidates. He actually made three interview blunders. He called Mr. Stern by his first name, which was too informal. He brought up the salary issue before he had been offered a job. He also assumed that since he knew Mr. Stern, he could ask a personal question and get away with it.

Keep "Chatter" to a Minimum

17 Jessie, whom you met at the beginning of this article, had a problem with not talking enough for the interviewer to get to know her. However, there is such a thing as saying too much during an interview! Megan found this out when she applied for a veterinary assistant's position. Megan had worked for

a year as a receptionist at an animal clinic and decided she wanted to become a vet's assistant. She saw an ad in the paper for a clinic that needed an assistant and was willing to train. She was ecstatic when they called her for an interview.

18 Things went really well at the interview until the veterinarian asked Megan to talk about her experiences at her current job. She rattled on about everything from funny dog stories to her "grumpy" boss. She thought her prospective employer would think her stories were funny, but he didn't.

19 "Answer each question, putting yourself in a positive light, and then look to the interviewer to see if she wants more," advises Tom Jackson in *Interview Express*. "Avoid long stories about yourself."

20 No matter how comfortable you are during an interview or how confident, keep in mind that you are conducting business. If you have the attitude that you must act as a professional, you'll be likely to ace the interview . . . and knock the competition out of the running.

Can You Spot the Blunders?

21 Read the following story about Donald's interview experience. List the blunders he made during the meeting.

22 "Since this is my second interview here," Donald thought, "I think I'll go casual—khakis and a sweater."

23 Donald felt good about going to the interview. He looked at his watch and noticed it was only 7:30. He didn't have to be there until 8:15. "I think I have time to stop for a quick breakfast," he thought to himself.

24 At the coffee shop, Donald ran into his friend Sara, and they decided to split a bagel. When he'd finished his last bite of bagel, Donald looked at his watch. "Yikes, it's 8 a.m.! I'll never make it to the interview on time!"

25 At 8:20, Donald raced into the office building. He'd been asked to bring a résumé, but he suddenly realized he'd left it at the coffee shop.

26 During the interview, the interviewer asked Donald to describe some of his classes. Donald told him in great detail what he had taken and what kinds of grades he'd received, and even some funny things that had happened in his classes.

27 The interviewer wanted to tell Donald about the company's future plans. Donald got a little bored, so he looked around the interviewer's office at his books, posters, and photos.

28 At the end of the interview, Donald thanked the interviewer for his time and told him he'd really like to have the job. He was feeling good. On his way out, Donald stopped at the front desk and joked with the receptionist, "I don't suppose you could put in a good word for me with the boss?"

29 List the things Donald did wrong. Answers: Dressing too casually, being late, not bringing items requested, talking too much about himself, losing eye contact, asking the receptionist an inappropriate question.

AND

30 • Before the interview, do some research about the company and the job so you can go to the interview as an informed applicant.

• Get plenty of sleep the night before and eat a good breakfast.

• Be on time.

• Dress in a clean, well-pressed, professional manner. And don't forget to polish your shoes.

• Be polite and courteous to the interviewer and all the office staff.

• Bring extra résumés and a notebook and pen.

• Extend a firm handshake and maintain eye contact.

• Give well-thought-out answers and ask appropriate questions. Anticipate what you may be asked and practice your answers.

• Thank your interviewer for his or her time, and express your interest in the job.

• Write a thank-you note or follow-up letter.

Don'ts

31 • Mumble or speak too quietly.

• Speak too loudly.

• Talk too much or too little.

• Fidget or slouch in your seat, chew gum, or take swigs out of a water bottle.

• You may accept a glass of water, coffee, or soda if offered, but don't let it detract from the interview.

• Argue with the interviewer or dominate the discussion.

• Speak poorly of previous jobs or supervisors.

• Beg or plead for the job, or ask inappropriate questions about other candidates.

RESPONDING TO THE READING

1. Why should you avoid responding to an interviewer's questions with only "yes" or "no" answers?

   You won't appear to be an effective communciator, you won't give enough infor-

   mation to sell yourself to the interviewer, and you won't seem interested in the job.

2. Why should you ask questions of your own at a job interview?

   Your questions will indicate your interest in the company and the job.

(continued)

RESPONDING TO THE READING *continued*

3. What are the author's suggestions regarding appropriate attire for job interviews?

Dress as you would expect to dress on the job for which you're applying.

4. Have you ever committed any of the interview "blunders" described in the article? Which ones? On separate paper, describe your experience. *Answers will vary.*

5. What method(s) of development is (are) used in paragraphs 11–12?

Exemplification and narration.

BUILDING VOCABULARY

The article you have just read above includes several words that your dictionary may label *informal*. Informal words are usually acceptable in the language of conversation but may be considered unsuitable for more formal communication. Examples include:

. . . he thought he was a *shoo-in* for the job. (paragraph 5)

. . . Nick decided to take matters into his own hands and get the *scoop* on the job. (paragraph 12)

If you have the attitude that you must act as a professional, you'll be likely to *ace* the interview. (paragraph 20)

[Don't] take *swigs* out of a water bottle. (paragraph 31)

1. What are the effects of informal language in written documents?

They create a casual, conversational tone.

2. In what kinds of documents would it be acceptable to include informal language? Think of different types of academic, professional, and personal documents.

E-mail messages, letters, and notes to friends and peers.

3. In what types of documents would informal language usually be inappropriate?

Business documents and academic assignments.

4. Do you think the informal language is inappropriate in the article above? Why or why not?

Answers will vary.

6 Cohesive Paragraphs

PROFESSIONAL PROFILE
Cindy Carswell, Certified Recreation Therapy Assistant

After earning her two-year degree, Cindy Carswell went to work as a Certified Recreation Therapy Assistant for a large state psychiatric institution. She is responsible for engaging patients in games and other activities that strengthen their problem-solving, interpersonal, and social skills and help promote psychological healing. Cindy's duties require her to write an initial assessment of each patient; then, she must compose weekly notes about the patient's progress. She also writes e-mail messages to colleagues and letters to community members regarding fundraising events for special programs. The following paragraph comes from a thank-you letter she sent to a restaurant owner:

> Your employee John Macon was most helpful to our group during our three visits to your establishment. He conducted a thorough tour of the restaurant, showed us the basics of food preparation, and demonstrated some principles of food preparation. He clearly explained the possibilities in food service careers and answered the group's questions in an open and friendly manner. While we dined, he checked on us frequently and described the merits of various dishes. His professionalism impressed and inspired the young people in our group.

This paragraph focuses on one specific reason—the attentiveness of a particular employee—for the writer's satisfying experience at the restaurant. Because it clearly explains just one main idea, it demonstrates cohesiveness, the topic of this chapter.

Within a longer composition, we must divide ideas into smaller logical units to help readers not only follow the train of thought but also see the relationships among different ideas. These smaller logical units of thoughts are paragraphs. Each unit of thought should present only *one* main idea to the reader, along with a complete explanation of that idea. A *cohesive* paragraph, one that "sticks together," is one that discusses only one idea. All of the sentences in the paragraph stick together to support that one point.

When a writer tosses too many different ideas into one unit, two problems result. First, the reader is forced to separate them, to sort them out from each other, which is a frustrating and confusing task. Second, the writer probably isn't fully explaining each separate idea with adequate layers of development (which are discussed in Chapter 4 of this book).

For example, read the following paragraph from an e-mail message:

The auction will take place on Saturday, September 25, at the maintenance storage center. To get there, take a right off Foxfire Drive at the Valley View Fire Department and follow the signs. It is open to the public.

The auction begins at 8:00 A.M. You can preview the items from 7:00 to 8:00. Terms of the sale are cash or approved check only. Items for sale include various heavy equipment, furniture, and computer components. Several very large machines will not be moved to the auction site. Anyone interested can see them at the maintenance garage on Hope Road.

This paragraph actually contains *four* different main ideas:

1. details about the date, time, and location of the auction,
2. terms of the sale,
3. on-site items for sale, and
4. off-site items for sale.

Each of those four ideas should be developed in a separate paragraph. Because they are all thrown together into one paragraph, several are not adequately explained. The writer gives sufficient details about the time and place of the auction but does not adequately explain the terms of the sale. For instance, she should add information about removing and returning items after the sale. Also, she does not offer enough layers of development about the items to be sold. What kinds of heavy equipment, furniture, and computer components will be auctioned? Will they be grouped in lots or sold individually? Will bidding begin at certain amounts? The lack of cohesiveness contributes to the problem of unanswered questions. Because the four main ideas are lumped together in one brief paragraph, the reader does not get enough information to fully understand any of them.

Writers should not confuse supporting details and information (the layers of development discussed in Chapters 4 and 5) with *main ideas*. Supporting details are always *subordinate* to the main-idea sentence; in other words, they always further explain or develop that idea. Paragraphs that are not cohesive include more than one *coordinate* main idea. The second main idea in a non-cohesive paragraph does not explain the first. Instead, it presents a new, different idea that needs more development of its own.

TYPES OF NON-COHESIVE PARAGRAPHS

A writer can produce two types of non-cohesive paragraphs. The first results from the writer's beginning with one idea and then veering away from the subject. The second type is the result of the writer's including two or more ideas that should each be developed separately.

Digressing from the Main Idea

Discussing something related to but off the original topic is a natural and common occurrence, for our brains constantly "free-associate." In other words, one thought leads us instantly to another related thought, which leads to yet another thought. This is how we think; so if we're not paying attention, we might write this way. The following paragraph from an Internet article is an example.

To better manage your paperwork, you must begin by acquiring good equipment. If you don't already have one, purchase a sturdy filing cabinet with two easily opened file drawers. No one needs more than two drawers for personal files. In one of these drawers, you'll store all of your current files. In the other, you'll place archival papers. Along with the filing cabinet, also purchase a box of hanging files and a box of manila folders. *Then, create your new filing system.*

That paragraph illustrates the simplest and most common form of non-cohesive paragraph. The writer got ahead of himself and tacked a new, un-developed idea onto the end of a paragraph that was developing a different main idea. The paragraph starts off fine by presenting a clear main idea that focuses on equipment. The next five sentences all "stick together" by providing more explanation about the types of and reasons for owning that equipment. However, the fifth sentence's mention of file folders caused the writer to forget his main idea and leap ahead to another topic— the filing system— as he composed the last sentence. That idea needs to be separated from the paragraph and developed with more layers.

It's very easy to get sidetracked as we write, to go off on tangents when related ideas pop into our minds. Unfortunately, even though writing this way makes perfect sense to the writer, who's doing the thinking, the reader will find the result difficult to follow. Therefore, writers must pay attention as they compose, making sure that each of their paragraphs keeps to one main idea. The following paragraph, which comes from a travel brochure, provides another illustration of how loss of cohesion occurs.

Two of Virginia's historic sites—the Yorktown Victory Center and the Yorktown Battlefield—help visitors understand the events of the Revolutionary War. Costumed actors at the Yorktown Victory Center re-create a 1770s farm and campsite. At Yorktown Battlefield, visitors can gaze out over the now-silent fields where General George Washington's troops roundly defeated those led by Lord Cornwallis, the British commander. *The British still rule in the nearby town of Colonial Williamsburg, where actors tell stories of early Americans' pursuit of freedom.*

The writer begins this paragraph by focusing on two specific historic sites. The last sentence, however, brings up a third site. This loss of cohesion was triggered by the third sentence's mention of the British. This led the writer to think of the British-operated Williamsburg, so she tosses in that site, too, without any further explanation.

Admittedly, the writer of this paragraph *could* present all three sites in one unit. She could revise the topic sentence to include all three, instead of just two, and add more layers of development to explain the last sentence. As it stands now, however, the paragraph promises the reader a discussion of the Victory Center and the Battlefield; therefore, the writer should move the sentence about Williamsburg to a different paragraph.

This next paragraph, from an e-mail message, offers another example of digressing from the main idea. This one, however, needs a different kind of repair. The section that violates the paragraph's cohesion is in italics.

The Computer Center staff members want to serve you to the best of our abilities. To reach this goal, we need your assistance. When you need help, please send your request to our new e-mail address (help@flash.com). Include in this request your name, office number, phone number, and a detailed description of your request or problem. This procedure will provide us with a recorded list of everyone's needs. *Our previous system was inefficient. It may have been easier for you to just grab us when you saw us in your area, but that created problems for us. We can't always remember additional requests when we're involved in other projects. And we do not want to overlook requests or forget their details. So we thank you for your cooperation.*

The italicized section appears to introduce a new idea, an explanation of the previous system. It could, however, remain in that particular paragraph if the writer were to rearrange the information, making it adhere to a recognizable method of development—in particular, the problem/solution method—and adjust the topic sentence. Notice how the following revision applies those two suggestions to create a cohesive, well-organized paragraph.

> The Computer Center staff members want to serve you to the best of our abilities. To reach this goal, we need your assistance to implement a new procedure to replace our previous, inefficient request system. It may have been easier for you to just grab us when you saw us in your area, but that created problems for us. We can't always remember additional requests when we're involved in other projects. And we do not want to overlook requests or forget their details. So now, when you need assistance, please send your request to our new e-mail address (help@flash.com). Include in this request your name, office number, phone number, and a detailed description of your request or problem. This procedure will provide us with a recorded list of everyone's needs. Thank you for your cooperation.

One final example comes from a letter from a deaf writer who discusses the controversy between signed English and American Sign Language (ASL). This non-cohesive paragraph needs a different set of corrections.

> I'm glad I learned signed English. My above-average reading comprehension and my solid writing skills are due to my knowledge of signed English. I learned ASL by communicating with other deaf people, and I use it in informal settings to talk to friends and family. I use signed English through an interpreter to communicate with my hearing acquaintances, including my college professors. These people would not be able to understand literal translations of ASL. For example, in a conversation with a hearing person, I would sign, "The bird flew in and sat on the fence." If I sign the same message using ASL, it comes out, "Bird fly fence sit." ASL is obviously faster to sign, but signed English uses the word order, verb tenses, articles, and plurals of standard English. ASL is more concept-oriented. *One other drawback of ASL is the impossibility of saying and signing a word at the same time.*

In this paragraph, the last sentence seems to introduce a new idea. However, it would integrate smoothly if the writer were to reorganize the whole paragraph by using methods of development (specifically, contrast and cause/effect), add transitions, and revise the topic sentence to more clearly state the main idea. Applying these three revisions results in a coherent, cohesive paragraph:

> My use of signed English and ASL in different situations illustrates the major differences between the two. Signed English, which uses the word order, verb tenses, articles, and plurals of standard English (and therefore takes longer to sign) has resulted in my developing above-average reading comprehension and solid writing skills. I use it through an interpreter to communicate with my hearing acquaintances, including my college professors. These people would not be able to understand literally-translated ASL, which is better suited to informal conversations with other deaf people or with my family and friends. ASL is faster to sign because it's concept-oriented. For example, in a conversation with a hearing person I would use signed English to say, "The bird flew in and sat on the fence." If I signed the same message using ASL, it comes out, "Bird fly fence sit." Despite its speed, though, ASL will not allow me to say and sign a word at the same time as I can with signed English.

**PRACTICE 6.1
Non-Cohesive
Paragraphs**

In each of the following paragraphs, underline the sentence or sentences that go astray from the main idea and disrupt the cohesiveness.

1. The Roth IRA, which was first introduced in 1998, allows investors to save for retirement while avoiding income taxes both before and after retirement. It allows you to build more wealth because, unlike the traditional IRA, you do not have to begin mandatory withdrawals at age 70½. Therefore, your money can continue to grow for a longer period of time. Furthermore, you can continue contributing earned income to your Roth IRA after retirement. This advantage is enough to make most investors seriously consider opening a Roth IRA account. <u>However, another benefit is just as valuable. The Roth IRA is an effective estate-planning tool.</u>

2. A balanced diet will help you stay fit and reduce stress. Every day, eat a variety of foods such as fruit, vegetables, bread, cereal, lean meat, fish, poultry, and low-fat dairy products. All are healthy foods that help the body deal with stress. <u>Eating regular meals in relaxed settings will also help you reduce stress.</u> Avoid excessive sugar, salt, fat, caffeine, and alcohol, which can all contribute to stress or nervous irritability.

3. Microsoft's Outlook Express 5 includes award-winning features that make it the best Internet mail client for regular users. Outlook Express is tops in its class; <u>however, Eudora Pro E-mail 4.2 includes many outstanding features, too.</u> Outback Express offers Identity Management so that several members of the same family or business can all have their own individual accounts. It allows you to sort and filter large volumes of incoming messages so you can better manage the flow. Also, it tracks your Internet connection and automatically redials if you are disconnected.

4. All walkways on our campus already meet the guidelines of the Americans with Disabilities Act. However, covering the major walkways will further benefit mobility-impaired students. Right now, accessible routes require them to travel longer distances. Often, these routes are twice as long as those for walking students. In inclement weather such as rain or snow, students who use wheelchairs are exposed to the elements even longer. <u>One major disadvantage of this proposal is the cost of installing the covers.</u>

Including Extra Main Ideas

A second type of non-cohesive paragraph results when the writer is not sure before or during composing what *one* idea he or she wants to discuss in the paragraph. This uncertainty produces a paragraph that rambles from idea to idea. For example, read the following excerpt from a memorandum.

> We bought a new Pitney-Bowes postage machine for the mailroom. Only employees who have been trained to use it may operate it. All of the switchboard operators, along with a few other people, received this training. This machine allows us to code postage costs to individual departments. So please write your department's name on the envelope or package. This machine will improve our record-keeping system. If you have questions, please call me.

This single paragraph discusses the following related but different ideas:

1. Authorized users
2. New mail procedures
3. Benefits of the new machine

All three of these points are underdeveloped. For instance, who are the "others" trained to use the machine? Where should you write the department name? How will the new machine improve record-keeping? The writer should create three different paragraphs and add more layers of development to explain each idea.

For another example, examine this paragraph from an article:

> Why do Americans feel so rushed and busy? We usually blame work for taking up too much of our time, but watching television is actually the culprit. Television viewing now consumes an astonishing 40% of Americans' free time. It has replaced many leisure activities, and experts predict that it will continue to push aside other worthwhile activities. Television has altered the whole structure of daily life. Television addiction is a serious problem, and overcoming it is the only way to get control of your time again.

This paragraph begins well with the idea that television consumes Americans' free time. It explains that problem in the next two sentences. However, the fifth sentence introduces a related but new idea, television's altering the structure of daily life. Then the sixth sentence zooms off to a completely different idea, television addiction. To correct the lack of cohesiveness, the writer should develop the fifth and sixth sentences in paragraphs of their own. In addition, he should add examples of the *worthwhile activities* mentioned in the fourth sentence.

Another non-cohesive paragraph comes from a report:

> Three satellite shops, located in area A, area C, and area D, serve the whole plant. Five special tool sets are being assigned to each area, with the additional one allocated to the power room. The special tool set for area B is being stored in area C until we decide whether to create another satellite shop. These sets are engraved like your individual tool sets with the company name and area. Each special set also includes foam tool control similar to your individual sets. They include tools needed on a less frequent basis, but you should feel free to use them as needed. All other shop equipment must be marked somehow to state the owner and location. If you find something unmarked, use our company stamp, stencils, or branding irons to label it.

This paragraph begins with a misleading topic sentence that leads the reader to believe the paragraph will be about the satellite shops. Instead, the bulk of the paragraph describes special tool sets, one item stored in those satellite shops. In the seventh sentence, the writer jumps to another idea, other equipment. To correct this paragraph, the writer should write a clearer topic sentence, one that states his focus on the special tool sets. Then he should move the sentences about other equipment to another paragraph, where he can develop them in more detail.

One final example comes from a resignation letter:

> Regretfully, I plan to resign from Peterson and Associates effective July 1. I have been part of this organization for the past nine years, and I have come to care deeply for my colleagues. I will treasure my memories of participating in this company's successes and improvements. I plan to

pursue the challenge of creating my own business, a personal errand service. I will be here throughout the month of June to help train my successor. I wish you all continued growth and prosperity for the future.

This paragraph seems to ramble; however, the writer could easily divide her thoughts into three paragraphs corresponding to the past, the present, and the future. Then she could add more details to develop each one.

PRACTICE 6.2
Non-Cohesive Paragraphs

For each of the following non-cohesive paragraphs, list the different main ideas in the blanks provided.

1. Littering highways is illegal in Florida, and offenders face expensive penalties. The state of Florida spends over one million dollars annually to clean up roadsides. Littering not only mars the beauty of our state, it also endangers both health and safety.

   Main idea 1: *Penalties for littering*

   Main idea 2: *Florida's response to littering*

   Main idea 3: *Drawbacks of littering*

2. Alzheimer's disease usually afflicts people between the ages of 40 and 60, and more women than men develop the disease. The German neurologist Alois Alzheimer discovered the disease. A form of presenile dementia, Alzheimer's withers the brain's frontal and occipital lobes. Early symptoms include memory loss and decreased concentration. People easily overlook them, though, because they resemble signs of natural aging. Other symptoms include language problems, poor judgment, and rapid mood swings. Treatment options are few.

   Main idea 1: *The Alzheimer's victims*

   Main idea 2: *Discovery of the disease*

   Main idea 3: *Physiology of the disease*

   Main idea 4: *Symptoms of the disease*

   Main idea 5: *Treatment options*

3. The College Planning Fund allows you to begin investing for your child's future right away. The monthly payments are affordable. The State Treasurer manages your fund, so you know it's a safe investment. You can create a fund for any child or grandchild under 17 years old. The fund has two parts: savings and loan. You can use it to pay for higher education anywhere, and it includes tax breaks.

   Main idea 1: *Cost of the fund*

   Main idea 2: *How the fund is managed*

   Main idea 3: *Uses of the fund*

   Main idea 4: *Two parts of the fund*

   Main idea 5: *Benefits of the fund*

4. Next time you pass through the lobby area, take a minute to look at the quilt hanging on the south wall. Master quiltmaker Beth Phillips made it. She used the intricate star pattern and hand-sewed the whole quilt. We're selling chances to win the quilt in a raffle fund-raiser. She also makes custom quilts and has other wall hangings for sale. She may teach a quilting class, so let us know if you're interested in signing up for it.

Main idea 1: *The quiltmaker*

Main idea 2: *How one quilt was made*

Main idea 3: *The quiltmaker's other projects*

Main idea 4: *A quilting class*

WRITING COHESIVE PARAGRAPHS

How can you make sure your paragraphs are cohesive? Do several things during the planning, writing, and rewriting stages.

Planning for Cohesiveness

Before you write, use invention strategies to get ideas (see Chapter 1). Decide on the one main point you wish to make. Then organize your ideas for the whole composition, before you begin to write. Plan the order in which you'll discuss them. Chapter 7 presents a thorough discussion of this procedure.

Composing for Cohesiveness

As you write your first draft, do the following:

1. For each paragraph, write a topic sentence that clearly states the main idea. This sentence will help you focus on one idea at a time.
2. Review your topic sentence as you write each developing sentence, to make sure you're sticking to that one idea.
3. Use methods of development (discussed in Chapter 5 of this book).

Revising for Cohesiveness

As this chapter has illustrated, you can repair non-cohesive paragraphs in different ways. Some need to be divided into separate paragraphs, and then each main idea should be explained with additional layers of development. Others need to be reorganized according to a particular method of development. Some need the addition of transitions to help the reader understand how the ideas are related to one another. Finally, some need a rewording of the topic sentence to include the ideas that seem unrelated.

Reevaluate each paragraph after you've completed the entire composition. Be willing to reorganize, to remove sentences that belong elsewhere or to divide one paragraph into two or more smaller paragraphs. Also, examine the length of your paragraphs. Very long paragraphs may not be cohesive. Check them carefully for digressions or too many main ideas.

PRACTICE 6.3
Checking Your Own
Paragraphs for
Cohesiveness

Choose one of the longest paragraphs from a document you've written. Turn the main-idea statement of that paragraph into a question. Does each sentence in the paragraph answer that question? A sentence that does not answer the question may not belong in the paragraph. If your paragraph is not cohesive, decide how you can correct it. *Answers will vary.*

TEST YOUR UNDERSTANDING

1. What does *cohesive* mean?

   Developing just one main idea.

2. Describe the two different types of non-cohesive paragraphs.

   A paragraph begins with one main idea and then switches to another. A paragraph

   rambles from one idea to another throughout.

3. What can writers do *before* they compose, to ensure cohesive paragraphs?

   Use invention strategies and organize ideas.

4. What can writers do *as* they write, to ensure cohesive paragraphs?

   Write clear topic sentences for each paragraph, review those topic sentences while

   composing, and use methods of development.

5. What can writers do *after* they write, to ensure cohesive paragraphs?

   Reevaluate each paragraph, especially longer ones, and check for digressions.

WEB ACTIVITY: Online Writing Labs

If you need assistance with a writing project, you can seek help from an online writing center. Colleges and universities across the country are creating these centers by hiring skilled writing tutors who can answer quick questions or provide more extensive feedback. Some even offer "real time" chat sessions, so that the writer and tutor can actually participate in an online discussion. Many of these centers are willing to offer their services to anyone, even nonstudents.

(continued)

WEB ACTIVITY: *(continued)*

1. Go to Dakota State University's Online Writing Lab at http://www.departments.dsu.edu/owl/default.htm.
2. Click on *How to Use the DSU OWL.*
3. Send to the address given an e-mail that asks for advice. You want suggestions about improving the memo you will be working on for this chapter's group project and writing activities—a memo about a community service organization. If possible, ask specific questions. To send your memo, attach the file that contains it to the e-mail message, or cut and paste it into the e-mail message itself, or type it into the e-mail message.
4. When you receive a reply from an OWL tutor, print it and submit it to your instructor.

GROUP PROJECT AND WRITING ACTIVITIES

As you studied Chapters 4 and 5, you researched and wrote a report about a community service organization. In this chapter, you'll convince two different audiences that they should support that organization with donations of time and effort or money.

With your group, discuss ways you could persuade the public to support the community service organizations you've chosen. As your group generates ideas, jot them in the space below.

Write a memo to your current co-workers urging them to donate their time, their money, or both to the organization you researched. In the first paragraph, introduce the organization and ask your co-workers for their support. In the middle paragraphs, explain the reasons why this organization is worthy of your readers' support. In the last paragraph, thank the readers for considering your request. Use the following format and headings when you begin your memo

TO: Employees of _____

FROM: _____ (Your name)

DATE: _____

SUBJECT: _____ (Name of organization)

_____

_____

_____

_____

_____

_____

_____

_____

_____

_____

_____

_____

_____

_____

_____

_____

_____

_____

_____

_____

_____

_____

_____

_____

_____

Prepare and deliver an oral presentation to convince your classmates that they can donate time or money to the organization you chose. See Appendix B for more information about preparing an effective oral presentation.

READINGS   How have computers been changing the way people work? As technology continues to advance, what other workplace changes can you predict for the twenty-first century?

In the next article, *Workforce* magazine editor Samuel Greengard has gathered the opinions of leading experts who forecast the ways technological innovations will change the way we work.

As you read this article, circle every word that's unfamiliar to you. Look it up and write the meaning in the margin. Put an exclamation point (!) next to any sentence or paragraph you find especially interesting. Put a question mark (?) next to any sentence or paragraph you don't understand.

How Technology Will Change the Workplace

Samuel Greengard

1   Over the last 20 years, the workplace has changed in more ways than we could've ever imagined. The Industrial Age has evolved into an Information Age—bits and bytes of data rocket around the globe 24 hours a day. To be certain, the very definition of work is undergoing fundamental redefinition. Increasingly companies, and human resources departments, are examining work processes, human capital and knowledge in radically different ways.

2   The next decade will bring even greater change. Technology will permeate almost every business practice and drive enormous strategic and practical progress. Gone will be most secretarial and administrative jobs. And managers will have to focus on measuring efficiency and productivity rather than tracking a group of employees and tasks.

3   Moreover, computers will automate and manage almost every type of process—succession planning, training, skills development, retirement and government compliance. When an employee requires specific training, a human resources computer system will trigger a message and ask the employee to enroll. Employees who aren't contributing to a 401(k) plan at the same

level as co-workers might be flagged for a specific, targeted educational program through the corporate intranet or via e-mail.

4   Thanks to more sophisticated intranets along with e-mail able to support audio, video and graphics, communications capabilities will be far more advanced than we can imagine today. The paperless office still might not exist, but we will be far closer to realizing the concept. Of course technology will drive change, but human change will also influence the direction of technology.

5   How will human resources be affected by this enormous paradigm shift? Here's what some of the nation's leading experts—authors, consultants, business leaders and practitioners—have to say about the workplace and technology of the future. While nobody has a crystal ball in hand, here are some of the technologies and issues worth following:

Workplace Flexibility

6   Technology already has changed the way we live and work. But even more profound changes lie around the corner. With greater numbers of telecommuters and virtual employees, companies will be forced to design new ways to measure and reward workers' contributions. They also will have to find ways to create greater balance within work and life issues.

7   The problem today is that we haven't yet learned to manage technology. All too often our cellular phones and notebook computers control us. Increasingly, we work all the time, everywhere. We use every available second to handle and prioritize voicemail, e-mail and paperwork. In the Information Age, it's becoming impossible to know when work is completed. And unless something changes, all this ultimately affects everything from customer service to burnout. Here's what some experts say.

Reginald Best, General Manager
Remote Access Products Division, 3Com Corp., Santa Clara, CA
3Com is a manufacturer of networking equipment.

8   "There are numerous reasons for creating more flexible work spaces and [allowing] telecommuting. The trend will continue because it allows companies to cut costs and gives workers more control over their careers and family lives. The ongoing advance of computers and telecommunications technology will create less structured work in the future—also fueling growth and outsourcing.

9   "Human resources professionals must help drive the social changes required to make this paradigm work. Managers must learn to evaluate employees on the basis of accomplishment rather than physical presence. Was the project completed on time? What was the quality of the project? How much revenue did the salesperson bring in? How many new accounts is the person responsible for? Some of this will require a cultural change, but there's also a need for software and systems that can track work and evaluate employees in a different way. A company's challenge is to guide management and to know who is adept at working within this new model and who isn't—and then use people and their talents accordingly."

Karol Rose, Principal
Work-Life Effectiveness Practice, Kwasha Lipton Group, a Division of
Coopers & Lybrand
Rose is an expert on work/life issues and is author of the book
***Work/Family: Program Models and Policies* (John Wiley, 1993).**

10   "The problem is that we use Industrial Age thinking in an Information Age. We measure and reward productivity based on time, which is a throwback to a manufacturing-based economy that produces widgets. Trying to equate hours worked with productivity is all wrong. Ultimately people get burned out. We have to create new measures of productivity. We need to put more power in the hands of managers and employees to negotiate flexible working agreements. When that happens, everyone benefits."

Global Business

11   As business goes global, technology will facilitate human interaction. It will allow people of different languages and cultures to work together seamlessly. Computers will translate language on the fly, allowing multinational and multicultural teams to work together seamlessly. A file that is sent to people of different languages will ultimately appear in each person's native tongue. But that won't be the only change. The Internet and intranets will allow even more work teams and strategic alliances than we see in today's business world.

Barbara Ells, Industry Analyst
Zona Research, Redwood City, CA
Zona Research provides market research and analysis on the Internet.

12   "The Internet allows any time, anywhere communication. You can disregard time zones as long as you have a common communications source. And that convenience has huge implications for global business. In the future, we'll see multicultural work teams that share information and collaborate on projects. As a result, language translation tools will become far more important—for Web pages, e-mail, word processing and other functions. It will be essential for information and documents to be accessible worldwide.

13   "In the future, workers will exchange information in many forms: text, images, video, audio and other media. That will necessitate the use of far more sophisticated tools for managing knowledge and searching for appropriate information. With such a far-flung employee base, most companies are going to rely on human resources to play a larger role in creating a sense of culture and community."

William Sheridan, Director of International Compensation Services
The National Foreign Trade Council (NFTC), New York City
The NFTC is sponsored by more than 600 multinational employers in every major industry group. It helps companies facilitate global commerce.

14   "Technology is creating a more culturally diverse workforce. Nationality or citizenship isn't a significant factor when a corporation is looking to create a work team or a strategic alliance. Increasingly, the language employees speak isn't as important as the common, technology-centered language they work

in. This is especially true for engineers, programmers and others involved in product development. Today's technology allows people to work across vast geographies in an almost invisible way. It drives down the cost of managing a project and generates a competitive advantage. Already, a few companies have established work teams that 'follow the sun': The project moves around the globe, from the United States to Asia and Europe and back to the United States, so that work is being done 24 hours a day. We'll see much more of this in the future, as communications capabilities and software become more sophisticated."

Work and Society

15   As workplace technology evolves, the way people interact and go about work will change. The rules of business will be rewritten, and the way knowledge is defined will change radically. Of course, the social implications are profound, and virtually no one will be spared.

16   Future work will require a high level of computer literacy. It will demand not only people who know how to use the Internet, a word processing program and a spreadsheet, but also individuals who understand the radically different conceptual framework in which tasks, projects and alliances will be handled. The good news is that computers should become far more intuitive and intelligent than they are today.

Joseph Coates, President
Coates and Jarratt, Washington, D.C.
Coates is coauthor of *2025: Scenarios of U.S. and Global Society Reshaped by Science and Technology* (Oak Hill Press, 1966). He is a business futurist and consultant.

17   "Organizations are moving to a new structure that links people by what they know rather than their job rifles or ranks. This [structural shift] puts huge demands on the organization to understand and use information technology effectively. An intranet lets you connect to information fast. You no longer have to wait hours or days for an answer. Looking forward, the challenge is to manage all the information and knowledge. For the old-line manager, all of this is very traumatic. The methods and techniques that got him where he is are no longer valid. For those who understand the paradigm shift and the technology, there are tremendous opportunities."

Seymour Siegel, Director
Technology Management Program, Pepperdine University School of Business and Management, Culver City, CA
Siegel is a leading observer in studying technology's impact on the workplace.

18   "The advent of networked computing has drastically changed the work environment. The nature of work 10 years ago was very different than today, and the changes will only accelerate over the next decade. This new workplace requires people who are comfortable with computers and technology and can use them to work in different ways. Unfortunately a lot of people are going to

be left behind. One of the biggest challenges for employers, Human Resources professionals and the rest of society will be to deal with this issue from a social policy point of view. It isn't going to be enough to create new job grades."

Workforce Development

19 The next decade will bring profound changes in the way human resources manages people, data and knowledge. Human resources departments will be asked to play a larger role in attracting and developing human assets. Like other systems, software will measure the payoff from training and more closely track organizational needs and deficiencies.

20 The next generation of client/server systems will capture valuable information and use it more effectively, rather than constantly duplicating it and reinventing it as needed. For example, if a work team in Brazil develops an innovative solution to a companywide problem, others in the organization will know about it instantly through the intranet. More powerful human resources computer technology—combined with the Internet, intranets and e-mail—will allow this to happen.

Row Henson, Vice President of HR Systems and Product Strategies
PeopleSoft, Pleasanton, CA
PeopleSoft is a vendor for human resources management systems.

21 "Tracking training and career development will become even more important. The problem has been that there's no way to measure the effectiveness of training. In the next decade, sophisticated computer-based training, used in conjunction with the Internet, will provide the mechanism to gauge learning and track competencies within an organization. In the future, people will seek out employment at companies where they can gain the most knowledge and are paid for their knowledge."

Brandon Hall, Editor and Publisher
Multimedia and Internet Training Newsletter, Sunnyvale, CA
Hall is an expert in the area of multimedia training.

22 "Corporate training is changing dramatically. The live workshop with an instructor is disappearing. In the future, almost all training will be delivered via computer and delivered over a network. Some of this will be in the form of distance learning through the Internet, allowing people in various geographic locales to study and learn together. In some cases, people will use videoconferencing and document-sharing capabilities; in other instances people will connect using satellites. We also will see an increased use of virtual reality training, which will allow people to learn in realistic, 3-D environments.

23 "The learning organization concept has been around for some time, but we will begin to see organizations exchange wisdom through training. In the past, training was viewed as an expense item. Managers hoped that employees would learn quickly so they could go back to work and do their job faster. Executives are finally understanding that increased organizational knowledge provides enormous returns."

Definition of Jobs

24 Today's databases will give way to a more sophisticated knowledge-based model. Pieces of information will not be as important as threads of knowledge. This will require far more sophisticated databases that use intelligent search techniques and perhaps even pattern recognition. As graphics and images become increasingly important, it will be necessary to find specific images contained in a database. Software that can recognize patterns could speed up research and information systems.

25 Of course, humans will remain at the hub of this new workplace. Increasingly, organizations will move away from a model of filling job openings and instead will be recruiting, promoting and assigning work teams based on specific knowledge requirements. Technology will manage this change and allow Human Resources to recruit in a radically different way. Today's job postings might be replaced with knowledge postings as companies seek specific expertise for special projects. Finally, new work processes will require Human Resources to create new benefits and incentives to attract and retain the best people.

26 Ultimately, that might translate into companies providing greater tuition reimbursements and special perks, as well as rewards for years of service.

Daniel Burrus, Founder and CEO
Burrus Research Associates Inc., Milwaukee
Burrus Research is a consulting firm that specializes in the impact of future technologies. Burrus is also author of the book *Technotrends* (HarperBusiness 1994).

27 "The toolbox of the 21st century is already here in the form of Web-based technology. It's now a matter of learning to use the tools effectively and changing the mindset. Today, we still reward people for hoarding knowledge. In the future, we must find ways to reward people for sharing it. Using an intranet, it's possible to see who posted a particular piece of knowledge or wisdom and reward him or her. Then, using the network, you can let everyone know that the person posting the knowledge was rewarded.

28 "Within such a model, you wind up with a culture in which people share, and you can compensate and reward those who are the most valuable. You also can retain much of their knowledge and wisdom if they leave. Technology is now giving us the ability to unleash the power of employees in new and dynamic ways."

Steve Ciesinsky, President and CEO
Resumix Inc., Sunnyvale, CA
Resumix is a vendor of human skills management software.

29 "We will see a continued migration toward a more dynamic workforce. It will be one in which companies rely heavily on temporary workers, part-time workers, consultants, specialists and outside contractors. The labor market isn't likely to resemble free agency in sports, but it will reflect some of the same qualities.

30 "The sharper companies will make use of technology to better understand the composition of their workforces. Human asset management will become

crucial. It won't be good enough to track only pay levels and benefits. [Companies] will need to know a person's skills, experiences, proficiencies and knowledge. As online recruiting grows and becomes more mainstream, we also will need more sophisticated tools for finding the right knowledge workers through résumés and Internet connections."

RESPONDING TO THE READING

1. What are two benefits of telecommuting?

   Companies can cut costs. Workers can gain more control over their own careers and personal lives.

2. What is one drawback of telecommuting?

   Sometimes it's difficult for the employee to separate work from personal life.

3. How will managers need to change the way they evaluate the performance of employees who telecommute?

   They will need to evaluate on the basis of accomplishments rather than physical presence.

4. What are some ways the Internet will change both the scope and the types of global communication?

   People of different languages and cultures can easily work together, workers can easily share information and documents, and work on a project can go on around the clock.

5. How will organizations change their structures to better match advances in information technology?

   People will be linked together on the basis of their knowledge rather than their rank.

6. How will technology change employee training?

   There will be more distance learning and virtual reality training experiences.

7. How will technology change the way companies define and fill job openings?

   Jobs will be defined by the knowledge the company needs. Companies will have to create new ways to keep the most knowledgeable people.

8. Which sentence disrupts the cohesiveness of paragraph 16?

   The last sentence.

9. Which sentence disrupts the cohesiveness of paragraph 21?

   The last sentence.

BUILDING VOCABULARY

New technology regularly adds new words to the English language. For example, Samuel Greengard's article includes new words such as *voice-mail* and *videoconferencing*. In addition, technology frequently adapts the meanings of existing words. For instance, the word *networked* (paragraph 18) has developed into an adjective that describes a system of interconnected computers. Many dictionaries may include only the noun or verb meanings of that word.

Technological advances created or altered the following words and phrases. Do you know the meaning of each word or phrase? Is each in your dictionary? If not, how could you find out the meaning?
Answers will vary.

1. bytes (paragraph 1) *A byte is the amount of computer memory needed to store*

   one character.

2. intranet (paragraph 3) *Computer network used by members of an organization*

   but inaccessible to those outside the organization.

3. telecommuters (paragraph 6) *People who work at home by connecting to a*

   company's office through a computer.

4. virtual employees (paragraph 6) *People who work for a company but are*

   rarely physically present on company premises.

5. virtual reality (paragraph 22) *Computer simulation.*

What computer-related terms are you using now that are not yet in your dictionary?

Have you sent and received e-mail messages? Do you know how they get from one computer to another?

The next article explains the "mystery" of an e-mail's journey.

As you read this article, circle every word that's unfamiliar to you. Look it up and write the meaning in the margin. Put an exclamation point (!) next to any sentence or paragraph you find especially interesting. Put a question mark (?) next to any sentence or paragraph you don't understand.

Journey of an E-Mail

John Dyson

1 Doug and Julie Young raise Dandie Dinmont terriers. They also publish a newsletter for fellow lovers of the breed. Not too long ago they wanted a picture of Mr. D, our family pet.

2 I could have sent the photo by ordinary mail, but that would have taken at least four days. Instead, sitting down at the computer in my den overlooking London's River Thames, I sent an e-mail. I typed in an address, young@montizard.com, composed a short message, then attached a photograph I'd scanned into my PC. Finally I clicked Send. Mr. D instantly vanished from my screen—headed to a farmhouse in rural Ohio.

3 Along with more than 150 million others around the world, I use e-mail all the time and can't imagine living without it. How it actually works, of course, was a mystery. So one day I decided to find out. Mounting my bicycle, I pedaled off to follow my dog through cyberspace.

Chopped Into Bits

4 The first stop was a brick office plaza between a canal and an elevated highway in Brentford, west London. This was one of the homes of Cable & Wireless, the company that connects my computer to the Internet by telephone lines. Escorted through security checks and card-swipe doors, I entered a brightly lit, windowless room with rows of fridge-size metal cabinets called racks, containing computers the size of TV sets, each costing as much as a car. In an adjoining control room, engineers, some of whom were wearing earrings, were monitoring rows of complicated numbers on video screens. As the racks tend to look the same, engineers give them names. "This is Marvin," said Jason Semple, pointing to one. "He's your postbox."

5 A burly 27-year-old, Semple hooked a finger over the spine of what looked like one of scores of videocassettes on a shelf. He slid out a circuit board glittering with tiny gold wires and silver connectors.

6 "When your PC dials our number, it's answered by one of these modems," Semple explained. "It checks your name and password with another computer, then asks what you want."

7 My computer had replied, "I've got mail."

8 Next, Mr. D was fed into a "mail server"—a bunch of computers filling five racks. One read my e-mail's destination and checked another, which stored Internet addresses like a gigantic phone directory.

9 The Cable & Wireless directory could do ten look-ups a second. It didn't find montizard.com, so it asked a bigger directory, storing ten million addresses in Europe and Africa. That didn't work either, so it asked one of 13

core directories (ten in the United States, two in Europe, one in Japan) holding every Internet address in the world.

10   Back came the answer: "Send mail to BuckeyeNet." This is the company connecting the Youngs to the Internet. BuckeyeNet's Internet address—209.41.2.152—was clipped like a dog tag to Mr. D's collar.

11   Next, something bizarre happened. Imagine a postal clerk who chops your letter into little bits and puts them in separate envelopes. This is done to every e-mail. All the bits and bytes representing Mr. D were instantly divided among about 120 packets. Every one was stamped with BuckeyeNet's address, plus my own address, so the jigsaw puzzle could be reassembled at the other end.

12   But they didn't go all at once. Instead, a single packet was sent off like a scout car, to knock on the door of BuckeyeNet, say hello and make a connection. The first stop was a gateway router, which would help the scout car find the way.

Kids With Flashlights

13   Picture the Internet as 65,000 interstate highways crisscrossing the globe and connected to smaller roads and streets. Like a cop with a walkie-talkie on every crossroad, the router learns the fastest way to get an e-mail to its destination. It knows all the routes and, by talking with other "cops" down the road every half-minute, it discovers where the delays are—say, heavy telephone traffic or a cut cable.

14   A Cable & Wireless router sent Mr. D's hello packet across London to the company's transmission center in Docklands, where another router fed it into the stream of e-mail packets heading for the westerly tip of Cornwall, the nearest part of England to America.

15   All this happened in four milliseconds—like a lightning flash.

16   I took a decidedly slower train to Cornwall and went to Porthcurno, a cliff-top village. There, in a barn-size room, is the base station of the transatlantic Gemini cable.

17   Take a hair-thin fiber of glass, wrap it in a protective jacket, then incorporate it with others in a rubbery protective tube. This is fiber-optic cable, known in the trade as pipe.

18   A flashing laser at one end fires digital on/off signals along the fiber. At about 120,000 miles a second—more than half the speed of light—they zip to the other end.

19   "It's the high-tech equivalent of two kids signaling each other with flashlights," explained Dave Shirt, operations director. With pretty quick fingers, I'd say: the lasers flash ten billion times a second.

More Gold Earrings

20   Mr. D's packet next jostled for elbowroom with a torrent of transatlantic electronic traffic—equivalent to 100,000 closely typed pages every second, or 400,000 simultaneous phone calls. Think that's a lot? At present six parallel lanes of traffic hurtle along every glass fiber. Newly laid cables will soon have

128 lanes, preparing for the explosion of Internet traffic when every movie ever made could be available online.

21   I returned to London, hopped a plane to New York and rented a car, then picked up Mr. D's trail again on a long, flat beach in Manasquan, N.J., where the Gemini cable comes ashore. Next the e-mail zipped along poles and beside railroad tracks before flashing into 60 Hudson Street, in downtown Manhattan. Time taken from London: approximately 40 milliseconds, or one-tenth of a blink of the eye.

22   This 22-floor art-deco building is a "telco hotel" where telephone companies own or rent space for equipment so they can connect to one another more easily. The scout packet was switched into high-capacity "fat pipes" crossing the continent. It also hit what engineers call ATM—asynchronous transfer mode.

23   Now Mr. D was diced yet again into dozens of identically sized cells which flashed through the back of a telephone exchange in West Orange, N.J., just west of New York.

24   But from there the cells had a really wild ride, zipping through pipe beside railroad tracks, into and out of Philadelphia, up the Ohio Valley, through Cleveland and into another telephone exchange at Willow Springs, outside Chicago. Here the bits came together, and the original packet was restored. It all took a fraction of a second.

25   Barely pausing for a breath, so to speak, the scout packet next raced through Chicago and Detroit, before landing in a building in Columbus, Ohio—headquarters of Fiber Network Solutions. There I met the company's co-founder, Kyle Bacon, a laid-back 27-year-old wearing two gold earrings.

26   Bacon, who used to duck classes to work on his university's computer system, helped set up a network that controls Internet pipes so businesses and industry have to pay the company to open the tap. That was three years ago. Now the company employs 45 people, and Bacon drives a silver BMW whose license plate reads FAT PIPE.

27   A router in the company switched Mr. D into a skinny pipe running direct to the home of BuckeyeNet—then a two-room office with a dirt parking lot, some five miles from rural Lancaster. BuckeyeNet has over a thousand clients and 13 computers. By way of comparison, the biggest Internet-access provider in the world, America Online, has some 19 million subscribers and servers covering football fields of floor space.

28   Dressed in shorts and, naturally, sporting a gold earring, Jonathan Sheline, 27, told me he'd set up the company after leaving the Army, where he'd served hitches in the infantry and counterintelligence. In just 18 months his net was one of the largest in the town. Our friends the Youngs are among its $17.95-a-month clients.

29   "Okay, I'm listening." BuckeyeNet's mail server unwrapped Mr. D's scout packet, which carried a message. "Helo," it said. "I am j.dyson at cwcom.net." "Helo" means hello in a computer language called Simple Mail Transfer Protocol (SMTP).

30　　　BuckeyeNet's mail server sent an acknowledgment to London, which took one-tenth of a second to arrive. Next the two computers negotiated the connection. Their conversation, using codes as well as plain text, went like this.

31　　　Ohio: Okay, I'm listening. SMTP is spoken here.
London: I have mail from j.dyson at cwcom.net.
Ohio: Pleased to meet you.
London: I've got mail for montizard.com.
Ohio (checking list of clients): Okay, I can handle that.
London: I'm ready to send data.
Ohio: Start mail input.

32　　　From London, five packets hit the road. If any crashed or failed to arrive, the Ohio dispatcher would let London know and they'd be sent again. When this bunch arrived, Ohio said: "I got the first five, give me five more."

33　　　Despite all the messages PingPonging across the Atlantic, the last bit of Mr. D straggled into BuckeyeNet's server less than half a minute after I had originally clicked Send. For me it had been nine hours in the air, four hours waiting for a connection and an hour and a half in cars. And my luggage was left behind. But Mr. D still had to go the last five miles.

34　　　When I arrived in their old farmhouse on nearly five acres outside Rushville, Doug and Julie Young were making breakfast for 35 dogs, 30 ferrets, two llamas and a parrot. Julie had an armful of cans, bowls and milk cartons, difficult to carry because they were all different sizes.

35　　　Meanwhile, from a big paper bag, Doug filled a container with pellets of dog food—the perfect metaphor for understanding why e-mails are minced and shredded into packets and cells. Like pellets, they pour more easily and therefore travel much faster.

36　　　A big, jovial man of 51, Doug uses e-mail to talk with breeders all over the world. When he clicked Get Mail, the BuckeyeNet server checked his mailbox and forwarded its contents down the phone line. The stream of bits materialized into Mr. D gazing imperially out of the screen from his kitchen chair, not a bit ruffled after his 4000-mile dash.

RESPONDING TO THE READING

1. Why is an e-mail message divided into smaller packets that travel separately?

   They must be in small pieces in order to travel quickly through cables and wires.

2. The author makes many comparisons, using figurative language such as analogies and similes to help the reader understand the e-mail process. Explain two of these comparisons. Why are they effective?

   The following comparisons all compare the process to things familiar to the reader

   and by creating mental images: "Imagine a postal clerk who chops your letter into

   (continued)

**RESPONDING TO
THE READING**
continued

little bits. . . . This is done to every e-mail." ". . . A single packet was sent off like a

scout car. . . ." "It's the high-tech equivalent of two kids signaling each other

with flashlights. . . ."

3. What is Internet "pipe"?

Fiber-optic cable.

**BUILDING
VOCABULARY**

A *thesaurus* can help writers discover the most accurate words for stating their ideas. It contains *synonyms*, words with similar meanings.

Use a thesaurus to find a synonym for each of the italicized words in the following sentences from the article. Substitute words that do not change the meanings of the sentences. Use a dictionary to help yourself decide on the right substitute. *Answers will vary.*

1. Next, something *bizarre* happened. (paragraph 11)

   strange

2. A flashing laser at one end *fires* digital on/off signals along the fiber. (paragraph 18)

   sends

3. Mr. D's packet next jostled for elbowroom with a *torrent* of transatlantic electronic traffic. . . . (paragraph 20)

   flood

4. At present six parallel lanes of traffic *hurtle* along every glass fiber. (paragraph 20)

   race

5. Now Mr. D was *diced* yet again into dozens of identically sized cells which flashed through the back of a telephone exchange in West Orange, N.J. . . . (paragraph 23)

   cut

6. A big, *jovial* man of 51, Doug uses e-mail to talk with breeders all over the world. (paragraph 36)

   friendly

7 Organizing Logical Units

PROFESSIONAL PROFILE
Phyllis Shuping, Buyer

After working for fifteen years in the plant of a furniture manufacturer, Phyllis Shuping decided to improve herself and expand her abilities. So she enrolled in her local community college and earned a degree in operations management, which enabled her to move into better positions at the company. She now serves as a buyer, spending most of her time researching, selecting, and purchasing the materials used in the plant. Her position requires her to write a variety of documents, including memorandums, letters, reports, and e-mail messages. In the following memo, she compares different propane companies to explain her recommendation that the company change suppliers.

MEMORANDUM

TO: Fred McMahon, Operations Manager
FROM: Phyllis Shuping, Buyer
DATE: June 1, 20xx
SUBJECT: Propane Report

As you requested, I have been investigating the propane we use for fork lifts, tow motors and boiler starter at our three plants. Last year, we used 31,014 gallons of propane, which we purchased from Quincy Propane and PLP Propane. My research has led me to conclude, however, that we should change suppliers and purchase our propane from Performance Propane.

Performance Propane offers a significantly lower price per gallon. While Quincy Propane charges $1.26 per gallon and PLP Propane charges $0.837 per gallon, Performance Propane charges only $0.794 per gallon. According to my calculations, we paid $26,323.92 to Quincy and $8,472.11 to PLP that year. Had we purchased the same amounts from Performance, the total cost would have been $24,625.12, a savings of over $10,000. The attached tables summarize our propane usage amounts and costs by plant.

Furthermore, Performance has already demonstrated exceptional customer service. Their friendly, knowledgeable representative assured me that the company can meet our needs. The Quincy representative was helpful, too, but the PLP representative did not return my phone calls. Performance also promises to furnish and install new propane storage tanks at no extra charge. Neither of our current suppliers has offered that service. Performance also offers either net/60 or net/30 payment terms, with an additional discount for net/30 terms. Neither Quincy nor PLP offers any discount.

Therefore, I recommend that we change suppliers from Quincy and PLP to Performance Propane immediately. We should make the change in the very near future to prevent costly refills by our current suppliers, and we should notify all Plant Managers to refrain from calling the current suppliers to service their tanks. If you have any questions or comments, please do not hesitate to contact me at extension 5055.

Phyllis's memo organizes the information logically, so the reader can easily understand her idea. Chapter 7 discusses the methods for clearly organizing one's thoughts before composing.

Writing can be compared to collecting butterflies. Writers have many thoughts and ideas, which act like "butterflies" flitting about in their minds. These "butterfly" ideas come in a variety of "types": some are large, some are small, some are blue, some are yellow, some are black, some are orange. Some are spotted, some are striped, some are solid. But they all fly together around in our heads, tumbling in and over each other, weaving in and out of our consciousness. When we compose, we seek to offer readers an understanding of what some of these "butterflies" in our minds are like.

Before we can do that, though, we must find a way to arrange them so that we can describe them logically to someone who can't see them. We must find a way to organize them before we present them to a reader. We might think of this organizing process as netting the butterflies and placing them in jars according to characteristics they share. For instance, we could place all of the blue butterflies in one jar. Or we could put all of the large butterflies in a jar. Or we could group the striped ones together. This helps the person examining our collection understand the butterflies better.

Prior to letting a reader examine our collection of ideas, we must determine the most logical way to group them. One expert on thinking says that "much of what we call 'intelligence' is our ability to recognize patterns."[1] Intelligent writing, therefore, is organized according to discernible patterns. When we prepare to write, we determine these patterns by finding logical *categories* for organizing ideas. Doing so will help our readers grasp what we want to say.

Organizing things into categories is a task we're all familiar with. The clothes in your dresser drawers, for instance, are probably divided into different categories. You might place socks in one drawer, underclothes in another, and shirts in another. In this case, the category you use to separate these articles of clothing is Type of Clothes. You store different types in different drawers, rather than jumbling them all together.

However, when it's time to do laundry, we reorganize those clothes, using a different category: Color. Now you might separate those same clothes into piles you label whites, pastels, and bright colors.

You may have categorized other things in your home as well. The food in your kitchen might be organized according to Type of Food (different cabinets for canned goods, spices, and cereals). The homework you need to complete could be separated according to Subject (different notebooks or folders for English, math, and biology). The bills you need to pay might be arranged according to Due Dates (electric bill and phone bill this Friday, rent and car payment next Friday, etc.).

Just as you sort items into categories to help yourself understand and manage them better, you must find categories for your ideas in order to help your reader comprehend them. When you present your thoughts in logical units, the reader can more easily grasp your meaning. This means that writ-

[1]Roger Von Oech, *A Whack on the Side of the Head* (New York: Warner Books, 1983), 55.

ers must spend some time determining the best organization plan for their entire compositions *before* they begin to write. After determining *what* they'd like to say, they must decide on the categories they'll use to arrange *how* they'll say it.

When writers skip this important step and begin to write without planning ahead, their compositions will often ramble or jump from thought to thought. At best, readers of such compositions will experience difficulty accessing specific information. At worst, they'll fail to understand the writer's ideas and feel confused or frustrated. For example, read the following passage from a report about the causes of violent behavior in young people.

> Children who exhibit violent behavior have often been subject to abuse. Child abuse has a reciprocal effect, so abused children often grow into abusive adults. Most parents can control their anger, but some cannot manage it constructively. An average of 35% of child abuse cases involve substance abuse.
>
> Drug and alcohol use reduces self-control and often exposes children to violence, either as victims or perpetrators. Four out of five high school students admit to drinking alcohol, and half say they've drunk alcohol within the last month. Alcohol is a major contributor to violent child behavior.
>
> Studies show that substance abuse and child abuse are linked. About 10 million American children are affected by parents who abuse alcohol and drugs.

That writer did not organize her thoughts before composing; instead, she just wrote down details in the order in which she thought of them. As a result, the article's focus keeps shifting, in a confusing manner. A list of topics discussed in each paragraph makes this disorganization clear:

Paragraph 1:	Child abuse
	Parents' substance abuse
Paragraph 2:	Parents' substance abuse
	Children's substance abuse
Paragraph 3:	Parents' substance abuse

Listing the topics in this way causes three clear categories to reveal themselves:

Child abuse

Parents' substance abuse

Children's substance abuse

The writer is offering three distinct causes of violent behavior, so the organizing category should be Causes. However, because the author did not determine this category *before* beginning to write, the information is all mixed up. For instance, she discusses parents' substance abuse in all three paragraphs, mixing these details with other types of information. As a result, the information is difficult to follow.

To improve this article, the writer should sort the details into the three categories listed above. But even then, she's still not ready to compose. The next step involves determining the most logical order for these categories. The writer says a connection exists between at least two of these causes: parents' substance abuse and child abuse. Because the first cause contributes to the second, she should discuss parent's substance abuse first. Child abuse, its result, is the logical topic for the second paragraph. The writer does not link children's substance abuse to child abuse; instead, she offers it as a separate cause. Therefore, she should present that cause last in a paragraph by itself.

Another example of a composition that lacks logical organization comes from a newsletter article that attempts to explain a fund created for a church:

> Trustees can allocate monies from the Howard Stanton Fund for large expenditures on the current building, such as maintenance or renovation. Scholarships for youth or adults are permissible with the Board of Trustees' approval. This could include fees for camps, workshops, or attendance at other church functions such as district meetings.
>
> The Board can vote to loan money to church members who experience hardships or disasters such as illness or fire. Anyone who needs the money must petition the board for assistance. Scholarships can't exceed $500 per applicant. The Board determines how much to loan for disaster relief and decides on repayment terms.
>
> For building expenses, the Board decides how much to use. The fund is also for seed money toward the purchase of a larger facility. This is why most payments must be in the form of loans that must be repaid.
>
> The exception is scholarships, which can't exceed $500 per year. If the entire $500 is not awarded, then the unused portion can be added to the next year's award.

Again, because the writer did not determine her organizing categories *before* composing, the details are jumbled and difficult to follow. A list of topics discussed in each paragraph reveals the disorganization:

Paragraph 1:	Use #1 (building expenditures)
	Use #2 (scholarships)
Paragraph 2:	Use #3 (disaster relief)
	Use #2 (scholarships)
	Allocation procedures
	Repayment terms
Paragraph 3:	Allocation procedures
	Repayment terms
	Use #4 (future facility)
Paragraph 4:	Allocation procedures and repayment terms for scholarships

When we examine the information included in the article about the Howard Stanton fund, clear categories emerge:

The four different uses of the fund

Allocation procedures

Repayment terms

However, the writer discussed two different uses of the fund in the same paragraph. She presents details about scholarships in paragraphs 1 and 2, mixing them with details about other topics, and then adds more information about them in the final paragraph. Explanations of the allocation procedures are mixed in throughout, often separated from the specific use they match. As a result, the information is very difficult to follow.

To improve the reader's understanding of this information, the writer should sort these details into clear categories. Her first category should obviously be Uses of The Fund. This category creates four separate paragraphs, one to describe each different use. Then, she should determine the best order for these four uses. Two of them concern building projects (present and future), so they should be discussed one after the other instead of being separated by two other unrelated uses. Next, the writer should determine what to do about the Allocation Procedures and Repayment Terms categories. Should she combine them and present them as a separate category of information at the end of the article? Or should she match them with and integrate them into her discussion of each separate use? The second option would be most effective because the allocation and repayment terms differ according to each specific use. Reorganizing the details this way would result in the following plan for the article:

Paragraph 1:	Use #1 (building expenditures)
	Description
	Allocation procedures
	Repayment terms
Paragraph 2:	Use #2 (future facility)
	Description
	Allocation procedures
	Repayment terms
Paragraph 3:	Use #3 (scholarships)
	Description
	Allocation procedures
	Repayment terms
Paragraph 4:	Use #4 (disaster relief)
	Description
	Allocation procedures
	Repayment terms

Regrouping the details in this way is more logical, and they will make more sense to the reader.

Now that we've established the importance of grouping like information together, let's look at how to discover and arrange the best categories for our ideas.

THE THESIS STATEMENT

Before you can decide on the most logical categories for your ideas, you'll need to determine what you'd like to say. What *one* major idea or concept would you like readers to know or to believe by the time they have completed reading your letter, your essay, your memo, or your report? That idea or concept is your **thesis.** Your **thesis statement** is the sentence in your document that clearly reveals this overall main point. For example, your thesis statement in a letter to your gas company might be

Foothills Natural Gas needs to correct the error in my last monthly statement.

Your thesis in your report about a professional organization to which you belong might be longer:

The Professional Society for Administrative Assistants seeks to promote professionalism among administrative assistants, provide professional development opportunities, and encourage communication and cooperation among its members.

Your thesis in your memo addressed to those you supervise might be one like this:

Every employee must wash his/her hands thoroughly after clocking in.

The thesis statement, which should always be clearly stated near the beginning of your composition, announces your main point. An effective thesis statement will possess the following three characteristics.

1. *It is stated in one declarative sentence.* This is the *one* point you want your reader to remember, so write one clear, precisely worded sentence to state that point. Never phrase the thesis as a question.

2. *It is stated assertively.* Omit phrases such as *I think that* or *I believe that* and just state the idea.

3. *It is specific.* It states an idea or an opinion that is not too broad or too vague, one that can be adequately explained or defended in the composition. In addition, it often includes the *reasons* why this idea is true or should be true.

Formulating a clear thesis statement is the first step toward logical organization of your ideas, for you have to know exactly what you want to say before you begin trying to say it. As a matter of fact, a good thesis statement will often suggest the most sensible organization pattern, the next section explains.

DISCOVERING CATEGORIES FOR IDEAS

Once you have determined your thesis statement, you're ready to decide how to collect and categorize the ideas you want to present. How do you know which categories to choose, to logically sort your thoughts? Unfortunately, there is often no right or wrong answer. Each subject might be organized in any of several different ways.

For example, if you decided to organize your personal collection of videotapes, how would you arrange them? Many people would sort them according to Genre, grouping tapes together according to their type (drama, comedy, horror, documentary, etc.). But that's not the only way to organize them. You could, instead, group them according to specific Actor or Actress. Using that category, you would place all of your Tom Cruise movies in one area, all of your Julia Roberts tapes in another, and your James Earl Jones movies in another. Or you could arrange them from Most Watched to Least Watched. You could even organize them according to Length. The category you chose would depend on your purpose.

When you write, a variety of different categories might suggest ways of arranging your thoughts. Your topic and thesis statement will sometimes dictate which categories you *must* use. Other topics and thesis statements will require you to apply logic to decide not only what categories you'll use to organize ideas, but also what order you should use to present these categories. In the following sections, thesis statements about different aspects of the Internet will illustrate how a thesis can either dictate certain categories or require you to determine them with your own powers of logical thinking. Using the same subject will demonstrate how your *focus* (thesis) affects the organization of your thoughts.

Natural Organization

Some subjects organize themselves. If you are recounting a series of events, for example, you will naturally arrange them in chronological order, from the first that happened to the last. For instance, suppose this is your thesis:

The Internet has expanded significantly over the past 40 years.

You would probably tell the story of how the Internet was created and how it has developed. Or suppose your thesis is this:

Our marketing team developed a new company web site last year.

You would recount how the team completed the project by conducting research, brainstorming ideas, and then designing the new page. In a report about a speech given by a computer company's CEO, your thesis might be as follows:

In his presentation, Bill McDonald described the new Internet technologies on the horizon and made several predictions about the future of online uses.

To explain this thesis, you would naturally describe Mr. McDonald's speech topics in the order in which he presented them.

However, even though narratives organize themselves, you will still need to determine how to divide a longer composition into smaller units. Usually, we relate one incident or describe one scene per paragraph.

Another type of subject that will also organize itself naturally is an explanation of a procedure. Like a narrative, the steps in a process arrange themselves in chronological order, so you present each step in order from the first thing done to the last. Here is an example.

You can download the free ICQ software by following three easy steps.

You will need to determine how to divide your explanation into smaller units. Usually, we explain each *major* step in a separate paragraph. The thesis above organizes the composition into three units.

Paragraph 1: Download and save the installation file.
Paragraph 2: Run the installation program.
Paragraph 3: Follow the registration instructions.

Because you will be explaining a procedure, you will naturally discuss the steps in the order in which they take place.

Other explanations of procedures, however, require additional logical thought. For instance, read this next thesis:

You can protect yourself against Internet fraud.

This thesis suggests that the writer will offer instructions but that these instructions are not a series of steps. Therefore, a chronological arrangement of the details is not possible. The writer must find a logical category to organize the separate pieces of advice. In this case, the category Types of Information to Protect effectively arranges the details:

Paragraph 1: Protect information about your personal identity (social security number, date of birth).

Paragraph 2:   Protect information about your location (address, telephone number, e-mail address).

Paragraph 3:   Protect information about your finances (credit card number, checking account number).

In addition to narratives and explanations of procedures, other types of thesis statements will clearly suggest how information can be categorized. For example, a thesis announcing that you'll present reasons suggests that you will discuss each separate reason in a separate unit. Let's look at this thesis statement:

Online banking will simplify your life.

The overall organizing category is Reasons. All you need to do now is determine the most logical order for presenting these reasons to the reader. Does it make more sense to arrange them from most important to least important, or vice versa? Or do the reasons themselves suggest a particular order, perhaps because of a cause/effect relationship between them? For example, the thesis just stated might suggest three reasons, each of which should be discussed in a separate paragraph:

Paragraph 1:   Generate electronic tax returns.
Paragraph 2:   Make electronic payments.
Paragraph 3:   Reduce paper record-keeping.

Are those three reasons presented in the best order? You might want to discuss tax returns *after* record-keeping because you compile the tax-returns data from the records. But what about electronic payments? Does it seem more appropriate to discuss that reason first—or last? Use logic to decide.

Logical Organization

Unfortunately, many of the compositions you'll write will not organize themselves. Instead, you will have to use logic to determine appropriate categories, as well as the best order for those categories. For example, examine the following thesis statement.

Parents can prevent their children from accessing pornographic or violent web sites by using new filtering software.

You could organize the information for this composition different ways. For instance, you could choose the category How It Works and explain procedures for installing and running these programs. You could choose Features of Filtering Software and describe their various functions and options. Or you could choose the category Brands of Filtering Software and describe different companies' products and their features.

These three different categories would produce three different organization plans. Yet much of the same information might appear in any of those three plans. For instance, you could mention specific brands as examples as you describe the steps of operation. However, using the Brands organization plan would allow you to discuss the different operating procedures of each. The organizing category and plan you choose should always depend upon your readers' needs. Always ask yourself which will help them best understand whatever they need to know.

Let's say you need to write a report about Internet Service Providers (ISPs), and your thesis is

Our area's best Internet Service Providers are Company A, Company B, and Company C.

Your first impulse might be to use the organizing category Internet Service Providers. So you'd determine which specific features of each company you should explain to your readers. Your plan might look like this:

Company A

Paragraph   1: Equipment
Paragraph   2: Price
Paragraph   3: Customer service
Paragraph   4: Technical support

Company B

Paragraph   5: Equipment
Paragraph   6: Price
Paragraph   7: Customer service
Paragraph   8: Technical support

Company C

Paragraph   9: Equipment
Paragraph 10: Price
Paragraph 11: Customer service
Paragraph 12: Technical support

However, you could arrange this information by using a different organizing category, one that would help the reader better understand how each company compares to or differs from the others. That category is Company Features, and using it would result in a plan that looks like this:

Equipment

Paragraph   1: Company A
Paragraph   2: Company B
Paragraph   3: Company C

Price

Paragraph   4: Company A
Paragraph   5: Company B
Paragraph   6: Company C

Customer Service

Paragraph   7: Company A
Paragraph   8: Company B
Paragraph   9: Company C

Technical Support

Paragraph 10: Company A
Paragraph 11: Company B
Paragraph 12: Company C

Even though you'd present the same information with either organization plan, the second plan would probably suit readers' needs better. It would let them see more easily the similarities and differences among the three different companies.

Here's another example of a thesis statement that lends itself to different organization plans.

> A researcher must maintain a healthy skepticism when looking for information on the World Wide Web.

This thesis statement leads readers to ask both how and why. To answer the question How? you might use the organizing category Signs of Unreliable Information. The organization plan would look like this:

Paragraph 1:   Lack of author information (name, credentials, contact information)

Paragraph 2:   Lack of information about sources

Paragraph 3:   Contradictory information

To answer the question Why? you'd organize the composition within the category of Reasons, in order to explain more about the types and origins of unreliable information. That organization plan might look like this:

Paragraph 1:   Freedom of speech

Paragraph 2:   Opinions disguised as facts

Paragraph 3:   Author's personal agendas/ulterior motives

In this case, notice how the information in the two plans differs, even though each could successfully develop that thesis statement. You would have to decide which plan better expresses your ideas and fulfills the readers' needs.

Some compositions, reports in particular, will require you to determine more than one organizing category. Because reports usually present different kinds of information about a subject, they need to employ different organizing categories for the specific details. For instance, examine the following thesis statement.

> Electronic grocery shopping is an exciting new online trend.

This thesis suggests a report, one that seeks to inform the reader about different aspects of the topic. Suitable categories might include How It Works, Companies, Reasons for Its Popularity (Advantages), and Disadvantages. After determining these organizing categories, the writer should decide next how to order them. Does it make more sense to explain *who* is providing the service before you explain *how* it is provided? Should you present advantages before disadvantages? These decisions result in a plan that might be as follows.

Paragraph 1:   Companies

Paragraph 2:   How the online service works

Paragraph 3:   Disadvantages

Paragraph 4:   Advantages

To avoid struggling to determine the best organizing category or categories, spend time refining your thesis statement. A clear, specific thesis statement will often suggest the best organization plan. A good example is the following one.

> Computers help scientists make more progress in research.

That thesis statement could be developed with different categories, including Examples of computer programs, or Reasons (Causes), or Effects, or Procedures. Too many choices for organization, though, may indicate that the main point should be reworded more precisely or more specifically. Compare the following thesis statement, which narrows each part of the general statement about computers to state one very specific idea:

> New networking technologies that help scientists collaborate with each other will result in new medical breakthroughs and discoveries.

This thesis easily indicates that the organizing category is Effects of the new technologies, so the plan of organization might be as follows.

Paragraph 1: Includes participation of those who don't have billion-dollar, high-tech equipment but who can study the data
Paragraph 2: Avoids duplication of effort
Paragraph 3: Fosters cooperation and sharing of immense amounts of electronic data between companies and countries

This plan organizes the information into a series of effects that all contribute to the end result—medical advances—mentioned in the thesis.

Now examine another vague thesis statement:

> Millions of people are buying cars on the Internet.

How would you organize the details that would develop this idea? Should you present the Causes of this new trend? The Effects of this trend? The Procedures, or an explanation of how to do it? Or should you give Examples of online companies or their customers? It's not easy to decide because the thesis statement needs some refining. When we revise it to make the focus clearer, the organizing category becomes clearer:

> Several online vehicle sales companies are revolutionizing the automobile industry.

This thesis suggests that the composition will use Examples of online companies, so the plan might look like this:

Paragraph 1: autobytel.com
Paragraph 2: carsdirect.com
Paragraph 3: carmax.com

As you describe each different company, you could explain how each has "revolutionized the automobile industry."

Here is another example of a thesis statement that needs improvement:

> In the twenty-first century, talking computers will be popular.

This thesis could be developed and organized with Descriptive Details or Reasons (Causes) or Examples of different programs. If we zero in on one particular aspect of the subject, we could revise the thesis:

> Talking computers will eventually replace written language with spoken language.[2]

[2]William Crossman, "The Coming Age of Talking Computers," *The Futurist* (December 1999): 42–48.

Not only does this revised statement express a much more interesting idea; it also points to the best organizing category: Causes (Reasons):

Paragraph 1: Reading and writing were invented only to compensate for limited human memory.

Paragraph 2: Reading and writing are slow and tedious.

Paragraph 3: Literacy is declining because the majority of the world's population doesn't like to read and write.

Paragraph 4: Spoken language is more user-friendly because it's easier and more natural.

Paragraph 5: Scientists are working hard to perfect oral-aural and visual computer technologies.

This plan presents a well-organized chain reaction of different causes that will ultimately lead to the end result described in the thesis statement.

Finally, beware of thesis statements that *seem* clear and specific but that will lead you down the wrong path of development and organization. The following one, for example, is misleading.

A company should invest considerable effort in designing an effective web site.

This thesis easily suggests the organizing category of Reasons. However, only one reason—increased profit for the company—really exists. Therefore, that's not an effective category. Improving the thesis clears up the confusion:

A web site that attracts both new and repeat customers includes three important features.

The new organizing category is Features:

Paragraph 1: It permits the customer to move around quickly and easily (pages load fast and are well organized).

Paragraph 2: It's interactive (includes online ordering, electronic payment, and e-mail alerts about specials).

Paragraph 3: It includes a database that stores customer information for future transactions and recommendations.

PRACTICE 7.1
Determining Logical Categories

Write down *one* logical category you could use to organize the information that would develop the following thesis statements. *Answers will vary.*

1. Recreation departments should perform criminal-background checks on all men and women who apply to coach children's sports teams.

    Organizing category: *Reasons*

2. Recreation departments can follow four easy steps to perform criminal background checks on men and women who apply to coach children's sports teams.

    Organizing category: *Steps*

3. Low-carbohydrate, high-protein diets—such as the Atkins diet—offer a popular way to lose weight.

   Organizing category: *Diets*

4. Many obese people have achieved amazing weight loss success with low-carbohydrate, high-protein diets such as the Atkins diet.

   Organizing category: *People (or Steps)*

5. In the twenty-first century, job hunters who don't know how to use the Internet will be at a disadvantage.

   Organizing category: *Disadvantages (or Advantages)*

6. Job hunters can use the Internet to find positions that match their goals and credentials.

   Organizing category: *Steps in a Process*

7. You can reduce your tax bill six different ways before December 31.

   Organizing category: *Ways (to reduce bill)*

8. Filing a tax return electronically offers several benefits to the taxpayer.

   Organizing category: *Benefits*

9. Teenage pregnancy rates are declining.

   Organizing category: *Causes*

10. Declining teenage pregnancy rates impact society in positive ways.

    Organizing category: *Effects*

11. Laser eye surgery may promise 20/20 vision, but you should understand the risks.

    Organizing category: *Risks*

12. Laser eye surgery offers certain patients a popular alternative to eyeglasses and contact lenses.

    Organizing category: *Benefits*

13. DVD technology creates a high-quality experience for viewers.

    Organizing category: *Reasons*

14. Films recorded on DVD are far superior to those recorded on videotape.

    Organizing category: *Points of Comparison*

Each of the following passages lacks organization. Determine the category (or categories) of information presented in each. Some are reports, so they will include more than one category.

A. To begin beekeeping, you need to purchase a hive. The hive contains a floor, a body, a super, racks, an inner cover, and a top. You also need full body covering, including coveralls, boots, gloves, and a hat. You need some other equipment, too, especially a smoker. These are the basics for your new hobby. Of course, you also need bees.

   The hive contains an opening near the bottom where the bees come in and out. When you order your bees through the mail, they'll send you one queen bee and about 3,000 worker bees. The bees raise their young in the body of the hive. They build honeycombs in the racks of the body. After they fill up the racks with honey, you can add a super. The honey that fills the super is honey you can keep. But you need a smoker because they won't let you just walk up and take their honey.

   The smoker calms the bees by distracting them from their surroundings. Your whole body needs to be protected. Your gloves should cover your arms up to your elbows, and your hat should include a veil. Bees will find any holes in your suit. You buy them in swarms that split from a hive that grew too big.

   Organizing categories: *Hive, Body Covering, Equipment, Bees*

B. Transferring the child support system from individual counties to a central office in Raleigh has caused major backups in child support payments. Even though one parent pays on time, the custodial parent does not receive the check until two or three weeks later. This is leading to bad credit for many families who can't pay their bills.

   Many families depend on these checks to buy food for their children or to pay for medical care. They may need the money for medicine. But they are forced to do without because Raleigh's computer system is backlogged.

   The central office said the delay is due to their miscalculation of the number of checks they had to process. They did not expect it to take so long to transfer the necessary data.

   The problem will not be solved anytime soon. Checks will continue to be late. So families who depend on the money are suffering because they can't afford many important necessities.

   Organizing categories: *Effects*

C. The RoamAbout wireless network allows hospital nurses to get immediate authorization for medications from doctors. Patients don't have to suffer while the nurse tries to track down the doctor for permission. Patients don't have to wait around because the RoamAbout saves time in processing information such as medical history. Any caregiver can access the patient's records instantly without having to wait for someone to locate a file. Patients get better care.

   Imagine the stress of going to the hospital. All you want is treatment for your illness or injury, but the clerk needs to get a lot of information from you. You finally finish the paperwork, but when you see the nurse, she starts asking you the same questions all over again. It makes you want to scream. But the RoamAbout solves the problem because it saves your answers to the questions. Therefore, treatment can begin immediately.

The RoamAbout is convenient, too. Doctors don't have to worry about being interrupted by their pagers as often.

Organizing categories: _Advantages_

D. The Westlaw web site is available to attorneys, paralegals, government personnel, and pre-law students. Colleges can purchase a subscription that allows students to look up statutes, cases, forms, public records, and other information.

You can access the site from any computer, but you have to know the password. Attorneys and their staffs use it extensively in their offices. The subscription is expensive but worth the price.

You can pay yearly or monthly. You can also get regular upgrades. Clients save money, too, because their legal representatives spend less time accessing necessary information.

The site is available twenty-four hours a day. Subscriptions are flexible and customized according to the needs of the customer. Therefore, rates vary. It saves anyone conducting legal research valuable time.

Organizing categories: _Who (can use it); What (it contains); How (to use it);_

and Why (you should have it)

CHOOSING NATURAL OR LOGICAL ORGANIZATION

Neglecting to determine categories for ideas is one way to ensure organization problems. Another common way to create organization problems is by trying to present ideas by using a natural organization pattern when a logical pattern should be used instead. Specifically, we often inappropriately arrange our thoughts in narrative form. Telling a story is easy and comes naturally, so it's tempting to present points within a chronological recounting of events. However, this form often buries ideas in unnecessary details and as a result, prevents readers from finding and understanding them. Try reading the following passage. The writer composed it to inform readers about a disease called Legg-Calve-Perthes.

My brother Brandon was as normal as any other five-year-old. He was an active kindergartner who played on a baseball team. But suddenly, he began complaining about pain in his leg. He started limping a little, but my parents couldn't find any bruises. He insisted that it hurt, so my mother took him to the pediatrician, who ordered blood tests and X-rays.

We didn't begin to worry until we found out they were looking for cancer and bone diseases. After all these tests, the terrible diagnosis was Legg-Calve-Perthes disease. Brandon's ball joint in his hip had disintegrated due to an insufficient blood supply. The cause was unknown.

Our family was devastated. We cried only in private, though, trying to be strong for Brandon's sake. He needed surgery, so we took him to a specialist, a pediatric orthopedist who told us that the ball joint was almost completely deteriorated. The doctor scheduled surgery, which would end with Brandon in a cast from the waist down. So our whole family went to Disney World before he had to go to the hospital. Even with Brandon in a wheelchair, we managed to enjoy ourselves. However, the whole trip was overshadowed with our fears and anxiety.

Brandon was very brave during the whole ordeal. The doctors cut a wedge of his bone and repositioned it, holding it in place with a steel plate and screws. Brandon spent three days on morphine to control the intense pain. When he began to recover, he went through morphine withdrawal. The other painkillers the doctors prescribed never completely deadened his pain.

Now, several months later, Brandon's ball joint is finally beginning to regenerate, so we're hoping he'll recover fully to lead a normal life. However, he will probably face osteoarthritis later in life.

The writer intended to educate his readers about a disease. However, he ended up writing a story about his brother's experience. Though he does offer a few facts about Legg-Calve-Perthes, the composition's focus is always on his brother and his family. As a result, information about the disease is buried among details about the experiences of the people involved, and readers don't get enough information to truly understand the disease.

This writer's focus on *one* individual who suffers from a disease causes him to exclude relevant information that did not happen to be part of that person's experience. For instance, the effects of Brandon's surgery included intense pain and morphine addiction. Are these common side effects for *all* who undergo this procedure? Are there other possible side effects from the treatment? The writer never tells because he's concentrating on Brandon.

To improve this composition, the writer should focus on the disease itself, reorganizing the information into categories. The new organization plan might look like this.

Paragraph 1: Symptoms
Paragraph 2: Tests for diagnosis
Paragraph 3: Treatment
Paragraph 4: Short-term and long-term prognosis

The writer could then use his brother's experiences as *layers of development* (see Chapter 4) within each section, but he should also include a wider range of experiences. Therefore, he'd need to add more information about symptoms, treatment options, and prognosis for Legg-Calve-Perthes patients in general.

When you choose narrative organization, carefully evaluate whether this is the best method for arranging your ideas. If you're writing a report for your supervisor to explain a work-related accident that injured an employee, you might be tempted to tell the story of what happened on the day of the accident. However, a better organization pattern for your information might involve considering your details in terms of a category such as Causes of the accident or Unsafe Conditions. Or instead of telling a story about your tour of a new store, consider grouping the relevant details on the basis of a category such as Innovative Features. Then you can discuss the features that will most interest your reader and omit information your reader doesn't want or need. For instance, you could focus on the state-of-the-art security system, the new cash register technology, and the new merchandise layouts, even though you didn't view them in that order during the tour.

Outlining

When people express their dislike for outlining, they usually give two reasons why they skip this step of the writing process. First, they say, outlining takes too much time. Inexperienced writers think they can decide on the best order for their ideas as they compose, so why spend extra time working that out before writing? Second, they argue that they don't usually stick to the original outline, so since they may end up changing it to match the finished paper, why bother with one to start with?

Unfortunately, both of these arguments are myths. Outlining is actually a critical step in the composition process, one that should not be omitted for these or any other reasons. An outline is a guide that improves logical arrangement of the writer's thoughts and prevents rambling or digressing.

Myth #1: Skipping the Outlining Step Saves Time. Failing to outline actually *adds* time to composition. Finding the language to express ideas is difficult enough. When we don't spend time determining a plan of organization *before* we begin writing, we force our brains to do two challenging mental tasks (organizing and composing) at the same time. Because this is more complicated, the composing is usually slower and often can be more frustrating. Separating the outlining stage and working out the organization of your ideas before you begin to write might actually *save* you valuable time in the long run, for composition uncomplicated by simultaneous organizing tends to be easier and, therefore, faster.

Myth #2: An Outline Is Useless Because the Final Paper Rarely Matches It. A builder never begins constructing a building without a blueprint, or plan, for the finished structure. However, if during construction the builder discovers a better way to do something, he can alter the blueprint to reflect the improvements. Similarly, writers should not begin compositions without an outline. Creating an outline of your ideas before you write will prevent you from

- digressing from your main point,
- rambling or jumping from thought to thought,
- mixing different kinds of information, and
- discussing an idea in the wrong place.

The outline is your best determination of the overall structure, but if you do discover a better way as you're writing, by all means go with the better plan. An outline is not cast in stone; it's a preliminary guide to help yourself get started.

Formal Outlines. When most people think of an outline, they picture one that includes Roman numerals. A formal outline uses a combination of Roman numerals, letters, and Arabic numbers. The following outline, for example, shows a possible plan of organization and development for a thesis statement mentioned earlier (see page 202).

A web site that attracts both new and repeat customers includes three important features.

  I. Fast-loading and well-organized
   A. Features and elements of fast-loading pages
   B. Organizational elements
    1. Buttons and links
    2. Columns and layouts
    3. Typeface and color

  II. Interactive
   A. Online ordering
   B. Online payment
   C. Online access to records/accounts
   D. E-mail alerts to specials

III. Database for information storage
A. Customer recommendations
B. Convenience of not having to reenter data

In this type of outline, the Roman numerals correspond to the major organizing units, while the letters and Arabic numbers list supporting ideas and examples.

This format is useful for separating ideas and indicating their relationships. It also helps writers evaluate whether or not they're adequately developing each idea. However, writers do not necessarily need to use this more rigid form for planning their compositions. Instead, they might choose a less formal approach.

Informal Outlines. When writers are determining the arrangement of their compositions, they can sketch ideas in an informal manner. The point of outlining before composing is to work out the organization of thoughts. Therefore, writers can use any system that provides a useful guide or map to follow as they compose. Such systems can be as brief as simply making a list of ideas in the order in which you want to discuss them. Or make a list of topics for each paragraph, as shown in the preceding sections of this chapter. Or use any other approach that makes sense to you. Because this planning is for your eyes only, you should develop a system that works for *you*.

One specific informal technique is called *branching*. This involves starting with a topic and then drawing "branches" of subtopics, supporting reasons, main points, cause/effect relationships, examples, or details radiating from that central topic. If you need to write a memo, for instance, to inform your employees of renovations to the building that houses their offices, you could first plan that memo by creating branches of subtopics (*reasons why, temporary changes, the noise*, and *permanent changes*) you'll need to explain. Then draw more branches from each subtopic branch to outline the specific details you need to present.

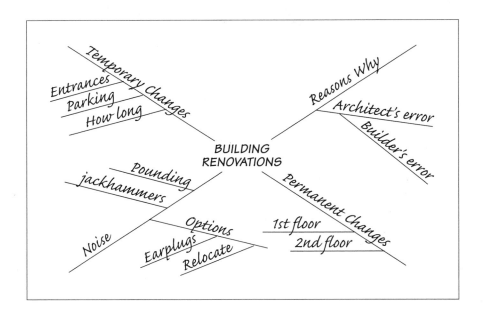

The plan shown divides the changes into two categories—temporary and permanent—and then adds specific types of changes in each category.

In the Why category, the builder's error is branched from the architect's error because of the cause/effect relationship between the two. The Noise category will explain two types of noise and then discuss two ways to deal with it.

For those writers who like a more visual layout of their ideas, the branching technique can be a valuable tool for discovering and arranging logical categories.

PRACTICE 7.2
Outlining

Choose three of the following thesis statements from this list and fill in each blank to state an opinion of your own. You may generate your own ideas or select one of the ideas shown in brackets. Then, in the spaces provided after the list, create formal or informal outlines for your three statements.

Parents can teach their children _____.

[money management; fire safety; telephone etiquette]

The Internet includes excellent sites for _____.

[genealogical research; bargain shopping; investment information]

_____ should win the championship this year.
[Fill in the name of a sports team]

_____ usually share several significant personality traits. [Successful students; Successful salespeople; Children prone to violent behavior]

Increasing numbers of young people are _____.
[smoking cigarettes; dropping out of high school; taking five years or more to earn a degree]

_____ is/are negatively impacting American society. [High divorce rates; High numbers of lawsuits; Indifference to politics]

The top two brands of _____ are Brand A and Brand B. [Fill in the blank with a type of product (car stereo, laundry detergent, snow skis, etc.). Then change *Brand A* and *Brand B* to the names of actual products.]

Answers will vary.

THESIS #1: _____

OUTLINE:

THESIS #2: _____

OUTLINE:

THESIS #3: _____

OUTLINE:

Using Organizational Markers

Organizational markers are different systems for arranging information on the page. They help your readers separate ideas visually and see their relationships quickly. Using these markers, which include different types of lists and headings, helps readers access and understand your thoughts more easily. Professional writing, such as memorandums and reports, will often include these types of markers to help busy readers find and understand specific pieces of information rapidly.

Lists.   Lists line up information in columns and then add a visual feature such as *bullet dots* (black dots) or numbering to help the reader distinguish the items from one another. The following selection from a newsletter article presents the writer's suggestions in the form of a bulleted list.

WANT MORE BUSINESS? PUT IT IN WRITING*

The written word can be a powerful and persuasive sales tool. Whether you're writing a yellow pages ad, a brochure or a personalized letter, keep these simple communication tips in mind.

- **Talk to your audience.** You may not be speaking face-to-face, but you can certainly write that way. Put yourself in the person's

*Lowe's Home Centers, Inc., "Want More Business? Put It in Writing," *Talk of the Trade* (April 1999): 1. Reprinted by permission.

mind-set, and convince him that you understand what's important to him. Then explain specifically how you can help him achieve his goals.

- **Don't beat around the bush.** Get to the point immediately, within the first sentence or paragraph. Let your target know that you respect his or her time by cutting out any unnecessary words or phrases. Edit sentences down to 20 words or less.

- **Write the way you speak.** Keep your message simple, and use words people use every day—such as "buy" instead of "purchase." And don't fill your message with technical jargon and statistics. Concentrate on the end result by explaining the specific benefits your product or service can provide.

- **Include a call to action.** If you don't ask for an order, you shouldn't expect to get it. Sum up your message by stating specifically what you want the target to do, whether it's purchasing a product or scheduling a meeting.

For those times when face-to-face sales meetings simply aren't possible, try expressing your message succinctly on paper. A few well-chosen words can go a long way toward boosting your business.

Separating each suggestion from the others by using list format, bullet dots, and bold print improves the document's readability.

Headings.   Headings, or minititles, for smaller sections of a composition also help readers separate information and find specific details quickly. An effective heading is a concise, accurate description of the topic discussed in that section. Headings are distinct from the rest of the text; they might be in bold print, underlined, or in larger letters. Look at the following example, an excerpt from a web site, which uses a distinctive typeface for headings.

PALM ISLAND RESORT*

Accommodations

Each of the 160 spacious villas features a full kitchen, living and dining room, laundry, and a screened porch overlooking the Gulf of Mexico.

Cuisine

Rum Bay Restaurant features specialty drinks, an enticing luncheon menu, and dinner entrees such as mahi-mahi, Cajun shrimp, and famous baby back ribs. Stop by the Island Store for sundries, casual clothes, or fresh meat and fish for a barbecue on one of the gas grills located near each pool area.

*Getaways: Palm Island Resort, http://155.212.1.116/scripts/faxidquery.idc?Lookup=437.

Activities

The resort's Recreation Department offers special daily kids' and family activities, as well as rentals such as bicycles, canoes, surf kayaks, hydro bikes, snorkeling equipment, Wave Runners, Windsurfers, and golf carts. Even the fishing is great.

An effective heading system also helps the reader understand the relationships between sections. A textbook, for instance, might have bold headings in capital letters for major sections of each chapter, with subsections of the chapter identified by subheadings in "caps and lowercase."

Combining Organizational Markers.   You can combine different types of organizational markers. Note how the following excerpt from a web site article uses headings, numbering, and bulleted lists.

SPECIFIC TECHNIQUES FOR ASSERTIVENESS*

1. Be as specific and clear as possible about what you want, think, and feel. The following statements project this preciseness:
   - "I want to . . ."
   - "I don't want you to . . ."
   - "Would you . . . ?"
   - "I liked it when you did that."
   - "I have a different opinion, and I think that . . ."
   - "I have mixed reactions. I agree with these aspects for these reasons, but I am disturbed about these aspects for these reasons."

   It can be helpful to explain exactly what you mean and exactly what you don't mean, such as "I don't want to break up over this, but I'd like to talk it through and see if we can prevent it from happening again."

2. Be direct. Deliver your message to the person for whom it is intended. If you want to tell Jane something, tell Jane; do not tell everyone except Jane. Do not tell a group of which Jane happens to be a member.

3. "Own" your message. Acknowledge that your message comes from your frame of reference, your conception of good vs. bad or right vs. wrong, your perceptions. You can acknowledge ownership with personalized ("I") statements such as "I don't agree with you" (as compared to "You're wrong") or "I'd like you to mow the

*"Specific Techniques for Assertiveness" from The Counseling Center of the University of Illinois at Urbana-Champaign, *Assertiveness* (1996). Reprinted by permission.

lawn (as compared to "You really should mow the lawn, you know"). Suggesting that someone is wrong or bad and should change for his or her own benefit when, in fact, it would please you will only foster resentment and resistance rather than understanding and cooperation.

4. Ask for feedback. "Am I being clear? How do you see this situation? What do you want to do?" Asking for feedback can encourage others to correct any misperceptions you may have as well as help others realize that you are expressing an opinion, feeling, or desire rather than a demand. Encourage others to be clear, direct, and specific in their feedback to you.

TEST YOUR UNDERSTANDING

1. What is a *thesis statement*?

   A sentence that states the overall main point of a composition.

2. What three characteristics should an effective thesis statement possess?

   One declarative sentence, assertive and specific.

3. What is the difference between natural organization and logical organization?

   Subjects that organize themselves are naturally organized. Subjects that require

   the writer to determine the most appropriate categories require logical

   organization.

4. Give an example of a type of composition that uses natural organization.

   A narrative or an explanation of a procedure.

5. Why is outlining an important step in the composition process?

   It will allow you, as you compose, to concentrate on determining the best

   language to express your ideas, and it will prevent organization problems such

   as digressions.

6. What is the difference between formal and informal outlines?

   Formal outlines use the traditional Roman numeral format and are often included

   in the document for the reader's examination. An informal outline uses a format

   developed by an individual writer. An informal outline is a tool the writer uses in

   preparing to compose; readers usually don't see it.

7. What are two types of organizational markers?

   Numbering or bullet dots; headings.

WEB ACTIVITY: Personality Quiz

To work well with many different types of people, you first need to understand *your own* personality type and how it influences your thoughts and behavior. You can take a personality quiz online to learn more about yourself.

1. Go to the Kaplan web site at http://www1.kaplan.com.
2. Click on *Mind Games* at the top of the screen.
3. Click on *Self-Quizzes*.
4. Click on *Test Yourself*.
5. Click on *Your Personality*.
6. Click on *The Kiersey Temperament Sorter*.
7. Complete the quiz and click the *Score Questionnaire* button.
8. Print the graphed results of your quiz, and click on the links that explain what your score means.
9. Do you agree with these results? Why or why not?

GROUP PROJECT AND WRITING ACTIVITIES

For Chapters 7, 8, and 9, you'll begin a new project that focuses on a needed improvement to your college campus. In this chapter, you'll interview another student for information and then describe a specific problem.

With your group, use one or more invention strategies (such as brain-storming or listing) to generate ideas about needed improvements to your college campus. Think about facilities or procedures that appear unsafe, inefficient, or inconvenient. Write as many ideas as possible in the space below.

With your group, select one of the needed improvements you discovered in the last activity. Together, use an invention strategy to generate more details and information about the problem. Record your ideas in the space below.

On your own, interview another student, one who has been inconvenienced, injured, or frustrated by the problem you selected. See Appendix A for more information about conducting successful interviews. Record details from that interview in the space below.

Collaborate with your group to compose a detailed description of the needed improvement. Focus only on the problem, thoroughly describing it and its effects on students, faculty, staff, and visitors to your college campus.

_____

_____

_____

_____

_____

_____

_____

_____

_____

_____

_____

_____

_____

_____

_____

_____

_____

_____

_____

_____

_____

READINGS How would you classify different types of employees? What kinds of workplace goals have you seen in your past or current co-workers?

The next article, from _The Futurist_ magazine, categorizes workers according to six different goals.

As you read this article, circle every word that's unfamiliar to you. Look it up and write the meaning in the margin. Put an exclamation point (!) next to any sentence or paragraph you find especially interesting. Put a question mark (?) next to any sentence or paragraph you don't understand.

Study Reveals Six Types of Workers

Cynthia G. Wagner

"Fulfillment Seekers" and "Paycheck Cashers" have different goals on the job.

1 Some people go to work because they need the money; others, because they need the challenge. Understanding these differences is increasingly important to employers trying to hire and retain effective workers. It's also important to young people looking for a job that meets their needs.

2 According to a recent poll sponsored by Shell Oil Company, the American work force includes six worker-personality types, each with a distinctive approach to work:

3 • **Fulfillment Seekers.** These workers want to make the world a better place and seek jobs that allow them to do so. According to the survey, most are white, married, and describe themselves as team players rather than leaders. Fulfillment seekers are evidently also fulfillment

Cynthia G. Wagner, "Study Reveals Six Types of Workers," originally published in the Feb. '99 issue of _The Futurist_. Used with permission of the World Future Society, 7910 Woodmont Ave., Bethesda, MD 20814 www.wfs.org

attainers, expressing high satisfaction with their work. Typical occupations include teachers, nurses, and public defenders.

4   • **Risk Takers.** Members of this group are anxious to get rich quick and perpetually seek opportunities for financial success. They tend to move frequently from one employer to the next, looking for better and better jobs. Risk Takers are young, male, fairly well educated, and (surprise) successful: Forty percent have household incomes of above $50,000. Typical occupations are software entrepreneurs and car salespersons.

5   • **High Achievers.** These are workplace leaders who take initiative. The majority of high achievers have typically planned their career path from a young age, and the planning seems to have paid off: High Achievers are the highest income group, with one fourth earning $75,000 a year or more. This group is predominantly male and highly educated, consisting of lawyers, surgeons, architects, etc.

6   • **Clock Punchers.** An overwhelming majority of people in this group say they ended up in their jobs by chance rather than by design, and their satisfaction level is the lowest of the six groups. Three-fourths say they would have made different career choices if they could do it all over again. Clock Punchers are predominantly female, have only a high school diploma or less, and earn under $30,000 a year. Jobs include cashiers, waitresses, and hospital orderlies.

7   • **Ladder Climbers.** Company loyalty is a key trait of these workers, who like the stability of staying with one employer for a long time. Having a stable income is more important to them than having a very high one. Most are female, have modest education but good income, with 48% earning more than $50,000. These are corporate middle managers and skilled blue-collar supervisors.

8   • **Paycheck Cashers.** These workers seek good incomes and benefits rather than the opportunity to stretch their capabilities or change the world; many are perfectly happy in their cubicles. Most are young, male, members of a minority (18% African-American, 10% Hispanic, 3% Asian), do not have a college degree, and work in blue-collar or nonprofessional white-collar jobs. Jobs in this group include factory work and entry-level word processing.

9   Shell's poll on workplace types was conducted in July 1998 by the Washington, D.C.-based survey research firm Peter D. Hart Research Associates, which interviewed a representative national sample of 1,123 randomly selected adults. According to Shell President and CEO Jack E. Little, the company's new quarterly polls are an attempt to initiate a dialogue on issues that are important to the public, addressing people's goals and values. "The results can provoke comment, insight, and discussion," he says.

10   Managers and human-resource directors may find the worker typology identified by Shell useful in their recruitment efforts. "As the labor market

tightens, employers are discovering that they're going to have to be more aggressive in their recruiting efforts," says business futurist Roger Herman, co-author of *Lean and Meaningful* and a contributing editor to *The Futurist*.

RESPONDING TO THE READING

1. Which of the six worker personality types best describes you in your current or previous job? Why?

   Answers will vary.

2. Which of the six worker personality types best describes your hopes for the career you plan to pursue upon completing your education? Why?

   Answers will vary.

3. What kind of organizational marker is used in this article?

   Bullet dots with subheadings.

4. On separate paper, create a formal or informal outline of this article.
   Answers will vary.

BUILDING VOCABULARY

Homonyms are words that sound alike but are spelled differently and have different meanings. Because they sound the same, writers can easily mix them up and use the incorrect word, for they are not interchangeable. For example, the words *their* and *they're* both appear in the article you have just read. *Their* is a possessive pronoun, and *they're* is a contraction for *they are*.

In the following sentences, circle the word in the brackets that fits the sentence's meaning.

1. [Your/You're] not going to believe what I saw today.

2. Mr. Quinn put those papers on [your/you're] desk.

3. [It's/Its] six o'clock.

4. The plant lost [it's/its] power supply at six o'clock.

5. Just leave the box over [their/they're/there].

6. [Their/They're/There] arriving on Delta Airlines.

7. The managers had [their/they're/there] annual review last week.

8. Joe has more experience [then/than] Frank.

9. Finish the report; [(then)/than] fax it to the Tokyo office.

10. She is stopping at the bank [(to)/too/two] make that deposit.

11. I tried to call him [to/too/(two)] days ago.

12. Are you going to apply for that job, [to/(too)/two]?

Have you worked with people who are difficult to get along with? How did these people make your job harder?

In the following article, management consultant Sandy Crowe offers specific advice about how to handle difficult people in the workplace.

As you read this article, circle every word that's unfamiliar to you. Look it up and write the meaning in the margin. Put an exclamation point (!) next to any sentence or paragraph you find especially interesting. Put a question mark (?) next to any sentence or paragraph you don't understand.

Tactics to Tame Tough People

Sandra Crowe

1 Harmony is easier to sing than to practice in a relationship. Especially if someone has already shown his "jerkiness." Someone in your company is singing off-key. Off-key means stubborn, antagonistic, complaining, insecure employees and co-workers. Do you work with someone who is hard to get along with? Here are seven guidelines for dealing with off-key people:

2 **1. Set the example.** What goes around comes around. When dealing with co-workers it's crucial to remember that what you do to and with them will be reciprocated. If you are playing argument games with an office mate, you can be sure it will come back to haunt you. It takes two to tango and to tangle. If the example you set is superior and consistent behavior, it will be followed.

3 **2. Don't get sucked in.** Recently I was in the grocery store in a great mood for no particular reason. As I approached the end of the checkout line I looked at the cashier and saw she had an "I'm having a bad life" look on her face. I decided not to speak to her, but unfortunately one of the items that I chose did not have a price on it and she had to call the manager. The moment between the time she called the manager and the time he came was an eternity. I began to look at her and smile. Really smile. She looked back at me and as she did that sourpuss frown slowly and carefully turned into a smile. She wasn't jumping for joy, but she was smiling. My emotion had been so much stronger than hers that she couldn't help but get pulled in. How easily

Sandy Crowe, "Tactics to Tame Tough People." Sandra Crowe, the author of *Since Strangling Isn't an Option*, is a speaker and consultant in the communications field. She can be reached at www.pivpoint.com or pivpoint@cyberrealm.net.

are you led into a co-worker's emotion? Do you let the complainers pull you in? Who is really in charge of your emotions? Lead with a smile.

4   **3. The more you understand, the more you can be in control.** How many times have you let someone else push your buttons? When he does, it says he knows you better than you know yourself. Frightening, isn't it? When someone else knows you better than you know yourself, he has the opportunity to take advantage of that knowledge. The bottom line is know yourself and be aware when the attempt is being made to control you. Personal awareness and understanding are 95% of the cure.

5   **4. Reward behavior you want to see repeated.** People will do what they get rewarded for. It is interesting to note that reward for one person may be punishment for another. Making you angry could be seen as a reward for some. The key is to reward yourself.

6   **5. Ignore the behavior you don't want to see repeated.** A few years ago I was doing a presentation for a group where I asked them what problems they were having in their team. One woman responded that sexually and racially descriptive terms were a problem for one member of their team. Every time they had a meeting he used the air time to make inappropriate remarks and every time he did people laughed with embarrassment. After the suggestion of silence was brought up she went back and requested that the other team members do the same. For the first time in 10 years the man received no attention and ultimately no reward. Within a week he had stopped.

7   **6. Confront in private.** Another word for confront is carefront. Carefront means to make the other person's ideas, thoughts and feelings as important as yours and be gentle in your delivery. When you address poor behavior, the environment of privacy is paramount. The way you conduct the interaction is more focused and direct. When doing so, use the following steps: Ask for permission to speak to the person alone. Tell him your perception of the situation using the words "From my perspective" or "In my opinion." Ask him for his. Move towards action for the future: "What do you suggest we do differently?" or "My suggestion is. . . ." Be sure to honor his perceptions as much as yours.

8   **7. Confront by asking, not telling.** When you come up against another person's ignorance, the inclination is to inform him of it. Resist this! Instead ask questions about how he did what he did or his strategy in approaching something. Don't ask why. It might make him more defensive. Ask what. It will cause him to give you information instead of justification. And who knows, you might even learn something in the process. No matter which tactic you use, the most important thought to remind yourself of is take it seriously, not personally. You can never

know what other issues trigger that response you hear. It is important to remember that even when people address their anger towards you, very often it is not about you. They are usually frustrated about other events. Even though you can never walk in someone else's shoes it helps to have compassion for him. Too often, taking it personally distorts the real issue. The best way to get tough is to get smart. Realize you have many options in dealing with difficult people. Saying what you have to say with acceptance and non-judgement will take you the farthest no matter what tactic you choose to use. When you do, dealing with them will be the easiest thing you've done all day. The most important unspoken aspect in dealing with any person in any situation is not what you say, but how you say it.

RESPONDING TO THE READING

1. Describe a former or current co-worker of yours who was (is) difficult to get along with.

   Answers will vary.

2. Have you ever used any of the author's seven tips in dealing with that co-worker? Which ones? Were they effective?

   Answers will vary.

3. Which of the author's tips should help you get along better with that co-worker?

   Answers will vary.

4. What kind of organizational marker is used in this article?

   Numbering, with subheadings.

5. On a separate piece of paper, create an informal or formal outline of this article. *Answers will vary.*

BUILDING VOCABULARY

A *suffix* is a word ending that changes the word's meaning or part of speech. The noun suffixes include *-ness, -ment, -tion, -er, -ar,* and *-or.* When attached to the ends of verbs or adjectives, these suffixes change those words to nouns. For example, the article by Sandy Crowe includes the following words:

manager [manage + er]

argument [argue + ment]

interaction [interact + tion]

awareness [aware + ness]

Adjective suffixes include *-less, -ful, -ish, -able, -ible, -ant, -ent, -ous, -y,* and *-ive.* When added to either nouns or verbs, these suffixes change them to adjectives. Examples from the article include:

defensive [defense + ive]

careful [care + ful]

Many adverbs are created by adding *-ly* to the ends of adjectives. For example:

unfortunately [unfortunate + ly]

racially [racial + ly]

The verb suffixes, *-ate, -en, -fy,* and *-ize,* change nouns or adjectives into verbs. For example:

frighten [fright + en]

motorize [motor + ize]

Add the appropriate suffix to change each verb or adjective to a noun.

1. happy *happiness*

2. behave *behavior*

3. help *helper*

4. advance *advancement*

5. demote *demotion*

Add the appropriate suffix to change each noun or verb to an adjective.

6. resource *resourceful*

7. contempt *contemptible*

8. child *childish*

9. select *selective*

10. ease *easy*

Add the appropriate suffix to change each noun or adjective to a verb.

11. strength *strengthen*

12. sympathy *sympathize*

13. legal *legalize*

14. diverse *diversify*

15. domestic *domesticate*

8 Interesting Openings

With only an associate in arts degree, Mark Radaskiewicz supervises twelve technicians in his position as Engineering Maintenance Team Leader for a multi–billion-dollar tire manufacturer. His responsibilities include leading teams during the installation of equipment, maximizing machine operations to meet production goals, and training personnel and monitoring their performance toward safety and production goals. To accomplish these tasks, Mark regularly writes memos, letters, e-mail messages, and reports. Most of his documents concern the efficiency and safety of plant operations. Read the following example, the opening of his report about an improved machinery lockout system he developed.

> I have developed a new method for locking out train-type machinery that will increase efficiency, improve safety, and save the company money. This new procedure will allow us to lock out and restore a machine much faster, so it will increase our available preventative maintenance time.
>
> It will provide an easy method for performing thorough audits of the lockout's integrity. It will also make the lockout system easier to understand; as a result, even someone without an in-depth understanding of the equipment can be assured of his or her safety.
>
> My new system includes a series of visual, logical steps to accomplish a lockout. A description of the procedure will reveal how it simplifies and improves our existing system.

Mark's paragraph achieves all four objectives of a successful opening, the topic of this chapter.

A good opening paragraph is crucial for the success of your composition. First impressions are important because readers often judge your document on the basis of your first few sentences. When readers can choose whether or not to read the rest of your composition, their decision is usually based on what you do (or don't do) in your introductory paragraph. When readers *must* read your composition, they are likely to decide on its effectiveness (its clarity and its interest) on the basis of those crucial opening statements.

PURPOSES OF THE OPENING

Whether you're writing a report, a memo, a letter, or any other document, you need to achieve several objectives at the outset. Every effective opening accomplishes four specific tasks:

1. It provides background information.
2. It states your thesis.
3. It establishes the tone of your composition.
4. It stimulates your reader's interest.

To achieve all four objectives, the length of your opening will vary according to your topic and the scope of the information you plan to include. Openings are at least one paragraph long, but they can be several paragraphs long—if, for instance, you need to offer a great deal of background information.

Give Background Information

The first purpose of the opening is to provide readers with any necessary background information they need in order to understand your topic or idea. The kind of background information you'll include depends on your subject. One type is historical detail that helps readers understand the past. For example, in a letter advocating the reintroduction of the wolf into certain wilderness areas, you may want to explain the animal's past history in those areas, including an explanation of why the wolf disappeared. In a report to your supervisor about a committee project, you might want to describe what tasks have already been completed.

Another type of background is a description of the current situation or circumstances of an issue or problem. You might need to give your reader information about what is happening *now*. For instance, a memo to co-workers about an equipment problem might need to explain the current status of that equipment. A report on the topic of computer security will probably need to orient the reader by a discussion of concerns confronting computer users today.

Background could also include an explanation of your topic's relevance or importance. Why should the reader be interested in this subject? Why is it meaningful? What are some of its effects? For example, in a memo about the need for salary increases, you might want to establish the exact number of employees who recently left your organization for higher pay elsewhere. In a letter to your local newspaper editor about the need for a traffic light at a busy intersection, you might want to note how many motorists are affected, as well as how often accidents occur at this location.

A final type of background information is definitions of terminology. To prevent confusion or misinterpretation, you'll want to make sure your reader knows the meaning of significant words. For instance, in an e-mail message about a new procedure, you may define specific terms you'll be using. Or in a report about the use of the drug Ritalin, you'll explain what this drug is, what conditions it treats, and its effects.

State Thesis

Another purpose of the opening paragraph(s) is to state your main idea or *thesis*. The thesis statement is the sentence that clearly and concisely identifies the main idea you want your reader to know or to believe after reading your paper. Stating your thesis in your opening paragraph focuses the reader's attention on that point.

Where should you state the thesis? In the first sentence of the composition? The last sentence of the introduction? Someplace in between? There is no one answer to that question. The best location for the thesis depends on your topic. You could announce your main point at the very beginning of your composition; however, you'll often find that preparing the reader with some background information is more effective. Readers may need some information about the topic or issue before they can understand your idea. If that's the case, the thesis is more appropriately stated later in the introduction.

Establish Tone

Tone is defined as the author's attitude toward his subject. In other words, tone describes the mood the writer was in when he or she composed the paper, a mood that transfers onto the page. The different kinds of tone include serious/scholarly, silly, humorous/lighthearted, sarcastic, angry, nostalgic, sentimental, and pleading. Writers can communicate a particular feeling about a topic through their choice of words and writing style. For instance, to create a scholarly, academic flavor, use more sophisticated vocabulary and complex sentence structures (see Chapter 3). Also, refrain from using slang or humor. In addition, distance yourself from the reader by not addressing him or her directly ("you") or referring to yourself ("I"). For example:

> In a statutory corporate acquisition, the stockholders of the acquired corporation are entitled to receive adequate consideration for their stock. This right is protected by state appraisal statutes, pursuant to which stockholders who are unhappy with the terms of the acquisition can exercise their dissenters' rights and thereby receive cash equal to the "fair value" of their shares.
>
> Stockholders of the acquired corporation also are protected by common-law fiduciary duties, which ensure that they receive a "fair price" for their shares. The term "fair price" grew out of the common law of corporate fiduciary duties as applied in affiliated acquisitions, in which a court is required to consider fair price as a part of its evaluation of the acquisition under the intrinsic fairness test. Even non-affiliated, arm's length acquisitions, however, generate a fair price requirement, as the directors of Trans Union Corporation learned in *Smith v. Van Gorkom*. Fundamentally, the Trans Union directors in *Van Gorkom* failed their common-law fiduciary duty because they did not take reasonable steps to ensure that the stockholders of Trans Union received a fair price for their stock in an arm's length transaction.[1]

The academic tone of this opening is created by long, formal sentences and sophisticated vocabulary.

For a more lighthearted or conversational flavor, you could include one or more kinds of humor (exaggeration, understatement, wordplay, irony, or satire) in your opening. Your style would tend to be more informal, including slang words or personal anecdotes and opinions. For example, this opening paragraph comes from a career advice web site:

> An anonymous writer once noted that "on the plains of hesitation lie the blackened bones of countless millions, who at the dawn of victory, sat down to rest, and resting, died."
>
> A rather chilling image, yes, but one that nonetheless embodies a principle every professional should take to heart. I may not be the

[1]Rutherford B. Campbell Jr., "Fair Value and Fair Price in Corporate Acquisitions," *North Carolina Law Review* (November 1999): 102–103. Copyright 1999 by the North Carolina Law Review Assoc. Reprinted with permission.

sharpest knife in the drawer, but if I can understand the implication, then you should as well: without an objective or goal in mind, you can't control your own destiny.

To be fair, goal-setting isn't easy. If it were as easy as following the directions on a box of cake mix, for example, then we'd all be as successful as Stephen Covey.[2] I've personally made countless attempts to motivate myself to change, from late night bouts with one of Covey's wonder tools to watching personal development "advertorials" on TV, all to no avail. (Perhaps the best thing I ever did was to marry a "Type A" individual who's made it a personal quest to coax goal-oriented behavior out of me. There's nothing quite like a stick in the rump every so often to keep you on track.)

I don't purport to know any universal methods of attaining self-actualization—for that, you'll need to consult the experts—but I can offer a few suggestions on how to get off your duff.[3]

The informal tone of this passage is created with the use of personal examples and humorous slang expressions such as *stick in the rump* and *get off your duff.*

To achieve an angry tone, choose words that convey anger. For example:

What would you call someone who unscrupulously cheats a helpless 75-year-old widow? Thief? Criminal? Shark? Vulture? When elderly Elsie Duncan, who lives on Social Security and a small pension, needed cash to fix the roof on her house, she was duped by a "predatory lender," a company who loaned her money based on her home equity. They pounced on her. They talked her into an obscenely high interest rate. They persuaded her to agree to excessive loan fees that destroyed her finances and mired her in debt. These unethical practices must stop. Our state needs a law to control the greedy jackals who would do this to a poor, old woman.

This writer is clearly annoyed. He communicates this irritation with short, clipped sentences and with many deliberately chosen, emotionally loaded words—such as *cheats*, *duped*, and *greedy jackals*—that clearly reveal his strong feelings.

Different tones are appropriate for different writing tasks. A letter to a member of Congress, complaining about lack of funding for school equipment, should be serious and formal. A humorous tone would be ineffective in such a letter. A memo to your supervisor requesting an adjustment to your work schedule should not reveal sarcasm or anger.

Regardless of the tone you wish to convey, establish that attitude in your opening paragraph(s) and stick to it throughout the entire composition. If you begin with a serious, no-nonsense approach to your subject, don't suddenly switch to a humorous approach in the middle of your paper. The expectations readers form about the writer's attitudes are based on the opening. You risk confusing or frustrating those readers if other parts of your composition fail to fulfill those expectations.

Interest the Reader

In today's hectic, fast-paced world, readers are busy and easily distracted by the many things competing for their attention. Good writing, therefore, must capture and hold readers' interest from the very beginning to entice them to

[2]Stephen Covey is the author of best-selling books about success, such as *Seven Habits of Highly Effective People.*
[3]Ken White, "Setting Goals: Advice from a Recovering Lump on a Log," *Achieve E-zine*, http://www.careerbuilder.com/content/achieve/archive/myc/management/jan_goals.html.

read and concentrate on a whole document. And that, of course, has to happen if the writing is to achieve its purpose.

So how can you pique your readers' curiosity and make them want to know more about your ideas? You can include in your opening one or more of several effective attention-getting techniques: tell a story, ask questions, establish the subject's significance, begin with a quotation, use contrast, give an example, explain your general topic, or surprise the reader.

Never begin a paper with phrases such as *"In this paper I am going to . . ."* or *"This report will prove that. . . . "* Readers will be yawning before they finish your first paragraph.

Tell a Story. Everyone loves a good story. Narratives, real or fictional, generate immediate interest in a subject. Therefore, stories effectively draw the reader into your topic. For example, read this opening from an article about deer hunting.

> One of Cliff Shelby's most memorable hunts involves a deer that walked away startled but unscathed. Earlier this season, the veteran Arkansas hunter closely followed a pair of does through the woods for nearly a quarter of a mile with muzzleloader in hand before approaching one so close that he was able to slap it on the rump. The surprised deer instantly bounded off into the undergrowth after an encounter that was undoubtedly puzzling to her. Shelby did it to prove a point—that you can successfully stalk deer afoot.[4]

Story openings engage the reader's interest by creating a scene that includes people participating in suspenseful or intriguing events.

Another example comes from a letter:

> It's 9:32 P.M., and you're in your office. You're at your computer, frantically typing an important report that you must deliver to a client by 8:00 A.M. the next day. With a sigh of relief, you finally finish it, save it, and then click the "Print" button. The inkjet printer starts to whirr, and you stand it front of it wearily, ready to grab the document. To your horror, the pages come out blank. The ink cartridge in your printer is empty.
>
> Do you have a replacement cartridge on hand? No, you postponed buying one because they are so expensive. You start to panic. What will you do now?
>
> If you were a customer of Ink Refills, Inc., this would never happen to you again. Our company provides previously used cartridges filled with high-quality ink at *half* the cost of new cartridges. We also provide bottles of ink that allow you to refill your cartridges yourself in emergency situations. Add your name to our growing list of satisfied customers, and you'll be able to afford to have on hand the supplies that will allow you to finish the job.

Whether your narrative is true, fictional, or hypothetical, all story openers should adhere to two important guidelines. First, they should be brief. Resist the urge to include a lot of descriptive details. Instead, concentrate on the plot (the events in the story). This story should not become your focus; instead, it should introduce your paper's focus. Second, the story should clearly illustrate or relate to your composition's main idea. In other words, it should have something to do with the topic you'll discuss.

[4]Tim Tucker, "All-but-lost Art of Stalking Adds More Thrill to the Hunt," *Outdoors* (January 2000).

Ask Questions.   Another technique for arousing your readers' interest is to begin by asking one or more questions that get them thinking about your topic. This method encourages readers to directly participate by mentally answering those questions. For example, the following opening is from a newsletter article:

Do you remember the last time you received a poorly written memo, letter or e-mail? What was your impression of the writer? According to Joseph Dobrian, author of *Business Writing Skills* (AMACOM, 1998), few things can damage one's professional image as much as a letter or memo marred by grammatical and typographical mistakes. Dobrian says that the main principle of effective writing boils down to three simple words: brevity, precision, and clarity. However, he offers these additional guidelines to improve your business writing.[5]

A second example is from a brochure advertising a stress management seminar:

Do pressures, deadlines, and difficult people leave you feeling frazzled? Do you suffer from low energy and fatigue during the day? Do you worry about your job when you're not at work?

Today, many professional women suffer from the anxiety and burnout of overstress. The results: mistakes, muddled thinking, even depression. Here's an opportunity for you to gain energy, confidence, and enthusiasm—and put your life and career in balance.[6]

Follow two guidelines when beginning with questions. First, keep each question brief and to the point. Second, don't ask too many questions. Readers are not reading your paper to be quizzed. So ask a few key questions to get them interested. Then move on to providing some answers.

Establish the Significance of Your Subject.   Another effective way to get your readers interested involves convincing them that your subject is important. Present to readers the data or statistics that reveal why this topic is significant and worthy of their attention. You can achieve this by stating who is affected, and where and how. For example:

As business people, we know our time is worth a lot. But do you realize just how valuable those few moments of spare time throughout the day are? If you make $50,000 each year, then 20 minutes a day for every working day of the year is worth $2,043 a year. None of us wants to throw that kind of money away.

You can make use of these pieces of time, this "scrap time," if you choose to. All it really takes is some forethought and planning.[7]

Another example comes from a newsletter for parents.

Sitting down together to eat does more than just feed the body. It also nourishes your family's soul. Need more convincing? Just consider this: A recent research study of more than 270,000 children in 600 communities found that eating together as a family is one of the factors that helps kids

---

[5]"How to Look Good on Paper," *The Office Professional* (October 1999): 1.
[6]Career Track, *Stress Solutions Workshop for Women* brochure, 2.
[7]Rebecca L. Morgan, "Salvage Scrap Time," iVillage Career, http://www.ivillage.com/content/ 0,1625,1300~43,00.html.

succeed in school and stay out of trouble. At family meals, parents can offer support, communicate with their children, and share advice. All three are important developmental assets for a child. Here are ten steps to making mealtime more rewarding.[8]

When establishing your topic's significance with data or facts, make sure your information comes from reputable, accurate sources. You will want to acknowledge those sources to increase your own credibility.

Begin with a Quotation.   A quotation is another way to get your reader interested in your ideas. The best quote is a short, clever, and thought-provoking saying, often from a famous or noteworthy person. For instance:

Jack Stack, author of *The Great Game of Business*, is famous for transforming the rusty old International Harvester into Springfield Remanufacturing Corporation by turning employees into fully involved team members. He had this to say about why teams are essential to organizational success: "You can sometimes fool the fans, but you can never fool the players."
Here are two strategies that players—that is, team members—can use to keep themselves energized, healthy, and productive at work.[9]

Another example comes from a memorandum:

Hippocrates said that "a wise man should consider that health is the greatest of human blessings." Holden Tile believes that our employees' mental and physical well-being is important, so we are committed to offering you opportunities to increase your fitness and reduce stress. Therefore, we recently established a corporate membership at the Maguire Wellness Center. We want to encourage all of you to take advantage of this excellent new employee benefit.

An effective quotation is always related to your topic. It either concisely summarizes your point or leads to that main idea. When offering a quote, always identify the speaker in order to properly credit that person.

Use Contrast.   When we contrast two things, we examine their differences. This can be an appropriate method for getting the reader wondering about your topic. One type of contrast explains changes over time; in other words, you note the differences between the past and the present. The following example from an article employs this type of contrast.

It wasn't long ago that being a stay-at-home Mom, or a Mr. Mom, would damage your career. Fortunately, this is no longer the case. Flexibility is becoming the norm, and as the '90s draw to a close, businesses are placing a higher priority on results than on face time. Smart companies are finding creative ways to conduct business by utilizing the talents of non-traditional workers. Some people even claim that you can advance your career while working from home on a part-time basis. But if you want to make the most of a flexible arrangement, you'll need to learn a few things first.[10]

[8]"Why Mealtime Matters: 10 Steps to Low-Stress, High-Reward Mealtimes," *Tots Tribune Newsletter*, Burke County Public Schools Family Connections, Morganton, North Carolina (Spring 1999): 4.
[9]Barbara Reinhold, "Making Work Better Through Teaming," http://www.midcareer.monster.com/articles/team/teaming.html.
[10]Pat Boer, "Making Flexible Work Arrangements Work For You," http://www.midcareer.monster.com/articles/flexible.html.

Another type of contrast explains two different views, opinions, attitudes, or perspectives:

> Technology is the best friend of every supervisor and manager today. It is one of the critical survival tools for the new millennium. Technology enables individuals and entire organizations to work smarter, faster, and more productively than ever before.
>
> Whether you work in a factory, shop or office, technology now links your workers with counterparts around the world. It levels the playing field by giving everyone the power of instant access to information. Without up-to-date technology, no workforce today can keep up or catch up with the competition.
>
> Unfortunately, this same technology can also alienate, intimidate and frustrate employees and customers alike. It can even create a sterile or hostile work environment by putting a premium on uninspired performance and a cookie-cutter mentality. As the 21st century commences, more and more leaders are discovering there can be a downside to today's love affair with technology. Can a workplace have too much technology? It's a question seldom asked. The answer is, "You bet!" Following are some of the most common signals technology on the job has gotten out of hand.[11]

Contrast may also involve revealing differences between the imagined and the real, or between expectations and actual experiences. For example, you could introduce a report about your tour of a new facility by describing what you had expected. Then you could go on to explain what you actually found.

Give an Example. When you give an example, you describe how the experiences of one particular person illustrate your main idea. Like the story method, this technique immediately engages your readers' interest by presenting them with a real person rather than an abstract idea:

> Bruce Craddock spent what he thought was an idyllic weekend fishing in a stream surrounded by tall grass. But within five days of his trip, Craddock experienced chills and a fever so severe he couldn't get out of bed.
>
> "I could barely lift my head off the pillow, I felt so bad," he recalls. At first, Craddock believed he had the flu—until he spotted a strange rash on his leg that slowly started to resemble a bull's eye.
>
> "I knew then it was more than just the flu," he says.
>
> Craddock's symptoms all pointed to Lyme disease, a potentially dangerous bacterial infection spread to humans by tiny deer ticks or black-legged ticks—often no bigger than a pinhead—that live in wooded and grassy areas. The disease initially mimics the flu but can result in arthritis and neurological problems if not detected and treated early.[12]

Still another example comes from a memorandum.

> Last year, my family and I could not afford a vacation, but our company policy states that I would lose any vacation days I did not use before the end of the year. So I took days off for no reason. This year, my family was presented with an opportunity to travel to Africa with a group from our church. We could have afforded the trip, but we were forced to turn down this offer because I did not have the necessary three

[11]Robert D. Ramsey, "How Much Technology Is Too Much?" *Supervision* (January 2000): 3. Reprinted by permission of © National Research Bureau; P.O. Box. 1, Burlington, Iowa 52601-0001

[12]"Lyme Time," *Health Scene,* Valdese General Hospital, Valdese, North Carolina (Summer 1999): 6.

weeks of vacation time. If I could have carried last year's vacation time over to this year, I could have participated in a rewarding and memorable travel experience with my children. My situation illustrates the deficiency in our current vacation policy, and I'd like to ask that you consider revising it to allow us to accumulate vacation days from year to year. A more flexible vacation policy should benefit the company with happier, more productive, more loyal employees.

When giving an example, stick to the details relevant to your main idea. Resist the urge to include information, however interesting, that does not relate to your topic.

Explain Your General Topic and Narrow to Your Specific Point.   Often the reader wants to learn more about how your main idea relates to a broader issue or topic. So you might begin a paper with a discussion of a general subject, gradually narrowing to your specific point about one aspect of this subject. Using this technique, you orient readers by showing them the "big picture" before zeroing in on one focal point. This first example comes from a newsletter article:

> There are many different definitions of success. For some people, success is measured by how high they rise in the corporate ranks. Others measure success by the size of their bank account or their accumulation of material goods. Still others gauge success in terms of relationships and personal satisfaction.
>
> Whatever your definition of success, it is likely that those whom you consider to be successful share many abilities and characteristics. Jeffrey J. Mayer, author of *Success Is a Journey: 7 Steps to Achieving Success in the Business of Life* (McGraw-Hill, 1999), identified some qualities shared by people who have succeeded in a wide variety of fields and endeavors.[13]

A second example is from a memorandum.

> This past fall, our company was involved in two very successful relief projects for the victims of Hurricane Floyd in eastern North Carolina. Those who assisted flood victims, along with the flood victims themselves, have expressed deep gratitude for our efforts. As the holiday season nears, we wondered what else we could do to help. We asked for your ideas, and the Engineering Department submitted a proposal that we decided to adopt as our company's charitable holiday project. This proposal involves sponsoring five needy families who lost their homes and possessions in the disaster.

This approach is often used in business documents such as memos and reports, where you must remind busy readers of an overall situation or concept before they can understand your specific idea. For example, the following opening begins another memorandum.

> A little over a year ago, a copier machine was installed in the first-floor workroom for the convenience of staff in that area. That copier has malfunctioned regularly, and a repairman has had to service it on a weekly basis. Overuse of this machine is causing the regular malfunctions, so we will need to implement some new guidelines for its use.

[13]"Learning from Others," *The Office Professional* (October 1999): 4.

Surprise, Shock or Startle the Reader.   Perhaps one of the best ways to pique your readers' immediate interest is to surprise, startle, or shock them. You can achieve this in several ways: with an attention-getting quotation, with startling statistics, or with a fascinating or unusual fact. The following example comes from a memorandum.

Forty percent of employees at Wilson Ferguson, Inc. recently confessed to feeling "out of place" at work either daily, weekly, or monthly. Fifty percent believe that being female inhibits advancement at our company. This startling information was revealed by the Diversity Opinion Survey we asked everyone to complete this past February. The Ethnic and Gender Diversity Task Force designed this survey to reveal attitudes and issues such as racism, prejudice, and discrimination that affect the working atmosphere at our organization. While the majority of you report being satisfied with the climate here at Wilson Ferguson, the survey did reveal several areas of concern that we plan to address in an upcoming series of diversity workshops.

Another memo also begins with a startling fact.

One office worker in the United States uses an average of 12,000 sheets of paper per year. To save money and to do our part to protect natural resources, we want to make sure we recycle all of the paper we use on the job. So we remind everyone to discard used paper in the recycling cans placed beside each desk.

Combining the Methods.   A writer can combine different methods for stimulating interest, in order to appeal to a variety of readers. This excerpt from an article, from an online career-development journal, provides a good example.

Looking for a job in a field in which you have no experience? If so, you'll run into a classic Catch-22:[14] You can't get a job without experience, but you can't gain experience without a job.

Close to 70% of Fortune 500 companies balk at hiring people without relevant experience. The training or reschooling of employees isn't necessary when the company has 200 résumés from people who have experience. So how do you get some experience?

There are several options for people looking to get started in new fields—from first time job seekers to those looking to change career tracks.[15]

That opening paragraph combines two different attention-getting techniques by first asking questions, then providing statistics that establish the topic's significance.

Another combination opening is from a letter.

Our state employees' newsletter quotes our governor as saying that "state employees are our most valuable resource. Thanks to their devoted service, our schools are open and our prisons are secure." I am one of

[14]The term *Catch-22* comes from the Joseph Heller novel of the same name. It refers to a no-win situation.
[15]Liz Schmid, "Catch-22: How To Get Experience When You Don't Already Have It," *Achieve E-zine,* http://www.careerbuilder.com/content/achieve/myc/choosing/apr_catch.html.

those state employees the governor was commending, but lately, I have felt anything but "valuable." This past March, in the course of my duties as Correctional Officer at the Morgan Correctional Institute, I was trying to break up a fight between two inmates when one of them charged me and threw me to the floor. I required spinal surgery and a two-week hospital stay for my injuries, and six months later, I am still undergoing physical therapy. I hope to return to work as soon as I am able, but I'm not sure I can continue to serve as a Correctional Officer. We have always endured too many stresses—including potential injury, high turnover and understaffing, and inmates' disrespect—in exchange for inadequate compensation. It's time to substantially increase Correctional Officers' salaries to better match the stress they face on the job.

This interesting opening paragraph has combined a quotation with an example and narration.

<table>
<tr><td>PRACTICE 8.1
Writing Openings</td><td>Each of the following paragraphs fails to achieve all four objectives for effective openings. Mark the needed revisions, in the list that follows each paragraph.</td></tr>
</table>

A. Speech pathologists use the Goldman Fristoe Test of Articulation to determine a child's speech therapy needs. This test involves showing the child a series of pictures and monitoring how he articulates certain sounds. It has been widely used since 1986; however, the test's creators recently revised it to suit a wider variety of cultural backgrounds.

☒ Add a technique to interest the reader.
☒ Add a clear thesis statement.
☒ Add more background information.

How would you describe the tone of this opening? *academic/*

professional, formal

B. I am writing this letter to complain about the ridiculous construction on the interstate in Washington County. Since construction began, it has been nothing but a headache to residents in our area. Motorists are sick of being forced to deal with blocked lanes, traffic jams, and accidents while they watch their tax dollars being wasted. I know you're probably a busy person, but hear me out. We are frustrated, and we want this nonsense to end.

☒ Add a technique to interest the reader.
☒ Add a clear thesis statement.
☒ Add more background information.

How would you describe the tone of this opening? *angry*

C. Pregnancy is a beautiful and enriching experience that changes a woman's life forever. I have researched the topic of pregnancy and would like to present an overview of people's concerns about pregnancy. I hope the reader will understand why prenatal care is crucial. Also, I hope my reader will understand possible complications, as well as what happens during labor and delivery. Hopefully, my paper can educate anyone who has questions about pregnancy.

☒ Add a technique to interest the reader.

☒ Add a clear thesis statement.

☒ Add more background information.

How would you describe the tone of this opening? *pleading and*

uncertain

D. Children afflicted with visual dyslexia view letters incorrectly. They do not suffer from vision problems; rather, they fail to accurately interpret letters, often seeing them upside down or backwards. As a result, the confusion and frustration caused by this condition create numerous difficulties for students in classroom settings. Thus, educators must use varied and appropriate methods of instruction and discipline in order to help these students overcome their disability and process information successfully.

☒ Add a technique to interest the reader.

☐ Add a clear thesis statement.

☐ Add more background information.

How would you describe the tone of this opening? *academic/*

professional, formal

E. Does your boss buzz around you all day like an annoying fly you'd like to swat? You know what you're doing on the job, but if your boss won't stay out of your hair, she doesn't trust you to work on your own. If she thinks you need constant hand-holding, the two of you are probably not on the same wave length when it comes to communication. This problem won't go away until you do something.

☐ Add a technique to interest the reader.

☒ Add a clear thesis statement.

☐ Add more background information.

How would you describe the tone of this opening? *casual, humorous*

Choose 3 of the following thesis statements and write two different opening paragraphs for each, using different techniques for interesting the reader. Try to use several of the eight different techniques discussed in this chapter. *Answers will vary.*

Techniques for Interesting the Reader
- Tell a story
- Ask questions
- Establish the significance of your subject
- Begin with a quotation
- Use contrast
- Give an example
- Explain your general topic and narrow to your specific point
- Surprise, shock or startle the reader

---

1. I am the most qualified candidate for the _____ position.

2. The hairstyles, makeup, and clothing you choose can make or break your career.

3. You can change your family's chaotic weekday mornings into a calmer, less stressful routine.

4. _____ is a sport now gaining more popularity in our area.

5. Stress management, a healthy diet, and regular exercise are the three pillars of an active immune system.

6. This company should offer a college tuition reimbursement benefit for employees.

7. I nominate my co-worker _____ for the Employee of the Month award.

TEST YOUR UNDERSTANDING

1. What are the four purposes of a composition's opening?

   To give background information, state the thesis, establish tone, and stimulate

   readers' interest.

2. What are two types of background information?

   Historical detail, description of a current situation, explanation of a topic's

   relevance or significance, definitions of terminology.

3. Where in your opening should you state your thesis?

   The best location depends on the topic and the opening technique, but most

   thesis statements are effective when placed near or at the end of the opening.

4. What is *tone*? Give two examples of different types of tone.

   Tone is the author's attitude toward the subject. Examples will vary: serious, silly,

   sarcastic, and so on.

5. What are the eight techniques for getting readers interested in your topic and thesis?

   Tell a story, ask questions, establish the significance of the subject, begin with a

   quotation, use contrast, give an example, explain the general topic and narrow

   to a specific point, or surprise the reader.

WEB ACTIVITY: **Leadership Potential**

If you have never had a leadership role, you may wonder how effective you'd be in positions of authority and decision making. If you have acted as a leader, you may have wondered if your leadership skills could be improved. You can take an online quiz to determine your potential to be a good leader.

1. Go to the Leadership Test at http://www.queendom.com/leadership.html.
2. Follow the directions to complete the test, and click on *Score*.
3. Print the results of your test.
4. What is your overall score? Do you agree with these results? Why or why not?

GROUP PROJECT AND WRITING ACTIVITIES

For these next activities, you'll be focusing again on the needed improvement to your college campus your group selected in Chapter 7.

With your group, use one or more invention strategies to generate possible solutions to the problem on your campus. Record as many ideas as possible in the space below.

With your group, select one of the solutions you generated in the last activity. Together, use an invention strategy to generate more details and information about this solution. Who would handle it? How? When? Where? How much would it cost? Record your ideas in the space below.

On your own, interview someone who could either help implement the solution you chose or who has had direct experience with that type of solution. For example, if the problem you selected is inefficient registration procedures and the solution is new computer software, you could interview a computer company representative who sells that software, or you could interview a student or staff member at another college who has actually used the software. See Appendix A for more information about conducting successful interviews. Record details from your interview in the space below.

_____

_____

_____

_____

_____

_____

_____

_____

_____

_____

_____

_____

_____

_____

_____

_____

Collaborate with your group to compose a detailed description of your proposed solution. Focus only on the solution, thoroughly explaining _who_ would implement it, _how_, _when_, and _where_ it would be done, and _how much_ it would cost. (Use separate paper, if you need extra space.)

_____

_____

_____

_____

_____

_____

_____

_____

_____

_____

_____

_____

_____

_____

_____

_____

_____

_____

_____

_____

Write the opening paragraph of a memo to your college president that will explain your proposed solution. Use one or more of the opening techniques discussed in this chapter.

READINGS

Do you hope to rise to management or administrative levels in your career field? What do managers and administrators do during a normal workday?

The following article, written by three business experts, describes a manager's typical day and defines several essential skills effective leaders must possess.

As you read this article, circle every word that's unfamiliar to you. Look it up and write the meaning in the margin. Put an exclamation point (!) next to any sentence or paragraph you find especially interesting. Put a question mark (?) next to any sentence or paragraph you don't understand.

What It Takes to Become a Successful Manager Today
William M. Pride, Robert J. Hughes, and Jack R. Kapoor

1 Everyone hears stories about the corporate elite who make salaries in excess of $250,000 a year, travel to and from work in chauffeur-driven limousines, and enjoy lucrative pension plans that provide for a luxurious lifestyle even after they retire. Although management can obviously be a very rewarding career, what is not so obvious is the amount of time and hard work that managers invest to achieve the impressive salaries and perks that may come with the job.

A Day in the Life of a Manager

2 Organizations don't pay managers to look good behind an expensive wood desk. Organizations pay for performance. Managers coordinate the organization's resources. They also perform the four basic management functions: planning, organizing, leading and motivating, and controlling. And managers make decisions and then implement and evaluate those decisions. This heavy workload requires that managers work long hours, and most don't get paid overtime for work in excess of forty hours a week. Typically, the number of hours increases as managers move up the corporate ladder.

3 Make no mistake about it: today's managers work hard in a tough and demanding job. The pace is hectic. Managers spend a great deal of time talking with people on an individual basis. The purpose of these conversations is usually to obtain information or to resolve problems. (Remember, a problem can be either negative or positive and is a discrepancy between an actual condition and a desired condition.) In addition to talking to individuals, a manager often spends a large part of the workday in meetings with other managers and employees. In most cases, the purpose of the meetings—some brief and some lengthy—is to resolve problems. And if the work is not completed by the end of the day, the manager usually packs unfinished tasks in a briefcase and totes them home to work on that night.

Personal Skills Required for Success

4 To be successful in today's competitive business environment, you must possess a number of different skills. Some of these are technical, conceptual, and interpersonal skills. But you also need to develop some "personal" skills in order to be successful. For starters, oral and written communication skills, computer skills, and critical thinking skills may give you the edge in getting an entry-level management position.

William M. Pride et al., "What It Takes to Become a Successful Manager Today," *Business* (Boston, Houghton Mifflin, 1999), pp.157–159. Copyright © 1999 by Houghton Mifflin Company. Reprinted with permission.

5   1. *Oral communication skills.* Because a large part of a manager's day is spent conversing with other managers and employees, the ability to speak *and* listen is critical for success. For example, oral communication skills are used when a manager must make sales presentations, conduct interviews, perform employee evaluations, and hold press conferences.

6   2. *Written communication skills.* Managers must be able to write. The manager's ability to prepare letters, memos, sales reports, and other written documents may spell the difference between success and failure.

7   3. *Computer skills.* Today most managers have at their fingertips a computer monitor that is linked to the organization's larger computer system. Most employers do not expect you to be an expert computer programmer, but they do expect that you should know how to use a computer to prepare written and statistical reports and communication with other managers and employees in the organization.

8   4. *Critical thinking skills.* Employers expect managers to use the steps for effective managerial decision making. They also expect managers to use their critical thinking skills to ensure that they identify the problem correctly, generate reasonable alternatives, and select the "best" alternative to solve an organization's problem.

The Importance of Education and Experience

9 Although most experts agree that management skills must be learned on the job, the concepts that you learn in business courses lay the foundation for a successful career. In addition, successful completion of college courses or obtaining a degree can open doors to job interviews and career advancement.

10   Most applicants who enter the world of work do not have a wealth of work experience. And yet there are methods that you can use to "beef up" your résumé and to capitalize on the work experience you do have. First, obtain summer jobs that will provide opportunities to learn about the field you wish to enter when you finish your formal education. If you choose carefully, part-time jobs during the school year can also provide work experience that other job applicants may not have. (By the way, many colleges and universities sponsor cooperative work/school programs that give students college credit for job experience.) Even with a solid academic background and relevant work experience, many would-be managers still find it difficult to land the "right" job. Often they start in an entry-level position to gain more experience and eventually—after years on the job—reach that "ideal" job. Perseverance does pay!

11   We include this practical advice not to frighten you but to provide a real-world view of what a manager's job is like. Once you know what is required of managers today—and how competitive the race is for the top jobs—you can decide whether a career in management is right for you.

RESPONDING TO THE READING

1. According to the authors, what are a manager's primary duties on the job?

   Planning, organizing, leading/motivating, and controlling.

2. What personal skills must an effective manager possess?

   Oral communication skills, written communication skills, computer skills, critical

   thinking skills.

3. Think of a time when a professional, social, or civic group to which you belonged faced a problem. Describe the problem and then explain how you, the group's leader, or the entire group used critical thinking skills to solve that problem.

   Answers will vary.

4. What is the authors' advice for gaining valuable work experience?

   While in college, choose summer and part-time jobs that help you gain experience.

5. In the opening paragraph, what technique do the authors use to interest the reader?

   Contrast.

BUILDING VOCABULARY

Although we sometimes alter their spellings, the English language has absorbed many words directly from other languages. For example, the foregoing article contains three words we adopted from French: *chauffeur* (paragraph 1), *limousine* (paragraph 1), and *résumé* (paragraph 10).

Look up each of the following words in your dictionary and identify the language that gave us the word. When your dictionary states that the word progressed through several different languages, identify the language whose version of the word is closest to the English version.

1. kindergarten   *German*

2. yankee   *Dutch*

(continued)

**BUILDING
VOCABULARY**
continued

3. savvy   *Spanish*

4. prairie   *French*

5. semester   *German*

6. cockroach   *Spanish*

7. raccoon   *Native American*

8. karma   *Sanscrit*

9. tattoo   *Polynesian*

What are the essential qualities of a successful leader? How do effective managers motivate employees and win their loyalty?

The next article, written by Bruce Spotleson of the *Las Vegas Business Press*, is a parable (a story that teaches a lesson) about leadership in the modern workplace.

As you read this article, circle every word that's unfamiliar to you. Look it up and write the meaning in the margin. Put an exclamation point (!) next to any sentence or paragraph you find especially interesting. Put a question mark (?) next to any sentence or paragraph you don't understand.

Finding Wisdom on Mount Potosi

Bruce Spotleson

1   I had been hiking on Mount Potosi in search of Chief Baccarat, the famous Yaqui oracle who resides in a cave there. When I finally came upon him, the old man was brewing herbal tea over a small fire, his white ponytail waving in the breeze.

2   "Welcome," he said, nodding. "The wind whispered that you were coming. You must have had Mexican food at lunch."

3   His omniscience once again amazed me.

4   "We live in turbulent times," I told the venerable sage. "Let me explain my challenge. We live in a place in which there is great turnover in our tribes. And it is very difficult to find quality warriors to pick up the spears of those who have gone. Although many are called for interviews, only a few are chosen. So, all-knowing one, I have come to seek your guidance. Can you show me the way?"

5   "Things are as they always have been," he responded calmly. "You see, my son, other than the ridiculous price you now must pay for a necktie, nothing ever changes. I cannot help you with the task of building your tribe, but I know you must treat them properly once you have them assembled. And on this I will speak."

Bruce Spotleson, "Finding Wisdom on Mount Potosi," *Las Vegas Business Press* (Feb. 16, 1998), 4. Reprinted by permission.

6   That having been said, the respected sage began to chant loudly. His eyes closed tight and he lapsed into a trance, speaking in measured words.

7   "Your minions must of course be taught, trained, supported. But since you spend so many of your waking hours at work together, it is also important to be able to counsel them. People today bring all sorts of troubles to the office with them. Of course, you should steer clear of any problems related to sex or religion. For in these matters you will not help."

8   "You must also have a desire to initiate activity," he continued. "People can bring you all sorts of good ideas, but nothing happens with them until their leader acts. They will be watching to see what you do with their suggestions. The wise chief says 'yes' very quickly to a good idea, but says 'no' very slowly to a poor idea. This protects the self-esteem of the members of the tribe, and avoids bad karma for yourself.

9   "You must have a general interest in improving things. You must believe in your heart that no product or service is ever good enough. Even your own ideas can be improved on. It will sometimes be hard for you to accept this, my cynical friend. But, yes, even the chief's ideas can be improved on."

10   "You must always have self-confidence in your abilities and goals. People don't want to be led by anyone who is wishy-washy, insecure or indecisive. If you have these unfortunate weaknesses, either keep them to yourself or volunteer for a line position.

11   "You must be able to inspire teamwork. This is tricky in your village these days, because so many of your tribes seem to always be changing—new faces all the time. But teams need time to find harmony. And you must provide the patience and stability in their world.

12   "You must be skilled in either oral or written communication. There is no way of getting around this—you need to be able to express your thoughts clearly to your tribe. Take a writing class or join a Toastmasters Club if you need to.

13   "But you also must be able to communicate to the tribe spontaneously. Share your honest opinions at meetings. Share yourself on a more individual basis.

14   "Remember that you must always be objective when there is a dispute among members of your tribe. Remind your warring peoples that the people on the other side of the building work as hard and care as much as their own unit does.

15   "A chief must always know his or her own strengths and weaknesses. Go with your strengths, but know which members of your tribe can supplement your weaknesses."

16   At this point, his eyes opened and he inhaled deeply. I envied his bliss.

17   "Finally, find a credible and tactful way of conveying to your tribe that change is a constant these days, and they will need to be able to roll with it. And ambiguity is a fact of your secular world. Tell them it is nothing personal or unique to your tribe. It is just the way the world is in the new millennium. Now, go in peace."

18   On this, I thanked him for the free advice. His silent smile bade me farewell.

19   When I returned to the office, I found a fax waiting on my machine. It was an invoice from a company called Baccarat Enterprises, with a scribbled note along the bottom.

20   "One more thing I forgot to mention," the oracle wrote. "There is no such thing as free advice."

RESPONDING TO THE READING

1. The author compares today's workplace to a unsettled world populated by warring tribes led by chiefs. What are some of the characteristics of these "tribes"?

   High turnover; few quality warriors capable of being effective leaders.

   _____

2. Choose one of the oracle's qualities of an effective leader; then think of someone you've worked for or worked with who demonstrated it. Briefly describe an incident in which the person exhibited this quality.

   Answers will vary. _____

   _____

   _____

3. Do you agree with all of the oracle's advice about leadership? Agree or disagree with each of the following three points. *Answers will vary.*

   Good leaders must counsel their employees and help them with their troubles.

   _____

   _____

   Good leaders must share themselves with their employees.

   _____

   _____

   A wise leader says "no" slowly to bad ideas in order to protect employees' self-esteem.

   _____

   _____

4. Because this whole article is a story, it does not begin with a separate opening. However, the writer still hooks the reader's interest in the first few sentences. How does he achieve this?

   He uses interesting descriptive detail, dialogue, and humor. _____

BUILDING VOCABULARY

When you look up an unfamiliar word in the dictionary, you'll often find several different meanings and variations for that one word. You have to look at the word's *context* (the other words, phrases, and sentences surrounding the word) to determine which definition applies.

Also, you may need to determine the word's part of speech in the sentence. Many words can function as different parts of speech (the word *right,* for instance, can be a noun, a verb, an adjective, or an adverb), so you'll have to observe how the word is being used before you can decide which definition applies.

For example, the word *sage* can be either an adjective or a noun, and the noun form has several different meanings.

"We live in turbulent times," I told the venerable *sage.* (paragraph 4)

In this sentence, the word is a noun, but the noun form has two different meanings: "a person venerated for wisdom," or "a plant used as an herb." The words that surround *sage* in the example sentence help you conclude that it refers to a person venerated for wisdom.

The following sentences all come from the article you have just read. Look up each of the italicized words in a dictionary and determine which definition best describes how it is being used.

1. We live in a place in which there is great *turnover* in our tribes. (paragraph 4)

   change in workers hired to do a job

2. His eyes closed tight and he lapsed into a trance, speaking in *measured* words. (paragraph 6)

   careful, restrained

3. Your *minions* must of course be taught, trained, supported. (paragraph 7)

   subordinates

4. Of course, you should *steer* clear of any problems related to sex or religion. (paragraph 7)

   maneuver or guide

5. You must be able to *inspire* teamwork. (paragraph 11)

   stimulate to action

6. There is no way of getting around this—you need to be able to *express* your thoughts clearly to your tribe. (paragraph 12)

   state

7. Go with your strengths, but know which members of your tribe can *supplement* your weaknesses. (paragraph 15)

   add to, in order to complete or to make up for a deficiency

9 Effective Closings

PROFESSIONAL PROFILE
Russell Barnes, Police Division Commander

Commander Russell Barnes is a married father of three children who supervises seven sergeants and forty-five officers and civilian employees in a large metropolitan police department. He oversees patrol and property crime investigations, and he also commands the S.W.A.T. Team. His position requires him to write a variety of documents, including memos, reports, letters, e-mail messages, and meeting notes. He also wrote the following article for *Police* magazine (January 1999):

That's a Hero; That's a Cop

It was 12:42 a.m., June 3, 19xx, and Officer Malcom Thompson, of the Kissimmee (Fla.) Police Department, was investigating a suspicious person report. He noticed someone who matched the description standing next to a cab, using the phone booth at a convenience store. Thompson, a 25-year veteran of police work, recognized him as a local career criminal, who had been discussed as a possible suspect in a recent string of hold-ups. He checked out the suspect on the radio.

I notified dispatch that I was on the way to offer backup as they confirmed that the suspect was indeed wanted for armed robbery. Earlier in the evening, the suspect had robbed two tourists, then carjacked a cab driver, whom he was holding hostage as he talked on the phone. He was armed with an eight-shot, .22-caliber revolver.

Thompson went to go hands-on with the suspect. No, he didn't wait for back-up. No, he didn't draw his firearm. He told the suspect that he was going to have to come with him.

The suspect shouted, "F— you, cop! I'm not going back to prison!" and pulled the revolver out of a pocket. He shot at Thompson six times. Three of the shots hit the officer in the head, throat and chest. The suspect then got into the cab, placed the revolver against the head of the cab driver and demanded that he drive away.

Despite being hit by what doctors would later call three fatal shots, Thompson did not surrender. He approached the cab, weapon now drawn, and fired six rounds at the suspect, who had climbed into the back seat of the cab and was trying to escape out the opposite side door.

Thompson's left eye was shattered, his left lung had collapsed, and he was bleeding profusely from the throat wound, but he continued around the cab. When he saw the suspect, with the revolver still clutched in his hand, attempting to crawl from the cab, Thompson fired six more times. Every police round fired was accounted for. They had all hit the suspect, who died in the parking lot—with two live rounds in his revolver.

As another officer and I applied direct pressure to his massive wounds and called for Fire Rescue, Thompson kept asking us if the bad guy was down. He was concerned

"That's a Hero: That's a Cop" by Commander Russell Barnes, *Police Magazine*, Jauary 1999. Reprinted by permission of Bobit Publications.

250

for the safety of responding officers. He told me he wanted his wife to come to the scene. He asked if his dog was all right.

While we tried to comfort our colleague, our squad members converged on the location. They began securing the crime scene, identifying evidence, contacting witnesses and setting up a landing zone for the medevac helicopter.

A few minutes later, the Fire Rescue guys arrived in the Orange County Sheriff's Office helicopter, Chase One, and began emergency medical treatment. Thompson was then airlifted to a waiting surgical team that worked for hours to stabilize him.

The Osceola County Sheriff's Office began helping us answer our calls for service, filling in for officers and dispatchers who were busy dealing with the tasks associated with an investigation involving a critically injured officer and officer shooting. Overall, it was an impressive display of teamwork.

Though Thompson lost the use of his left eye and will not likely be able to return to full police duty, he survived and is still as tough as ever. He freely admits his mistakes. But Thompson displayed what we try to teach recruits in the academy, and new officers in the F.T.O. program: the will to survive.

Hopefully Thompson, a defensive tactics and firearms instructor, will be able to talk about his experience with new recruits. For my part, whenever I teach officer survival in the academy or meet a new officer who didn't know him, I'll point to one of my partners and say, "That's a hero. That's a cop."

Commander Barnes's fine article ends with a good closing paragraph. This chapter explains how to end your own compositions effectively.

People are accustomed to clear endings. We don't like to hang up the phone until both speakers have said goodbye. We like predictable endings in our popular music: either a crescendo building to a dramatic climax, a final long note, or repetition while the tune fades. We like our movies and television shows to end satisfactorily, with all of the loose ends tied up and all of the characters getting the rewards or punishments they deserve.

As readers, too, we expect clear, satisfactory endings in compositions. We want to feel a sense of closure when we finish reading. We want thoughts and ideas to be wrapped up neatly and logically.

As writers, though, we often find closure difficult to achieve. Once we've thoroughly explained all of our ideas, we're not sure how to end. We feel as though we've said all we wanted to say. So we're tempted to simply tack on a little summary that merely repeats the points we've already discussed. Repetition and summary, though, tend to be dull, lifeless ways to end a paper. Yet, the closing is not the place to introduce brand new ideas either.

TECHNIQUES FOR CONCLUDING A COMPOSITION

The better way to end the compositions you write is to use your closing paragraph(s) as an opportunity to share with the reader the *consequences* or *implications* of your ideas. Assume that you've persuaded your reader to accept the idea or belief stated in your thesis. Then ask yourself, "So what?" The answer to that question becomes your closing. For example, in a memo that describes required hand-washing procedures for employees who handle food, your closing might explain how this requirement will increase customer confidence, reduce complaints, and therefore increase the company's profits. In a report that informs the reader about a new cancer drug, you might predict how this drug will change the future of treatment for this disease. In a letter complaining about a faulty product, you might suggest that the manufacturer replace the item or refund your money.

When deciding how to explain consequences or implications, writers can choose from five effective techniques for concluding their compositions: describe effects, make predictions, make recommendations, complete a circle, or ask questions to keep the reader thinking.

Describe Effects

One way to end a composition is to describe the effects of your ideas. These effects could be short-term, long-term, or both. Upon completing your paper, ask yourself this question: "Now that I've established my point about this topic, what changes will (or did) it cause?" For example, in a report about a new computer technology, the closing paragraph might mention all of the ways it's changing your business or industry. In a report that describes various metal detectors available for purchase, you could conclude with a paragraph about the overall benefits of buying and using one.

Here is an example from a letter an apartment complex manager wrote to her tenants. After listing all of the rules governing usage of the apartment complex's swimming pool, the letter concludes as follows:

> Management will strictly enforce these rules, and we hope you understand that we adhere to them for your benefit. They are made so the pool will be a safe and pleasant place to relax. With your help, we can maintain our reputation as a considerate, neighborly community.

The author offers two effects—safe, enjoyable pool experiences and an overall neighborly atmosphere—of complying with the rules.

Another example comes from a memorandum. The author describes renovations to the company parking lot and explains changes that will affect employees. He ends this way:

> I want to thank everyone for your patience while construction proceeds. Although we will all be slightly inconvenienced while the changes are taking place, the end result will bring 50 new parking spaces to the lot, an addition that should help reduce most of our parking problems.

This memo briefly notes the beneficial effects of the situation.

A third example is from a letter of complaint to an optometrist's office. The writer describes the unsatisfactory service he received and then concludes with this paragraph:

> Because of your receptionist's rude, unfriendly response to me, I will not patronize your office again. I'm sure any of the other doctors' offices will treat me with the courtesy that paying customers deserve. Furthermore, I will not recommend your office to any of my friends or relatives.

This letter ends with the long-term effects of the writer's displeasure.

Make Predictions

Another effective way to conclude some compositions is by making some predictions. These predictions should arise naturally out of the information you've presented in your paper. For instance, in a letter to a member of congress about the poor condition of roads near your home, you might speculate that more accidents and injuries will occur if these roads are not repaired. In a report about mortgage loan rates, you might make some predictions about future trends.

One example comes from an investment company's newsletter. The article explains "small cap" stocks and compares them to "large cap" stocks. The article concludes with the following paragraph.

> Thanks in part to current economic conditions, in part to the surge in Internet and other technology issues, the outlook for small caps may be improving. Profits for small companies in the Russell 2000 Index are expected to rise by 31% in 19xx, compared with 19% for stocks in the S&P 500. Should these expectations become reality, small cap stocks may deserve consideration.[1]

This closing makes predictions about the future of the stocks described in the article.

Another example comes from a letter from a heating and air conditioning company representative to a prospective customer. The letter describes a particular heating/cooling system and discusses the advantages of that system. To conclude, the writer ends with a prediction.

> We're confident that you'll find our heating/cooling system to be the most efficient and economical choice for your company, and we look forward to installing your new HC-1000 in the near future.

A final example is from a memorandum that proposes expanding a department's computer system by adding more memory and new software programs. The writer ends with this prediction:

> If we upgrade our current computer system, we will be able to serve a larger number of customers faster and more efficiently. I speculate that making these few improvements could result in revenue increases of as much as 50% over the next two years. Obviously, a return that high is worth the investment.

Make Recommendations

A third way to present the implications of your ideas is to recommend that readers do something in response. You might ask that they change a belief or a behavior. For instance, you could suggest that they write a letter, join a group, buy a particular product, or make a certain decision. In an editorial about why readers should help save a historic battleship, you might ask them to donate money or to volunteer their time to an organization. Following a review of an innovative new product, you could recommend that readers consider using it.

The following example is from a memorandum that explains the company's participation in a United Way fundraising drive. After establishing the reasons for contributing and describing donation procedures, the writer recommends a course of action.

> Though you are not required to contribute, I urge you to support this worthy organization and help our company reach its goal of 100% participation. Please return your contribution or your pledge card to me by noon on Friday, September 29.

[1]"Is It Time To Think Small?" *Envision* newsletter, Enterprise Group of Funds, Inc. (Spring 1999): 2

The next example comes from a report. The author compares and contrasts three different brands of office furniture. After describing each company's product and noting its advantages and disadvantages, she concludes with a recommendation.

> After thoroughly researching our options, I have concluded that the Gregorio Tucci designer furniture best fulfills all of our selection criteria. This company's products offer comfort and a professional look for a reasonable price. Therefore, I recommend that our firm furnish our new offices with the Gregorio Tucci line.

A job application letter offers another example of the recommendation technique. After explaining her relevant education and experience, the writer ends with a suggestion about the reader's response.

> I would be interested in meeting with you to further discuss my qualifications. Perhaps we could arrange an interview to talk about the ways I can benefit your company. To schedule a convenient time, please contact me after 3:00 P.M. at my home phone number, (404) 232-6801. I look forward to hearing from you.

Complete a Circle

Another good technique for wrapping up a paper involves referring to something you mentioned earlier in the composition, often in the opening, thus circling back and closing a loop. This method leaves readers feeling as though the ending is tied neatly to the beginning, so it gives them a satisfying sense of closure.

One example comes from an online journal that offers career advice. The author explains three ways—temping, volunteering, and interning—to add valuable work experience to your résumé. In the opening, she refers to a lack of job experience as a "Catch-22" or no-win situation (the complete opening is on page 235 in Chapter 8). After explaining the three options, she ends with the following paragraph.

> Bottom-line: looking for a job without relevant experience isn't really a Catch-22. There are plenty of ways to tailor your résumé to a certain position or function, and then land that job you really want.[2]

The second reference to a Catch-22 brings the composition back to where it began, leaving readers with the feeling of completing a circle.

Another example comes from a credit union newsletter about loans for computer purchases. The opening asks readers, "Are you the only person you know who isn't online yet?" The article explains the advantages of owning a home computer and summarizes details about the loan. Here is the concluding paragraph:

> So now, with a credit union home computer loan, there's no reason not to be online with the rest of your friends and family members. Call us today, and you'll be surfing the web in no time!

This closing circles back to the question posed at the beginning of the article.

One final example is from a letter that encourages the reader to purchase refilled inkjet printer cartridges. In the opening, the writer narrates a hypothetical story about the stress of running out of ink during an important printing job (the complete opening appears on page 230 in Chapter 8). The

---

[2]Liz Schmid, "Catch-22: How To Get Experience When You Don't Already Have It," *Achieve E-zine*, http://careerbuilder.com/content/achieve/myc/choosing/apr_catch.html.

letter goes on to describe the product, its cost, and available payment terms. The writer concludes with

> Never panic in front of your printer again! Become an Ink Refills, Inc. customer today, and let us save you money *and* unnecessary stress.

This closing reminds readers of the story in the opening, so it gives them a sense of closure.

Ask Questions

One final technique for ending a paper involves asking the reader questions. These questions ask readers to keep thinking about your topic even after they have finished reading the paper. This technique is also effective for nudging readers toward a particular course of action.

This first example comes from a brochure that describes the merits of an automobile dealer's service department. After explaining the reasons why readers should have their vehicles serviced there, the brochure ends with this paragraph:

> We'll take good care of your car the next time it needs service. After all, who knows your Toyota better?

Another example is from a memorandum that requests a more flexible vacation policy for employees (the complete opening appears on pages 233–234 in Chapter 8). After explaining the benefits of changing the policy so that employees can carry over unused vacation time from one year to the next, the writer concludes with

> As you can see, everyone will benefit from a revised vacation policy. Happier employees will create a more friendly, customer-oriented atmosphere, and productivity will increase for our company. Everyone wins, so why not make the change?

A collection letter offers a final example. After it reminds the reader of a past-due balance and offers payment terms, it ends this way:

> I have enclosed our latest sale catalog, where you will find some outstanding discounts on some of our most popular items. When you send in your next payment on your account, why not take advantage of these special deals by placing your next order?

PRACTICE 9.1
Writing Closings

For each of the following brief compositions, write the type of closing paragraph indicated.

In his recent reelection campaign, our mayor promised us a "new library for a new century." He has kept his promise by pushing forward the plans to finally expand the outdated Summerville Public Library facilities. This month, we finally began the renovation process. While construction takes place over the next six months, we will offer limited services in a temporary location, but the newly designed and enlarged building will be worth the short-term inconvenience.

The temporary site will be at 500 Oak Street, across the street from Dr. Miller's office. It will house the entire children's collection, along with adult materials such as New Fiction and Current Periodicals. We will also offer our computers with our online catalog and public access to the Internet. The Children's Department will continue to offer its regular programming schedule, including Saturday morning storytimes. Hours of operation at this temporary site will be 9:00 A.M. to 6:00 P.M., Monday through Saturday.

When the renovated library building reopens in January, we will offer:

- A 200 percent increase in space for the Children's Department.
- A new roof, which will prevent the leakage problems that have damaged books for several years.
- New paint, new carpet, and new furniture.
- Fifteen new computers.

Add an *effects* closing for this composition:

Answers will vary.

_____

_____

_____

_____

_____

_____

_____

_____

Recently, I stopped for gasoline at the new Gate gas station/convenience store on Park Drive. I pulled up to the gas pump, got out, and lifted the nozzle. As I did this, a cheerful voice suddenly said over a loudspeaker, "Good morning! Welcome to Gate!" When I finished pumping the gas and went inside the store to pay, a cashier greeted me with a warm smile and a friendly hello, rang up my purchase, thanked me, and wished me a pleasant day. The whole experience made me feel like a valued customer, and I will definitely buy gas at that establishment in the future. But it also made me think about how we can implement a more customer-oriented attitude here at Townsend Shoes. I recommend that we make a few small changes to make our customers feel welcome and therefore, increase their loyalty to our store.

First, I propose that we train all employees to smile and greet all customers the moment they enter the store. I have been in other stores where the floor staff says hello as you first walk in. This small effort makes customers feel welcome and invites them to browse.

Second, I propose that we ask all employees to not only offer each customer assistance as usual, but also introduce themselves by their first names. For example, when a customer enters, our employee would say, "My name is Mary. Is there something I can help you find?" This small detail will personalize our employee-customer relations and help the customer feel more welcome.

Finally, we should instruct Townsend employees to thank all customers—whether they make a purchase or not—for coming in and wish them a good day as they leave the store. This courtesy, also, should help them feel that we value their patronage. It will also remind them that Townsend Shoes is a friendly place to shop.

Add a *recommendations* closing.

Answers will vary.

_____

_____

_____

_____

_____

_____

"I can't possibly go back to college! I can't afford it! Besides, I have a family and a full-time job. Where would I find the time?"

Have you said these words? Are these the reasons why you're still postponing the education that will lead you to a more satisfying, better-paying career? Then let the friendly, caring professionals at Johnson Community College show you how to overcome all of these obstacles to a brighter future for yourself and your loved ones.

Many forms of financial aid can help you afford college today. Our financial aid experts will help you put together a combination of grants, loans, scholarships, and on-campus employment to help you finance your educational goals.

We also offer a variety of scheduling options so that you can fit your classes around your other obligations. Sign up for day or evening classes, or you can even take advantage of our many tele-courses and Internet courses that allow you to complete assignments when it's convenient for you. Our experienced advisers will help you design a schedule that's right for you.

Add a *questions* closing.

Answers will vary.

_____

_____

_____

_____

_____

_____

Girl Scout Troop 512 of Rockville is always looking for good fundraising projects to finance our many activities and outings. So when we heard that clubs could rent a booth at the Plant City Strawberry Festival, we signed up to participate. We charged $2 per glass for lemonade shakers, a blend of freshly squeezed lemons, sugar, water, and ice. We worked the booth for eight hours but made only $306 in profit because of a few problems we encountered.

One of these problems was too few workers. We scheduled four volunteers for each two-hour shift, but that wasn't enough people to fill the demand! Lemonade shakers are made to order from scratch, so they take some time to prepare. We needed more hands to cut lemons, squeeze lemons, measure sugar, scoop ice, pour water, and make change. The long wait probably discouraged many potential customers, and if we'd had more help, we could have served people faster and made more money.

The other problem was the cost of supplies. We did not allow ourselves enough time to shop around for the best prices, so we ended up paying too much for cups, lemons, and sugar. Probably, if we'd bought our supplies in bulk, we could have reduced our initial investment and wound up with more in profits.

Add a *predictions* closing.

Answers will vary.

_____

_____

_____

_____

_____

_____

_____

You probably begin each school year with at least one shy kid cowering at his desk at the back of your classroom. This kid has no friends. He feels insecure in his new environment. He's afraid he's not as smart or likable as the other kids. And he's afraid of you, afraid the teacher will make things even worse by exposing his failures to the rest of the kids in the class. Back in 19xx, in your 6th grade math classroom at Wilson Middle School, that kid was me. I had just moved to the area, didn't know anyone, and was terrified that I would remain an outcast. But you quickly put my fears to rest, and this week, as I graduate from high school, I wanted you to know how much you influenced and inspired me.

You helped me believe I could learn. Other teachers were not as patient with me, and several of them left me with the impression that I was stupid and could not understand math. That's why I was afraid you'd somehow brand me a slow learner in front of the other students. Not only did you not do that, you worked with me until I understood. I finally felt I could learn, and I didn't stop feeling that way after I left your class. My successes in your classroom inspired me to work harder in all my other classes through the years, and I'm graduating on the honor roll.

My academic successes made me feel less shy, so I was able to make friends a little more easily. I had always found it difficult to meet new people, but a few of the other students in your classroom actually asked me for help when they saw that I understood the material. That led to a few friendships I'm proud to say I still maintain today.

Finally, I've decided to become a teacher because of your example. I see the impact that a teacher can have on students' lives, and I want to be able to help others as you helped me. I plan to enroll in Johnson Community College in the fall, and I will begin working toward a degree in math education. So I have you to thank, too, for helping me choose the right career for me.

Add a *circle* closing.

Answers will vary.

_____

_____

_____

_____

_____

_____

TEST YOUR UNDERSTANDING

1. Why do readers expect compositions to end with satisfactory closings?

   They like to experience closure and a logical wrap-up of ideas.

2. What is a common but dull way of ending a composition?

   Summary.

3. What are five different ways you can explain the consequences of your ideas in your closing paragraphs?

   Describe effects, make predictions, make recommendations, complete a circle,

   ask questions.

WEB ACTIVITY: **Online References**

Thanks to the Internet, you can consult a variety of online reference works as you compose. On your home and office computers, bookmark web sites containing a dictionary, a thesaurus, an encyclopedia, a collection of quotations, and a grammar handbook. Then, as you write, you can quickly find information or answers to your questions.

1. In this chapter, find a word that is unfamiliar to you. Go to the *Merriam-Webster Dictionary* web site at http://www.m-w.com/dictionary. Follow the directions to look up the word, and print the screen containing the definition.
2. Go the *Roget's Thesaurus* web site at http://humanities.uchicago.edu/forms_unrest/ROGET.html. Follow the directions to search **headwords** for the word *speech*. Print the screen containing synonyms for that word.
3. Go to the *Electric Library Encyclopedia* web site at http://www.encyclopedia.com. Follow the directions to locate an article about a noteworthy historical figure whom you admire. Print this article.
4. Go the *Guide to Grammar and Writing* web site at http://webster.commnet.edu/hp/pages/darling/grammar.htm. Click on *Notorious Confusables* in the list of topics, and follow the directions to find out if the word *lays* is used correctly in the following sentence: She *lays* in the sun without wearing sunscreen. Print the screen that contains the answer.
5. Go to the *Bartlett's Familiar Quotations* web site at http://www.bartleby.com/99. Find quotations about success and print them.

GROUP PROJECT AND WRITING ACTIVITIES

In Chapters 7 and 8, you described a needed improvement on your college's campus and proposed a solution to the problem. In this chapter, you'll present your ideas to some of your college's decision makers.

With your group, use one or more invention strategies to generate a list of possible objections (arguments) to the solution you proposed in Chapter 8. Record as many ideas as possible in the space below.

Collaborate with your group to compose a memorandum to your college president. Briefly describe the problem; then try to persuade him or her to implement your recommended solution. Use the opening paragraph you wrote as one of Chapter 8's activities. Make sure you address the president's possible objections to your proposal. Use one of the techniques described in this chapter to conclude your memo.

TO: _____ , President

FROM: _____

DATE: _____

SUBJECT: _____

_____

_____

_____

_____

_____

_____

_____

_____

_____

_____

_____

_____

_____

_____

_____

_____

_____

_____

_____

_____

_____

_____

_____

_____

_____

_____

_____

_____

_____

_____

_____

_____

With your group, prepare and deliver to your classmates an oral presentation about the needed campus improvement and your proposed solution. Invite representatives from your college's student government to hear your presentation. Divide your presentation so that each group member speaks. See Appendix B for more information about preparing effective oral presentations.

READINGS

What information does the Internet offer job seekers? Do you know how to use the World Wide Web for assistance in your job search?

The next article, written by a member of the National Association of Business Economists (NABE), explains how to use the Internet to locate career advice and employment opportunities.

As you read this article, circle every word that's unfamiliar to you. Look it up and write the meaning in the margin. Put an exclamation point (!) next to any sentence or paragraph you find especially interesting. Put a question mark (?) next to any sentence or paragraph you don't understand.

Using the Web to Advance Your Career

John J. Casson

1 Are you using the World Wide Web to advance your career? You should. A large number of business, government and nonprofit organizations are utilizing the Web to recruit employees. In addition, an extensive amount of information about pursuing a career and searching for employment can be found on the Web.

2 The career-related resources on the Web that are of most use. . . can be divided into a dozen categories: (1) employer sites, (2) job listings, (3) management recruiters, (4) entrepreneurial ventures, (5) résumé postings, (6) hompage portfolios, (7) e-mail communications, (8) networking opportunities, (9) search assistance, (10) career advice, (11) educational programs, and (12) retirement information. Descriptions of these resources follow, and the names of some Web sites where they can be found are listed in the appendix to this article.

Employer Sites

3 Are you interested in obtaining a position with a particular employer? Thousands of private, public and nonprofit organizations utilize a portion of their Web sites to recruit employees. The "career," "employment" or "job" links located in the site map and the directory or homepage of an organization's Web site can be used to learn about positions that the employer wants to fill. Companies ranging from Abbott Laboratories to the Zygo Corporation are among the many business organizations that recruit directly on the Web. A large number of federal, state, local and international government agencies and nonprofit organizations also use their Web sites to recruit employees. Links to many of these sites can be found in directories such as America's Employers and Hoover's Top Employers.

4 In addition to providing the titles and brief descriptions of positions that they want to fill, the Web sites of employers can be an important resource in other ways. Such sites usually contain information about an organization's products or services, human resource policies, benefit programs and recruitment contacts. Much of this information can be of help in determining whether you would want to apply for a position with an organization. It also can be incorporated into your letters of inquiry, employment interviews and follow-up correspondence. Many organizations also furnish facilities on their Web sites for submitting employment applications, résumés, and messages.

Job Listings

5 You don't have to limit your search to the sites of individual employers to find job openings on the Web. A great many business, government and non-profit organizations list positions that they want to fill on one or more of the

John J. Casson, "Using the Web to Advance Your Carreer," *Business Economics*, (Oct. '99), 84. Reprinted by permission.

many compilations of employment opportunities that are on the Web. America's Job Bank identifies about one million openings posted with state employment agencies. More than a quarter-million job openings can be found on CareerPath and the Job Factory. The National Association of Business Economists Employment Opportunities in Business Economics is one of many listings of vacancies in specific occupations that can be found on the Web. There also are sites that provide compilations of job openings in the public and nonprofit sectors and with organizations in other countries.

Management Recruiters

6 Many executive search firms have established Web sites. Some provide information about the managerial and professional positions that they are attempting to fill and/or solicit résumés from experienced executives. Futurestep, LAIcompass.com and Leaders-Online are among the subsidiaries that management recruiters have established for the purpose of recruiting on the Web. You can obtain information about, as well as links to, executive search firms on such sites as the Recruiters Online Network and SearchBase.

Entrepreneurial Ventures

7 Are you interested in becoming a consultant or running some other type of business? Information and opportunities can be found on the Web. Advice for entrepreneurs is furnished on the Web sites of the U.S. Small Business Administration and SmallbizNet. Nation's Business provides information, a directory of resources and links to Web sites of interest to aspiring business owners. If you are searching for consulting opportunities, you can offer your services on Web sites such as the Alliance of Consultants, Experts.com and the NABE Consultants and Services Registry.

Résumé Postings

8 Would you welcome an offer of employment? You can make your qualifications known to a great many organizations by posting your résumé on Web sites such as Career Mart and JobOptions. Employers and recruiters are able to search electronically through such extensive compilations of résumés for "key words" that indicate that the qualifications of an individual may match the requirements for a position. NABE members can post their résumés on the Positions Wanted section of the association's Web site. Instructions on how to convert paper résumés into electronic résumés can be found on Career Mosaic, Tripod's Résumé Builder and many other Web sites.

Homepage Portfolios

9 Do you have your own Web site? You can modify or create your own homepage in order to furnish information that could be of interest to prospective employers and/or consulting clients. In addition to your résumé, your Web pages could contain a portfolio of material that furnishes evidence of your qualifications for job openings or consulting assignments. This could include

samples of your work, such as written reports and audio and video recordings of your presentations, as well as letters of recommendation, news media clips and photographs. Instructions and facilities for creating homepages are provided by many Internet portals and service providers such as America Online and Lycos.

E-mail Communications

10   The Internet has provided you with an important new means of communication. E-mail can be used to inquire about employment opportunities, submit cover letters with résumé attachments and conduct follow-up correspondence with prospective employers. You also can use e-mail to supplement telephoning, meetings and letter writing as means of establishing and maintaining networking contacts. Numerous Internet service providers such as Excite Mail and Net@address offer free e-mail accounts as well as facilities for searching for e-mail addresses. The e-mail addresses of NABE members can be found in the Association's latest Membership Directory.

Networking Opportunities

11   Do you want to expand the scope of your networking activities? This can be accomplished by participating in chat rooms, message boards and news groups. There are a multitude of such discussion groups and their areas of interest vary widely. Included are industrially and occupationally focused groups as well as those that offer practical advice and encouragement to individuals searching for employment. Participating in such groups may enable you to obtain information about job openings, career possibilities and prospective employers. Directories of discussion groups can be found on Web sites such as deja.com, Liszt and Reference.COM.

Search Assistance

12   Have your job hunting skills atrophied? A wealth of information and practical advice about searching for employment can be obtained on sites such as The Riley Guide and The Wall Street Journal. This can include suggestions about finding job openings, networking techniques, preparing paper and electronic résumés, corresponding with employers, answering interview questions and negotiating job offers. Many of these sites also provide career information and links to lists of employment opportunities, résumé postings and other related Web sites.

Career Advice

13   Are you thinking about a career change? Several Web sites furnish an extensive amount of career advice. This can include information about assessing personal aptitudes and interests, prerequisites for various careers and the employment outlook and salary ranges for many occupations. Sites such as the Career Resource Center, MSU Career Resources on the Web and What Color Is Your Parachute also furnish suggestions about searching for employment

as well as links to other career and employment related Web sites. NABE is one of many professional associations that furnish occupational information on their Web sites.

Educational Programs

14   Would an advanced degree such as a doctorate or specialized training help your career? Information about a multitude of educational and certification programs can be found on the Web. Petersons and Gradschools.com are among the sites that contain directories of full-time, part-time and distance learning graduate school programs. Detailed descriptions of these and other programs can be found on the Web sites of individual universities and other educational institutions. Many also provide facilities on their Web sites for requesting additional information about their programs and submitting applications for admission.

Retirement Information

15   Are you concerned about what you should do after the end of your professional career? A great deal of retirement-related information can be found on the Web. There are sites that can be of help in determining when and where to retire. Some, such as the Administration on Aging, International Society for Retirement Planning and Quicken provide retirement related advice, including information about pensions, estate planning and managing investments. If you are uncertain about what to do when you stop working, you may find inspiration on sites that contain descriptions of opportunities for volunteers, vacation destinations and hobbies. Some sites such as the AARP Webplace furnish a wide range of information, while others such as Elderhostel provide a narrower focus on subjects of interest to retirees.

Expanding Benefits

16   You can obtain a great deal of information on the World Wide Web that can be of help throughout all stages of your career. Unfortunately, finding this information can be difficult. There is an overabundance of career-related sites on the Web, and the quality and quantity of information that they provide vary widely. Web sites often change: some will be modified, new ones will appear, and others will be abandoned. Consequently, you will need to be discerning, selective, and assiduous in using the Web to advance your career. The effort will be increasingly rewarding. In the years ahead, the number of organizations recruiting employees and the amount of career related information on the World Wide Web will continue to grow.

APPENDIX

Employer Sites
Abbott Laboratories www.abbott.com/career/index.htm
Zygo Corporation www.zygo.com/employment/openings.htm

America's Employers www.americasemployers.com
Hoover's Top Employers www.hoovers.com/features/topemps.html

Job Listings
America's Job Bank www.ajb.dni.us
CareerPath http://new.careerpath.com
Job Factory http://jobfactory.comEmployment
Opportunities in Business Economics www.nabe.com/mem/eoprn.htm

Management Recruiters
Futurestep, Inc. www.futurestep.com
LAIcompass.com www.laicompass.com
LeadersOnline www.leadersonline.com
Recruiters Online Network www.recruitersonline.com
SearchBase www.searchbase.com

Entrepreneurial Ventures
U.S. Small Business Administration www.sbaonline.sba.gov
SmallbizNet http://www.lowe.org/smbiznet/sites/index.htm
Nation's Business www.nbmag.com/about.htm
Alliance of Consultants http://allianceofconsultants.com
Experts.com www.experts.com
NABE Consultants and Services Registry www.nabe.com/publib/registry.htm

Résumé Postings
Career Mart www.careermart.com/resumebank.html
JobOptions www.joboptions.com
NABE Positions Wanted www.nabe.com/mem
Career Mosaic www.careermosaic.com/cm/cm39.html
Tripod's Résumé Builder www.tripod.com/explore/jobs_career/resume

Homepage Portfolios
America Online http://hometown.aol.com
Lycos www.lycos.com/press/jump.html

E-Mail Communications
Excite Mail www.mailexcite.com
Net@address www.netaddress.com

Networking Opportunities
deja.com www.deja.com
Liszt www.liszt.com
Reference.COM www.reference.com

Search Assistance
The Riley Guide www.dbm.com/jobguide
The Wall Street Journal http://careers.wsj.com

Career Advice
Career Resource Center www.careers.org
MSU Career Resources on the Web www.metro.msus.edu/links.html
What Color Is Your Parachute www.jobhuntersbible.com

Educational Programs
Petersons www.petersons.com/graduate
Gradschools.com www.gradschools.com

Retirement Information
Administration on Aging www.aoa.dhhs.gov/aoa/pages/finplan.html
International Society for Retirement Planning www.isrplan.org/links.htm
Quicken http://quicken.excite.com/retirementAARP
Webplace www.aarp.org
Elderhostel www.elderhostel.org

RESPONDING TO THE READING

1. **What are a few different ways you can use the Web to find available positions at particular companies?**

   Visit Employer web sites, sites that compile and list job openings, and search firms'

   web sites.

2. **What two ways can you use the Web to help employers find *you*?**

   Post your résumé on an employment web site, create your own home page, network

   in online discussion groups.

3. **How can e-mail help in your job search?**

   Use it to inquire about job openings, to submit attachments such as your résumé,

   and to send follow-up up correspondence to prospective employers.

4. **How can you use Web networking to advance your career?**

   Join discussion groups to obtain information about job openings and prospective

   employers.

5. What kinds of career advice are available on the Web?

Advice about the job search, networking, résumé preparation, job interview

preparation, and negotiation of job offers.

6. What technique does the author use to conclude this article?

Prediction.

BUILDING VOCABULARY

The rapid growth of the Internet has added many new words and altered the meanings of many others in the English language. For example, the word *attachment* (paragraph 10) used to refer to something attaching one thing to another; or to a bond of affection; or to an accessory, such as a vacuum cleaner attachment. With the expansion of e-mail, we found it necessary to add yet another definition of the word: a file transmitted electronically along with an e-mail message.

The sentences below are from the article you just read. Look up each italicized word in your dictionary. Is the word or phrase a brand new addition to the language, or does it expand the meanings of a word or phrase already in use?

1. The "career," "employment" or "job" links located in the *site map* and the directory or homepage of an organization's Web site can be used to learn about positions that the employer wants to fill. (paragraph 3)

   New term for an outline of a web site's contents.

2. You can modify or create your own *homepage* in order to furnish information that could be of interest to prospective employers and/or consulting clients. (paragraph 9)

   New term for a file available for access via the Internet.

3. Instructions and facilities for creating homepages are provided by many Internet *portals* and service providers such as America Online and Lycos. (paragraph 9)

   Existing word that means "doorways, entrances, or gates."

4. This can be accomplished by participating in *chat rooms,* message boards and *news groups.* (paragraph 11)

   Both new terms for online communication tools.

5. Many of these sites also provide career information and *links* to lists of employment opportunities, résumé postings and other related Web sites. (paragraph 12)

Existing word that means "units in a connected series." _____

6. What Internet-related words are you using now that do not yet appear in your dictionary?

Answers will vary. _____

Have you ever worked in a cubicle? What were some of the advantages of working so closely to your fellow employees? What were the disadvantages?

In the following article, newspaper columnist Lenore Skenazy makes some observations about workplace cubicles.

As you read this article, circle every word that's unfamiliar to you. Look it up and write the meaning in the margin. Put an exclamation point (!) next to any sentence or paragraph you find especially interesting. Put a question mark (?) next to any sentence or paragraph you don't understand.

Small Cubicle Is Closing In at the Office

Lenore Skenazy

1   It's a small world after all! Just about big enough for you, your computer and a Dilbert* mug—if you hold it in your lap.

2   Why? The venerable office cubicle is going the way of Monica's middle.** It's shrinking before our very eyes. Five years from now, says office-design guru Kristin Hill, "It won't be uncommon to see today's 7-by-8-foot cubicle turn into a 6-by-6, or even a 5-by-5." The cubicle will become less like an office and more "like a locker."

3   Of course, in high school we didn't actually work in our lockers. But that's not the point. The point is that businesses know a good thing when they see one, and what they see here is lots of freed-up square footage.

4   While cynics may see this windfall morphing into an even bigger office for Boss Man, complete with private kitchen and shower (which is what happened at my old job, by the way), Hill insists the future is more democratic than that.

5   The extra inches shaved from everyone's elbow room will be harvested to create bigger, happier common areas filled with team-building recreational equipment, says Janis Reiters, Hill's partner at Design Management in Natick, Mass. "If you can go play Ping-Pong, climb the walls or bungee-jump through the atrium, you'll be able to clear your head."

6   Or break it open.

*Dilbert is a comic strip character who works in a cubicle.
**Monica Lewinsky testified to having a romantic relationship with United States President Bill Clinton and then became a spokesperson for a weight loss center.

Lenore Skenazy, "Small Cubicle is Closing In at the Office," *New York Daily News*, (Jan. 25, 2000). © New York Daily News, L.P. reprinted-reproduced with permission.

7   While the idea of watching my betters boinging up and down holds obvious appeal (just kidding, boss!), the larger trend of team sports infiltrating the workplace is worrying indeed.

8   "It makes me feel like I was back in seventh-grade gym class and they were making me climb the rope," frets my pal Jim. Jim never got very far off the knot, but he did get pretty far from Philadelphia, where the humiliation occurred. And isn't that the whole point of adulthood, scurrying away from the Playground of Mortification?

9   But now for us nonjocks, the playground is scurrying back. Here in the same building as the Daily News [offices], the Internet company DoubleClick is fashioning a fabulous basketball/volleyball court for its kids, er, workers. How ya gonna score points with your co-workers if you can't score points with your co-workers?

10   Bad enough most companies hold a picnic each year where, after you've been chained to a desk for 12 months, you're supposed to suddenly play softball and not wheeze when you run. Now the game is year-round! For this we're giving up pencil sharpener space!

11   So maybe you're wondering who's to blame for the modern office maze. There really is one individual, a near-genius who also invented a heart pump and automatic tree harvester—Robert Propst, who dreamed up the corporate cubicle 31 years ago.

12   Back then, most people worked in offices with doors if they were big shots, or in a roomful of desks if they weren't. Propst found this appalling. Individual offices wasted space. But the bullpens were worse because of what he dubbed the "idiot salutation" syndrome.

13   "Every time somebody goes by, you say, 'Hello Joe!'" he once explained, wasting time that could be better spent making long-distance phone calls to friends.

14   Next thing you know, Propst came up with the idea of little, insulated booths previously only seen at Peep World. And now it's an $11 billion business (cubicles, not Peep World).

15   Luckily for us, even as the cubicle shrinks, most of us can still find space for a mini-dartboard with Propst's picture in the middle. Bungee jumping? For this we give up space?

RESPONDING TO THE READING

1. Robert Propst said he created the cubicle to improve working conditions, not to make them worse. He once said, "An organization that . . . wants to pack the maximum number of people in a minimum amount of space can wreck the mental health of employees." Do you think working in cubicles could "wreck mental health"? What are some of the disadvantages of working closely with others in a cubicle environment?

Answers will vary. Disadvantages include lack of privacy, noise or other distractions, cramped work space.

RESPONDING TO THE READING *continued*

2. What are the advantages of cubicles, especially when you compare them to the large rooms filled with desks known as "bullpens"?

Answers will vary. Advantages include easy access to co-workers, social benefits,

more sharing of information, more clearly defined personal work space.

3. What technique is used in the closing paragraph?

Ask questions.

BUILDING VOCABULARY

Words in the English language often expand their meanings as we find new uses for them. For example, the word *cubicle* once meant a small sleeping compartment. We expanded the meaning of that word to describe small partitioned office spaces.

Using your dictionary for help, explain how the meaning of each italicized word below has been changed.

1. Five years from now, says office-design *guru* Kristin Hill, "It won't be uncommon to see today's 7-by-8-foot cubicle turn into a 6-by-6, or even a 5-by-5." (paragraph 2)

The word has evolved from meaning "spiritual teacher" *to meaning* "recognized

leader in a field."

2. While cynics may see this windfall *morphing* into an even bigger office for Boss Man, complete with private kitchen and shower (which is what happened at my old job, by the way), Hill insists the future is more democratic than that. (paragraph 4)

The word has evolved from meaning "undergoing a transformation via computer

animation" *to* "being transformed in general."

3. But the *bullpens* were worse because of what he dubbed the "idiot salutation" syndrome. (paragraph 12)

The word has evolved from meaning "a fenced enclosure for confining bulls" *to*

"a large, open area filled with desks for many workers."

4. Next thing you know, Propst came up with the idea of little, *insulated* booths previously only seen at Peep World. (paragraph 14)

The word has evolved from meaning "preventing passage of heat or electricity

with non-conducting material" *to* "apart and protected from view."

10 Confidence and Assertiveness

PROFESSIONAL PROFILE
Starla Hoke, Paralegal

Starla Hoke, a married mother of one son, works as a paralegal for a law firm specializing in real property. She coordinates, schedules, and conducts loan closings and property settlements, performs title exams, and disburses monies on behalf of clients. Her duties require her to write often; she corresponds frequently with lenders, insurance agencies, appraisers, surveyors, clients, and attorneys. She also drafts a variety of legal documents, including property deeds, release agreements, and descriptions of property. This sample comes from a letter regarding a dispute between a seller and the buyers of a piece of land.

> Because you knew about the problem with the water supply to the property and did not disclose this problem in the offer to purchase contract, you will need to resolve it in order to avoid further litigation. Until adequate water is supplied to the property, Mr. and Mrs. Jones cannot proceed with the construction of their new home. Apparently, you can rectify this situation by purchasing and installing a jet system. According to the plumber we contacted, it costs approximately $1000. You may also need to attach a supplementary water pump system to the water line from the water department if the jet system is not effective. Either or both solutions should satisfy Mr. and Mrs. Jones and prevent them from filing a lawsuit in court.

Starla's statements are confident and assertive. Chapter 10 explains how to achieve confidence and assertiveness in your own writing.

Effective writing is always confident and assertive. Confidence is the sincere belief in the ideas being communicated. Assertiveness is the ability to declare these ideas true and valid.

Of course, to write confidently, you must first have confidence in your ideas. If you are unsure about your topic, if you don't fully understand it, or if you harbor any doubts about your thesis or main points, this uncertainty will surface in your writing. So you must take the time to think through your ideas, subject them to intense scrutiny, test their validity, and discuss them with people who disagree or hold differing viewpoints. Only when you truly *believe* in your idea can you communicate it assertively to a reader.

This chapter discusses four ways to achieve confident writing: by avoiding certain apologetic or hedging phrases, by choosing confident words, by stating ideas using the more confident declarative sentence structure, and by using certain typefaces to emphasize and reinforce ideas.

273

COMMUNICATING CONFIDENTLY

A reader will often evaluate writers' thoughts according to how confidently they present those thoughts. If a composition reveals doubt, timidity, or uncertainty, the reader may reject its ideas because of not being sure the *writer* even believes them. Thus, the document will not convince the reader and will not achieve its purpose.

Avoid Hedging, Apologies, and Disclaimers

Adding certain phrases to your sentences will result in writing that seems timid and unsure. The term *hedging* effectively describes the first group of phrases we are about to list. To *hedge* in speaking or writing means to avoid a firm commitment: for instance, by qualifying a statement—wording it so as to allow withdrawal or escape from your position. Here are some common hedging phrases:

It seems to me

I think

I believe

I feel that

In my opinion

All of these phrases inject a note of uncertainty into your writing by calling attention to the fact that these are *your* thoughts alone. They indirectly suggest that your thoughts do not necessarily represent prevailing wisdom. Therefore, they call into question the truth, or validity, of your statements.

Furthermore, hedging phrases are redundant, adding unnecessary words to your sentences. Because you are writing the statement, you obviously believe it, think it, or feel it; therefore, it's unnecessary to say that you do.

Note how the revisions of the following examples result in much more confident statements.

Hedging:	*I believe that* good leaders are born, not made.
More confident:	Good leaders are born, not made.
Hedging:	*I think that* careful attention to financial details will allow us to meet our objectives.
More confident:	Careful attention to financial details will allow us to meet our objectives.
Hedging:	*I really feel that* our training program is one of the best in the industry.
More confident:	Our training program is one of the best in the industry.

Another type of hedging word is the *qualifier,* a word that limits an idea or makes it less positive. Common qualifiers include *probably, maybe, seems,* and *some.* Overuse of these words will result in timid, wimpy writing. Notice how the removal of qualifiers in the following statements increases their confidence.

Hedging:	He *probably* needs to find some type of psychological counseling.
More confident:	He needs to find some type of psychological counseling.
Hedging:	Flexibility *seems to be* the key to affordable airline fares.
More confident:	Flexibility is the key to affordable airline fares.

> *Hedging:*   *Maybe* we need to revise that policy.
> *More confident:*   We need to revise that policy.

Hedging also includes "fence-sitting," or refusing to take a stand about an issue. If you're "sitting on the fence," undecided about which side to choose, you haven't yet made a commitment one way or the other. This indecision will reduce the reader's confidence in your writing. As the following statements illustrate, when writers haven't made firm decisions about their topics, their statements will clearly reveal their uncertainty.

> *Hedging:*   Raising prices may or may not be the solution, but the problem is certainly there.
> *More confident:*   Raising prices will not solve the problem.
> *Hedging:*   Some type of action needs to be taken to fix this situation. *[What action? Taken by whom? This writer needs to give more thought to his topic before he can improve this sentence.]*

Apologies and disclaimers are another group of phrases that undermine the confidence of writing. An apology is an acknowledgment of some weakness or deficiency, usually in the writer's understanding or information. Similarly, to *disclaim* means to disown, which involves rejecting responsibility for a statement. Common apologies and disclaimers include phrases such as these:

I don't really know much about this, but . . .

I'm not really sure, but . . .

I'm no expert, but . . .

I don't have a degree in this, but . . .

By including such phrases, you immediately destroy your credibility for the reader, who will probably dismiss your thoughts as unreliable. *If you really don't know enough about the topic, don't write about it until you gather more information.* On the other hand, if you *do* understand the topic and can offer appropriate evidence to support your ideas, present those ideas confidently.

Don't water down your writing with hedging, apologies, and disclaimers! Instead, state your idea as if it is a truth that everyone accepts (or should accept). When you write, take a stand, believe in your position, and avoid phrases that cast doubt upon your viewpoint.

PRACTICE 10.1
Eliminating Hedging, Apologies, and Disclaimers

Rewrite the following statements to increase their assertiveness.
Answers will vary.

1. I strongly believe that metal detectors will help make our high school safer.

   Metal detectors will help make our high school safer.

2. We were somewhat startled by the information in the report.

   We were startled by the information in the report.

3. I guess we could hire another groundskeeper, but that may not be the most cost-effective approach.

   We should not hire another groundskeeper because that is not the most

   cost-effective approach.

4. I do feel that we should create a system to track this data for future reference.

   We must create a system to track this data for future reference.

   _____

5. I'd need to do more research, but it seems to me that we might want to extend our business hours.

   Apparently, we need to extend our business hours.

Choose Assertive Words

To achieve an assertive style, choose assertive words. Use bold, even forceful, words to clearly reveal the strength of your convictions. For example, read the following passage from a book that explains how honesty will reduce stress and improve mental health.

Parents, out of a *confused* mixture of fear, love, and anger, try to care for children the best they can, using the *mind-sets* they have been given by their own parents. They constantly warn their children to be careful, do this, don't do that, and watch out for a dangerous world. The results for millions of us have been *tragic*. We have been taught to be *paranoid* and *guarded* in life as our parents' way of trying to ensure our survival after they are gone. In turn, we attempt to convince our own children of the correctness of believing in the rules of safety, so that they will act according to the principles we teach them. . . . It's important to us to *stringently dictate* protective rules and to instill faith in the necessity of rules for control of self and others.[1]

This writer assertively communicates his viewpoint by choosing words (shown in italics) that effectively reveal his strong feelings about his subject.

Selecting bold, assertive words requires consideration of two qualities. First, the right word will be the most specific word. Look at the following list:

plain

unattractive

ugly

hideous

If you want to state your judgment about the appearance of a new building in your community, you will want to choose from that list the adjective that most specifically communicates your opinion. Chapter 2 of this book discusses specific word choices in more detail.

After you've narrowed your choices according to their specificity, the second step involves considering any *connotations* attached to those words. The connotative meaning of a word refers to the emotion or feeling we have assigned to that word beyond its denotative, or dictionary, definition. Many words have taken on either positive or negative connotations that writers can use in order to help convey their opinions. For example, compare the words *policeman* and *cop*. The latter word is sometimes used in a derogatory, disrespectful way.

[1]Brad Blanton, *Radical Honesty* (New York: Dell, 1994), 30.

In the short list you just looked at, the first two words (*plain* and *unattractive*) are more gentle, even euphemistic, choices. The last two words (*ugly* and *hideous*) are blunt and much more harsh. If you really hate the new building, they'd be the best choices for revealing your feelings.

Now consider this list:

could

should

must

Each verb in this list is a little more forceful than the one that comes before. The word *could* phrases an idea as a questionable suggestion; *should* makes it a little more assertive by injecting the writer's opinion; and *must* is the most assertive, leaving out any room for debate. Now compare the following three statements.

Timid:	We *could* ask for a raise.
More confident:	We *should* ask for a raise.
Most assertive:	We *must* ask for a raise.

Note how the assertive verbs in the following passage from a memo create an authoritative, confident tone:

> Too often, unauthorized vehicles clog the service area behind the building. This *interferes* with delivery trucks and persons seeking handicapped parking. Employees who are not authorized to park in this area *must park* in the lower lots. This *applies* to all employees. Unauthorized vehicles *will be towed.*

Finally, consider inserting into your writing some assertive adverbs that strengthen the confidence of your statements. These adverbs include words such as *clearly, obviously, definitely, absolutely,* and *certainly.* Such words, as the following statements illustrate, leave no room for doubt about your confidence in an idea:

> *Clearly*, one of the major issues for our company is thriving in the world of e-commerce.

> We *obviously* need to schedule more staff during our busy 4:00–7:00 P.M. period.

The following examples both illustrate how bold word choices (in italics) of all parts of speech create assertive writing. The first, from a telephone company's sales letter, includes effective verbs, nouns, and adjectives:

> It's not often we can point out a *great deal* like this to one of our customers. The BellSouth Complete Choice plan *is truly* a *super* buy for you, for one flat rate—just $28.70 a month—you can get your local phone service and the features you need. You already know how useful calling features can be. Look at everything you can get with this one *value-packed* package. . . . The Complete Choice plan is *perfect* for busy households, growing families—it could be *perfect* for you. And this is the *perfect* time to order.[2]

[2]Gloria R. Cockerham, BellSouth sales letter.

This next example is from an attorney's letter to an insurance company.

It has come to our attention that you *surreptitiously* tape-recorded telephone conversations with our client. You *covertly* recorded our client's statements without her knowledge, permission, or consent. Such conduct is *profoundly objectionable* and *violates* the code of ethics that governs our communication. We *will not tolerate* such *clandestine abuse* and *disrespect.*

Now consider the following examples, which become much more assertive with a few substitutions and additions.

Not confident: Don't continue to work in a job that's going nowhere.

More assertive: Don't continue to *slave away* in a *dead-end* job.

Not confident: Predatory lenders are those who loan money based on your home equity and then make large profits on fees and rates at your expense.

More assertive: Predatory lenders *unscrupulously* loan money based on your home equity and then *rob* you with *obscenely* high fees and rates.

Not confident: This year, corrections officers received a 3% salary increase along with a one-time $150 performance bonus.

More assertive: This year, the state legislature *insulted hard-working* corrections officers with a *measly* 3% salary increase along with a *paltry* $150 performance bonus.

As you search for more assertive words when you write, beware of two specific dangers: overgeneralizing and insulting the reader. Even though you should phrase your ideas as truth, you also should avoid unfair or inaccurate generalizations and absolutes. In particular, be careful with words such as *all, always, never, none, no one, every,* and *everyone.* These words leave no room for exceptions, which might make your statement untrue. The following statements are invalid because of their overgeneralizing words (in italics):

Everyone feels overwhelmed by too many voice mail and e-mail messages.

All children who watch TV violence behave in aggressive ways toward others.

In your choice of words that most accurately convey your attitudes and opinions, you must also avoid *insensitive* words or phrases, ones that might offend, insult, or ignore any of your readers and their needs. Chapter 11 of this book fully discusses this topic.

PRACTICE 10.2
Using Assertive Words

Rewrite the following sentences to increase their assertiveness.
Answers will vary.

1. If you hired me, I could be an asset to your company because of my management experience.

   My management experience will benefit your company.

2. That insurance company is not being fair with you.

   That insurance company is cheating you.

3. A lawyer may be helpful, and you might choose to discuss these matters with him.

   You definitely need to consult a lawyer.
   _____

4. I attended an interesting and informative seminar.

   That amazing seminar taught me the secrets of getting rich.
   _____

5. We should consider limiting the content of X-rated web sites to protect our children.

   We must ban X-rated web sites to protect our children.
   _____

6. The defendant's family members were disappointed when they heard the judge's verdict.

   The defendant's family members were stunned by the judge's harsh verdict.
   _____

   _____

7. You seem unsure about the proper procedure for completing a timecard.

   Your timecard is incorrect.
   _____

Write Assertive Sentences

Another technique for writing more assertive prose is to use assertive sentence structure in phasing the vast majority of your ideas. The four different kinds of sentences are declarative, imperative, interrogative, and exclamatory. A declarative sentence, which ends with a period, declares or states with authority an idea *(You'll need to read Chapter 12 by next week)*. An imperative sentence is one that gives a command or makes a request *(Please read Chapter 12 by next week)*. It, too, ends with a period. An interrogative sentence asks a question and ends with a question mark *(Can you read Chapter 12 by next week?)*. An exclamatory sentence exclaims an idea, expressing it as a strong feeling *(Chapter 12 will delight and amaze you!)*. This type ends with an exclamation point.

The declarative and imperative sentence types express ideas most assertively. The period at the end of a statement adds a note of finality and truth. So by relying predominantly on this sentence structure, you will write more assertive prose.

In contrast, the interrogative sentence, because it's a question, adds a note of uncertainty, indecisiveness, or pleading to your writing. Notice, for instance, how the following example becomes much more assertive when converted to an imperative sentence:

Interrogative: Will you forgive us while we work out the "bugs" in our system over the next few weeks?

Imperative: Forgive us while we work out the "bugs" in our system over the next few weeks.

Though you can insert an occasional question into a document, you should not overuse this type of sentence. When you do ask the reader a question, make sure you always answer it with a declarative statement. One exception to this rule is the rhetorical question you may ask in a closing paragraph, to keep readers thinking about the topic even after they put down your composition.

The exclamatory sentence may seem assertive, for the exclamation point at its end emphasizes the idea. When used sparingly, the exclamatory sentence can be effective in calling attention to a particular point. However, when overused, it produces the opposite effect. Too many statements punctuated as exclamations will add a note of overreaction, even hysteria, that the reader may interpret as insecurity or overemotionalism. For example, read the following e-mail message, which includes too many exclamatory sentences.

> Our web site has undergone so many changes, we can't tell you about all of them in a single e-mail—you'll just have to see for yourself! So click over to http://www.smarthouse.com and check out YOUR new web site! In the next few weeks, we'll be adding even more features and information, so look often! Also, send us your feedback so we can make it even better!! Enjoy your new site!!!

Every sentence in this message ends with one or more exclamation points. The writer intends to communicate enthusiasm, but instead, he seems overly excited, particularly when using multiple exclamation points.

If you're using assertive words, as discussed in the previous section, you will not need to rely on exclamatory sentences to communicate the strength of your convictions.

PRACTICE 10.3
Writing Assertive Sentences

Rewrite the following sentences to increase their assertiveness.

1. Wouldn't we all like to see neatly mowed lawns when we drive through the neighborhood?

   We would all like to see neatly mowed lawns when we drive through the

   neighborhood.

2. Please don't leave trash on your patio. It attracts bugs and mice! Clear off the leaves, too. They're a fire hazard! Don't leave trash outside your front door. It's unsightly! If you track dirt into the breezeway, clean it up!

   Please don't leave trash on your patio. It attracts bugs and mice. Clear off the

   leaves, too. They're a fire hazard. Don't leave trash outside your front door. It's

   unsightly. If you track dirt into the breezeway, clean it up.

3. Did you know you can call us with your questions as late as eleven o'clock?

   You can call us with your questions as late as eleven o'clock.

4. If you're tired of being overweight, why not sign up today?

If you're tired of being overweight, sign up today.

Use Varying Typefaces for Emphasis

If even after using assertive words in declarative sentences, you feel compelled to further emphasize your ideas, use capital letters or varying typefaces to make words, phrases, or whole sentences stand out. For example, read the following passage from a mayoral candidate's campaign brochure.

IT'S TIME FOR A CHANGE IN LEADERSHIP. The current mayor's 12 years of service is enough. Our town needs new ideas, new voices, and a fresher perspective. If you agree, please support my campaign and get involved in this election. THANK YOU. I do APPRECIATE your vote on **October 5.**

This writer uses capitalization, underlining, and bold print to stress his points. You can also use italics or even different colored fonts to achieve the same effect.

However, use these typefaces sparingly and only to emphasize one specific phrase or thought. Don't type an entire document in capital letters, in an attempt to stress your ideas; the result will be a composition that's difficult to read, one that seems to shout at the reader. When overused, varying the appearance of words in your message can have the same negative effect as too many exclamation points.

TEST YOUR UNDERSTANDING

1. Give two examples of hedging phrases.

It seems that, I think, I believe, I feel that, In my opinion.

2. Give one example of a common apology or disclaimer.

I don't really know much about this, but; I'm not really sure, but; I'm no expert, but; I don't have a degree in this, but.

3. What are two important qualities of assertive words?

Specific, appropriate connotations.

4. What two sentence types express ideas most assertively?

Declarative and imperative.

5. Why should you avoid overusing exclamatory sentences?

They suggest overreaction, overemotionalism, even hysteria.

6. How do variations such as capital letters, bold print, underlining, and italics contribute to a sentence's assertiveness?

   They add emphasis to certain words or phrases.

WEB ACTIVITY: Grammar

If you need to review the rules for grammar and punctuation, the Guide to Grammar and Writing web site offers brief tutorials and interactive quizzes that allow you to check your understanding of this important information.

1. Access the Guide to Grammar and Writing web site at http://webster.commnet.edu/hp/pages/darling/grammar.htm.
2. Choose from the list a topic you need to review. Your instructor may want to recommend a topic for you.
3. Read the tutorial and complete the quiz or quizzes.
4. Have the computer "grade" your quiz or quizzes. Review your incorrect answers; then print the quizzes to submit to your instructor.

GROUP PROJECT AND WRITING ACTIVITIES

For the last two chapters, you'll focus on a company that has provided you with good service or a quality product.

With your group, use one or more invention strategies to generate a list of businesses or companies in your area that have satisfied you with either good service or a quality product. Write as many ideas as possible in the space below.

On your own, choose one of the companies in the list that has just been generated and interview one of its owners, employees, or customers. Find out more about the company's goals, methods, and competition. See Appendix A for more information about conducting successful interviews. Record details from that interview on separate paper or in the space below.

On your own, write a letter to the company's owner or manager to praise its product or service.

READINGS   What strategies do you use to help yourself cope with stress? Should you do more about managing the stress in your life?

In the next article, six experts explain some effective strategies for stress management.

As you read this article, circle every word that's unfamiliar to you. Look it up and write the meaning in the margin. Put an exclamation point (!) next to any sentence or paragraph you find especially interesting. Put a question mark (?) next to any sentence or paragraph you don't understand.

Handle Stress like an Expert

Megan Othersen Gorman

1   According to the American Institute of Stress in Yonkers, N.Y., as many as 90 percent of visits to primary-care physicians are stress-related. Adults, children and apparently even pets are susceptible. No one is immune to the ill effects of stress—not even scientists schooled in how to prevent it.

2   Stress results when our bodies react to a challenge—mental or physical— by increasing metabolism, elevating blood pressure, boosting heart and breathing rates, and pumping three to four times more blood to the muscles than normal. This fight-or-flight response works fine when we do just that— fight or flee. But most often, we do neither. And that's what gets us into trouble. A surplus of unused adrenalin coursing through our bodies can lead to a host of psychological and physical problems.

3   Unless, that is, we learn to handle pressure like a pro. Here, leading stress authorities tell us how they do just that.

The EAT (Energy-Action Team) Plan

Susan Mitchell, a registered dietician and co-author of I'd Kill for a Cookie: A Simple Six-Week Plan to Conquer Stress Eating

4   "My No. 1 stress-less strategy is to graze," says Mitchell. "When I'm anxious, I can't stomach big meals. But when I eat small snacks, I feel better, my energy level improves, and I can better deal with stress."

5   Several years ago the stress of a divorce and the death of several family members left Mitchell with no appetite. But, using her experience as a nutritionist, she and colleague Catherine Christie ultimately devised positive ways to deal with the situation. The result is their EAT (Energy-Action Team) Plan, a multistep approach to minimizing stress that includes eating healthfully (to boost energy, immunity and mood) and exercising regularly (to burn calories and increase endorphins).

6   Ironically, Mitchell notes, the grazing approach works equally well for those of us who *overeat* when we're stressed. "If you eat small portions throughout the day, you're not as hungry as you would be otherwise," she says. "So you're less vulnerable to your cravings."

Megan Othersen Gorman, "Handle Stress Like an Expert," © Copyright 1998 *Cooking Light ®
Magazine.* For subscriptions call 1-800-336-0125.

The Immunity Connection

Janice Kiecolt-Glaser, director of the health psychology division at The Ohio State University College of Medicine, Columbus

7 It isn't just the traumatic that taxes our immune systems and can make us sick, but also the mundane—say, a bad workday or a minor tiff with your mate. Thankfully, though, Kiecolt-Glaser has uncovered strategies to help you protect yourself from the negative effects of stress—one of which is to surround yourself with good friends. "Across our studies, close personal relationships are strongly associated with better immune function," she says. "They provide a buffer in times of stress. So if I've had a bad day, the first thing I do is talk with my husband."

8   Besides finding a confidant, you can counteract stress's influence on your resistance to illness by getting ample sleep, exercising and eating well. "People under stress tend to have poor diets—they consume more junk food, caffeine and alcohol—at the very time when good nutrition is most important," she says.

The Solitude Solution

Peter Suedfeld, psychology professor at the University of British Columbia in Vancouver

9 "When you're alone and quiet," says Suedfeld, "negativity decreases while alertness increases. As a result, you might find that solitude and reduced stimulation restore your ability to think clearly, be creative and maintain an emotional calm."

10   Some people seek solitude behind closed doors, while others take solitary walks. Suedfeld prefers to read, though he sometimes takes a quirkier route: relaxing in a flotation tank in total darkness. "For me, it's a good method of decompressing," he says.

11   Suedfeld believes social support can help ward off some kinds of stress. "But overload requires solitude," he says.

The Strong Survive

Salvatore R. Maddi, professor of psychology and social behavior at the University of California, Irvine, and president of the Hardiness Institute

12 According to Professor Maddi's theory of stress management, it's the hardiest who survive. Maddi defines hardiness as a conglomeration of characteristics that make people try to solve stressful problems rather than fall victim to them.

13   Maddi's theory of hardiness originated from a 12-year study of Illinois Bell Telephone employees between 1975 and 1987. During that period, the phone industry was deregulated and the company was dramatically reduced in size. "Stress was rampant, but a third of the employees actually thrived," Maddi says. "We called them the 'hardy' ones."

14   Maddi himself exemplifies the model. "I struggle, like everyone, against the inclination to allow stressors to direct my life," he says. "But I know in the long run, the best life isn't earned that way. Trying to remain comfortable by avoiding stresses is not only unrealistic, but will also force you to shrink your life to the size of a postage stamp. What's important is to solve stressful problems, turning them from potential disasters into opportunities."

15   Maddi tries to keep what he calls the three C's foremost in his mind during pressure-cooker times: *commitment* (being actively involved in life rather than hanging back and feeling alienated; *control* (trying to influence outcomes instead of being passively influenced by them); and *challenge* (continuing to learn from positive *and* negative experiences).

The Gender Influence

Harriet Braiker, psychologist and author of The Type E Woman: How to Overcome the Stress of Being Everything to Everybody

16   The Type E woman is the female counterpart of the Type A man, the guy most vulnerable to stress-related illness. But while the destination—burnout— might be the same for both personality types, the paths they take to get there are often different. "Type E Women are continually anticipating the needs of others at their own expense," Braiker says. "The classic Type E is a woman with multiple roles; she's a career woman, or a dedicated volunteer. You don't have to be married to be a Type E, but if you are, there's typically an intrinsic conflict between what it takes to be a good mother or wife and what it takes to succeed in the other things you do.

17   "I used to be a Type E," Braiker admits. "But now I'd characterize myself as very high-achieving. I still have multiple roles—wife, mother, and psychologist—but I've learned to practice what I preach: I don't say yes to everybody. I delegate tasks. And it's very clear to me what my priorities are."

18   Those would be Braiker's husband and her nine-year-old daughter—not a June Cleaver-clean kitchen floor.

The Relaxation Response

Dr. Herbert Benson, president of the Mind/Body Medical Institute, affiliated with Harvard Medical School

19   Despite highly respected research showing that what he calls the relaxation response helps treat stress-related disorders, Benson avoided using his own therapy for some 20 years. "I was fearful I wouldn't be viewed as objective if I practiced it myself," he says. "But when I got older, more established—and more stressed—I began to think, *This is silly.*"

20   Here's how to do it: Choose a word or phrase (*ocean* or *peace* or *Hail Mary*, for instance). Sit quietly in a comfortable position, close your eyes and relax your muscles. Breathe slowly, repeating your focus word or words in your mind as you exhale. If everyday thoughts intrude, let them go, and return to the repetition. Continue for ten to 20 minutes.

21   Essentially a physiological antidote to the fight-or-flight syndrome, the relaxation response downshifts all the bodily systems that gear up in stressful situations.

RESPONDING TO THE READING

1. Which of the strategies described in this article have you tried? Were they effective? Why or why not?

   Answers will vary.

   _____

   _____

2. Which of the stress management strategies would you be interested in trying?

   Answers will vary.

   _____

3. Describe a person you know who demonstrates *hardiness*.

   Answers will vary.

   _____

   _____

   _____

4. Describe a woman you know who fits the definition of a *Type E.*

   Answers will vary

   _____

   _____

   _____

   _____

5. Rewrite each of the following sentences from the article to increase their assertiveness. *Answers will vary. Sample answers:*

   "Across our studies, close personal relationships are strongly associated with better immune function. . . ." (paragraph 7)

   Across our studies, close personal relationships obviously improve immune

   function. . .

   "As a result, you might find that solitude and reduced stimulation restore your ability to think clearly, be creative and maintain an emotional calm." (paragraph 9)

   As a result, you'll find that solitude and reduced stimulation will allow you to think

   clearly, be creative and stay calm.

   _____

**RESPONDING TO
THE READING**
continued

Suedfeld believes social support can help ward off some kinds of stress. (paragraph 11)

Suedfeld says social support wards off stress.

_____

During that period, the phone industry was deregulated and the company was dramatically reduced in size. (paragraph 13)

During that period, the government deregulated the phone industry and the

company's workforce was slashed in half.

_____

"Type E women are continually anticipating the needs of others at their own expense. . . ." (paragraph 16)

Type E woman sacrifice themselves for others.

**BUILDING
VOCABULARY**

Review the types of context clues explained on pages 73–74. Then identify the context clue that helps you understand the italicized word in each of the following sentences from the article.

1. It isn't just the traumatic that taxes our immune systems and can make us sick, but also the *mundane*—say, a bad workday or a minor tiff with your mate. (paragraph 7)

   Exemplification _____

2. Maddi defines *hardiness* as a conglomeration of characteristics that make people try to solve stressful problems rather than fall victim to them. (paragraph 12)

   Definition/restatement _____

3. Maddi tries to keep what he calls the three C's foremost in his mind during pressure-cooker times: *commitment* (being actively involved in life rather than hanging back and feeling alienated); *control* (trying to influence outcomes instead of being passively influenced by them); and *challenge* (continuing to learn from positive *and* negative experiences). (paragraph 15)

   Definition/restatement _____

4. Here's how to do *it* [relaxation response]: Choose a word or phrase. . . . Sit quietly in a comfortable position, close your eyes and relax your muscles. (paragraph 20)

   Explanation _____

What kinds of people and situations increase your stress on the job? What strategies do you use to cope with these stressors?

In the next article, author Richard Carlson explains how to cope more effectively with common workplace stressors.

As you read this article, circle every word that's unfamiliar to you. Look it up and write the meaning in the margin. Put an exclamation point (!) next to any sentence or paragraph you find especially interesting. Put a question mark (?) next to any sentence or paragraph you don't understand.

Don't Sweat the Small Stuff at Work
Richard Carlson

1 Most of us spend a good part of our lives at work. And whether we work for a giant corporation or a smaller company, work can be, and usually is, stressful. It's simply a fact of life.

2 The sources of stress vary from job to job. There can be unrealistic deadlines and expectations, difficult and demanding bosses, ridiculous meetings and memos, back-stabbing and criticism, harassment, uncertainty and rejection. In addition, there are insensitive or selfish co-workers, poor working conditions and long commutes. So the question isn't whether stress exists in the workplace, but how to deal with it. Basically, you have two choices: You can surrender to stress or learn to respond in new, more productive ways.

3 If you've read any of my earlier books, you know that I'm an optimist. I believe that practically anyone can make improvements in the quality of her life by making small daily changes in attitude and behavior. If you can learn to treat the smallest hassles with more perspective, wisdom and patience and a better sense of humor, you'll begin to bring out the best in yourself as well as in others. You'll also find, soon enough, that nearly all stuff is small stuff. Here are some ways to get started. I believe that when you try these small steps, you'll not only find work less stressful, but when stress does arise, you'll be able to deal with it with much more grace and ease.

1. Avoid the Phrase "I Have to Go to Work"

4 Of course, you do "have to" go to work to earn money. But remember that your words paint a picture of your expectations. When you *have* to do something, it implies that it's not a choice, that you'd rather be somewhere else. So, when you say "I have to go to work," you are in a subtle way setting yourself up for a bad day.

5 I'm not suggesting you jump for joy or yell out "Yippee, I get to go to work," but something just a little more upbeat. You might also think about the signals you send your children. I don't want to send the message to my children that "work is a bummer and here I go again." Yuck!

6 You'll be surprised and relieved when you change the way you talk about going to work. First, you'll begin to catch yourself as you begin to complain.

From *Don't Sweat the Small Stuff at Work* by Richard Carlson, Ph.D. Copyright © 1998, Dr. Richard Carlson. Reprinted by permission of Hyperion.

Then you'll stop and rephrase your statement to something a bit more positive, like "I'm going to earn some money today so we can do some of the things we enjoy." That sends a subtle reminder to your brain that you're going to have a good day. And when you expect to have a good one, you very seldom disappoint yourself.

2. Don't Make Too Many Promises

7   Some of the promises we make to others may not even seem like promises. Statements like "I'll call you later today," "I'll stop by your office" or "Call me if you ever need me to take your shift" sound innocent enough when we say them. By trying to please, you may have overburdened yourself with tasks that no one would have asked you to do in the first place.

8   I used to engage in this habit virtually every day. Someone would ask me to do something simple, like "Can you send me a copy of that article you were talking about?" I'd automatically say "Sure, no problem." I'd even write myself a note so I wouldn't forget. By the end of the day or week, I was so busy trying to deliver on my promises, I'd often be short of time or forced to hurry on things I really needed to do. Obviously, the more promises you make, the more pressure you have to keep them.

9   I'm not suggesting you stop making promises altogether. Instead, what I'm suggesting is that certain ones don't need to be made in the first place. And if they're not made, you will have less pressure to keep them! I have learned to evaluate each request. For example, if I'm asked for a copy of an article, I might suggest an alternate way for the person to obtain it.

3. Absorb the Speed Bumps of Your Day

10   Rather than labeling the issues that come up during a typical workday as problems, I think of them as speed bumps. Depending on how you approach and deal with the bump, it can be a miserable experience or a temporary slowdown—no big deal.

11   As with a speed bump, if you get stressed out and speed up, you'll hit the bump with a loud thump! If, however, you approach the bump softly and wisely, you'll be over it in no time.

12   Thinking of problems as speed bumps encourages you to say things like "I wonder what the best way to get through this one might be?" This fosters a healthy detachment, so you can look at the problem objectively rather than reactively, and find the path of least resistance. In other words, you assume there is an answer; you just need to find out what it is.

13   My guess is that if you experiment with this one—simply thinking and labeling your issues on the job as speed bumps instead of problems—you're going to be pleasantly surprised at how much more manageable your day is going to seem. You'll slow down and look for a solution, until you find one. That approach makes the workday a lot less bumpy.

4. Become Less Self-Absorbed

14 All of us have a tendency to become somewhat self-absorbed. With a job, spouse and children in the picture, we have a lot on our minds. And at times, we may get carried away with our own issues and our own problems. In the worst cases, however, people take themselves extremely seriously. They speak but don't listen. They consider their problems the most important ones. They value their own time—but no one else's. This mind-set is not to be confused with self-esteem. Having confidence in yourself is virtually the opposite. A person with high self-esteem feels good about herself, and because she already has what she needs, her natural instinct is to reach out to others in an unselfish way. She's extremely interested in hearing what other people have to say and in learning from them.

15 By contrast, self-absorbed individuals are so taken with their own problems, ambition and needs that they come to see others only as instruments to get something they want. Being so focused on themselves makes them not only unappealing to co-workers, but also creates high levels of stress. In fact, self-absorbed people sweat the small stuff more than any other group. It seems that nothing is ever good enough. They are stuck in their own problems and their own perspective. After a while, few people want to help or support them. It's difficult to cheer on an arrogant person. In fact, it's tempting to want to see him fail.

16 For these reasons, it's a good idea to make an honest assessment of your own level of self-absorption. If you feel you've drifted in that direction, make an adjustment. Train yourself to stop talking and ask other people about their lives. You'll find it's a relief from your stress, connects you to your co-workers and keeps you up to speed on office politics. You'll break out of your own little world and do a better job.

5. See Beyond the Roles

17 It's almost inevitable that you will sometimes see people as their role instead of as a unique human being doing business in that role. You see the banker as a uni-dimensional person with control over your bank account, or the baker as the person who ran out of pecan pies for Thanksgiving. But a baker has a life of her own, her own stories and dramas to deal with. The flight attendant is tired and can't wait to get home. The person pumping your gasoline has a family, insecurities and problems of his own. The corporate executive probably argues with her husband and has plenty of problems unknown to the rest of us. Whether it's your staff or your boss, every person has a rich life beyond the office.

18 I recently heard a story about a woman's boss who was so locked into roles that he actually put his pencils in his outbox for his secretary to sharpen! It would have taken him a few seconds to do it himself, but in his mind it was her role and ". . . she was going to do it." He was either oblivious or simply didn't care how this made her feel.

19   When you see people as human beings first, they often treat you better, listen to you and make allowances for you that others don't enjoy. You open the door for richer, more nourishing and genuine interactions. People will like you and trust you. They will often go to great lengths to help you.

20   Had the man in my example treated his secretary more as a fellow person and less as her role, she probably would have sharpened the silly pencils anyway. As it was, however, the way he handled it made her feel like dirt and she ended up quitting the job. Sadly for him, she had been an excellent secretary. One small consolation was that the boss later realized how badly he had treated her. I hope he learned his lesson.

21   My suggestion is simply to remember that each person is special, and is so much more than what they do. Each person you meet has feelings—sadness, joy, fears and all the rest. Simply knowing this and keeping it in mind can transform your life in some simple yet powerful ways. You can brighten other people's days by merely smiling and making eye contact. You can contribute to making the world a nicer, friendlier place for others and for yourself.

6. When You Solicit Advice, Consider Taking It

22   One of the most interesting dynamics I've observed is the tendency of many people to share a problem but completely ignore the advice they receive in response. The reason I find this so interesting is because, as I have listened to conversations over the years, I've been impressed over and over again by a great deal of the creative advice I have heard. So often, it would appear that the advice being given would solve the problem at hand easily and quickly.

23   I don't know exactly why so many of us tend to dismiss the advice we receive. Perhaps we are embarrassed that we need help, or we hear things we don't want to hear. Maybe we are too proud to admit that a friend or family member knows something we don't. Sometimes the advice we receive requires effort or a change in lifestyle. There are probably many other factors as well.

24   I'm the first to admit that I do many things wrong. But one of the qualities I'm most proud of—and am certain has helped me a great deal in both my personal and professional life—is my ability to really listen to advice, and, in many instances, take it. I'm absolutely willing to admit that I don't have all the answers I need to make my life as effective and peaceful as possible. Not only do I often benefit from the advice I receive, but the person offering it to me is thrilled that I'm actually willing to listen and even take the advice. People have suggested that I talk too much—and they were right. I've been told I needed to become a better listener—and I did. People have suggested that I take a certain course or try a certain diet, and I have. And it really helped. As long as I remain receptive and nondefensive, I can almost always learn something. Sometimes, one simple suggestion can make a world of difference.

7. Don't Get Stressed by the Predictable

25 In most jobs, there are certain predictable pressure points. The first few times they happen, or if you're caught off guard, it's understandable that they can create some anxiety or stress. However, once you factor them into your awareness, and you can predict how events are typically played out, it's silly to be annoyed and upset. Yet I find that many people continue to feel bothered, even after they see how the game is played.

26   I met an accountant, for example, who gets annoyed every March and April because his hours are increased and he can't leave the office at five. He jumps up and down and complains about how "unfair" it is, even though it's absolutely predictable. It would seem to me that virtually all accountants who prepare income tax returns for a living would be the busiest during tax season. What am I missing?

27   I met a police officer who took it personally when people drove faster than the speed limit. He would get frustrated and dish out harsh lectures, apparently forgetting that it was his job to catch people speeding to create safer roads. Again, this is a predictable part of his work.

28   Before you say, "Those are silly examples," or "I'd never get upset over something like that," take a careful look at your own situation. I've seen a similar pattern in many fields. In some industries, for example, there are built-in delays. You'll be waiting on suppliers, orders or someone or something else in order to do your job, so it will always seem as if you're running late and in an enormous hurry. While it's true you have to wait until the last minute to get everything you need, it's entirely predictable. Therefore, if you can make the necessary allowances for the inevitable, you won't have to feel the pressure. To be surprised and resentful that you're constantly waiting for others is foolish. It is the worst kind of stress—self-induced. You'll be much happier if you make allowances in your mind, attitude and behavior for the predictable pressures.

8. Get It Over With

29 I've created a habit for myself that has undoubtedly saved me thousands of hours of unnecessary stress and worrisome thinking. The habit I'm referring to involves attending to the most difficult or uncomfortable parts of my day first, before anything else.

30   For example, I may have to resolve a conflict, make a difficult phone call, turn someone down and disappoint him, or do something else that I wish I didn't have to do. I've made a commitment to myself that, whenever possible and practical, I make the phone call first—before anything else. I get it over with! That way, I avoid all the stress that would have been inevitable had I waited. But even more than that, I find I'm usually more effective in dealing with the situation because I'm fresher and more alert. I haven't spent the day dreading or rehearsing my conversation. This makes me more responsive to the moment, a key element in solving most problems effectively and gracefully.

31   I'm sure there are exceptions, but I've yet to experience a single scenario where I've regretted this decision. I know for sure that this strategy has helped me to keep calmer and, overall, happier while I'm engaged in my work.

9. Don't Sweat Your Critics

32   To be honest, if I became upset by my critics, I can guarantee that you wouldn't be reading this book today. The truth is, critics are a fact of life, and criticism is something all of us must face. Sometimes the criticism we receive is valuable, even helpful. Other times, it's utter nonsense. Either way, learning to see criticism as "small stuff" is incredibly useful in our efforts to live a life of reduced stress.

33   I've been criticized for being everything from a Pollyanna to simplistic, naive and unrealistic. I've even had a few people accuse me of attempting to harm people with my message of cheer! For as long as I can remember, a certain percentage of people have told me, "You couldn't possibly be that happy" or "Your life must be easier than mine." There's just no way around it. Someone is always going to have an objection to something you are doing.

34   I asked a fellow author who is extremely calm and nonreactive how he handles bad reviews and criticism. He answered, "I always try to see if there is a grain of truth in what is being said. Quite honestly, there often is. In these instances, I try to learn what I can, and then let go of it. Very often my greatest growth comes directly after a dose of criticism. On the other hand, I've learned that if there's nothing to the criticism, it will simply fade away. The worst thing to do is take it personally and become defensive."

35   Everyone is entitled to his opinion. Something you find funny I might think of as boring, or vice versa. No matter how hard any of us try, no matter how positive our intentions, there will always be someone there to criticize us. Welcome to the human race. When you make the decision to stop sweating your critics, your ego and self-image won't be hurt anymore, and work will seem a great deal less stressful.

RESPONDING TO THE READING

1. Do you contribute to your own stress by doing any of the nine things the author describes in this article? Which ones?

   Answers will vary.

   _____

   _____

   _____

2. How can you apply the author's advice to your situation to reduce stress?

   Answers will vary.

   _____

   _____

3. Underline the particularly assertive words in the following sentences:

There can be <u>unrealistic</u> deadlines and expectations, <u>difficult</u> and <u>demanding bosses</u>, <u>ridiculous</u> meetings and memos, <u>back-stabbing</u> and <u>criticism</u>, <u>harassment</u>, <u>uncertainty</u> and <u>rejection</u>. (paragraph 2)

Had the man in my example treated his secretary more as a fellow person and less as her role, she probably would have sharpened the <u>silly</u> pencils anyway. As it was, however, the way he handled it made her feel like <u>dirt</u> and she ended up quitting the job. (paragraph 20)

BUILDING VOCABULARY

A *thesaurus* can help writers discover the best words to state their ideas. It contains *synonyms*, words with similar meanings.

Use a thesaurus to find a synonym for each of the italicized words in the following sentences from Richard Carlson's article. Substitute words that do not change the meanings of the sentences. Use a dictionary to help yourself decide. *Answers will vary.*

1. I used to *engage* in this habit virtually every day. (paragraph 8)

   take part

2. For example, if I'm asked for a copy of an article, I might suggest an alternate way for the person to *obtain* it. (paragraph 9)

   get

3. Whether it's your *staff* or your boss, every person has a rich life beyond the office. (paragraph 17)

   employees

4. However, once you factor them into your awareness, and you can predict how events are typically played out, it's *silly* to be annoyed and upset. (paragraph 25)

   pointless

5. Therefore, if you make the necessary *allowances* for the inevitable, you won't have to feel the pressure. (paragraph 28)

   modifications

6. You'll be much happier if you make allowances in your mind, attitude and behavior for the predictable *pressures*. (paragraph 28)

   stresses

7. I asked a fellow author who is *extremely* calm and nonreactive how he handles bad reviews and criticism. (paragraph 34)

   unusually

PROFESSIONAL PROFILE
John King, Systems Administrator

John King is a married father of three who works as a systems administrator. His responsibilities include round-the-clock monitoring of servers that host web site files for his company's clients, procuring hardware and software to meet the company's needs, and troubleshooting and resolving all problems with the computer system. He writes many e-mail messages and information-technology plan documents, which outline strategies for systems improvements. Here is one of his e-mail messages to his company's employees.

Kindly do not download and install any software on your systems without checking with and receiving approval from management or myself. Whilst we typically do not exercise any rigid controls over the software that you have on your systems (e.g., instant messaging software), we cannot justify the time it takes to resolve and rebuild systems that crash due to the downloading of software such as AOL Instant Messenger. At this time we will, however, ask that no one use AOL's Instant Messenger, as it crashed a system yesterday and caused the IS Dept to spend upwards of two hours researching, resolving and rebuilding the system. In addition, if anyone is going to do any heavy downloading of other material, check with the above mentioned folks before doing so. The copying of web sites must absolutely be cleared through Ralph before commencing such a process. Any downloading or uploading of materials that is not related to company business is prohibited and must be cleared through management. For your information, we do monitor web traffic, and we can tell how much bandwidth is being used specifically by your machine.

Thanks for your cooperation.

John's message shows tact and sensitivity, two characteristics of all effective writing. Chapter 11 explains how to achieve those qualities in your own writing.

Let's say you arrived at work one day to find the following e-mail message from a co-worker addressed to you:

You were supposed to send me the Franklin report yesterday. You need to get your act together and send it to me by 9 o'clock this morning. Any idiot knows that Mr. Franklin doesn't tolerate slackers who goof off instead of doing their jobs. If we lose his business because of you, there'll be hell to pay.

What would be your reaction to this message? You'd probably be angry and defensive, even if you were in the wrong. Even if you *are* late in finishing the report, this e-mail is probably not going to get you to finish it any faster. Because your co-worker threatens you, insults you with words such as *idiot, slacker*, and *goof off*, and offends you with curse words, you won't be inclined to do what he wants, even if he has a valid request.

Writers should always strive to phrase their ideas and opinions with confidence, as Chapter 10 of this book recommends. However, we must balance this assertiveness with an awareness of our readers' needs, goals, and feelings. Though we do want to present our thoughts unequivocally, we must also take care to avoid offending or insulting readers, as we don't want to cause them to reject our ideas. Instead, we want to make sure we state our ideas with sensitivity and tact, always tailoring a composition to the specific reader.

This means that a careful consideration of the reader must be an important step in planning any composition. First, a writer needs to think about his reader's *priorities*. For instance, a writer who wants his co-worker to send him a report should keep in mind that the co-worker may be responsible for many other projects, all of equal or greater importance. Yet that co-worker probably wants to complete all assigned tasks, so that he'll be viewed as competent.

Next, identify the reader's *needs*. Ask yourself why he might find your ideas useful or interesting. In the case of the e-mail about the late report, perhaps the reader is unaware of the report's due date. He may not understand the report's importance. Therefore, one of his needs could be information about the problem. Also, he might need assistance or input from others in order to finish the report.

Then consider any *objections* he might have to your ideas. Your co-worker responsible for sending you a report may be overwhelmed with other obligations that have delayed him in fulfilling your request. He may object to insufficient preparation time or to lack of help. How will you address and overcome these concerns?

Finally, what language will most sensitively convince him to believe you? Your conclusions about your reader's priorities, needs, and potential objections will determine the words you choose. For instance, think again about that co-worker who's supposed to write a report for you. What is the most sensitive way to remind him of his past-due obligation? Because his behavior is creating problems for you, you might be tempted to suggest that he's an *idiot*, a *slacker* who *goofs off*. But the derogatory meanings of those terms will anger him. Also demeaning are the accusations that he doesn't know what's he doing. Instead of insulting *him*, it's best to stay focused on the problem of the tardy report.

Here is a revision of the earlier message. This version considers the reader.

As you recall, we agreed that you'd send me the Franklin report yesterday. I have not yet received it, and I wanted to remind you that the data you're collecting for us is critical to the development of our marketing strategy,which we'll be discussing in this afternoon's meeting with Mr. Franklin. I'm sure you're busy with many projects right now, but I'll need that report this morning. If you need any assistance, please call me or Anne Davis.

This revised message, which illustrates specific things to do—and not do—to persuade a reader to accept your ideas, has a better chance than the first version of achieving its purpose.

MATCH YOUR POINTS TO YOUR READER

The most effective composition will always match the writer's ideas to the reader's priorities and needs. Therefore, the first way to compose with sensitivity is to include only those points, ideas, opinions, and arguments that are directly relevant to your reader. Let's say, for example, that you wish to write about improving accessibility for disabled customers at a new shopping center in your community. You could offer many reasons in support of your opinion, including the following:

1. Discrimination and possible lawsuits
2. Loss of revenue
3. Danger to all patrons
4. Negative reputation in the community
5. Concern for people with disabilities

Types of Readers

Not all of the five arguments just listed will affect all readers. To select appropriate points to include, you'll need to think more about your specific reader. If she's an owner of the shopping center, she'll be a businessperson interested in making money. She'll also want to avoid anything—such as lawsuits—that will reduce profits. Therefore, the most effective arguments for this reader are 1, 2, and 3. You probably wouldn't use these same arguments in a general letter addressed to the citizens who patronize the shopping center. If they have no financial interest in that shopping center, they're likely to be more interested in potential dangers to themselves (reason 3) and to feel concern for those who face discrimination and restrictions (reason 5).

For a second illustration, consider writing a memo to propose a change in a procedure to your supervisor at work. To decide what points to present, first consider who the reader is. He's in a position of responsibility. He wants to make cost-effective decisions that will satisfy his customers. What arguments will convince him that he ought to make your proposed change? The ones that point out how your proposal will save the company money, generate more business, or deliver your product or service faster or more efficiently to the customer. He'll be less likely to be swayed by arguments that focus on benefits to his employees, unless you show him how these benefits will lead to increased productivity, profits, and happier customers, his three main priorities. It's not that you shouldn't mention the lighter workload and reduced stress that the change will bring to you and your co-workers. You just want to place more emphasis on the points that match your reader's major goals.

Types of Arguments

When matching points to a specific reader, it's a good idea to consider whether or not that particular individual will be most affected by logical arguments, emotional arguments, or a combination of the two. *Logical arguments* are based on hard facts and empirical evidence. For example, if you want your reader to buy a certain brand of paper towels, you could explain how that brand's physical makeup results in greater absorbency, or how it's more cost-effective than other brands because it provides more towels for less money. These are the logical arguments that support your recommendation. In addition, you could also add emotional arguments to your appeal. If your reader has children, for example, you could argue (as many television commercials do) that buying this specific brand makes you a better parent because the quick, easy cleanup will prevent you from getting upset about messes your kids make. *Emotional arguments* target readers' needs for love, friends, fun, power, and influence. As you're deciding on the most appropriate points to include, categorize each as either logical or emotional. This will help you tailor specific arguments to specific readers.

**PRACTICE 11.1
Matching Points
to Reader**

For each different reader, select the two or three most appropriate arguments from the list.

Thesis: You should learn ballroom dancing.

Reasons:

A. Improved cardiovascular health

B. Improved physical appearance (weight loss, muscle tone)

C. Expanded social life

D. Potential career

E. Fun and entertainment

F. Improved business and networking skills

Answers will vary.

1. A group of senior citizens: *A, C, E* _____

2. A single mother: *B, C, E* _____

3. A teenager: *B, D, E* _____

Thesis: The City Council should put an end to driving on the beach.

Reasons:

A. Danger to pedestrians

B. Possible lawsuits

C. Environmental damage

D. Increased tourism

E. Increased revenue for city

1. Business owners near the beach: *D and E* _____

2. The city's mayor: *A, B, D, E* _____

3. Readers of the city's local newspaper: *A, C, E* _____

MAKE CONCESSIONS

We don't write for readers who already know the information we're presenting or who already agree with our viewpoint. Doing so would be "preaching to the choir," a waste of time and effort. Because we write, then, to inform our readers or to convince them to believe what we do, we can assume one of two things about them: (1) they haven't yet made up their minds or formed their own opinions about the topic; or (2) they support the opposing viewpoint, which is why we need to persuade them to change their minds. In either case, our readers are likely to have at least a few preconceived ideas and opinions about our topic before they begin reading.

Keeping this in mind, you can write more successful compositions if you offer your readers *concessions,* or acknowledgments of their pre-existing opinions, disagreements, and objections. Obviously, you have to consider your reader carefully to choose appropriate concessions. Just as you match your points to your reader's goals and priorities, you must match your concessions to your reader's most likely objections. You have to anticipate her arguments and as you write, acknowledge that they exist. For instance, if you were to write that letter to the shopping center owner about improving access, you would acknowledge her specific concerns about this suggestion. She is likely to resist the idea because of the cost of your proposed changes. She may also object because the shopping center already complies with laws regarding handicapped accessibility. Furthermore, she may know of other disabled individuals who have shopped at the center without complaint. In your letter, you would want to mention these concerns.

Advantages and Disadvantages

Right now, as you read this chapter, you may be objecting to the whole notion of concessions. You might be thinking of two potential dangers that could weaken your composition. First, you might object to concessions because of your concern that they will remind readers of the opposing arguments. Second, you may be inclined to object because you fear you'll mention arguments that readers haven't even considered, thus adding even more support for their opposing viewpoints. Yet although these potential dangers do exist, the advantages of concessions almost always outweigh the disadvantages.

Including concessions will actually strengthen your composition in three specific ways. First, they demonstrate your understanding of the *whole* issue, not just one side. As a result, readers will see you as a more credible source of information and will more willingly accept your ideas. Second, concessions will help you establish your goodwill toward readers by acknowledging *their* viewpoints. Offering a concession is the written equivalent of *listening* to your readers, giving them a chance to have their say. As a result, they'll be more likely to consider your views because you seem sensitive to their opinions. Finally, concessions are valuable because they allow a writer to respond to and refute specific objections to his or her ideas. After acknowledging a particular concern or disagreement, the writer can very thoroughly present all of the evidence that argues against it. This will show readers how each of their particular concerns might be addressed.

To understand the effects of omitting concessions, read the following letter:

> Sick and tired of having your life endangered by drivers who are too self-important to put their phones down and pay attention to the road? So are we.
>
> The odds that you'll slam your jalopy into some hapless driver—or your local guardrail—increase 400 percent when a cell phone is being used. Those are about the same odds of having an accident as when you're legally drunk.
>
> Driving and Talking is dangerous. We know it. You know it. Even the cell phone industry flacks know it, though they'll never admit it.
>
> . . . Help us get everyone to "Drive Now, Talk Later"—before you or someone you love gets T-boned by a moron talking to his broker on a cell phone.[1]

One quick reading of this letter reveals the writers' total lack of consideration for their readers. Any cell phone user would undoubtedly have some

---

[1]From *In Our Humble Opinion by* Tom Magliozzi and Ray Magliozzi, copyright © 2000 by Tom Magliozzi and Ray Magliozzi. Used by permission of Perigee Books, a division of Penguin Putnam Inc.

valid objections to its points. For instance, many people don't use cell phones just to look important; rather, they need them for professional or personal responsibilities. Also, plenty of people manage to drive safely while talking at the same time. Furthermore, drivers have always chatted with other passengers in the vehicle without causing accidents.

The lack of concessions in this letter show that the writers really don't understand the whole issue. Also, because the writers make no effort to overcome readers' concerns and disagreements, those readers probably won't take the proposals in the letter seriously.

Guidelines

If you still fear that concessions will undermine your arguments, make sure you adhere to the following guidelines to reduce the potential dangers.

Keep Concessions Brief.   Mention the argument or objection, but don't elaborate on it. The more detail you include, the greater the chance that you might reinforce or augment the reader's opposition. Usually, a brief one-sentence statement will acknowledge the argument sufficiently. Then move on immediately to refute it with your own evidence and explanations.

Match Each Concession with the Appropriate Point.   A concession should address a point's specific argument. For example, in the letter about cell phones, the authors make the following points:

1. People who talk on the phone while driving are "self-important."
2. Driving and talking increase the chances of causing an accident.

To determine the best concessions, think of the argument a cell phone user would give for each point:

Point	Concession
1. People who talk on the phone while driving are "self-important."	1. Many people use cell phones to take care of professional or personal responsibilities.
2. Driving and talking increases the chance of causing an accident.	2. Plenty of people manage to talk while driving safely.

Don't End with Concessions.   Concessions are more effective when you present them at the beginnings of paragraphs and then prove them invalid with your own ideas and evidence. When you end a paragraph with a concession, you're leaving the reader with that contrary thought rather than with your viewpoint. Match the concessions you need to make to each of your points; then thoroughly refute each with a fully developed paragraph (see Chapters 4 and 5 of this book). Whatever you do, don't save all of your concessions for the end of your composition; the reader will finish it thinking of the opposing viewpoint rather than your own.

Signal the Beginning and End of a Concession.   Certain transition words signal to the reader when a concession begins and ends. Here are some common words and phrases used to introduce a concession:

Admittedly,   It's true that
Granted,   Yes,

Of course,	I agree that
I concede that	I understand that

Follow your concession with another clear transition to signal that you will now refute that point. These transitions include words such as *however, but,* and *on the contrary.*

The following passages provide effective examples of concessions (in italics). Transition words are in boldface.

I realize that I plan to move before my year's lease has expired; **however,** I am moving only because my company is transferring me to another state.

Admittedly, adding a 401(k) plan to our employee benefit package will cost you money. **However,** you will ultimately save more money in the long run, due to decreased employee turnover.

It's true that the highway needs repairs, **but** you should not close lanes for miles when crews can work on only a small section of the road at a time.

I know you think you'll benefit more by continuing your current relationship with Montgomery Paper Products; **on the contrary,** we'll offer you unsurpassed customer service and a larger inventory to choose from.

To fully understand the opposing viewpoint, consider debating your topic with someone who disagrees with your thesis. Your opponent's arguments will help you know what concessions to include in your composition.

PRACTICE 11.2
Concessions

Add concessions that match each of the points in the following outlines.

Thesis: You should extend the due date for our next assignment by one week.
Answers will vary.

1. We face tests and project deadlines in our other classes, too.

   Concession: *You shouldn't have waited until the last minute to begin working*

   on them.

2. This is a complex assignment that requires more preparation time.

   Concession: *You should have planned ahead and scheduled time to spend on it.*

3. You'll receive higher-quality work if we have more time to complete the assignment.

   Concession: *More time does not necessarily produce better work. Even with an*

   extended deadline, you might still put off the assignment until the night before it's

   due.

Thesis: Our state legislature should raise the minimum age for obtaining a driver's license to eighteen.

1. Young, inexperienced drivers cause too many accidents.

   Concession: *Instead of preventing them from driving, we should give them more*

   instruction and practice time. Without practice, they won't be any more competent

   at eighteen than they are at sixteen.

2. If they can't drive until they're eighteen, high school students will focus on school rather than on getting a job to pay for a car.

   Concession: *Plenty of high school students successfully juggle a job and school.*

3. Fewer drivers on the road will mean less traffic.

   Concession: *The number of drivers aged sixteen to eighteen is too small to*

   make a significant impact on traffic.

AVOID OFFENDING OR INSULTING YOUR READER

Can you remember the last time someone insulted either you personally or a group with which you were affiliated? Your first reaction probably was to become defensive, maybe even angry. Your next reaction probably was to reject all of the ideas and opinions of the person who insulted you. Readers experience the same reaction when they are offended by a composition. As writers, then, we must take care to avoid insensitive language, for no matter how brilliant our ideas, an insulted reader will dismiss them outright. Thus, the composition will not fulfill its purpose.

This section presents three specific types of insensitive language—name calling, statements that create a condescending or dismissive tone, and emotionally-loaded terms—that will threaten the success of your composition.

Name Calling

The first type of insensitive language is name calling, using derogatory labels to describe people or groups. Writers use this technique in an attempt to cast doubt upon or to destroy the credibility of an opponent's ideas by attacking that individual's intelligence or character. In reality, though, this most blatantly insensitive tactic usually produces the reverse effect. Name calling only brands the *writer* as immature, petty, and hostile.

For example, the cell phone letter refers to cell phone users as "morons." In an editorial about shaking hands, the writer claims that people who give "limp" handshakes believe they are superior to everyone else; therefore, they are "too good to bother giving a firm handshake."[2] Not surprisingly, both of

[2]Bree LeMasters, "The Illustrious Art of Handshaking," *The Observer* (September 18, 1997), http://www.tufts.edu/as/stu-org/observer/1997/september18/observations/4.htm.

these writers sound like mean, overemotional children, and the logical points they include are completely overshadowed by their insults.

Here are a few more examples of name-calling (in italics):

The customer service *jerk* I spoke to told me his computer screen did not show my latest payment.

The entire educational system in this country stinks (pretty much). The people who run the education business *are money-grubbing, self-serving morons.* The people who do the teaching are—for the most part—*egomaniacs who don't have the faintest idea* of what education should be all about.[3]

These *animal supremacist imbeciles* find it impossible to accept the need for change in the animal world. They find it unbelievable that any actual species should become extinct, no matter the nature, dangerous reality, or hopelessness for survival of that species. Such *absurd thinking* has even led to federal legislation imposing *insane* penalties on *the rest of the intelligent human population* in the form of such *inanities* as the Endangered Species Act. . . .[4]

You cannot build up yourself or your ideas by tearing someone else down. You will only damage your own credibility when you resort to childish attacks upon others. So focus on exposing the flaws in *ideas,* not in the people who believe them.

Condescending or Dismissive Tone

The second type of insensitive language includes statements implying that the reader or his or her idea is ignorant, uninformed, illogical, or wrong. Such statements will produce an arrogant, condescending tone of "talking down" to readers, suggesting that they are inferior. Writers never convert readers by implying that those readers are stupid. The following statements include examples of insensitive phrases (in italics).

You seem to be having difficulty understanding that we aren't interested in working overtime every week.

I have an answer for a few *supposedly bright individuals* who want [18-wheeler] trucks off the roads. Unless you have a railroad spur into your back yard, you need trucks. *Yes, you, the same idiot* that complains about the noise my reefer (refrigeration unit) is making on a 90-degree day in mid-July is the same person complaining about his or her ice cream being soft or his milk being sour. *How do you think it gets to the market anyway? Do you think they have cows in the back room or something? Think before you speak.*[5]

Religion is something to stop people from spending their time contemplating the secrets of the universe/meaning of life. . . . Religion is simply an *easy answer* to unanswerable questions. It's a way to comfort people of all their fears about the unknown. As said by Trent Reznor in the song "Happiness in Slavery": "*The blind* have been blessed with security." Religion is, essentially, a collection of *false explanations* to make people complacent with their lives.[6]

---

[3]Tom Magliozzi, "The Allegory of the Epiphany at the Fountain," *Car Talk,* http://cartalk.cars.com/About/Rant/r-r.html.
[4]WhatWhat (July 17, 1999), http://www.whatwhat.com.
[5]"Replies to Bad Truck Driver Law," http://www.bitchaboutit.com/ReadPages/truck_replys.htm.
[6]"My Opinion on Religion," http://members.xoom.com/ddisturbedd/religion.htm.

Women, by far, are the worst about handshakes. Maybe it stems from that whole *"dainty lady" thing* from bygone days when gloves restricted movement. However, I don't see too many gloved females except on sub-zero days. My theory is that the *faux-delicacy* of the limp [hand]shake is reflective of when women had their hands kissed by men. Then, it was appropriate to offer a light hand with closed fingers. Last time I checked, no guys . . . were kissing a girl's hand upon introduction.[7]

Avoid any suggestion that the reader is mentally deficient or unenlightened.

Emotionally Loaded Words

Chapter 10 of this book discussed the denotative (dictionary) and connotative (emotional) meanings of words. The connotative meanings of words help us communicate our thoughts and feelings about a topic accurately and confidently. They also help us urge the reader to feel a certain way about that topic. If you use the word *inexpensive* to describe a couch, you are suggesting to the reader that the buyer found a good deal. If you describe the same couch as *cheap*, you suggest not only that its price was low, but also that its quality is poor. Some readers will even attach the extra meanings of "tawdry" or "shoddy" to that particular adjective. Also, compare the words *assertive* and *aggressive*. Favorable connotations are attached to the former, while the unfavorable suggestions of "pushy" and "overbearing" are attached to the latter.

For another example, look at the following sentence, which comes from the *Why I Hate McDonald's* web site:

. . . neither [my daughter] nor I eat the *dead cow flesh* or the *deep-fat fried chunks of chicken gristle* that they offer in their *Crappy Meals*.[8]

This statement is obviously very harsh because of the emotionally loaded words (in italics), which the writer chose to encourage the reader to form a negative reaction to her subject. These words are indeed forceful and assertive. However, words like *dead cow flesh, gristle,* and *crappy* are clearly derogatory and insulting. Fans or employees of McDonald's reading this sentence would become defensive, even angry; therefore, the composition would not convince them to change their minds.

Assertive word choices must be tempered by consideration of the *reader's* feelings. Using language that is bold but offensive will cause the reader to reject your ideas. Often, we need to tone down a statement by choosing words more sensitive to that reader. For example, you might revise the example sentence as follows:

. . . neither [my daughter] nor I eat the poor-quality hamburger meat or the rubbery, processed chicken that they offer in their Happy Meals.

Though this revision obviously is much less forceful, it is much more sensitive to the reader who may happen to like McDonald's food.

Another example of emotionally loaded language comes from an animal activist web site. In an essay about experiments on monkeys, the author uses very emotional words and phrases.

It is impossible to *inject a virus* into a monkey, or *insert feces* into a newborn's lungs, or *sew an eye shut*, or inject *an individual* with PCP and at the

[7]LeMasters, "The Illustrious Art."
[8]Anne Kathleen Murphy, "The Crappy Meal Toy Scam," *Why I Hate McDonald's* web site (January 5, 1997), http://members.aol.com/AnneDroidz/mcdsux.html.

same time pretend to possess a concern for their well-being. The lines are clearly drawn.

The researchers themselves acknowledge that they are engaging in research on *beings* very similar to humans. Throughout history, during *other times of holocaust*, those not directly affected have kept their mouths shut. Such silence has amounted to a culpable, tacit approval.

Only *the brave* have spoken out, only *the true champions of human dignity and humanity* have *risked their personal reputation and safety* by *challenging the power* of the state to *harm others*.

Make no mistake, the United States government will not cease its *holocaust* of monkeys and apes until citizens make it clear that there are political risks in not doing so. The people who would harm a primate have a mindset similar to those who were willing to experiment on Jews, Poles, Gypsies, and homosexuals in *Nazi Germany* or low income people of color in this country.[9]

The writer uses this kind of language intentionally to stir the reader's sympathy for the animals.

On a final note, remember that all vulgar, sexist, and racist language is also emotionally loaded and offensive. Refrain from ever including curse words, gender-related insults, or racial slurs in your writing.

PRACTICE 11.3
Sensitive Language

Rewrite the following sentences to increase their sensitivity to the reader. *Answers will vary.*

1. Americans are truly the laughing stock of the world. Despite their own weakened and pathetic state, they feel the need to loudly inform anyone within reach of CNN of the "superiority" of their way of life.[10]

   The rest of the world often disagrees with the notion of American superiority.

   _____

2. I'm sick of precious trees being murdered so you can stuff my mailbox with useless junk mail that serves no purpose but to choke our already-overflowing landfills.

   Please stop sending us unsolicited paper advertisements. Because they just wind up

   in our already-overflowing landfills, they destroy trees for no reason.

   _____

3. You'd be totally crazy to elect another crooked ex-lawyer to represent you in Congress.

   Congress already contains too many former attorneys.

[9]"Primate Experimentation: A National Disgrace," *Ignorance is Bliss* web site http://www.angelfire.com/ar2/bliss/.

[10]*Assault on America* web site (March 18, 1997), http://www.geocities.com/CapitolHill/Lobby/1867/assault.htm.

4. . . . they certainly don't need to spend millions on "counseling" [the students who witness school shootings] and other mental babysitting upon which our weak-kneed society would seem to have become dependent (at least according to certain social wimps).[11]

   Our society mistakenly believes that counseling will solve everything. Students who

   witness school shootings don't necessarily need counseling.

   _____

   _____

5. The opening [of the Fox Network's coverage of a hockey game] was just horrid. It consisted of the old Sabres logo dissolving in .gif style from a horrible-looking blue blob, followed by some really cheesy music and clips. . . . Fox has destroyed everything that makes hockey enjoyable to watch.[12]

   The quality of the opening for Fox Network's hockey game coverage was poor. It

   consisted of the old Sabres logo dissolving in .gif style from an unpleasant blue

   background, followed by some ineffective music and clips.... Fox obviously needs to

   revise this opening.

   _____

   _____

6. The food is skimpy. A prawn in the dining room is about the size of a grub worm. They do offer some light dishes, like the salads that couldn't even be recognized. Where did these greens come from? I guess bitter chlorophyll biodegradable matter is in these days.[13]

   The food was unexpectedly poor. The prawns were very small, and light dishes such

   as the salads contained greens that were bitter and wilted.

   _____

7. Trying to reason with him was as worthwhile and satisfying as talking to my coffeemaker.[14]

   He did not comprehend my arguments.

   _____

---

[11]WhatWhat (May 6, 1999), http://www.whatwhat.com.
[12]Assault on America web site (March 27, 1997), http://www.geocities.com/CapitolHill/Lobby/ 1867/assault.htm.
[13]*Carnival Curse, I Mean Cruise* web site, http://members.aol.com/kgoldman12/carnival.html.
[14]Murphy, "The Crappy Meal Toy Scam."

TEST YOUR UNDERSTANDING

1. What is the difference between a logical and an emotional argument?

   Logical arguments are based on hard facts and empirical evidence. Emotional

   arguments target readers' needs for love, friends, fun, power, and influence.

2. What is a concession?

   An acknowledgement of the opposing argument.

3. Give two examples of words that signal the beginning of a concession.

   Admittedly, Granted, Of course, I concede that, It's true that, Yes, I agree that,

   I understand that.

4. What are two specific types of insensitive language?

   Name calling and condescending/dismissive language.

5. Why do some writers mistakenly use name calling?

   They believe it will cast doubt upon or destroy an opponent's ideas.

6. Why are readers usually offended by a condescending tone?

   They don't like the suggestion that they are inferior or wrong.

7. Why must writers carefully consider the connotations of the bold, assertive words they choose?

   If those words offend the reader, the reader will reject a writer's ideas.

WEB ACTIVITY: Resources for Business and Technical Writers

You may want to bookmark a web site you can turn to for advice as you compose documents on the job. The Internet provides many useful sites that offer resources for business and technical writing.

1. Search the World Wide Web for sites about business and technical writing.
2. Choose one particular site and explore its resources. What kind of information or advice does it offer?
3. Find and print information, advice, or an example from that web site that will help you as you compose your comparison of two companies in this chapter's Group Project and Writing Activities section.

GROUP PROJECT AND WRITING ACTIVITIES

In Chapter 10, you praised a company that provided you with good service or a satisfying product. In this chapter, you'll compare that company to its competition and convince others that they should patronize it.

Together with your group, use one or more invention strategies to generate a list of the company's competitors. Record as many ideas as possible in the space below.

On your own, write a report that compares and contrasts this company to one of its major competitors. Explain the two companies' similarities *and* differences.

Together with your group, create commercials for the all of the companies selected by the group's members. Either videotape your commercials or perform them live for your classmates.

READINGS Have you ever tried deliberately to define your personal values and to identify behaviors you believe to be right or wrong? Have you ever worked for a company whose corporate values did not match your personal values?

In the following article, human relations experts discuss the topic of ethics in the workplace.

As you read this article, circle every word that's unfamiliar to you. Look it up and write the meaning in the margin. Put an exclamation point (!) next to any sentence or paragraph you find especially interesting. Put a question mark (?) next to any sentence or paragraph you don't understand.

Personal Values and Ethical Choices

Barry L. Reece and Rhonda Brandt

1   *Ethics* are the rules that direct your conduct and moral judgments. They help translate your values into appropriate and effective behaviors in your day-to-day life. Personal ethics determine how you do business and with whom. Kickbacks and payoffs may be acceptable practices in some parts of the world yet may be viewed as unethical practices elsewhere. Where will you draw the line between right and wrong?

2   As competition in the global marketplace increases, moral and ethical issues can become cloudy. Although most organizations have adopted the point of view that "Good ethics is good business," exceptions do exist. Some organizations encourage, or at least condone, unethical behaviors. Surveys show many workers feel pressure to violate their ethical standards in order to meet business objectives. Thus, you must develop your own personal code of ethics.

3   Every job you hold will present you with new ethical and moral dilemmas. These challenges can surface almost daily for people who direct and supervise the work of others. It may be tempting to tell employees to "do whatever is necessary" to get a job done on time, or to look the other way when employees engage in unethical or illegal acts. Simply taking credit for the accomplishment of others or displaying favoritism when establishing the work schedule represents a lapse in ethical conduct.

4   As a laborer, salesperson, or office support worker, you too will be faced with ethical choices. Faced with the demands of overtime, balancing work and family, and layoffs due to downsizing, workers seem to feel more pressure to act unethically. A survey sponsored by Professional Secretaries International discovered an alarming frequency of unethical behaviors including breaching confidentiality about hiring, firing, or layoffs, removing or destroying information, and falsifying documents. Other studies indicate that underpaid employees who feel unappreciated are more prone to steal from their employers, with the price tag reaching over $120 billion a year—and climbing rapidly.

How to Make the Right Ethical Choices

5   In today's turbulent, fast-paced, highly competitive workplace, ethical dilemmas surface frequently, and telling right from wrong has never been more difficult. Here are a few guidelines to help you make right ethical choices.

Reece, Barry L. and Rhonda Brandt, excerpts from *Effective Human Relations in Organizations.* Copyright © 1999 by Houghton Mifflin Company. Reprinted with permission.

Learn to Distinguish Between Right and Wrong

6 Although selecting the right path can be difficult, a great deal of help is available today. Many current books and articles offer good advice. The book *The Measure of Our Success* by Marian Wright Edelman presents a collection of "lessons for life" that can offer guidance in making ethical choices. A few examples follow:

- There is no free lunch. Don't feel entitled to anything you don't sweat and struggle for.
- Never work just for money or for power. They won't save your soul or build a decent family or help you sleep at night.
- Be honest. Struggle to live what you say and preach. Act with integrity.
- Sell the shadow for the substance. Don't confuse style with substance; don't confuse political charm or rhetoric with decency or sound policy.

7 Help in making the correct ethical choices may be as close as your employer's code of ethics, ethical guidelines published by your professional organization, or advice provided by an experienced and trusted colleague.

Make Certain Your Values Are in Harmony with Those of Your Employer

8 You may find it easier to make the right ethical choices if your values are compatible with those of your employer. Many organizations have adopted a set of beliefs, customs, values, and practices that attract a certain type of employee (see the [Lotus statement]). Harmony between personal and organizational values usually leads to success for the individual as well as the organization. These **shared values** provide a strong bond among all members of the work force.

LOTUS DEVELOPMENT CORPORATION'S
OPERATING PRINCIPLES

These Operating Principles are intended to serve as guidelines for interaction between all employees. Their purpose is to foster and preserve the spirit of our enterprise and to promote the well-being of all concerned.

Commit to excellence
Insist on integrity
Treat people fairly; Value diversity
Communicate openly, honestly, and directly
Listen with an open mind; Learn from everything
Take responsibility; Lead by example
Respect, trust, and encourage others
Encourage risk-taking and innovation
Establish purpose before action
Work as a team
Have fun

Lotus's Operating Principles © 2000 Lotus Development Corporation. Used with permission of Lotus Development Corporation.

---

9   **Item:** When selling their long-distance telephone service, employees of Working Assets assure their customers that 1 percent of every phone bill will be donated to liberal causes such as Greenpeace, the American Civil Liberties Union, gun control, abortion rights, and protection of redwoods. One marketing campaign read, "Be Socially Responsible. Talk on the Phone." Chief Executive Officer Laura Sure says that people are looking for other reasons to make a choice beyond the cost of services rendered.

10   **Item:** In a Duke University survey of 650 M.B.A. graduates of eleven top schools, 70 percent indicated that they would not work for certain industries because of ethical or political concerns. About 82 percent said they would shun tobacco companies, 36 percent would avoid firms with environmental problems, 26 percent would refuse to work for liquor marketers, and 20 percent would not get involved with defense contractors. Dan Nagy, who conducted the survey for Duke's Fuqua School of Business, says, "Today's students have strong values and limit the compromises they're willing to make for money."

11   **Item:** Lotus Development Corp. was awarded *Personnel Journal*'s coveted Optimas Award, Quality of Life Category, for its continual re-evaluation of its values relative to its workers. One of Lotus's operating principles, treating people fairly and valuing diversity, led to the creation of an innovative benefits policy that offers medical, dental, vision, and hearing insurance benefits to gay and lesbian partners of employees. Russell Campanello, vice president of human resources for Lotus, stated this about the company's prior plan: "Our benefits program was out of synch with our stated values around not discriminating based on sexual orientation. It has to reflect the needs, interests and values [of the workers] because that's what makes [the relationship] mutual."

12   Research conducted by the Families and Work Institute indicates that work/family decisions continue to be a battlefield for clashing values. Increasingly, employees want the opportunity to openly discuss family issues such as child care, requests for a flexible schedule, or care for an ailing parent. Johnson & Johnson is one of several companies that is training managers to sensitize them to values priorities that are different from their own.

Don't Let Your Life Be Driven by the Desire for Immediate Gratification

13   Progress and prosperity have almost identical meanings to many people. They equate progress with the acquisition of material things. One explanation is that young business leaders entering the corporate world are under a great deal of pressure to show the trappings of success. This is the view expressed by John Delaney, who is a professor at the University of Iowa and has done extensive research on ethics. He says, "You're expected to have the requisite car and summer house to show you're a contributor to society, and many people do whatever it takes to get them."

14   To achieve immediate gratification often means taking shortcuts. It involves pushing hard, cutting corners, and emphasizing short-term gains over

the achievement of long-term goals. M. Scott Peck, author of the best-selling book *The Road Less Traveled*, discusses the benefits of delaying gratification: "Delaying gratification is a process of scheduling the pain and pleasure of life in such a way as to enhance the pleasure by meeting and experiencing the pain first and getting it over with. It is the only decent way to live."

15   If delaying gratification is "the only decent way to live," why do so many people seek immediate gratification? The answer to this question is somewhat complex. Some people feel pressure from friends and family members to climb the ladder of success as quickly as possible and display the trappings of success such as a new car, boat, or house. They fail to realize that the road to peace of mind and happiness is not paved with Rolex watches, Brooks Brothers suits, and a Lexus.

RESPONDING TO THE READING

1. List some workplace behaviors that violate your own personal code of ethics.

   Answers will vary.

2. As a consumer, do you make decisions about purchasing a product based on the values of its manufacturer? Give an example of a time when you either bought a product or boycotted one because you wanted to support or to protest the company's values.

   Answers will vary.

3. Did money influence your decision to enter the career field you're pursuing now? Are potential earnings the most important reason why you selected this career, or are other rewards more important to you?

   Answers will vary.

4. Agree or disagree with M. Scott Peck's statement: "Delaying gratification is a process of scheduling the pain and pleasure of life in such a way as to enhance the pleasure by meeting and experiencing the pain first and getting it over with. It is the only decent way to live." Explain your answer.

   Answers will vary.

_____

_____

_____

_____

5. Identify the concession in paragraph 6.

"Although selecting the right path can be difficult. . . ."

_____

BUILDING VOCABULARY

When you learn a new word through your reading, what's the best way to find the proper way to pronounce that word? You can, of course, always ask people you know if they know the correct pronunciation. You can also buy "talking dictionary" computer software. Or you can learn the pronunciation guide in your dictionary, which uses various symbols to represent the word's sound. For example, for the word *requisite* (paragraph 13), the dictionary may represent the pronunciation as here:

rĕk´ wĭ-zĭt

Do you know how to pronounce the following words from the article? For each word, write the dictionary's pronunciation, then practice saying the word aloud.

1. condone (paragraph 2) *symbol styles vary* _____

2. confidentiality (paragraph 4) _____

3. rhetoric (paragraph 6) _____

4. decency (paragraph 6) _____

5. colleague (paragraph 7) _____

6. synch (paragraph 11) _____

7. acquisition (paragraph 13) _____

Have you ever told a lie on behalf of your supervisor? Has a supervisor ever asked you to do something illegal or unethical?

The following article offers advice about protecting yourself when your colleagues violate laws or ethical standards.

As you read this article, circle every word that's unfamiliar to you. Look it up and write the meaning in the margin. Put an exclamation point (!) next to any sentence or paragraph you find especially interesting. Put a question mark (?) next to any sentence or paragraph you don't understand.

Coping with a Crooked Boss: How to Protect Yourself from Becoming an Accessory to Office Crimes

Anna Mulrine and Joannie M. Schrof

1   Betty Currie shuttled Monica Lewinsky into and out of the White House. Rose Mary Woods took the blame for the missing minutes on the Watergate tapes. Fawn Hall hid documents in her underwear for Oliver North. If that sounds like extraordinary behavior for a secretary, consider this: A full 88 percent of secretaries say they have told lies on behalf of their supervisors. A survey of 2,000 conducted by the International Association of Administrative Professionals also found that roughly a quarter have watched bosses fake expense reports, a fifth have seen information destroyed or carted off, and a third have observed time sheets doctored. Some have even been asked to hire a prostitute.

2   Most people never blow the whistle—and it's no wonder, says Ellen Bravo, executive director of 9to5, National Association of Working Women. "As a secretary, your success is tied to your boss's," she says. "Unfortunately, if they're axed, you may be, too." Here's how any employee can negotiate the slippery slope before loyalty becomes culpability in a court of law.

3   ***Have "ethics chats" before you need them.*** Most employees get into trouble by not broaching the issue of ethics with a boss until they find themselves knee-deep in unexplained packages and faked documents, says Bravo. One option is to check out the boss before you sign on, as one Iowa secretary did. Tired of working for an employer who lied to clients daily, she hired a headhunter to find her a new job. "I told her I faced strong 'ethical challenges' in my current job, and I wanted to find a fair company," she said. "Now I work for one." Janet Near, coauthor of *Blowing the Whistle*, suggests establishing an understanding with your boss during your first week on the job ("How can I ensure that our office doesn't inadvertently violate any ethical standards?"). If you haven't had that talk already, use Betty Currie as a springboard. You might say, "I realize that if anything like that happened here—although of course it never will at this fine firm—I wouldn't know what steps to take," suggests Bravo.

4   ***Play the loyal protector.*** If you suspect wrongdoing, accusing your boss of illegal conduct shouldn't be your first course of action. Because many bosses truly are unaware that their behavior breaks any rules, says Near, the best approach is to say, "I want to alert you to something that might not look good to other people." This might get through to a truly oblivious boss—and tip off a dishonest person that you're on to the behavior.

Anna Mulrine and Joannie M. Schrof, "Coping With a Crooked Boss: How To Protect Yourself from Becoming an Accessory to Office Crimes," Copyright, September 28, 1998, *U.S. News & World Report.* Visit us at our Web site at www.usnews.com for additional information.

5   ***Start a paper trail.*** Even if the talk goes well, protect yourself. Los Angeles labor attorney Robert W. Barnes says you might even precede a conversation with a friendly memo saying: "I'd like to learn more about the process here. I was hoping you could explain to me why the approach you've asked me to take with bids is better than the approach I thought we used."

6   ***If good cop doesn't work, play bad cop.*** Nefarious bosses often couch untoward requests in vague language, says Nan DeMars, author of *You Want Me To Do WHAT?* Her advice: "Skinny it right down for them, and paraphrase it back—'In other words, Phyllis, you want me to lie to the tax auditors?'" Most employers will back off; if they don't, emphasize that their behavior makes you *uncomfortable*. (You have good reason for discomfort. You can be held personally responsible—by the company or by the law—for carrying out actions you know to be wrong.)

7   ***Know where to turn.*** If your boss is an incorrigible criminal (for example, DeMars says, if the response to your ethical concerns is "Just get it done!"), most companies have someone to turn to—internal auditors, ombudsmen, or (the latest rage) "ethics officers." If your company isn't supportive, contact an attorney who will be. And if you've found yourself ferrying your boss's paramours and their packages through the office, you may even want to file a case of your own. "If we're talking about a secretary asked to facilitate an extramarital affair," says Joan Ackerstein, a Boston employment attorney, "you could argue hostile work environment and the boss could be charged with sexual harassment." Just what President Clinton needs—one more lawsuit.

RESPONDING TO THE READING

1. According to the authors, what two things can you do to avoid uncomfortable ethics violations *before* they occur?

   Check out the company or supervisor before you agree to work there, and have an

   ethics chat with your supervisor during your first week of work.

2. How will a "paper trail" protect you if your colleagues are engaging in illegal or unethical behaviors?

   It will demonstrate that you question unethical behaviors of your co-workers and do

   not participate in them.

3. Where can you go for help if your boss ignores your concerns about ethical violations?

   Speak to internal auditors, ombudsmen, "ethics officers," or an attorney.

4. What are the arguments *against* taking any or all of the authors' advice? Do the authors acknowledge these arguments anywhere in their article? Write a concession for each of the five suggestions offered. You'll have to think of some of these concessions yourself.

You might be risking your job (or making it more difficult to work with others at the

company) if you speak up about ethics violations. One concession is . . . "many

bosses truly are unaware that their behavior breaks any rules" (paragraph 4).

Other concessions will vary. One sample: Your supervisor may not listen to you or

simply tell you what you want to hear before continuing the unethical behavior.

BUILDING VOCABULARY

To add more creativity to your writing, you can use words that are *metaphoric*. A *metaphor* creates an interesting visual image for the reader as it compares two things. Metaphoric words or phrases make concise points by saying that one thing is another. For example, the article contains the sentence

Most people never *blow the whistle*, and it's no wonder. . . . (paragraph 2)

The author uses the metaphoric phrase *blow the whistle* to mean "expose wrong-doing." The people don't literally blow a whistle, of course, but this phrase suggests an interesting scene to the reader.

A second example is in the sentence

Here's how any employee can negotiate the *slippery slope* before loyalty becomes culpability in a court of law. (paragraph 2)

In this sentence, slippery slope is a metaphoric expression that compares unethical situations to a dangerous, difficult-to-navigate place.

Each of the following sentences from the article contains a metaphoric word or phrase. Circle that word or phrase; then briefly explain the comparison.

1. A survey of 2,000 conducted by the International Association of Administrative Professionals also found that roughly a quarter have watched bosses fake expense reports, a fifth have seen information destroyed or carted off, and a third have observed time sheets doctored. (paragraph 1)

compares altering documents to being "repaired" by a physician

2. "Unfortunately, if they're axed, you may be, too." (paragraph 2)

compares being fired to being hit with an axe

3. Most employees get into trouble by not broaching the issue of ethics with a boss until they find themselves knee-deep in unexplained packages and faked documents. (paragraph 3)

compares dealing with large quantities to standing in water

4. Start a paper trail. (paragraph 5)

compares a series of documents to a pathway

5. "Skinny it right down for them, and paraphrase it back. . . ." (paragraph 6)

compares getting to the heart of a matter to stripping away excess fat

APPENDIXES

APPENDIX **A** # Conducting Successful Interviews

When you need to collect information for a writing project, other people can be excellent sources. To access their expertise, you'll need to conduct successful interviews. Improve your interviewing skills by preparing beforehand and by knowing what to do—and not do—when asking others to share their knowledge with you.

BEFORE THE INTERVIEW

Whether you'll be conducting the interview in person or by telephone, contact your interviewee and arrange a date, time, and location for your meeting. If the interview will take place in person, choose a location that will allow you to keep distractions and interruptions to a minimum. Agree on a time limit for the meeting, so that you and your interviewee can schedule accordingly.

After arranging the details of your meeting, you'll need to make some preparations. Good advance work allows you to collect the information you need more quickly and efficiently. First, inform yourself about the topic. Learn as much as you can about the subject from sources such as books and magazines. This study will provide you with background information that will help you understand your interviewee's statements and avoid wasting the time asking about fundamental ideas and issues.

Next, make a list of questions you'd like to ask your interviewee. Arrange these questions in order from most important to least important. That way, you'll get the most critical information even if the interview has to be cut short.

The final preparation step involves gathering the materials you'll need for note-taking. You can either write information on paper or tape it. Tape recording is the better method, for two reasons. It allows more interaction between you and your interviewee. Because you won't be frantically scribbling down what your interviewee is saying, you'll be free to respond and converse with him or her. Also, taping the interview will allow you to incorporate direct quotations into your composition. You can transcribe the tape and use your interviewee's exact words. If you choose to tape record the interview, make sure you test your equipment ahead of time. Also, plan to take extra cassette tapes and batteries.

DURING THE INTERVIEW

Interviewees who feel comfortable and appreciated will be more likely to share their knowledge with you. Therefore, your own good manners and attentiveness will help you acquire the information you need.

Always be punctual for your appointment, and thank the interviewee for his or her time and information. If you'd like to tape record the session, ask for your interviewee's permission before you turn on the equipment. Most people will not object, but asking for permission is a necessary courtesy. As the interviewee answers your questions, listen carefully and show interest in what he or she is saying. You can convey your interest by smiling, nodding, looking at the interviewee, and asking follow-up questions. Unless the interviewee expresses a willingness to continue, make sure you end the interview at the pre-established time. As you conclude, thank the interviewee again and offer to send him or her a copy of the composition you are writing.

Before leaving, verify the spelling of the interviewee's full name and write down the date of the interview. You'll need this information later to properly document the individual's remarks. Also, get the interviewee's contact information, including phone number and mailing (or e-mail) address. Ask if you may contact the person if you need further information.

AFTER THE INTERVIEW

Following the interview, promptly mail or e-mail your interviewee a written thank-you note. If he or she expressed an interest in reading your completed composition, don't forget to send a copy when it's finished.

APPENDIX B Preparing Effective Oral Presentations

Oral presentations are an effective communication tool, for several reasons. They allow you to deliver information to several people at the same time. They capitalize on people's ability to process spoken information faster than written information. Also, because they often include question-and-answer sessions, discussion sessions, or both, they usually lead to an enhanced understanding of the information.

To be an effective speaker, you'll need to seize and hold your audience's interest throughout your presentation. To accomplish this, prepare your presentation in four key steps.

1. Plan to include only necessary information.
2. Clearly organize this information.
3. Use audiovisual aids.
4. Practice your delivery of the information.

PLAN TO INCLUDE ONLY NECESSARY INFORMATION

Your audience members will usually be busy people with a lot on their minds. Yet because they are attending your presentation, they either want or need the information you will share. They will become bored, restless, and disinterested, however, if they perceive that your presentation is not addressing their needs. Because your presentation will be unsuccessful if your audience stops listening, you need to think carefully about their goals and priorities, just as you consider the reader's needs when writing a composition. Then you can decide on the appropriate scope of information you'll need to present. The best presentations are always specifically tailored to that particular group of listeners.

ORGANIZE YOUR INFORMATION

If the audience cannot follow your information, they will become frustrated and lose interest. If they do not listen, your presentation cannot fulfill its purpose. Therefore, you'll need to think carefully about how you will organize your ideas so your audience can understand them. Effectively organized presentations contain three parts—an opening, a body, and a closing—along with a few additional features that assist audiences in following the thought progression of oral information.

In the **opening**, get the audience interested immediately. All of the techniques you can use in a composition to grab your reader's attention (see Chapter 8 of this book) also work well in the openings of oral presentations.

So as you begin, state the topic and purpose of your presentation then clearly identify your overall main point (thesis), the idea you want your audience to understand or to believe by the end of your presentation. Finally, identify yourself and explain why your education, training, or experience makes you a credible source of information. Mentioning your qualifications will help your audience understand *why* they should listen to you.

Next, determine how you will organize the **body** of your speech. Just as you organize your thoughts prior to writing, you'll need to determine how you can arrange them in logical categories that will make sense to your listeners. Chapter 7 of this book, which illustrates how to organize written information, applies to oral presentations, too. After you choose an organization plan, take the time to create a formal or an informal outline that you can use as a guide during your actual presentation.

Unlike readers, who can go back and reread if they miss a point, your audience will have only one chance to hear and understand the information you present. Therefore, you'll need to insert a few additional features into your organization plan, to make sure they comprehend your ideas. Use **transition words** (such as *first, second, third, next, then*) to help the audience follow you from one point to the next and understand the relationships of one section of your talk to another. Also, use **emphasis** to call attention to important points. You can emphasize an idea or a piece of information by directly stating that it's significant, by repeating it, by writing it (on the chalkboard, overhead, or easel pad), or by altering the tone, volume, or rate of your voice (for example, speaking very slowly and loudly).

Finally, include periodic previews and summaries. A **preview**, which is a statement about what you'll discuss later in your presentation, assists the audience in grasping the overall structure of your speech. A **summary**—a brief recap or overview of what you've already said—reinforces your points and repeats important information for anyone who did not hear it the first time.

The **closing** of your presentation, like the closing of a composition, provides a satisfactory feeling of closure for your audience. Briefly present the consequences or implications of your ideas (see Chapter 9 of this book for techniques that work for oral presentations as well as compositions) and if possible, allow the audience to ask questions.

USE AUDIOVISUAL AIDS

After organizing your information, think about how you can incorporate audiovisual aids into your presentation. Audiovisual aids include the following:

diagrams	photographs
graphs	charts
drawings	audio recordings
demonstrations	dramatic productions
lists or outlines	performances

You can integrate these audiovisuals into your presentation through the following mediums:

Handouts

Slide shows

Computer slide shows (such as PowerPoint)

Videotape

Audiotape

Overhead transparencies

CD-ROM

Live performance

Chalkboard, whiteboard, or easel pad

Posterboard

Audiovisual aids are essential to any effective oral presentation, for several reasons:

- Many of your audience members will understand information best when it's represented visually.

- Audiovisual aids effectively reinforce and summarize information.

- Audiovisual aids illustrate important relationships in information or data. For example, a graph clearly shows trends, and a chart clearly reveals comparisons.

- Audiovisual aids add interest to your presentation by giving your audience additional sensory experiences.

Always prepare high-quality, professional-looking audiovisual aids for your audience. Before your presentation begins, set up and test the equipment you'll be using.

PRACTICE YOUR DELIVERY

Delivery refers to your oral style, the way you speak to the audience. Because your delivery affects your audience's interest and attention, *how* you speak is just as important as what you say. In other words, your speaking behaviors—including your voice, your nonverbal communication, and any displays of anxiety—will either encourage or inhibit your audience's understanding.

Voice

Audiences become easily bored when listening to a speaker with a monotonous voice, so practice varying your pitch and tone to communicate enthusiasm and various emotions. Slightly raise your volume until everyone in the room can hear you. Work to eliminate distracting filler words such as *uh, um, you know,* and *OK.*

Nonverbal Communication

To keep the audience interested, try to move around a little instead of standing rooted in one spot. Use your facial expressions and body language to illustrate and reinforce your points. Try to eliminate nervous gestures, such as a leg-jiggling or fiddling with an object; if your audience is focusing on your behavior, they will find it more difficult to concentrate on what you're saying.

Nervousness

Outward displays of nervousness will distract your audience and lead them to focus on you and your behavior rather than on the information you're presenting. Almost everyone feels anxious before speaking in public, but you need to increase your confidence in order to deliver a successful presentation.

To feel more comfortable about being "on stage," you must rehearse your presentation as many times as possible before you actually deliver it. The more you practice, the more confident you'll feel. Practice also improves performance, and it results in a smoother, more polished event. You can also increase your confidence by remembering that *you're* the expert. No one in the audience knows as much as you do about the topic; they have come to your presentation because they want or need the information. During the presentation itself, slow down and breathe deeply to help control anxious feelings. Try to focus on what you're saying rather than on yourself.

Finally, remember that public speaking, like anything else, improves with practice.

Eleven Serious Errors in English

This book has illustrated all of the qualities that are always present in clear, accurate compositions. Grammatical correctness is, without a doubt, the final (or twelfth) characteristic of effective writing. A composition that adheres to grammatical rules is easier to understand. The reader does not have to stumble over errors or stop and make mental corrections in order to figure out the meaning of a sentence. Also, grammatical correctness prevents confusion and misinterpretation. Therefore, you will want to review the most common, most serious, grammatical mistakes that can undermine the quality of your documents.

ERROR #1: SENTENCE FRAGMENTS

A sentence is a complete thought containing both a subject and a verb. A **sentence fragment** lacks either a subject or a verb or does not express a complete thought. A fragment looks like a complete sentence because it begins with a capital letter and ends with a period, but it cannot stand by itself until the missing element or elements have been added. Though we commonly speak using sentence fragments, we should not write them. They are grammatically incorrect.

Fragments That Lack Subjects

One kind of sentence fragment lacks a subject, the noun or pronoun that performs the action.

> Missing the point. *(Who missed it?)*
> Guarantees delivery in two days. *(Who guarantees it?)*

Fragments That Lack Verbs

Another kind of fragment lacks a verb.

> The player who won the award. *(The clause* who won the award *is an adjective that describes which player, so this fragment has no verb.)*
> Probably this week. *(What about this week?)*

> The most common type of verbless fragment, though, is one that contains *part* of a verb, but not all of it.

> The cat licking its paw.
> This two-story house designed for a large family.

Simply adding the necessary helping verb will correct the fragment:

The cat *was licking* its paw.

This two-story house *was designed* for a large family.

Fragments That Lack a Complete Thought

A third kind of fragment is one that expresses only part of a thought. Two types of these fragments are **phrase fragments** and **dependent clause fragments**. Neither can be separated from the sentence to which it belongs.

Phrase Fragments.   Phrases, which come in many types, are always *parts* of sentences because the whole group of words in the phrase acts as one part of speech in the sentence. When phrases stand alone, they become fragments. In the following examples, the information in parentheses gives one or more possible parts of speech for each phrase, depending on the context of the rest of the sentence.

On my way to work in the rain. *(adverb)*

Folding napkins. *(noun or adjective)*

Spinning out of control. *(noun or adjective)*

To set a good grade on the test. *(noun or adverb)*

A caring but firm woman. *(adjective or noun)*

Phrases must be combined with other elements to form complete sentences:

On my way to work in the rain, I skidded into the back of a truck.

The servers always disliked folding napkins.

Spinning out of control, the model airplane crashed to the floor.

She studied all night to get a good grade on the test.

My son's teacher is a caring but firm woman.

Dependent Clause Fragments.   Dependent clause fragments look deceptively like complete sentences because they are groups of words that contain both a subject and a verb. However, they always begin with a certain kind of word—such as a relative pronoun or a subordinating conjunction—that causes the whole group to act as just one *part* of a complete sentence. Therefore, they cannot stand alone.

Who loves to go fishing.

Who is a relative pronoun in a clause that could act as an adjective. Therefore, that clause is only part of a complete sentence such as "My brother is a boy who loves to go fishing." The clause acts as an adjective modifying the noun *boy*.

RELATIVE PRONOUNS

who

whom

which

that

If it's not raining.

The word *if* turns this whole group of words into an adverb. That is, it should be part of a sentence such as "If it's not raining, she'll play golf." The clause becomes an adverb that modifies the verb *play*.

Because I can't be in two places at one time.

The word *because* turns this whole group of words into an adverb. It should be part of a sentence such as "You must give Megan a ride because I can't be in two places at one time." The clause becomes an adverb that modifies the verb *must give*.

WORDS THAT CREATE ADVERB CLAUSES

after	before	than	whenever
although	if	unless	where
as	since	until	wherever
because	so that	when	while

What I want.

This whole group of words can act as a noun. It should be part of a sentence such as "I can't decide what I want." The clause serves as a noun functioning as a direct object of the verb *can't decide*.

WORDS THAT BEGIN NOUN CLAUSES

that	who	what
which	whatever	whoever
whichever	whose	where
when	why	how

Correcting Sentence Fragments

There are two ways to correct a sentence fragment:

1. Add the missing element.
2. Attach the fragment to the sentence before or after it.

Fragment: Maybe a mouse or a moth. *(No verb)*
Correction: Maybe a mouse or a moth chewed the quilt. *(Adds the verb chewed)*

Fragment:	Got away with it. *(No subject)*
Correction:	He got away with it. *(Adds the subject* he*)*

Fragment:	Flooding the bathroom floor. *(Incomplete phrase fragment)*
Correction 1:	The water flooded the bathroom floor. *(Rewritten as a sentence, adding the subject* water*)*
Correction 1:	Flooding the bathroom floor, the water poured from the tub. *(Attaches the phrase to a sentence after it)*

Fragment:	Since I arrived home ill from Tennessee. *(Incomplete dependent clause)*
Correction 1:	I arrived home ill from Tennessee. *(Removes the word that creates the dependent clause)*
Correction 2:	I've been ill since I arrived home from Tennessee. *(Attaches the clause to a sentence that comes before)*

GRAMMAR PRACTICE 1.1

Rewrite each sentence fragment to create a complete sentence. If the sentence is already complete, write the word *Complete*. *Answers will vary.*

1. Successful entrepreneurs share some common characteristics.

   Complete

   _____

2. Have a lot of energy.

   They have a lot of energy.

3. Someone who seems to find the time for work and research and for sports, hobbies, and family.

   An entrepreneur seems to find the time for work and research and for sports,

   hobbies, and family.

4. And volunteers for worthwhile causes.

   An entrepreneur even volunteers for worthwhile causes.

   _____

5. Entrepreneurs enjoy trying new activities.

   Complete

6. Constantly look for ways to improve their businesses.

   They constantly look for ways to improve their businesses.

   _____

7. Because the entrepreneur is someone who couldn't stand to do a boring job.

   The entrepreneur is someone who couldn't stand to do a boring job.

   _____

8. The typical entrepreneur is a "people person."

   Complete

9. Who is always ready with a warm handshake and a smile.

   The typical entrepreneur is a "people person" who is always ready with a warm

   handshake and a smile.

10. And not easily discouraged.

    An entrepreneur is not easily discouraged.

11. If success were easy.

    If success were easy, everyone would be successful.

12. Entrepreneurs are well-organized.

    Complete

13. Taking charge.

    Entrepreneurs enjoy taking charge.

14. When they make a mistake.[1]

    When they make a mistake, entrepreneurs learn from that mistake.

    _____

GRAMMAR PRACTICE 1.2

Correct the fragments in the following article by adding the missing elements or by changing punctuation and capital letters to combine sentences.

Sleep and Dreams[2]

We have seen that the brain is active in all sleep stages, but dreams

differ from other mental activity in sleep, Because they are usually

[1]Winning with Small Business Course, Lesson Three: Waking Up to Your Opportunities is reprinted by permission of the author, Bill FitzPatrick. Website: Success.org
[2]Bernstein, Douglas A., Alison Clarke-Stewart, Edward J. Roy, Thomas K. Srull, and Christopher D. Wickens, *Psychology*, 4th edition. Copyright © 1997 by Houghton Mifflin Company. Reprinted with permission.

story-like, lasting from seconds to minutes. Dreams may be organized or chaotic, realistic or fantastic, boring or exciting. Sometimes, dreams lead to creative insights about waking problems. For example, after trying for days to write a story about good and evil in the same person, Author Robert Louis Stevenson dreamed about a man who drank a potion that turned him into a monster. This dream inspired *The Strange Case of Dr. Jekyll and Mr. Hyde*.

Although they often seem bizarre, Dreams often contain a certain amount of logic. In one study, for example, when segments from dream reports were randomly reordered, Readers could correctly say which had been rearranged, And which were intact. A second study showed that dream reports commonly describe one person transforming into another, Or one object turning into another object, but transforming of objects into people or vice versa are rare.

Daytime activities can clearly influence the content of dreams. In one study, People wore red-tinted goggles for a few minutes just before going to sleep. Although they did not know the purpose of the study, The next morning they reported more red images in their dreams than people who had not worn the goggles. It is also sometimes possible to intentionally direct dream content, Especially during lucid dreaming in which the sleeper is aware of dreaming *while a dream is happening.*

Research leaves little doubt that everyone dreams during every night of normal sleep. Even blind people dream, Although their perceptual experiences are usually not visual. Whether you remember a dream depends on how you sleep and wake up. Recall is better if you awaken abruptly, And lie quietly while writing or tape-recording your recollections.

Why do we dream? Theories abound. Some see dreaming as a
fundamental process./By which all mammals analyze and consolidate
information that has personal significance or survival value. Indeed,
research suggests that nonhuman animals do dream.

ERROR #2: RUN-ON SENTENCES

A sentence is defined as a complete thought that contains a subject and a
verb. A **run-on sentence** contains two complete but closely related sentences
(independent clauses) that are not separated with adequate punctuation.
Therefore, they "run together."

He bought tickets to the game I didn't want to go.

Bob did the research, Phil wrote the report.

I recommend hiring a new assistant however, Mr. Patel may want to wait
until June.

You need to exercise it will improve your cardiovascular health.

The lack of appropriate punctuation in the example sentences makes them
difficult to read. Usually, a reader has to stop and reread a run-on sentence to
mentally correct where one thought ended and another began.

Writers correct run-on sentences four different ways: by creating two separate sentences, by inserting a semicolon, by adding a coordinating conjunction, or by turning one of the sentences into a dependent clause (one that
cannot stand alone) with the addition of a subordinating word.

Create Two Separate Sentences

The easiest way to correct a run-on sentence is to divide it into two separate
sentences, each of which ends in a period.

He bought tickets to the game. I didn't want to go.

Bob did the research. Phil wrote the report.

I recommend hiring a new assistant. However, Mr. Patel may want to wait
until June.

You need to exercise. It will improve your cardiovascular health.

This separation will correct the mistake; however, it results often in short,
monotonous sentences and in a loss of direct connection between the two related ideas. The *reader* is forced to figure out the relationship between them.
Therefore, this type of correction, though the simplest, often results in less sophisticated writing that is more challenging to read. The next three correction
methods communicate better how the two thoughts are related.

Insert a Semicolon

The second way to correct a run-on sentence involves inserting a semicolon
between the two independent clauses.

He bought tickets to the game; I didn't want to go.

Bob did the research; Phil wrote the report.

I recommend hiring a new assistant; however, Mr. Patel may want to wait until June.

You need to exercise; it will improve your cardiovascular health.

The semicolon indicates to the reader that the two ideas are related. However, it still does not indicate *how*.

Add a Coordinating Conjunction

A more sophisticated way to correct a run-on sentence involves adding a coordinating conjunction to indicate the relationship between the two sentences.

COORDINATING CONJUNCTIONS

and	but
or	for
nor	so
yet	

He bought tickets to the game, but I didn't want to go.

Bob did the research, and Phil wrote the report.

Note: When they link independent clauses, coordinating conjunctions are always preceded by a comma.

Add a Subordinating Word

The most sophisticated way to correct a run-on sentence is to turn one of the independent clauses into a dependent clause with the addition of a subordinating word. This technique retains the link between the two thoughts while also clearly stating the relationship between them.

SUBORDINATING CONJUNCTIONS

after	before	unless
although	if	until
as	order that	when
as if	since	whenever
as long as	so that	where
as soon as	than	wherever
because	though	while

He bought tickets to the game, even though I didn't want to go.

After Bob did the research, Phil wrote the report.

You need to exercise regularly because it will improve your cardiovascular health.

GRAMMAR PRACTICE 2.1

Correct all of the run-on sentences that follow. If a sentence does not need correction, write the word *Correct* on the blank line. *Answers will vary.*

1. You can apply creative thinking to solve common problems.

   Correct

2. A businessman who loaned a friend $5,000 was worried that he would not get his money back his friend tended to forget his debts.

   A businessman who loaned a friend $5,000 was worried that he would not get his

   money back. His friend tended to forget his debts.

3. The businessman wanted something in writing to record the debt an obvious solution was to get his friend to sign an IOU however, the friend might not cooperate.

   The businessman wanted something in writing to record the debt. An obvious

   solution was to get his friend to sign an IOU; however, the friend might not

   cooperate.

4. He thought about the problem and came up with several solutions.

   Correct

5. The most creative solution was to write to his friend, reminding him that he owed $10,000 his friend immediately replied.

   The most creative solution was to write to his friend, reminding him that he owed

   $10,000. His friend immediately replied.

6. In his response, the friend protested that he owed only $5,000 the businessman got his written IOU his worries were over.[3]

   In his response, the friend protested that he owed only $5,000. The businessman

   got his written IOU, and his worries were over.

[3]Ang Seng Chai, *Problem-Solving the Creative Way,* from *New Straits Times,* May 18, 1996.

GRAMMAR PRACTICE 2.2

Correct all of the run-on sentences in the paragraph below.

The Internet was born in the Cold War of the 1960's. The government of the United States wanted a computer network that would allow communication even during bombing attacks. The Department of Defense began the project; the Advanced Research Projects Agency (ARPA) completed it. They named the network ARPAnet. Four computers formed the ARPAnet by the end of the sixties. The first electronic message traveled through the ARPAnet in the early 1970's. In the late seventies, Usenet and an e-mail network were installed and integrated into the ARPAnet. In the eighties, scientists who wanted a quick method for data exchange installed the Domain Name System. This system allowed users to contact remote computers. By this time, people were calling the network the Internet. During the late 1980's, the military separated itself from the ARPAnet, and organizations began to create standards for the Internet. In the 1990's, the Internet became an international communication network. Many people now exchange information and communicate using the Internet.

ERROR #3: COMMA ERRORS

Commas are probably the most misunderstood punctuation mark. Yet there are seven very clear rules that explain when they are necessary. To avoid comma errors in your own writing, memorize these rules. Then, when you are tempted to insert a comma, you can check yourself by thinking of the rule that requires a comma in that particular sentence.

Rule 1: Commas Separate Items in a Series.

Items in a series can be words, phrases, or clauses.

Carol designs, builds, and sells wooden deck furniture.
Please pick up milk, cheese, soda, and potato chips.
We enjoyed relaxing on the beach, shopping at the mall, and eating out every night.
The attorney interviewed him about where he went, what he did, and when he returned.

Rule 2: Commas Separate Two or More Adjectives Before a Noun.

If you could insert the word *and* between two adjectives and the sentence would still make sense, separate those two adjectives with a comma.

A smart, athletic senior won the scholarship.

I bought the newest, smallest laptop computer.

We ate at a crowded Chinese restaurant. *(no comma)*

Take the first right turn after you exit the highway. *(no comma)*

Rule 3: Commas Separate Two Independent Clauses Joined by a Coordinating Conjunction.

When two complete sentences (each with its own subject and verb) are linked together with a coordinating conjunction (*and, or, but, for, nor, so, yet*), a comma precedes the coordinating conjunction.

The candidate reconsidered her decision to run for office, and she dropped out of the race.

Air bags save lives, but they can injure very small children.

You can pay the balance now, or you can wait until you receive your next bill.

Many comma errors occur when writers mistakenly put commas in sentences that do not contain two separate subject/verb relationships. The following sentences contain compound verbs, but they are not compound sentences. Therefore, commas are unnecessary.

The candidate reconsidered her decision to run for office and dropped out of the race.

Air bags save lives but can injure very small children.

You can pay the balance now or wait until you receive your next bill.

Rule 4: Commas Separate Nonessential Clauses and Phrases That Interrupt the Rest of the Sentence.

Commas need to come before and after extra information inserted into a sentence.

Bill, who has a lot of experience, is our first choice for the job.

No one, not even the president, wants to work on Memorial Day.

The marketing team, working all night, finally readied all of the packages for mailing.

Todd, her youngest son, bought her the necklace.

Look out for clauses and phrases that are *essential* to understanding the entire sentence. Do not separate them with commas.

The applicant who has the most experience will be our first choice for the job.

Every person signing up for the soccer team must get a physical exam.

Rule 5: Commas Separate Introductory Elements of a Sentence.

No, I didn't understand the diagram.

By the end of the day, the staff was exhausted.

Hoping for a big turnout, we plastered posters all over town.

Because he has diabetes, he cannot eat the cake.

For instance, you could walk a mile every day after work.

Rule 6: Commas Separate Information in Names, Titles, Dates, and Addresses.

The company opened for business on August 1, 2001, in Orlando, Florida.

Alice Henson, Ph.D., Dean of Health Sciences, testified last Friday.

Rule 7: Commas Punctuate Direct Quotations.

"By the end of this year," Mr. Roberts said, "we'll generate six million in revenue."

According to this week's *Wall Street Journal,* "Investors should quickly recover their losses."

GRAMMAR PRACTICE 3.1

In the following paragraphs, circle the boldfaced commas that are incorrectly placed.

The main educational advantage of co-op programs, according to faculty and students, is that classroom theory is tested in the workplace. Jason Sherman of Drexel says, the lessons he learned in his corporate communications class—how to write watertight reports, communicate with managers, and organize work teams—were immediately useful in his job, as a marketing assistant at a construction-industry, consulting firm. The job required him to conduct market research, present his findings to supervisors, and complete group projects. And subsequent classes build on knowledge, gained at work. Researching and assembling billion-dollar, project proposals on the job, for instance, enabled Sherman to see the relevance of a proposal-writing unit in an entrepreneurship course, later on.[4]

Coaches start planning for competition-day chemistry from the moment they select a team, and that can mean they send some superb athletes home. "The last thing my team needs, is some hot-shot superstar worried about a better shoe contract," says men's soc-

[4]Joellen Perry, "A Fat Paycheck and Work Experience, Too." Copyright, August 30, 1999, *U.S. News and World Report.* Visit us at our web site at www.usnews.com for additional information.

cer coach, Bruce Arena. Instead, he opts for players known as "great chemists," those like charismatic Alexi Lalas, who have a knack for inspiring a group, and lifting spirits. "The first day Lalas joined our team, everyone played at a whole new level, because they like him, and respond to him so well," says Arena.[5]

GRAMMAR PRACTICE 3.2

All commas have been removed from the following article. Insert them where necessary.

Presentation aids can be powerful, but they can also deceive. They can raise challenging ethical questions. For example, the most famous photographer of the Civil War, Mathew Brady, rearranged bodies on the battlefield to enhance the impact of his pictures. Eighty years later, another American war photographer carefully staged the now celebrated photograph of Marines planting the flag at Iowa Jima. Fifty years after that, *Time* magazine electronically manipulated a cover photograph of O. J. Simpson to "darken it and achieve a brooding, menacing quality." On the one hand, these famous images may be fabrications: They pretend to be what they are not. On the other hand, they may bring home the reality they represent more forcefully. In other words, the form of the photos is a lie, but the lie may work to reveal a deeper truth. Are these photographs unethical, or are they simply artistic?

Perhaps we can agree that with today's technology, the potential for abuse looms quite large. Video editing easily produces illusions of reality. Consider how moviemakers depicted Forrest Gump shaking hands with Presidents Kennedy, Johnson, and Nixon. Or call to mind the image of the late Fred Astaire dancing with a vacuum cleaner in a recent television commercial. In movies and ads, such distortions can be amusing. When they purportedly convey real-life images, as when

[5]Joannie M. Schrof, "Team Chemistry Sets," *U.S. News Online,* http://www.usnews.com/usnews/issue/5team.htm.

television networks and newspapers "stage" crashes and other visuals to make their stories more dramatic without letting us in on the artifice, they can be quite deceptive.

All these practices may relate to the ancient adage "Seeing is believing." People are taught by tradition to be vulnerable to the "reality" revealed by their eyes. Our position on these ethical issues is the following:

- As a speaker, whenever you manipulate images so that they reveal your message more forcefully, you should alert your listeners to the illusion.

- You should be prepared to defend the illusion you create as a "better representation" of some underlying truth.

- As a viewer, you should cultivate a healthy skepticism concerning visual images—for you, seeing should no longer be the same as believing.

- Whenever important claims are made, and visual images are offered in support of them, you should ask for further confirmation and for additional evidence.[6]

ERROR 4: SEMICOLON ERRORS

Semicolons have only two purposes. They separate independent clauses, or they separate items in a series when those items contain commas. You might think of the semicolon as a punctuation mark that communicates balance: what comes before and what comes after are always related and equal.

Semicolons Separate Two Independent Clauses

A semicolon divides the two equal parts of a compound sentence.

You wash the dishes; I'll sweep the floor.

Retirement planning should begin early; people who start investing during their twenties often accumulate millions.

[6]Michael Osborn and Suzanne Osborn, *Public Speaking,* 5th ed., (Boston: Houghton Mifflin, 2000), 265–266. Copyright © 2000 by Houghton Mifflin Company. Reprinted with permission.

I'd love to get a pet; however, I just don't have the time to properly care for one.

The report was poorly written; furthermore, it included inaccurate data.

Note: Don't forget that in a compound sentence, two independent clauses joined by a coordinating conjunction (*and, or, but, for, nor, so, yet*) are separated by a comma. For example: *The report was poorly written, and it included inaccurate data.*

Semicolons Separate Items in a Series

If the items in a series contain commas, adding more commas to separate them would probably create confusion. Therefore, use semicolons when the list is more complex.

My ten-day business trip will include stops in Seattle, Washington; Chicago, Illinois; and Charlotte, North Carolina.

This workshop targets a variety of people such as business executives, including Human Resources managers; financial professionals, including stockbrokers and accountants; and attorneys.

GRAMMAR PRACTICE 4.1

Circle the highlighted semicolons that are incorrectly used in the paragraph below:

The United States Census Bureau's continued use of racial categories meets with both support and criticism. These categories are White; Black; Hispanic, including Mexican Americans, Puerto Ricans, Cubans, and South Americans; Asians, including Chinese, Koreans, Japanese, and Filipinos; and Native Americans. Those who support racial categories hold that in order to ensure that individuals of all races and national origins are treated fairly; we must categorize people according to their similar characteristics. They say the current system is needed to create minority voting districts; and to administer an array of federal laws and programs designed to ensure that minorities get equal housing; education; health care; and employment opportunities. Groups that are working to build race pride; such as the American Indian Movement; also oppose efforts to get rid of racial categories. On the other hand, critics say the use of these categories only intensifies and reinforces the beliefs and actions of racists. They believe that eliminating racial categories will cause the breakdown of racial barriers; in addition, it will promote a race-free consciousness. A growing number of geneticists and social scientists reject the view that "racial" differences have an objective or scientific foundation. The American Anthropological Association (AAA) notes that many people confuse race, ethnicity, and ancestry; therefore, it recommends that the Census Bureau drop the term *race* and replace it with *ethnic origins.*[7]

ERROR 5: SUBJECT/VERB AGREEMENT ERRORS

In the English language, subjects and verbs are either singular or plural. **Singular** means that the word refers to only one person or thing, and **plural** means that the word refers to more than one person or thing.

SUBJECTS		VERBS	
Singular	**Plural**	**Singular**	**Plural**
she	they	dances	dance
manager	managers	is	are
man	men	does	do

In a sentence, the subject and verb must agree (or match) in number. The writer must pair a singular subject with a singular form of the verb, and a plural subject with a plural verb. Agreement errors occur most frequently in sentences that contain compound subjects, collective nouns as subjects, pronouns as subjects, or an insertion between the subject and verb.

Compound Subjects

Two singular subjects joined by the word *and* form a compound subject. Compound subjects are plural, so they must be matched with a plural verb.

Her <u>brother and sister</u> *fight* all the time.

The <u>Bahamas and Key West</u> *are* my favorite vacation destinations.

Note: Two singular subjects joined by the words *or* or *nor* are not treated as plural: *Her brother* or *her sister* picks *her up at school every day.*

[7]Adapted from Barry L. Reece and Rhonda Brandt, *Effective Human Relations in Organizations* (Boston: Houghton Mifflin, 1999), 397–398.

Collective Nouns

Collective nouns refer to a group of people or things. When functioning as subjects, they are singular if the verb refers to the whole group acting as a unit.

The <u>public</u> *wants* details about celebrities' lives.

Our <u>Social Committee</u> *arranges* fun events.

<u>Sixty dollars</u> *is* the average ticket price.

Pronouns

Some pronouns are singular, and some are plural.

Singular		Plural
each	no one	several
either	nobody	few
neither	anyone	both
one	anybody	many
everyone	someone	
everybody	somebody	

<u>Each</u> of us *needs* a canteen of water.

<u>Everyone</u> in the audience *was* laughing.

<u>Several</u> of the players *have* the flu.

<u>Few</u> *realize* how difficult it is to ice skate.

Several pronouns (*some, all, most, any, none*) can be either singular or plural, depending on the words to which they refer.

<u>Some</u> of the play *was* dull.

<u>Some</u> of the actors *were* nervous.

<u>Most</u> of my family *has* red hair.

<u>Most</u> of my cousins *have* freckles.

Insertions Between the Subject and the Verb

Often, a phrase that separates subject and verb will result in a subject/verb agreement error:

The <u>planets</u> in our solar system *varies* widely in size.

The subject of this sentence is *planets,* not *solar system.* The word *planets* is plural, so the verb should be in a plural form: *vary.*

To avoid subject/verb agreement errors, disregard the phrase that separates the subject from the verb; then choose the appropriate verb.

Many <u>citizens</u> [in this state] *oppose* the governor's plan.

This <u>system</u> [of manually typing forms] *needs* to be automated.

<u>Joe</u>, [along with the other nurses,] *is* volunteering at the Blood Drive.

GRAMMAR PRACTICE 5.1

Circle the correct choice in each set of brackets.

Beginning at about two months, the distress and contentment that newborns experience [start, starts] to evolve into more complex feelings such as sadness and joy, envy and empathy, shame and pride. Sadly, children who do not play much or are rarely touched [develop, develops] brains 20 to 30 percent smaller than normal for their age because of the lack of stimulation. This [underscore, underscores] the importance of effective parenting—that is, finding time to cuddle a baby, talk with a toddler, and provide small children with stimulating experiences. The words filtered through your brain before you were three [determine, determines] your potential adult vocabulary, and the foundations for math and logic [was, were] set before you were four. This early, powerful development, or lack thereof, [serve, serves] as the basis for your success or failure at various endeavors throughout your life.[8]

GRAMMAR PRACTICE 5.2

Correct the subject/verb agreement errors in the following passage:

Should the emotion of love be allowed to flourish in a business setting? Wal-Mart Stores, Inc., *says* ~~say~~ the answer is no if the romance involves coworkers who are married to other people. Two Wal-Mart employees *were* ~~was~~ fired when a manager learned they were dating. One was separated from her husband but not divorced. At that time, Wal-Mart Stores had a policy that said married employees cannot date coworkers. This policy has since been modified to ban dating between supervisors and their subordinates. The Richards Group, a Dallas advertising agency, *has* ~~have~~ a similar policy. New employees are told at the outset that dating someone from the agency—married or single—*is* ~~are~~ not

[8]Reece and Brandt, 99.

tolerated. Stan Richards, founder of the company, ~~believe~~ *believes* that office romances interfere with providing good service to clients. Those who support Richards's position ~~says~~ *say* that workplace romances often result in lower productivity when the couple ~~take~~ *takes* extra-long lunches or long breaks. If fellow staffers ~~feels~~ *feel* that the couple is not doing their share of the work, feelings of anger or jealousy may develop.

George Mitchell, chief executive officer of Mitchell Energy & Development Corporation, ~~take~~ *takes* a very different view of romance in the office. He says, "People meet and get married, and you can't really stop that. It's the way the world goes." Bill Gates, CEO of Microsoft Corp., would no doubt agree. He married Melinda French, a Microsoft employee he met at work. There ~~is~~ *are* more women in the workplace than ever before. People with similar talents, backgrounds, and aspirations often ~~meets~~ *meet* on the job. An increasing number of men and women ~~works~~ *work* long hours and has less leisure time than they used to have.

Corporate America ~~seem~~ *seems* to be getting more comfortable with love in the workplace. A large number of companies now ~~employs~~ *employ* married couples. Steelcase, Inc., the Grand Rapids, Michigan, office furniture manufacturer, ~~have~~ *has* over 300 married couples on its payroll. And most executives seem unconcerned about office romances. Nearly three-quarters of the CEOs who participated in a *Fortune* magazine poll said romances between workers is "None of the company's business."[9]

ERROR 6: PRONOUN AGREEMENT ERRORS

Pronouns are words that substitute for and refer to another noun or pronoun. Like verbs, they can be either singular or plural.

[9]Reece and Brandt, 249.

Singular Pronouns			Plural Pronouns	
I	you	he	we	they
my	your	she	our	their
mine	yours	his	ours	theirs
myself	yourself	her	us	them
	it	him	ourselves	themselves
	its	hers	yourselves	
	itself	himself		
		herself		

These pronouns must agree in number with the word to which they refer. If that word is plural, you must use the matching plural pronoun form; if the word is singular, use the matching singular pronoun form.

Each participant must bring *his or her* photo ID.

The children left *their* lunchboxes on the bus.

Try to understand your co-worker's perspective. *She* may be busy juggling many responsibilities.

When the word to which the pronoun refers is another pronoun, the same guidelines for determining subject/verb agreement apply.

Singular		Plural
each	no one	several
either	nobody	few
neither	anyone	both
one	anybody	many
everyone	someone	
everybody	somebody	

Everyone in the play forgot *her* lines at least once.

Each of the firemen was checking *his* own safety equipment.

Several of the participants brought *their* lunch.

Both of the girls like to do the work *themselves*.

To avoid the inclusive but awkward *his or her* pronoun phrase, reword a sentence to use plural forms.

A person should brush *his or her* teeth three times a day.

People should brush *their* teeth three times a day.

When a school principal discovers a weapon on *his or her* campus, *he or she* must act immediately.

When school principals discover weapons on *their* campuses, *they* must act immediately.

GRAMMAR PRACTICE 6.1

Circle the correct pronoun in each set of brackets.

People with low self-esteem tend to maintain an external locus of control. This means that [he or she, (they)] believe [his or her, (their)] behavior is controlled by someone or something in [his or her, (their)] environment. When you hear a person say, "It's not my fault. He made me do it," you can be assured that [(he or she), they] probably has low self-esteem. Rather than taking responsibility for [his or her, (their)] own choices, such people blame other people or events for controlling [him or her, (them)]. Even when they succeed, they tend to attribute [his or her, (their)] success to luck rather than to [his or her, (their)] own expertise and hard work. This often results in reliance on the approval of others. This seeking of others' approval often pressures [him or her, (them)] into behaving contrary to [his or her, (their)] deepest convictions. When a person relies too heavily on validation from external sources, [(he or she), they] can lose control over [(his or her), their] life.[10]

GRAMMAR PRACTICE 6.2

Correct the pronoun errors in the following passage:

Good manners is a universal passport to positive relationships and respect. One of the best ways to develop rapport with another person is to avoid behavior that might be offensive to ~~them~~ *him or her*. Although it is not possible to do a complete review of this topic, some of the rules of etiquette that are particularly important in an organizational setting are covered here.

1. *When you establish a new relationship, avoid calling a person by their first name too soon.* Jacqueline Thompson, author of *Image Impact*, says assuming that all work-related associates prefer to be addressed informally by ~~his~~ *their* first name is a serious breach of etiquette. Use titles

[10]Adapted from Reece and Brandt, *Effective Human Relations*, 101–102.

of respect—Ms., Miss, Mrs., Mr., or Dr.—until the relationship is well established. Too much familiarity can breed irritation. When the other party says, "Call me Susan," or "Call me Roy," it is all right to begin using ~~their~~ *his or her* first name. Informality should develop by invitation, not by presumption.

2. *Avoid obscenities and offensive comments or stories.* In recent years, standards for acceptable and unacceptable language have changed considerably. Obscenities are more permissible in everyday conversation than ~~it was~~ *they were* in the past. But it is still considered inappropriate to use foul language in front of a customer, a client, or, in many cases, a co-worker. . . . Never assume that another person's value system is the same as your own. Foul language and off-color stories can do irreparable damage to interpersonal relations.

3. *Watch your table manners.* Business is frequently conducted at breakfast, lunch, or dinner these days, so be aware of your table manners. When you invite a customer to lunch, do not discuss business before the meal is ordered unless they initiate the subject. Begin eating only when the people around you have their plates. If you have not been served, however, encourage others to go ahead. . . . Thank the server when ~~they serve~~ *he or she serves* your meal.[11]

ERROR #7: APOSTROPHE ERRORS

Apostrophes have only two purposes: to form a contraction or to indicate possession. Many apostrophe errors occur when writers use them for incorrect reasons.

Contractions

A **contraction** combines two words into one to shorten them. The apostrophe indicates where letters have been removed.

I am	=	I'm
is not	=	isn't

[11]Adapted from Reece and Brandt, *Effective Human Relations,* 293–294.

you are	=	you're
will not	=	won't
there is	=	there's
she would	=	she'd

Possessives

Apostrophes also create the possessive form of nouns, which indicates ownership.

Greg's glove

Shakespeare's plays

house's roof

our money's worth

one year's experience

Note: In plural possessive nouns, place the apostrophe *after* the s unless the plural is irregular.

my parents' house

babies' bottles

the Joneses' car

men's cologne

Most apostrophe errors occur when writers mistakenly use apostrophes to form plurals. Ordinarily, create plurals by adding only *s* or *es,* with no apostrophe:

hero	=	two heroes
Monday	=	all Mondays
dollar	=	fifty dollars

GRAMMAR PRACTICE 7.1

Circle all of the incorrectly used apostrophes in the following passage:

Earlier this year, the airport broke ground for construction of a new international terminal just south of the existing airfield. Airline's will pay for the new facility by charging an additional fee for each plane ticket because the airport satisfied the term's of an agreement signed three years' ago.

Unfortunately, some airline operators' aren't happy with the term's of that 1997 agreement. It provided for money for a fourth airside at the north terminal, scheduled to open next month, and for construction of the new international facility.

Concerned about their bottom line's, some airline giants', such as Delta and United, want the airport either to take back excess gate's the airline's have leased at the existing terminal or to postpone the opening of the international terminal.

Those large airline's, which have contracted for more space than they now need, lease the excess to other carrier's that plan eventually to move to the new airside or the international terminal. And that would force the larger carriers' to find new tenant's to lease the space that would become vacant.

That may be in the airlines' financial best interest's, but it may not be in Central Florida's interests. When the airport's governing board meet's June 7 to discuss that issue, it should'nt agree to any construction delay that ends' up making the international terminal more expensive.[12]

ERROR #8: INCONSISTENT VERB TENSE

Verbs in the English language indicate time through different **tenses.** Every verb has six tenses, and each of these six tenses also has a progressive form, which indicates ongoing action.

	Singular	Plural
Present	writes	write
Present Progressive	am writing	are writing
Present Perfect	has (have) written	have written
Present Perfect Progressive	has been writing	have been writing
Past	wrote	wrote
Past Progressive	was writing	were writing
Past Perfect	had written	had written
Past Perfect Progressive	had been writing	had been writing
Future	will write	will write
Future Progressive	will be writing	will be writing
Future Perfect	will have written	will have written
Future Perfect Progressive	will have been writing	will have been writing

[12]"Keep Airport Flying High," *The Orlando Sentinel* (May 17, 2000), A-16. Reprinted by permission.

When you write, you use various tenses to show the reader what has already happened, what is happening now, and what will happen in the future. However, sometimes writers inadvertently shift verb tenses when they shouldn't. This type of error is particularly common in narratives or stories. The writer begins in the past tense because the event happened in the past. In the retelling, though, as the writer relives the events to re-create them on the page, he or she begins to think of the events in the present tense, as though they're happening again right now. In the following paragraph, notice how the italicized verbs are sometimes in the past tense and sometimes in the present.

I *was* very angry and frustrated the last time I visited your office. I *arrived* on time for my 11:30 appointment, and the receptionist *told* me to have a seat. I *sit* down, thinking I'll have to wait only a few minutes. Only one other person *is waiting*. I *am* on my lunch break, so after about 15 minutes, I *started* getting a little anxious. I *am getting* restless in my seat, but the receptionist *has disappeared*. A half hour *passed*. The receptionist finally *reappears*, so I *get* up and *ask* how much longer I'll have to wait. She *says* you were called to handle an emergency, and I *should reschedule* my appointment.

Throughout this passage, the verbs incorrectly shift back and forth from past to present. Because this entire series of events happened in the past, the writer should change all of the present tense verbs to past tense.

GRAMMAR PRACTICE 8.1

Correct the inappropriate tense shifts in the following passage:

Education has a special significance for me. I was raised in Mexico until the age of seventeen. Three years ago my family moved to the United states where I enter [entered] school as a junior without knowing a word of English. It is [was] not easy sitting in class attempting to learn a subject while simultaneously learning the language. I could not communicate with the Americans, and the Mexicans want [wanted] nothing to do with me. I often feel [felt] completely alone.

While things were difficult at school, they were worse at home. No one in my family could speak English, so no one helps [helped] me. My parents were oblivious to what I was going through at school. All they know [knew] is that they needed help with the children at home. I often feel [felt] like giving up and throwing everything out the window.

After all, my family was happy with me staying home helping out.

knew   *could*   *continued*
Somehow I ~~know~~ I ~~can~~ not give up. I ~~contunue~~ to plug along and
learned
~~learned~~ to be patient with myself and hold on to my desire to learn.
                    helped
This attitude ~~helps~~ me find people who could help me and support

me with my school work.[13]

ERROR #9: MISPLACED MODIFIERS

Modifiers are words, phrases, or clauses that explain or describe another word in the sentence. If a modifier doesn't come right before or right after the word it modifies, confusion can result. **Misplaced modifiers** are separated from what they explain or describe:

At only two years of age, my grandmother taught me to swim.

The italicized phrase is the modifier that is supposed to describe *me* in this sentence. However, because it immediately precedes *my grandmother,* the sentence says that the grandmother was only two when she conducted these swimming lessons!

She sent an e-mail to the president *that made everyone mad.*

This sentence incorrectly states that the president—rather than the e-mail—angered everyone.

Last year, I walked the same streets my father walked *for the first time.*

The italicized phrase should modify the first *walked.* Its placement at the end of the sentence causes it to modify the second *walked,* which does not correctly state the writer's meaning.

Misplaced modifiers can also create ridiculous images in the reader's mind:

Running down the street, my Poptart crumbled as I tried to catch the bus.

In this sentence, the Poptart is running down the street!

To correct a misplaced modifier, either move the modifier so that it's attached to the word it modifies, or reword the sentence completely to correct the error.

Misplaced:	I watch my children through the window playing in the sand.
Correction 1:	Through the window, I watch my children playing in the sand.
Correction 2:	As they play in the sand, I watch my children through the window.
Misplaced:	The lottery winner was a teacher at the high school, who cried tears of joy.
Correction 1:	The lottery winner, who cried tears of joy, was a teacher at the high school.
Correction 2:	When the teacher at the high school won the lottery, she cried tears of joy.

[13]Dave Ellis, *Becoming a Master Student* (Boston: Houghton Mifflin, 2000), 30.

Misplaced: In the bathtub, he discovered his son's collection of live frogs.

Correction 1:   He discovered his son's collection of live frogs in the bathtub.

Correction 2:   He looked into the bathtub and discovered his son's collection of live frogs.

Note: A dangling modifer is a related error to watch out for. When a modifier "dangles," the word it should modify has been left out of the sentence.

While walking down the beach, her tension and stress melted away.

In this sentence, the tension and stress are walking down the beach because the sentence lacks the real subject: *she.* (*Correction:* While walking down the beach, *she* felt her tension and stress melt away.)

GRAMMAR PRACTICE 9.1

Rewrite each of the following sentences to correct the misplaced or dangling modifier.

1. I painted a truck for a man in orange and blue stripes.

   I painted orange and blue stripes on a truck for a man.

2. Giving up time with friends and family, money becomes the priority of many executives.

   Giving up time with friends and family, many executives make money their priority.

3. Some companies provide benefits for workers such as onsite day care centers.

   Some companies provide for workers benefits such as onsite day care centers.

4. Entering the workforce in large numbers, the challenges women faced were formidable.

   Entering the work force in large numbers, women faced formidable challenges.

5. Joe is rude to everyone unlike his mother.

   Unlike his mother, Joe is rude to everyone.

6. We discussed the memo that was accidentally shredded in our weekly management meeting.

   In our weekly management meeting, we discussed the memo that was accidentally

   shredded.

7. The pastor incorrectly read the vows as he married a couple for the second time.

   For the second time, the pastor incorrectly read the vows as he married a couple.

   _____

8. To convince him to apply for the job, the salary had to be increased.

   To convince him to apply for the job, the company had to increase the salary.

   _____

9. After receiving the second notice of nonpayment, my check was discovered to be missing.

   After receiving the second notice of nonpayment, I discovered my check was

   missing.

ERROR #10: PARALLELISM ERRORS

When you write a sentence that contains a series of words, phrases, or clauses, each item of that series should be parallel, or matching in structure. Parallelism errors occur when the writer mixes different forms. This type of error makes it more difficult for the reader to understand relationships between the sentence parts.

> I enjoy golfing, tennis, and to hike.

This sentence mixes three different forms for the three items in the series. We can correct this parallelism error by choosing one form for all three items.

> *Correction 1:*   I enjoy golf, tennis, and hiking.
> *Correction 2:*   I enjoy golfing, playing tennis, and hiking.
> *Correction 3:*   I like to play golf, to play tennis, and to hike.

Another example illustrates nonparallel phrases:

> We searched for the missing file in the drawers, on the desks, and going through our briefcases.

The first two items in this series are prepositional phrases, but the last item breaks that pattern. It, too, should use the prepositional phrase structure.

> We searched for the missing file *in the drawers, on the desks,* and *in our briefcases.*

One final example demonstrates nonparallel clauses:

> She told us that the memo is due and to finish the report.

Both clauses in this sentence should begin with the same word to balance the two items in the series.

> She told us that the memo is due and that the report must be complete by July.

GRAMMAR PRACTICE 10.1

Identify and correct the parallelism errors in the following passage:

Typically, a workplace operates under two sets of rules: a formal system, which includes the publicly acknowledged reporting structure, rules, and regulations; and ~~what the~~ *a* political system ~~is~~, which is the dynamic informal network of friends and influence. Most people have an attitude of resentment about having to play office politics in order to get ahead. They want to be judged by their performance, skills, and ~~by knowing things~~ *knowledge* as they strive to succeed in their chosen careers. However, when you reach a certain level, everyone is smart, ~~works hard~~ *hard-working*, and competent. Then the standard may be "who you know, not what you know."

Office politics is part of being an effective team player in most organizations. It is nothing more than getting to know people on an informal basis and ~~to learn~~ *learning* their strengths and weaknesses. It involves getting to know who can get things done, whose opinion is respected, and ~~the people~~ *who is* ignored and why. The better you understand the values and attitudes underlying others' behaviors, the better you will be able to adjust your behavior accordingly. At the same time, the informal network allows you to share your talents and ~~that~~ ~~you can~~ *ability to* do things that might not be discovered merely by looking at the work you produce. The goal of the team is not to work within your personal comfort zone but ~~getting~~ *to get* things done quickly while taking into account members' emotions and personalities so the team can produce quality decisions. This often requires you to play the political game.[14]

[14]Adapted from Reece and Brandt, *Effective Human Relations,* 169.

ERROR #11: AWKWARD WORDING

Awkward wording describes a general category of errors that result when inaccurate combinations of words garble the meaning of a sentence. These errors often stem from wordiness (see Chapter 3 of this book) or from imprecise word choices (see Chapter 2 of this book). They can also be the by-product of other grammatical mistakes such as misplaced modifiers or faulty parallelism. Regardless of their cause, they always sound like wrong notes in a musical performance, and they undermine the sophistication of your writing.

> I quit watching Channel 5 quite a while ago as I could no longer take the action-packed drama as to what was going to be up next.

The wording of this sentence makes it difficult to discern the writer's exact meaning. Imprecise word choices such as *take, drama* and the clause *what was going to be up next* obscure the writer's intentions. Rewording the sentence makes it much clearer:

> I quit watching Channel 5 when I could no longer stand to watch their overly dramatic promotions that tease viewers and trick them into tuning in to a show.

> Here's another example of awkwardness created by imprecise words:

> Poignant local actions in the past have righted deteriorating conditions before large areas have suffered. I am confident this project will accomplish this effort once again.

What do these sentences mean? A variety of inaccurate word choices makes them incomprehensible.

Another sentence illustrates how wordiness, along with comma and parallelism errors, creates awkwardness:

> The organization works to educate and alert the public to the problem of illegal pornography, and to encourage communities to express themselves in an organized way to law enforcement officers, and to urge vigorous enforcement of obscenity laws.

The best way to find awkwardly worded sentences in your writing is to ask someone to read your composition aloud to you. When that reader stumbles over your wording or has to stop and reread, he or she has identified for you an awkward sentence that probably needs revision.

To correct an awkwardly worded sentence, first try to determine if a grammatical error is causing the problem. Correcting that error may untangle the sentence. Next, try completely rewording the sentence to find accurate words that will state what you mean.

For example, look at this awkward sentence:

> While the telecommunication and information revolutions are reshaping the way we work an awareness of what is possible is critical.

To improve this sentence, first find and correct the errors. Add the missing comma and change passive voice to active voice:

> While the telecommunication and information revolutions are reshaping the way we work, it is critical that we understand the possibilities.

Next, change the sentence's first word, which is not precise:

> Because the telecommunication and information revolutions are reshaping the way we work, it is critical that we understand the possibilities.

That revision is better, but it still sounds awkward. A complete rewording is probably necessary:

> If we keep informed about the innovations in telecommunication and information management, we can continue to improve the way we work.

GRAMMAR PRACTICE 11.1

Photocopy a composition you wrote and ask someone to read it aloud. Use the photocopy to follow along as the person reads. On this photocopy, highlight each sentence the reader stops to reread. Rewrite each of those sentences to eliminate their awkwardness. *Answers will vary.*

Index

A

A- prefix, 129
Ab- prefix, 129
-able suffix, 224
Active voice, 78–81
Addresses, commas with, 336
Adjectives
   commas with, 335
   definition of, 48
   overusing, 50
   subordinate relationships and, 110
   suffixes for, 224–225
   for vivid writing, 48–51
Adverbs, 224
   clauses, 327
Agreement
   pronoun, 343–346
   subject/verb, 81, 88, 340–343
Allegories, 38
American Heritage College Dictionary, 104
-ant suffix, 224
Apologies, avoiding, 274–276
Apostrophes, 346–348
-ar suffix, 224
Arguments
   concessions and, 301
   types of, 298–299
Assertive writing, 273–295
   definition of, 273
   sentence structure in, 279–281
   typefaces in, 281–282
   word choice in, 276–279
-ate suffix, 224
Auden, W.H., 5
Audiovisual aids, 322–323
Awkward wording, 354

B

Background information, 227
Barnes, Russell, 250–251
Bartlett's Familiar Quotations, 260
Bennett, Ralph Kinney, 99–105
Body, of speeches, 322
Brainstorming, 7–8
Branching technique, 208–209
Brandt, Rhonda, 310–314
Buchanan, Buffie, 41
Bulleted lists, 211–212. *See also* lists
Business writing, 308

C

Cantore, Jean Ann, 161–166
Career exploration, 21
Career Intelligence: The 12 New Rules for Success (Moses), 152–161
Carlson, Richard, 289–295
Carswell, Cindy, 167
Casson, John J., 263–270
Categories, logical, 192–195. *See also* classification
   determining, 202–205
   organization of, 197–202
Cause and effect
   development, 135–136
   transition words, 147
Chronological order, 197
Classification, 137–138
   of ideas, 196–205
   logical units for, 192–195
   transition words, 147
Clichés, 56
Closings, 250–272
   completing circles for, 254–255
   concessions as, 301
   consequences and implications in, 251–252
   describing effects in, 252
   for oral presentations, 322
   predictions in, 252–253
   questions in, 255
   recommendations in, 253–254
   techniques for, 251–260
Clue words, 110
   for concessions, 302
   transitions, 146–151
Clustering, as idea generation, 9–10
Coherence, 130–166
   cause/effect for, 135–136
   comparison/contrast for, 135
   description in, 132–133
   development methods for, 130–143
   exemplification as, 133–134
   narration in, 131–132
   process analysis for, 134–135
Cohesion, 167–190
   checking for, 175
   composing for, 174
   definition of, 167
   extra main ideas and, 171–174
   main idea digressions and, 168–171
   planning for, 174
   revising for, 174
Collective nouns, 341
Commas, 334–338
   between adjectives, 335
   between independent clauses, 335
   after introductory elements, 335–336
   missing, 88–89
   in names, titles, dates, addresses, 336
   around nonessential clauses, 335
   with quotations, 336
   in series, 334
Communication skills, 94–104
Comparison and contrast, 135
   as context clue, 73–74
   engaging reader interest with, 232–233
   transition words, 146
Complex sentences, 84
Compound sentences, 84
   semicolons in, 338–339
Concessions, 299–303
   guidelines for, 301–302
Condescending tone, 304–305
Confident writing, 273–295
   avoiding hedging, apologies, disclaimers in, 274–276
   definition of, 273
Context clues for word definitions, 39–40, 73–74, 288
Contractions, 346–347

Contrast. *See* comparison and
contrast
Coordinate relationships, 109–110
Coordinating conjunctions, 332
commas with, 335
"Coping with a Crooked Boss: How
to Protect Yourself from Becoming an Accessory to Office
Crimes" (Mulrine, Schrof),
315–318
Creativity and originality, 1–40
divine inspiration method in, 2–3
idea generation in, 3–21
Crowe, Sandra, 221–225
Cubing, 13–15

D

D'Angelo, Philip, 1–2
Dangling modifiers, 352
Dates, commas with, 336
Declarative sentences, 279
Definitions, as context clue, 74
Delivery, speech, 323–324
Dependent clauses, 84
as sentence fragments, 326–327
Description transition words, 146
Detail
categories of, 194–195
descriptive, 132–133
factual and sensory, 45–48,
132–133
general *vs.* specific, 43–45
organizing, 200–202
subordination of, 168
in vivid writing, 42–48
Development
cause/effect for, 135–136
choosing methods of, 143–146
by classification, 137–138
combining methods of, 140–141
comparison/contrast for, 135
by division, 136–137
division for, 136–137
identifying methods of, 142–143
layers of, 108–118
methods of, 130–143
narration as, 131–132
problem/solution method,
139–140
reasons as, 138–139
transitions in, 146–151
Dictionaries
determining correct definition in,
249
online, 260
pronunciation in, 314
talking, 314
using, 104–105
Digressions, 168–171
Directive process analysis, 134–135

Dis- prefix, 129
Disclaimers, avoiding, 274–276
Discussion, as idea generation, 4–5
Dismissive tone, 304–305
Divine inspiration method, 2–3
Division of ideas, 136–137
transition words for, 147
"Don't Sweat the Small Stuff at
Work" (Carlson), 289–295
Drawing, as idea generation, 6
Dyson, John, 186–190

E

Effects, describing, 252. *See also*
cause and effect
Electric Library Encyclopedia, 260
Emotional arguments, 298
Emotionally loaded language,
305–306
Emphasis
in speeches, 322
typefaces for, 281–282
-en suffix, 224
-ent suffix, 224
-er suffix, 224
Examples
assertive, 278
as context clues, 73
development through, 133–134
engaging reader interest with,
233–234
transition words, 146
Exclamatory sentences, 279–280
Explanations, as context clue, 74

F

Factual details, 45–48, 132–133
Fence-sitting, 275
Figures of speech, 55–57
"Finding Wisdom on Mount Potosi"
(Spotleson), 246–249
Fragments, sentence, 325–331
correcting, 327–328
dependent clause, 326–327
phrase, 326
Freewriting, 11–13
-ful suffix, 224
-fy suffix, 224

G

General *vs.* specific
language, 43–45
sentences, 108–118
Gorman, Megan Othersen, 284–288
Grammar, 88–89
errors, 325–354
in freewriting, 12
online, 260, 282

Greengard, Samuel, 178–185
Group projects, 22–25, 60–63,
92–94, 118–120, 151,
176–178, 215–218, 239–242,
260–262, 282–283, 309
Guide to Grammar and Writing, 260,
282

H

"Handle Stress Like an Expert"
(Gorman), 284–288
Headings, 212–213
Hedging, avoiding, 274–276
"Higher Calling" (Osborne),
120–124
Hoke, Starla, 273
Homonyms, 123–124, 220–221
Homophones, 58
Hot Jobs, 150
"How Technology Will Change the
Workplace" (Greengard),
178–185
"How to Drive the Stakes Through
the Hearts of Time Vampires"
(Kennedy), 69–74
Hughes, Robert J., 243–246

I

-ible suffix, 224
Idea-generating strategies, 3–21
brainstorming, 7–8
clustering, 9–10
cubing, 13–15
drawing, 6
freewriting, 11–13
journalism method, 16–18
lists, 15–16
meditation, 10–11
questions, 18–20
talk, 4–5
Ideas. *See also* development
categorization of, 196–205
digressing from main, 168–171
dividing, 136–137
including extra main, 171–174
main, 106
organizing, 205–215
outlining, 206–211
thesis statements, 195–196
Idioms, 98–99
Il- prefix, 129
Im- prefix, 129
Imperative sentences, 279–280
In- prefix, 129
Independent clauses, 84
commas with, 335
as run-on sentences, 331–334
semicolons between, 338–339
Informal language, 166

Informational process analysis, 134–135
Internet terminology, 269–270. *See also* Web activities
Interrogative sentences, 279–280. *See also* questions
"Interview Tips and Bloopers" (Cantore), 161–166
Interviews, 318–319
   tips and bloopers in, 161–166
Ir- prefix, 129
-ish suffix, 224
It is sentences, 77–78
Its/it's, 220
-ive suffix, 224
-ize suffix, 224

J

Jargon, 161
Job Options, 150
Job searches, 150–151
   interviews in, 318–319
Johnson, Jamie, 106
Journalism method of idea generation, 16–18
"Journey of an E-Mail" (Dyson), 186–190

K

Kapoor, Jack R., 243–246
Kennedy, Dan S., 69–74
King, John, 296

L

Language, vivid, 41–74
   adjectives in, 48–51
   details in, 42–48
   figures of speech in, 55–57
   general *vs.* specific language, 43–45
   precise word choice in, 57–60
   strong verbs in, 51–55
Layers of development, 108–118
Leadership ability evaluation, 239
Learning
   lifelong, 117–118
   styles of, 60
-less suffix, 224
Lifelong learning, 117–118
Lists
   commas in, 334
   as idea generation, 15–16
   as organizational markers, 211–212
   semicolons in, 339
Logical arguments, 298
Logical organization, 191–225, 198–202
-ly suffix, 224

M

Meditation, as idea generation, 10–11
-ment suffix, 224
Merriam-Webster Dictionary, 260
Metaphors, 31, 317–318
   definition of, 55
   for vivid language, 55–56
Misplaced modifiers, 350–352
Modifiers, misplaced, 350–352
Monster.com, 150
Moses, Barbara, 152–161
Mulrine, Anna, 315–318

N

Name calling, 303–304
Names, commas with, 336
Narration, 131–132
   engaging interest with, 230
   organization of, 197, 205–206
   transition words, 146
Natural organization, 197–198
Needs, reader, 297
Nervousness, speeches and, 323–324
-ness suffix, 224
Non- prefix, 129
Nonverbal communication, 323
Noun phrases, 327
Nouns, collective, 341
Numbered lists, 213–214

O

Objections, reader, 297
   concessions to, 299–303
Online writing labs, 175–176
Openings, paragraph, 226–249
   background information in, 227
   gaining reader interest in, 229–236
   for oral presentations, 321–322
   purposes of, 226–236
   thesis statement in, 227–228
   tone establishment in, 228–229
-or suffix, 224
Oral presentations, 321–324
Organization, 191–225
   category selection for, 192–195
   choosing type of, 205–215
   clustering and, 9–10
   headings as, 212–213
   idea categorization in, 196–205
   lists as, 211–212
   logical, 198–202
   markers for, 211–214
   natural, 197–198
   for oral presentations, 321–322
   outlining in, 206–211
   thesis statement in, 195–196

Originality. *See* creativity and originality
-ous suffix, 224
Outlining, 206–211
   formal, 207–208
   informal, 208–209

P

Paragraphs
   anticipating reader's questions in, 107–108
   cause/effect, 135–136
   classification, 137–138
   closing, 250–272
   coherent, 130–166
   cohesive, 167–190
   comparison/contrast, 135
   complete, 106–129
   definition of, 106
   description in, 132–133
   development layers in, 108–118
   division, 136–137
   exemplification in, 133–134
   extra main ideas in, 171–174
   narration in, 131–132
   non-cohesive, 168–174
   opening, 226–249
   problem/solution, 139–140
   process analysis, 134–135
   reasons in, 138–139
   topic sentences, 107, 144
   transitions in, 146–151
Parallelism, 352–353
Passive voice
   sentences, 78–81
   wordiness in, 83
Perry, Collin, 124–129
"Personal Values and Ethical Choices" (Reece, Brandt), 310–314
Personality quizzes, 215
Phrase fragments, 326
Planning
   category selection in, 192–195
   for cohesiveness, 174
   for oral presentations, 321
Possessives, 347
"Power of Goal Setting" (Sommer), 26–30
Predictions, 252–253
Prefixes, 68
   negative, 129
Previews, speech, 322
Pride, William, 243–246
Priorities, reader, 297
Problem/solution method, 139–140
   transition words for, 147
Process analysis, 134–135
   dividing into steps, 197
   transition words, 146

Professional Careers Network, 150
Professional organizations, 92
Pronouns
  agreement errors, 343–346
  relative, 326
  singular and plural, 341, 344–346
Pronunciation, 314
Punctuation, 88–89
  apostrophes, 346–348
  commas, 334–338
  periods, 331
  semicolons, 331–332

Q

Questions
  in assertive writing, 279
  closing with, 255
  engaging interest with, 231
  as idea-generation strategy,
    18–20
  journalism method, 16–18
Quotations, 232
  commas with, 336
  online, 260

R

Racist language, 306
Radaskiewicz, Mark, 226
Re- prefix, 68
Readers
  anticipating questions of,
    107–108
  expectations of, 144
  getting the interest of, 229–236
  knowledge level of, 107
  matching writing to, 297–299
  needs of, 297
  objections of, 297
  offending/insulting, 303–308
  priorities of, 297
  topic sentences and, 144
  types of, 298
Reasons, development by, 138–139
  transition words for, 147
Recommendations, making,
    253–254
Redundancy, 82
Reece, Barry L., 310–314
Reference works, online, 260
Relative pronouns, 326
Restatement
  closing with, 254–255
  as context clue, 74
Revision for cohesiveness, 174
Riley Guide, 150
Robinson, Osborne, Jr., 120–124
Roget's Thesaurus, 260
Romero, Raul, 75
Run-on sentences, 331–334

S

Saftner, T.J., 94–99
Schrof, Joannie M., 315–318
Semicolons
  errors with, 338–340
  between independent clauses,
    338–339
  in run-on sentences, 331–332
Sensitivity, 296–318
  concessions in, 299–303
  condescending/dismissive tone
    and, 304–305
  emotionally loaded words and,
    305–306
  name calling and, 303–304
  vs. assertiveness, 278
Sensory details, 45–48
Sentences
  assertive, 279–281
  complex, 84
  compound, 84
  declarative, 279
  exclamatory, 279–280
  fragments, 325–331
  general *vs.* specific, 108–118
  grammar and, 88–89
  graphing relationships among,
    108–118
  imperative, 279
  interrogative, 279–280
  it is, 77–78
  long, 86–87
  passive voice, 78–81
  punctuation and, 88–89
  rules for clear, 75–105
  run-on, 331–334
  short, 85–86
  simple, 84
  spelling and, 89
  strong verbs in, 75–81
  there is, 76–77
  topic, 107, 144
  varying length of, 84–87
  wordiness in, 81–84
Series. *See also* lists
  commas in, 334
  parallelism in, 352–353
  semicolons in, 339
Sexist language, 306
Shock, engaging reader interest
    with, 235
Shuping, Phyllis, 191–192
Significance, establishing, 231–232
Similes
  clichéd, 56
  definition of, 55
  for vivid language, 55–56
Simple sentences, 84
Skenazy, Lenore, 270–272
Slang, 98–99

"Small Cubicle Is Closing In at the
    Office" (Skenazy), 270–272
Smith, L. Lynn, 130
Sommer, Bobbe, 26–30
Speeches, 322–324
Spell-checkers, 89
Spelling, 89
  in freewriting, 12
Spotleson, Bruce, 246–249
Storytelling, 230
"Study Reveals Six Types of Work-
    ers" (Wagner), 218–221
Subjects (sentence part)
  compound, 340
  matching with verbs, 81, 88,
    340–343
  missing, 325
  passive voice and, 78–80
  sentence fragments and, 325
Subordinate relationships, 109–110
  run-on sentences and, 332–333
Subordinating conjunctions,
    332–333
Suffixes, 224–225
Summaries, speech, 322
Surprise, engaging reader interest
    with, 235
Synonyms, 58
  thesaurus use for, 190, 295

T

Tact, 296–318
"Tactics to Tame Tough People"
    (Crowe), 221–225
Talk, as idea generation, 4–5
"Talk the Talk: How Well Do You
    Communicate?" (Saftner),
    94–99
Technical writing, 308
Tenses, verb, 348–350
Their/they're, 220
Then/than, 220–221
There is sentences, 76–77
Thesauruses, 190, 260, 295
Thesis statements, 195–196
  logical organization of, 198–202
  misleading, 202
  natural organization of, 197–198
  in opening paragraphs, 227–228
  refining, 200–202
"Time Flies!" (White), 64–68
Time management, 64–74
-tion suffix, 224
Titles, commas with, 336
To be/to have
  sentences, 76–77
  as weak verb choices, 51–55
Tone
  condescending/dismissive,
    304–305

definition of, 228
establishing, 228–229
Topics
    engaging reader interest with, 234
    idea generation for, 3–21
To/too/two, 221
Transitions, 146–151
    for concessions, 302
    in speeches, 322
Twain, Mark, 57
Typefaces, for emphasis, 281–282

U

Un- prefix, 129
"Using the Web to Advance Your
    Career" (Casson), 263–270

V

Verbs
    to be/to have, 51–55
    matching with subjects, 81, 88,
        340–343
    missing, 325–326
    plural, 340
    sentence fragments, 325–326
    singular, 340
    strong, 75–81
    suffixes for, 224–225
    tenses, 348–350
    using strong, 51–55
Visualization, in idea generation,
    10–11
Vocabulary building
    context clues, 39–40, 73–74, 249,
        288
    dictionaries for, 104–105, 249
    expanded word meanings, 272
    foreign words, 245–246
    homonyms, 123–124, 220–221
    idioms, 98–99
    informal words and, 166

Internet terminology, 269–270
jargon, 161
metaphors, 31, 317–318
negative prefixes, 129
parts of speech and, 249
precise language and, 57–60
prefixes, 68
pronunciation and, 314
suffixes, 224–225
synonyms, 190, 295
technology words, 185
thesaurus use in, 190, 295
word connotations, 276–279
Vulgar language, 306

W

Wagner, Cynthia G., 218–221
Web activities
    business/technical writing, 308
    career exploration, 21
    grammar, 282
    job searches, 150–151
    leadership ability evaluation, 239
    learning styles, 60
    lifelong learning, 117–118
    online reference works, 260
    online writing labs, 175–176
    personality quizzes, 215
    professional organizations, 92
*Webster's Third New International Dic-
    tionary,* 104
Welty, Eudora, 32–39
"What Ever Happened to Customer
    Service?" (Bennett), 99–105
"What It Takes to Become a Success-
    ful Manager Today," 243–246
White, Jerry, 64–68
"Winning for Zora" (Perry), 124–129
Word choice
    assertive, 276–279
    awkward, 354
    emotionally loaded, 305–306

general *vs.* specific language,
    43–45
idioms, 98–99
insulting, 278
jargon and, 161
name calling, 303–304
precise, 57–60
racist, 306
sensitivity in, 278, 296–318
sexist, 306
thesauruses in, 190, 260, 295
tone and, 228–229, 304–305
vivid language, 41–74
vulgar, 306
Wordiness
    avoiding, 81–84
    in *it is* sentences, 79–80
    passive voice and, 83
    redundancy, 82
    in *there is* sentences, 76–77
"Worn Path" (Welty), 32–39
Writing
    assertive, 273–295
    closings, 250–272
    coherent, 130–166
    for cohesiveness, 167–190
    creativity and originality in, 1–40
    idea-generating strategies for,
        3–21
    openings, 236–239
    outlining in, 206–211
    sensitive, 278, 296–318

Y

-y suffix, 224
Your/you're, 220

Z

Zorich, Chris, 124–129